CONSTITUTIONAL FOUNDINGS IN SOUTHEAST ASIA

This volume focuses on the making, nature and role of the first modern constitutions at the founding of the modern nation-states in Southeast Asia. These historical essays add richly to our understanding and appreciation of the founding moments and to the theory and practice of constitutionalism in these states. This volume makes three significant contributions. First, it helps plug the wide knowledge gap in comparative constitutional history in Southeast Asia. Second, it furthers our understanding of contemporary constitutional practice and also anticipates possible developmental trajectories in light of the foundational values embedded in and manifested through these constitutions. Third, through the comparative historical study of these early constitutions, plausible theoretical insights may be gained to further our understanding of Southeast Asia's constitutional history. The book is essential reading for those wishing to obtain a deeper understanding of the constitutional foundings of Southeast Asia.

Constitutionalism in Asia series

NUS National University of Singapore | Centre for Asian Legal Studies Faculty of Law

Constitutionalism in Asia

Series Editors: Kevin YL Tan and Li-ann Thio

Asian constitutionalism is one of the most diverse, rapidly developing and challenging subjects of contemporary legal study. The continent is immensely diverse in its political ideology, religion, culture, language, economic development and colonial history. It has produced a great multitude of constitutional traditions, from authoritarian regimes to mixed communitarian and liberal constitutional models, and from regimes involving the military and monarchy to secular and theocratic constitutions. At the same time, its experience with courts and constitutions spans the gamut from rights-based to dialogical and good governance approaches, particularly where good government is sought through political process and public avenues rather than through the courts. With respect to judicial review and human rights, Asia provides a rich resource in examining how universal standards and local particularities interact. This series seeks to build on the growing academic interest in Asian constitutionalism by interrogating the normative, historical, empirical and conceptual dimensions of constitutionalism, through the lens of the Asian experience. It is expansive in scope and coverage and includes comparative studies between two or more Asian countries; comparisons between Asian and non-Asian jurisdictions; and critical single jurisdiction case studies. The series provides an excellent resource for scholars and students working in the field of Asian legal and constitutional studies, and comparative constitutional law more generally.

Published volumes:

Constitutionalism in Asia: Cases and Materials (edited by Wen-chen Chang, Li-ann Thio, Kevin YL Tan & Jiunn-rong Yeh)
Pluralist Constitutions in Southeast Asia (edited by Jaclyn L Neo & Bui Ngoc Son)

Link to Series website:

https://www.bloomsburyprofessional.com/uk/series/constitutionalism-in-asia/

Constitutional Foundings in Southeast Asia

Edited by
Kevin YL Tan
and
Bui Ngoc Son

•HART•
OXFORD • LONDON • NEW YORK • NEW DELHI • SYDNEY

HART PUBLISHING
Bloomsbury Publishing Plc
Kemp House, Chawley Park, Cumnor Hill, Oxford, OX2 9PH, UK

HART PUBLISHING, the Hart/Stag logo, BLOOMSBURY and the Diana logo
are trademarks of Bloomsbury Publishing Plc

First published in Great Britain 2019
First published in hardback, 2019
Paperback edition, 2020

A catalogue record for this book is available from the British Library.

Library of Congress Cataloging-in-Publication data

Names: Tan, Kevin, editor. | Bui, Ngoc Son, editor.
Title: Constitutional foundings in Southeast Asia / edited by Kevin Y. L Tan, Ngoc Son Bui.
Description: Chicago: Hart Publishing, 2019. | Series: Constitutionalism in asia |
Includes bibliographical references and index.
Identifiers: LCCN 2018060049 (print) | LCCN 2018060298 (ebook) |
ISBN 9781509918935 (EPub) | ISBN 9781509918928 (hardback)
Subjects: LCSH: Constitutional law—Southeast Asia—History. | BISAC: LAW / Public.
Classification: LCC KNC524 (ebook) | LCC KNC524.C655 2019 (print) | DDC 342.59—dc23
LC record available at https://lccn.loc.gov/2018060049

ISBN: HB: 978-1-50991-892-8
PB: 978-1-50994-612-9
ePDF: 978-1-50991-894-2
ePub: 978-1-50991-893-5

Typeset by Compuscript Ltd, Shannon

Table of Contents

List of Contributors .... *vii*

1. *Southeast Asian Constitutional Foundings: A Constitutional-History Perspective* *1*
   Kevin YL Tan and Bui Ngoc Son

2. *Keeping Close to Shore: Preserving Colonial Legacies in the 1935 Philippine Constitution* *11*
   Leia Castañeda Anastacio

3. *The Origins of the 1945 Indonesian Constitution* *49*
   Koichi Kawamura

4. *Timor-Leste's Post-Revolutionary Constitution: From Foundations to Practice* *77*
   Leigh-Ashley Lipscomb

5. *The Making of Myanmar's 1947 Constitution: Geography, Ethnicity, and Law* *111*
   Maitrii Aung-Thwin

6. *A Foreign Commission for Domestic Needs: The Constitutional Founding of Malaysia* *139*
   H Kumarasingham

7. *Foundational Moments: The 'Singapore Constitution'* *161*
   Kevin YL Tan

8. *The Making of Brunei's 1959 Constitution* *191*
   BA Hussainmiya

9. *Not Meant to Last: Vietnam's First Constitution* *225*
   Stein Tønnesson

10. *The Lao Constitution of 1947/1949: Creating a Nation-State* *257*
    Martin Stuart-Fox

11. *The First Constitution-Making in Cambodia: Colonialism, Modernism, Nationalism and the Implications* 275
Teilee Kuong

12. *The 1932 Compromise Constitution: Matrix of Thailand's Permanent Constitutional Instability* 297
Eugenie Mérieau

Index 319

List of Contributors

Kevin YL TAN is one of Singapore's leading constitutional law scholars and its foremost legal historian. He graduated from the Faculty of Law of the National University of Singapore with an LLB (Hons), and obtained his LLM and JSD from the Yale Law School. He specialises in constitutional and administrative law, the Singapore legal system, law and society, legal history and human rights. He is the author and editor of over 40 books on the law, history and politics of Singapore, including *Constitutionalism in Asia* (Hart, 2014); and *The Singapore Constitution: A Contextual Analaysis* (Hart, 2015). He is currently Adjunct Professor at the Faculty of Law, National University of Singapore and Professor at the S Rajaratnam School of International Studies, Nanyang Technological University. He is also Executive Editor of the *Asian Journal of Comparative Law* and Consulting Editor of the *Asian Yearbook of International Law*.

BUI Ngoc Son is an Assistant Professor at the Chinese University of Hong Kong Faculty of Law. His areas of interest include comparative constitutional law and comparative law. He holds law degrees from the University of Hong Kong (Ph.D) and Vietnam National University-Hanoi (LL.M; LL.B). He is the author of *Confucian Constitutionalism in East Asia* (Routledge 2016) and articles published or forthcoming in the *American Journal of Comparative Law*, the *Law & Social Inquiry*, the *International Journal of Constitutional Law*, the *University of Illinois Law Review*, the *Fordham International Law Journal*, the *Washington University Global Studies Law Review*, the *George Washington International Law Review*, the *Washington International Law Journal*, among others. He was previously a research fellow at the Centre for Asian Legal Studies in the National University of Singapore Faculty of Law.

CONTRIBUTORS

BRUNEI – Abdul HUSSAINMIYA is an Honorary Visiting Professor at the Southeastern University of Sri Lanka and a Research fellow at the International Centre for Ethnic Studies in Colombo. Prior to that, he was an Associate Professor of History at the Universiti Brunei Darussalam, Brunei where he taught for 28 years from 1988 to 2016. He received a PhD at the University of Peradeniya and MA (transferred to PhD Programme) at Monash University. He previously taught at Peradeniya and Colombo universities in Sri Lanka. He also held many visiting positions, including: Visiting Professor at National Museum of Ethnology, Osaka, Japan; Visiting

Fellow at Northern Illinois University; Visiting Scholar at New Zealand Asia Institute, University of Auckland, New Zealand and Visiting Fellow at the Universiti Kebangsaan Malaysia (UKM). He is the world's leading scholar on the constitutional history of Brunei and he has published extensively in these areas. Of particular note in this regard are two of his books, *The Brunei Constitution of 1959: An Inside History* (Brunei Press, 2000); and *Sultan Omar Ali Saifuddin III and Britain: The Making of Brunei Darussalam* (Oxford University Press, 1995). His other research interests are on Malay Manuscripts Studies, Classical Malay Literature, Malay Diaspora, History of Brunei, History of South and South-East Asia, comparative Education-South and Southeast Asia, and Biographical Studies of Brunei Sultans since Sultan Hashim Jalil-ul-Alam.

Cambodia – Teilee KUONG was formerly Associate Professor at the Centre for Asian Legal Exchange of Nagoya University, Japan. He was educated at the Ho Chi Minh City University of Economics before proceeding to Nagoya University where he obtained his PhD. His academic interests are in the areas of international economic law, comparative law, international cooperation in promoting the rule of law, and recent legal and political developments in Cambodia and Vietnam. His recent publications focus on national building and constitutionalism in Cambodia, legal education, international cooperation in promoting legal reform in Cambodia and the development of the Extraordinary Chambers in the Courts of Cambodia. He was a visiting scholar of Harvard Yenching Institute, a United Nations Center for Regional Development scholar, and a visiting fellow at Kansai University Faculty of Law.

East Timor – Leigh-Ashley LIPSCOMB is an independent scholar specializing in the history and culture of East and Southeast Asia, with a particular interest in human rights and humanitarian law, transitional justice, gender and nation building. She is currently collaborating with Professor David Cohen (Stanford) on a project analysing the politics of justice in Timor-Leste, with a focus on access to justice for vulnerable groups. Previously she worked with the United Nations Mission in Timor-Leste, where she was the Acting Coordinator of the Monitoring and Protection Unit of the Human Rights Division. Prior to working with the United Nations, Lipscomb was a researcher for the UC Berkeley War Crimes Studies Center and served as Special Assistant to the Legal Advisor to the Truth and Friendship Commission between Indonesia and Timor-Leste and as Researcher for the national prosecution team of the Serious Crimes Unit in Timor-Leste. Earlier in her career she developed a human rights education curriculum for primary school students in rural Japan, and helped develop a scholarship for higher education for Filipina women in honour of Corazon Aquino. She holds a PhD and MA from UC Berkeley in Asian Studies, and a BA from University of Virginia in Asian Studies. She is fluent in English, Bahasa Indonesia and Tetum.

INDONESIA – Koichi KAWAMURA is a Deputy Director of Southeast Asian Studies Group I of the Area Studies Centre at the Institute of Developing Economies Japan External Trade Organization (JETRO). He holds a BA in Political Science from the School of Political Science and Economics, Waseda University, and an MA in International Affairs from the Elliott School of International Affairs at The George Washington University. Kawamura was Visiting Research Fellow at the Centre for Asia Pacific Studies, Gadjah Mada University, Yogyakarta, Indonesia from 2002 to 2004. His research interests include Indonesian politics and comparative politics. His recent publications include works on elections, the presidential system, and democracy in Indonesia. He is also the author of 'President Restrained: Effects of Parliamentary Rule and Coalition Government on Indonesia's Presidentialism'.

LAOS – Martin STUART-FOX is Emeritus Professor of History at the University of Queensland (UQ). After completing a BSc in evolutionary biology, he worked in Papua New Guinea, Hong Kong and Laos before joining United Press International as a foreign correspondent covering the Second Indochina War. On returning to Australia he tutored and lectured in Asian history at UQ while undertaking an MA (on the rationale for an evolutionary theory of history) and PhD (developing an evolutionary theory of history). As Head of History at UQ, Professor Stuart-Fox taught courses on History, Time and Meaning, and Theory of History at the Honours level. On the subject of Laos he has written more than fifty articles, and seven books, including *Laos: Politics, Economics and Society* (Lynne Rienner Publishers, 1986), *Buddhist Kingdom, Marxist State: The making of modern Laos* (White Lotus Press, 1996, 2002), *A History of Laos* (Cambridge University Press, 1997), and *The Lao Kingdom of Lan Xang: Rise and Decline* (White Lotus Press, 1998). He has also published books and articles on the history of relations between China and Southeast Asia, Cambodia, Buddhism, and the theory and philosophy of history. Professor Stuart-Fox is a Fellow of the Australian Academy of the Humanities.

MALAYSIA – H KUMARASINGHAM is Lecturer in British Politics at the School of Social and Political Science at Edinburgh University. A New Zealander, he read History and Politics and obtained his PhD in Comparative Politics at Victoria University, Wellington. Kumarasingham's interests are expansive and his work ranges across politics, history and law. He writes on the history and politics of the former British Empire; South Asian studies, constitutional history and politics; executive power; state-building and decolonisation; and the Westminster model and its export across the world. He has held a wide variety of appointments at universities in Munich, London, Cambridge and Sydney. He is a Fellow of the Royal Historical Society and a Senior Research Fellow at the Institute for Commonwealth Studies, University of London. Among his recent works are: *Constitution-Making* *in Asia: Decolonisation and State-Building in the Aftermath of the British Empire* (Routledge, 2016); and *Constitution-Maker: Selected Writings of Sir Ivor Jennings* (Cambridge University Press, 2015).

MYANMAR – **Maitrii AUNG-THWIN** is Associate Professor of Myanmar/Southeast Asian history and Convener of the Comparative Asian Studies PhD Program at the National University of Singapore. His current research is concerned with nation-building, legal geography, infrastructure, and Buddhist networks in South and Southeast Asia. His publications include: *A History of Myanmar since Ancient Times: Traditions and Transformations* (2013), *The Return of the Galon King: History, Law, and Rebellion in Colonial Burma* (2011) and *A New History of Southeast Asia* (2010). Dr Aung-Thwin served on the Association of Asian Studies Board of Directors (USA) and he is currently a trustee of the Burma Studies Foundation (USA) and editor of the *Journal of Southeast Asian Studies*.

PHILIPPINES – **Leia Castañeda ANASTACIO** is Research Fellow at the Harvard Law School's East Asian Legal Studies program and was previously Visiting Research Scholar at the History Department of Dartmouth College. Leia holds a BA and JD from the Ateneo de Manila University in the Philippines and received her LLM and SJD degrees from Harvard Law School. Achieving first place in the 1993 Philippine Bar Examinations, she was awarded Harvard Law School's Yong Kim' 95 Memorial Prize in 2008 and the American Society of Legal History's William Nelson Cromwell Foundation Dissertation Prize in 2010. She is the author of *The Foundations of the Modern Philippine State: Imperial Rule and the American Constitutional Tradition in the Philippine Islands, 1898–1935* (Cambridge University Press, 2016).

THAILAND – **Eugenie MÉRIEAU** is a Postdoctoral Fellow at the Chair of Comparative Constitutionalism, University of Göttingen, Germany, where she teaches Comparative Constitutional Law, Political Sciences and Human Rights. Fluent in Thai, she spent many years in Thailand where she held various positions including researcher for the King Prajadhipok's Institute (under the Thai Parliament) and consultant for the International Commission of Jurists. Her most quoted article is 'Thailand's Deep State: Royal Power and the Constitutional Court (1997–2015)' (2016) 46(1) *Journal of Contemporary Asia* 445–466.

VIETNAM – **Stein TØNNESSON** is Research Professor at the Peace Research Institute Oslo (PRIO), of which he was Director from 2001 to 2009. Previously, he had been Professor of Human Development Studies at the Centre for Development and the Environment at the University of Oslo and before that, Senior Research Fellow at the Nordic Institute for Asian Studies (NIAS) in Copenhagen. His 1991 doctoral thesis (University of Oslo) was on the international history of the Vietnamese Revolution in 1945. His main areas of research are Vietnam, nation-building in Southeast Asia, the disputes in the South China Sea, and the use of social media in armed conflicts in Myanmar. His book *Vietnam 1946: How the War Began* (University of California Press, 2010), was translated into Vietnamese as Việt Nam 1946: Chiến Tranh Bắt Đầu Như Thế Nào? (Nhà Xuất Bản Chính Trị Quốc Gia, 2013).

Constitutional Foundings in Southeast Asia is accompanied by a webpage where the first constitutions discussed in this volume can be accessed openly:

https://www.bloomsburyprofessional.com/uk/constitutional-foundings-in-asia/

1

Southeast Asian Constitutional Foundings: A Constitutional-History Perspective

KEVIN YL TAN AND BUI NGOC SON

INTRODUCTION

THIS BOOK EXAMINES the making, nature, and role of the first modern Constitutions in 11 countries in Southeast Asia: the Association of Southeast Asian Nations (ASEAN) States and East Timor. As almost all the countries in this book were former colonies of the various European powers, we take the 'first' Constitutions to be those that were drafted during the transition from colony to independent State. Thus, the Constitutions covered in this volume include those of: Philippines (1935); Indonesia (1945); Vietnam (1946); Myanmar (1947); Laos (1947/1949); Cambodia (1947); Malaysia (1957); Singapore (1958–1965); Brunei (1959); and East Timor (2002). The choices for Singapore and Brunei may appear odd since the Constitutions considered were not those that were drafted exactly at the point of independence. Brunei became independent from Britain only in 1984 but the Constitution being studied is that of 1959 which was an earlier effort to edge the absolute monarchy towards greater democracy. In the case of Singapore, it became independent twice, first from Great Britain in 1963 as a constituent State of the Federation of Malaysia, and then again in 1965 when it seceded from the Federation as a unitary State. Thailand, the only Southeast Asian State never to have been colonised is 'represented' here by the contested versions of its 1932 Constitution which ostensibly transformed Siam into a constitutional monarchy.

This book is the outcome of an interdisciplinary project. While it draws on constitutional scholarship to understand the process and substance of constitution-making, it integrates knowledge in cognate disciplines, particularly historical studies and political science to better understand the process of constitution-making and the relationship between constitutions and state-building. Consequently, contributors of the book include both constitutional law scholars and historians. For each country, we asked contributors to offer three things. First, to provide an *exploratory description* of the process and substances in making the first modern Constitution in the respective country. Questions posed, and hopefully answered include: How was the constitution-making body formulated? Who were in that body? How was the Constitution drafted? What were the constitutional questions that the drafters considered? How were these questions debated in the constitution-making body and among the public? How was the Constitution approved? Second, contributors were asked to provide an *explanatory analysis* of the internal and external factors surrounding the making of the Constitution. What are the internal factors (eg, political-legal tradition, colonialism, revolution, social-economic condition, political conflicts, social division, ideology, local intellectual environment) which influenced the making of this Constitution? What are the external factors (for example foreign constitutional experiences and constitutional ideas, international bodies, or international experts)? What are the interactions between the internal and external factors? Third, we asked contributors to offer *some reflections* on the role of the first constitutional document in the founding of the modern nation-state and the subsequent state-building process in the country. How did the constitution impact the founding of state-institutions (legislature, government, courts, etc.)? Does the constitution still influence the subsequent constitutional development and even contemporary constitutional design and practice? If yes, how is this?

Contributors presented their chapters in the two-day workshop held in Singapore by the Centre for Asian Legal Studies at the National University of Singapore Faculty of Law on 9 and 10 November 2017. Following the workshop, the country rapporteurs were invited to revise their papers in light of the comments received.

It is not our intention to summarise the country studies in this introduction but rather to address common themes in the Southeast Asian experiences of constitutional foundings, and locate these experiences within the general study of constitutional history. We make two claims. First, constitutional history is important to understand constitutional law and constitutionalism, but the study of constitutional history requires us to move beyond looking purely at what courts do and how they interpret Constitutions (juriscentric originalism) and western liberal conceptions of government and constitutionalism. Second, the inquiry into constitutional foundings in the Southeast Asia requires us to consider a range of historical issues, including: the historical conditions and functions of the foundational Constitutions; the historical internal and external factors that influence the process and substances of foundational constitution-making; and the possible lasting impact of the foundational constitutional values in the subsequent constitutional trajectory. We pursue this dual argument in two parts. Part I addresses the issues regarding the significance of constitutional history and constitutional history studies, while Part II discusses general themes regarding the foundational constitution-making in the region. Part III concludes.

I. THE STUDY OF CONSTITUTIONAL HISTORY

Why should we be concerned about the first Constitutions in Southeast Asia, most of which were drafted decades ago? For a start, it is a truism that the development of constitutional law and constitutionalism in the region cannot be detached from history. Thus, it is important for us to study constitutional foundings in Southeast Asia to understand not only constitutional history but also contemporary constitutional development and constitutionalism in the region, especially since they are informed by foundational values embedded through these first constitutions. In fact, the significance of history in constitutional development and constitutionalism has been repeatedly underscored. Long ago, the German philosopher GWF Hegel argued that constitutionalism is the self-determination of identity of a given people, and is an ongoing social and historical process.[1] In the same vein, the Kenyan scholar Okoth-Ogendo posits constitutionalism 'can become a tradition only if it forms part of the shared history of a people.'[2] Similarly, Michael W Dowdle argues that 'in identifying a political identity, history provides the best source material for constitutionalism' since it 'is history that distinguishes the collective "people" of one particular terrain from those of another.'[3] Felix Frankfurter, who served as an Associate Justice of the United States Supreme Court, also considers the US Constitution 'most significantly not a document but a stream of history.'[4]

Unfortunately, while there has been heightened growth in Asian constitutional scholarship in recent years, most scholars tend to focus on contemporary constitutional issues, leaving Asian constitutional history largely understudied.[5] Hart Publishing has published single books on the Constitutions of five Southeast Asian States, namely Indonesia, Malaysia, Thailand, Singapore, and Vietnam.[6] All these volumes contain very useful historical introductions and contextual

[1] GWF Hegel, *Outlines of the Philosophy of Right*, trans., T. M. Knox; ed., Stephen Houlgate (Oxford University Press, 2008), 263.

[2] WO Okoth-Ogendo, 'Constitutions without Constitutionalism: Reflections on an African Political Paradox,' in *Constitutionalism and Democracy: Transitions in the Contemporary World*, ed. Greenberg et al (Oxford University Press, 1993), 65.

[3] Michael W. Dowdle, 'Constitutional Listening,' (2012) 88 *Chicago-Kent Law Review* 151–152.

[4] Quoted in Sanford Levinson, *Constitutional Faith* (Princeton University Press, 1988), 33.

[5] There are, of course, exceptions but these have been few and far between. See Kevin YL Tan, 'The Making and Remaking of Constitutions in Southeast Asia: An Overview' (2002) 6 *Singapore Journal of International & Comparative Law* 1–41; and ch 1 'Constitution- Making and State Building' of Wen-chen Chang, Li-ann Thio, Kevin YL Tan & Jiunn-rong Yeh, *Constitutionalism in Asia: Cases and Materials* (Oxford: Hart, 2015).

[6] Timothy Lindsey, *The Constitution of Indonesia: A Contextual Analysis* (Oxford: Hart, 2011); Andrew Harding, *The Constitution of Malaysia: A Contextual Analysis* (Oxford: Hart, 2012); Andrew Harding and Peter Leyland, *The Constitutional System of Thailand: A Contextual Analysis* (Oxford: Hart, 2011); Kevin Tan, *The Constitution of Singapore: A Contextual Analysis* (Oxford: Hart, 2014); Mark Sidel, *The Constitution of Vietnam: A Contextual Analysis* (Oxford: Hart, 2009).

study and add richly to our knowledge about constitutional experiences in Southeast Asia. However, this body of literature has three major limitations.

First, these books focus mainly on the individual constitutions of the single countries and lack substantive comparisons or identifying commonalities and differences in constitutional responses to the challenge of founding new States. Second, these books focus more on contemporary constitutional issues than the historical context of making the first Constitutions and their relevance to the trajectory of state-building in the respective countries. Third, this body of literature has yet to cover all the constitutions of Southeast Asia – Brunei, Cambodia, Laos, Myanmar, the Philippines, and East Timor. Beyond the Hart series, there are some books about the Constitutions of these jurisdictions, but they are also country-focused books and substantively lack historical constitutional comparison.[7] This book, therefore, seeks to fill the gap in the knowledge about constitutional history in Southeast Asia.

This book also taps into the scholarship associated with the recent revitalisation of the comparative study of constitutional history. A regular forum in this area has been active,[8] to address the lack of study into 'the comparative dimensions of constitutional history.'[9] Some specialist periodicals in this area have been published regularly.[10] Early comparative writings about constitutional history focused mainly on royal institutions in Europe in the Middle Ages.[11] In addition, RR Palmer's book *The Age of the Democratic Revolution* is identified by the author as:

> an attempt at a comparative constitutional history of Western Civilization at the time of the French and American Revolutions; but "constitutional" is to be understood in a broad sense, without much emphasis on formal provisions, and in close connection with the political, social, and intellectual currents and the actual conflicts at the time.[12]

[7] BA Hussainmiya, *The Brunei Constitution of 1959: An Inside History* (Bandar Seri Bagawan: Brunei Press, 2000); Hor Peng, Kong Phallack, Jörg Mendel, eds., *Cambodian Constitutional Law* (Phnom Penh, Konrad-Adenauer-Stiftung, 2017); Andrew Harding, *Law, Government and the Constitution in Malaysia* (Kuala Lumpur: Malayan Law Journal, 1988); Thio Li-ann, *A Treatise on Singapore Constitutional Law* (Singapore: Academy Publishing, 2012); Andrew Harding, *Constitutionalism and Legal Change in Myanmar* (Oxford: Hart, 2017); and Rufus B Rodriguez, *Constitutionalism in the Philippines* (Manila: Rex Book Store, 1997).

[8] In recent years, the University of Illinois College of Law Programme in Constitutional Theory, History and Law; the University of Bologna School of Law; and the Centre for Constitutional Studies and Democratic Development have jointly held annual conferences on 'Constitutional History: Comparative Perspectives.' For information about the recent workshop in 2017, see https://calendars.illinois.edu/detail/7?eventId=33286731.

[9] Ibid.

[10] They are the *Journal of Constitutional History/Giornale di Storia Costituzionale*: www.storiacostituzionale.it/index.html; and the *Historia Constitucional*; www.historiaconstitucional.com/index.php/historiaconstitucional.

[11] Gordon Griffiths, *Representative Government in Western Europe In The Sixteenth Century: Commentary And Documents For The Study Of Comparative Constitutional History* (Oxford: Clarendon Press, 1968); and H Mitteis, HF Orton, *The State in the Middle Ages: A Comparative Constitutional History of Feudal Europe* (American Elsevier, 1975).

[12] RR Palmer, *The Age of the Democratic Revolution: A Political History of Europe and America, 1760–1800: The Challenge*, updated edition (New Jersey: Princeton University Press, 2014) 3.

In recent years, scholars have produced some significant work in this field, such as one comprehensive study of the history of the German Constitutional Court from a comparative (American) perspective.[13] Justin Collings suggests that to translate 'comparative history' into 'comparative constitutional history,'[14] three approaches are possible: (a) 'perspectival histories' (an author's own perspective on a single jurisdiction); (b) 'thematic histories' (a single theme across jurisdictions); and (c) 'relational histories' (multiple jurisdictions within a single chronological frame).[15] This book falls within the third of Collings' categories.

The general inquiry of constitutional history in Southeast Asia is still underdeveloped and thus hampered by two limits. The first is jurisdictional. Studies have focused on single jurisdictions and have always linked back to colonial antecedents. The second is substantial in that few studies have looked beyond how history is used in judicial decision-making.[16] Our modest attempt in this volume in understanding the history of foundational constitution-making in Southeast Asia hopes to add to this scholarship.

II. CONSTITUTIONAL FOUNDINGS

This historical inquiry into constitutional foundings moves beyond juriscentric originalism: how courts should interpret the constitution according to the understanding of the foundational generation.[17] Rather, this inquiry is broadly concerned with the historical conditions and functions of the foundational Constitutions; the internal and external factors that influence the process and substances of foundational constitution-making; and the possible lasting impact of the foundational constitutional values in the country's subsequent constitutional trajectory.

A. Conditions and Functions of Constitutional Foundings

A theory of 'constitutional foundationalism' holds that (a) a Constitution is the culmination of a liberal revolution; (b) this foundational constitution-making is

[13] Justin Collings, *Democracy's Guardians: A History of the German Federal Constitutional Court, 1951–2001* (Oxford: Oxford University Press, 2015).

[14] Justin Collings, 'What Should Comparative Constitutional History Compare?' (2017) *University of Illinois Law Review* 475.

[15] Ibid.

[16] The organisers of the Illinois-Bologna Conference note that: 'In some nations, notably the United States, constitutional history plays an important and sometimes decisive role in the resolution by courts of questions of constitutional law. The conference will take up the place of constitutional history in constitutional adjudication.' see https://calendars.illinois.edu/detail/7?eventId=33286731.

[17] See, eg, Randy E Barnett, *Restoring the Lost Constitution: The Presumption of Liberty* (New Jersey: Princeton University Press, 2004).

a clean break with the past; and (c) the making of such a Constitution is foundational to the creation of a new democratic constitutional order.[18] The Southeast Asian experiences of constitutional foundings do not resonate with these constitutional foundationalist claims.

To begin with, foundational constitution-making in Southeast Asia is not solely the result of a liberal revolution. The process of decolonisation resulted in various different conditions impacting the foundational moments: revolution (in Vietnam and later Laos); evolution (in Singapore and Malaysia); royal determination (Thailand); and segregation (East Timor). Even when constitution-making is the culmination of a revolution, this revolution is not necessarily a liberal one. For example, the making of Vietnam's 1946 Constitution was the culmination of a communist revolution that ended French colonialism in Indochina.[19]

A related observation is that foundational constitution-making in Southeast Asia is not necessarily a radical repudiation of the past. Many first Constitutions in the region continue the colonial and traditional legacies. The monarchy, for example, was retained in the cases of Thailand, Laos, Cambodia and Brunei.[20] The traditional communitarian values continue to inform the first Constitution of Indonesia.[21] In Laos, the citizens' family duties, the role of Buddhism as the state region, and the institution of King's Council are reflective of the State's traditional values.[22] As the making of the foundational constitutions in the region is not the codification of values and achievements of liberal revolutions, they are not necessarily a fundamental framework for the creation of a democratic constitutional order. In fact, no democratic constitutional governments were created following the making of the first constitutions in Southeast Asia although the Philippines might be considered somewhat of an exception here. Instead, different types of constitutional orders were created after the making of the foundational constitutions in the region.

Few Southeast Asian experiences of constitutional foundings accord with theories of 'constitutional constructivism' in which constitution-making in transitional contexts is characterised by incremental change as societies move from authoritarian to liberal democratic rule while preserving continuity with its past.[23] While gradual constitutional construction and constitutional continuity

[18] See Bruce Ackerman, *The Future of Liberal Revolution* (New Haven: Yale University Press, 1992) 16.; see also, Hannah Arendt, *On Revolution* (London: Penguin, 1977). For critical discussions, see Gary Jeffrey Jacobsohn, 'Theorizing the Constitutional Revolution' (2014) 2 *Journal of Law and Courts* 1–32.

[19] See chapter on Vietnam.

[20] See chapters on Thailand, Laos, and Cambodia.

[21] See chapter on Indonesia.

[22] See chapter on Laos.

[23] See Ruti Teitel, 'Transitional Jurisprudence: The Role of Law in Political Transformation' (1997) 106 *Yale Law Journal* 2070; and Ruti Teitel, *Transitional Justice* (Oxford: Oxford University Press, 2000). For related accounts, see Andras Sajo, 'Preferred Generations: A Paradox of Restoration Constitutions' (1992–1993) 14 *Cardozo Law Review* 847; Venkat Iyer, 'Restoration Constitutionalism in the South Pacific' (2006) 15 *Pacific Rim Law & Policy Journal* 40.

are relevant, we do not see the incremental and continuing constitutional evolution culminates in the creation of liberal constitutionalism in Southeast Asia. The functions of the foundational constitutions in Southeast Asia are not to limit governmental powers in the name of individual liberty.

In contrast, in some cases, constitutional foundings are informed by communitarian constitutional values that are explicitly averse to liberal constitutionalism. For example, in Indonesia, the Javanese 'Family Principle' philosophy was transformed into a national ideology at its founding. The 'Family Principle' is the very anti-thesis of individualism, which renders the 1945 Constitution a communitarian and authoritarian constitution. The nationalists summoned Nazi doctrine of the totalitarian state, and models of the Soviet Union and the Chinese Nationalist Party government to legitimatise the 'Family Principle'.[24] On the other hand, the constitutional founding in East Timor drew on international legal and constitutional norms and ideals,[25] an example of what has been termed transnational or international constitutionalism.[26]

It is hard to make generalisations about the roles and functions of foundational constitution-making in Southeast Asia, varied and inter-mixed as they are. This is especially so in a colonial context when independence is won in different ways. For sure, new constitutions signal new beginnings and almost all constitutions may be considered to be foundational documents in the sense that they represent a break from the past, at the very least in terms of sovereignty. At the same time, they may be drafted to express nationalistic ideas and ideals and traditional values, and as a symbol and document to unify the nascent State. In many cases, it is a mix of all these functions.

B. Historical Factors in Constitutional Foundings

What historical factors influenced the process and substance of constitution-making? As the country studies show, different factors determined the course of constitution-making in each of the Southeast Asian countries. What might usefully be offered by way of analysis is perhaps for us, as comparativists to consider two broad factors: internal and external.

Internal factors inform the way foundational constitution-making is initiated, organised and carried out, and what goes into the Constitution. This kind of neo-functionalist enquiry takes serious account of the historical and political factors of constitutional development.[27] In the case of Southeast Asia, an unavoidable factor – indeed the 'elephant in the room' – has been the

[24] See chapter on Indonesia.

[25] See chapter on East Timor.

[26] Jiunn-Rong Yeh and Wen-Chen Chang, 'The Emergence of Transnational Constitutionalism: Its Features, Challenges and Solutions' (2008) 27 *Penn State International Law Review* 89.

[27] Ruti Teitel, 'Comparative Constitutional Law in a Global Age' (2004) 117 *Harvard Law Review* 2581.

decolonisation process. Except Thailand, the end of colonialism provided the impetus for the making of the first constitutions in Southeast Asia. Another influential factor is internecine political struggles. Political struggles among competing forces (eg the 'revolutionary' and royalist forces in Thailand; the Royal Lao government and the Lao Issara government in Laos; the Vietminh and non-communist forces in Vietnam) drove and shaped the process and substance of foundational constitution-making.[28] Other influential internal factors include: socio-economic conditions, intellectual environment, religion, and traditional values. For example, in Vietnam, the famine of 1945, the diversity of intellectuals (Confucianists, communists, western-educated intellectuals, religious leaders, and royalists) and anti-colonialist movements were relevant and significant factors that shaped its constitution-making processes and also the contents of its 1946 Constitution.

External factors include the influence of foreign or external players. Among such factors are foreign constitutional advisors, foreign constitutional texts and movements, foreign governments, international law and international or transnational actors, such as the United Nations. In some cases, constitution-making was influenced by ideas, values, and institutions of the former colonial powers (eg French influences in Cambodia, Laos, and Vietnam; the American influence in the Philippines; and the British influence in Singapore and Malaysia). However, external influences are not limited to colonial ties. Drafters of Vietnam's 1946 Constitution were also influenced by English and American constitutionalism. In the case of Thailand, as constitution-making was free from colonial domination, constitution-makers drew inspirations from different constitutional models (including the Soviet, French and Chinese models).[29]

Mechanisms of external influences on domestic constitution-making include: coercion, competition, learning, and acculturation.[30] Constitution-makers may be coercively influenced by their former colonists (eg Laos and Cambodia). Countries may also consciously borrow from foreign constitutional models to modernise the domestic political and legal systems (eg Thailand).[31] Countries may incorporate foreign experiences into their Constitutions to socialise themselves to the 'civilized world' to gain more international recognition (eg Vietnam). The incentive to adopt transnational constitutional values to compete for foreign investments is less relevant as this is more associated with economic globalisation.[32] Oftentimes, it is a mix of externalities given that constitutional

[28] See chapters on Thailand, Laos, and Vietnam.

[29] See chapter on Thailand.

[30] Benedikt Goderis & Mila Versteeg, 'Global Diffusion of Constitutional Rights' (2014) 39 *International Review of Law & Economics* 1.

[31] Nelson Tebbe & Robert L Tsai, 'Constitutional Borrowing' (2010) 108 *Michigan Law Review* 459; and Sujit Choudhry (ed), *The Migration of Constitutional Ideas* (New York: Cambridge University Press, 2009).

[32] Benedikt Goderis & Mila Versteeg, 'Global Diffusion of Constitutional Rights' (2014) 39 *International Review of Law & Economics* 1.

bargains need to be hammered out through negotiations among key political actors of all ideological stripes. Reaction to external influences is not always positive. Resistance is common in transnational constitutional interactions. This stems from a range of factors, such as nationalism, the protection of sovereignty, the expressive nature of Constitution, and the fear of western hegemony,[33] such as was the case in Indonesia, whose founders resisted western constitutional ideas and institutions in favour of traditional communitarian values.[34]

C. The Legacies of Constitutional Foundings

The legacies of the constitutional foundings have, in some cases, a lasting effect on the subsequent constitutional trajectory of their respective countries. In some cases, the founding constitutional legacies continue to provide the ideas, inspirations for constitutional debates and mobilisation many years after their promulgation. Take the case of Vietnam for example. During the 2013 constitution-making process, many actors called for a return to the values of the 1946 Constitution. These actors included retired political leaders and senior officials; incumbent senior officials; liberal assembly delegates; distinguished legal scholars, intellectuals in different fields; ordinary people; and dissidents. They made their demands utilising various different fora: congressional forum, popular forums (state-owned popular medias, unofficial websites, and Facebook), and scholarly forums (national law journals and conferences, workshops, and seminars) and using the first Constitution of 1946 as the platform, they called for a constitutional referendum; a change of the nation's name from Socialist Republic of Vietnam to Democratic Republic of Vietnam; a multiparty system; a semi-presidential system of government; judicial independence; and private ownership of lands.[35]

Foundational Constitutions may also inform and impact subsequent constitutional design. In Laos, we find some traits of its 1947/1949 Constitution in that of its socialist Constitution of 1991. For example, the name of its national legislature (National Assembly) is retained as well as the institution of vote of no confidence, which is most unusual in a communist state.[36] In Cambodia, despites radical differences, 'many traits of the 1947 Constitution can be found among the provisions of the 1993 Constitution. These include the restoration of

[33] Vicki C Jackson, 'Constitutional Comparisons, Convergence, Resistance, Engagement,' (2005) 119 *Harvard Law Review* 113–14; Kim Lane Scheppele, 'Aspirational and aversive constitutionalism: The Case for Studying Cross-Constitutional Influence Through Negative Models' (2003) 1 *International Journal of Constitutional Law* 296. For a recent account, see Ran Hirschl, Opting Out of 'Global Constitutionalism' (2018) 12 *Law & Ethics of Human Rights* 1.

[34] See chapter on Indonesia.

[35] See chapter on Vietnam. See also Bui Ngoc Son, 'Restoration Constitutionalism and Socialist Asia' (2015) 37 *Loyola of Los Angeles International and Comparative Law Review* 67.

[36] See chapter on Laos.

an elective mechanism for choosing the King; the establishment of a Supreme Council of Magistracy; and the principles for elections and functioning of the Senate, when it was reintroduced by a constitutional amendment in 1998.[37] The attachment to the founding constitutional legacies in constitutional debate, mobilisation, and design in Southeast Asia echoes Schepelle's observation that:

> Constitutions in their moments of creation cannot be inspired solely by imagined futures. Perhaps even more crucially, they encode imagined pasts. Though they may look abroad for models, constitution drafters ultimately understand and react most of all to what they take to be the crucial histories of their own countries.[38]

Reference back to the founding constitutional legacies may also be instrumental in gaining more legitimacy and social support for new constitutional designs as societies often prefer continuity to change. This may be done even if past constitutional experiences prove flawed, as in the case of Indonesia. In such situations, constitutional actors are not harking back nor clamouring for a particular constitutional form or arrangement, but rather for what might be regarded as ideals, values and other social meanings embedded in the foundational document and the process of its drafting.

III. CONCLUSION

This book makes a first small step towards a Southeast Asian contribution to the general scholarship on constitutional history in two ways. First, the inquiry into constitutional history is not necessarily associated with judicial institutions and constitutional adjudication. We believe that it is necessary to expand the scope of constitutional history studies to the study of the history of constitution-building generally. Secondly, as many of our case studies show, constitution-making in post-colonial conditions brought into play many other political and social factors, not least of which was the need for the nascent country to build both a State and a nation. The Constitution could be used to galvanise the disparate peoples of the new State but also to organise government in a way that would give the State enough authority and capacity to govern.

We end with a word of acknowledgement. Thanks to the Centre for Asian Legal Studies at the Faculty of Law, National University of Singapore, for supporting this project and to the scholars who generously contributed to the workshop and to this volume. Last but not least, we thank Hart Publishing for its continuing support of our efforts to contribute usefully to the study of Constitutionalism in Asia.

[37] See chapter on Cambodia.

[38] Kim Lane Scheppele, 'A Constitution Between Past and Future' (2008) 49 *William & Mary Law Review* 1379.

2

Keeping Close to Shore: Preserving Colonial Legacies in the 1935 Philippine Constitution

LEIA CASTAÑEDA ANASTACIO

INTRODUCTION

WHEN THE PHILIPPINE Constitutional Convention opened on 30 July 1934, the *Tribune*'s Vicente Ruiz Navarro recalled, 'the sun shone suavely while the cool breeze from Manila bay came in tender rhythm inland' as though 'all of God's creation was in a happy mood proclaiming the reign of peace all over the country.'[1] To Filipinos and Americans invested in the success of the long-gestating Philippine state, the Convention's inauguration was 'destined to be one of the events that will remain glorious in the life of the people of this country,' marking not only the day Filipinos 'began to exercise the most fundamental right of a free country, the right to draw up their own constitution under which they would create a new government and provide for their own independence,' but also 'the vital turning point in the political, social, and economic life of the people who, under the liberty law, have been vested with some transitory rights to define to a great extent their policies of government, improve their social standard, and formulate a new but progressive plan for economic development.'[2]

The Convention brought Filipinos closer to realising the sovereignty they first sought when revolutionaries revolted against Spain in 1896. Thwarted when Spain ceded the Philippine Islands, Puerto Rico, and Cuba to the US through the 1898 Treaty of Paris that ended the Spanish-American War, Filipino revolutionaries resumed their struggle against their new American conquerors.

[1] Jose M Aruego, *The Philippine Constitution: Origin, Making, Meaning, and Application*, 7 vols. (Manila: Philippine Lawyers Assoc. 1972) 119 [hereinafter 'Aruego, *Origin*'].

[2] V Ruiz Navarro, *The Philippine Constitutional Convention*, 2 vols. (Manila: General Printing Press, 1934) 111–112 [hereinafter 'Navarro'].

To Americans, the Convention signalled the near-completion of a successful experiment in republican and constitutional empire. Portrayed as exceptional compared to their traditional imperial contemporaries' despotic and exploitative colonialisms, President William McKinley's so-called 'benevolent imperialism' undertook to create in Filipinos sovereign capacity after the American fashion as they governed the Islands within the popular and legal limits of their democratic and constitutional traditions.

If American colonialism's goal was to teach, how well did Filipinos learn? The 1935 Constitution indicated that they assimilated a great deal, for it embodied applications of early twentieth-century American ideas and institutions to a Philippine setting shaped by 300 years of Spanish colonial rule. Transplanting American liberal constitutionalism to the Philippine terrain engaged some dimensions of the tradition over others, producing an interesting variant that the constitution preserved. Like the Government of the Philippine Islands, the Philippine Commonwealth and the independent Philippine Republic that followed have a unitary structure that divided power among executive, legislative, and judicial branches, but was dominated by the executive. Like its predecessor, the future Philippine government would be an activist bureaucratic apparatus directed towards social engineering and economic development and whose interventions met mostly mild resistance from the Bill of Rights. In this sense, it resembled less the night-watchman state created by the American Founders, but more the progressive New Deal incarnation of the US federal government, vesting those at its helm with tremendous power over national life.

Unpacking the story of the 1935 Philippine Constitution, this chapter explores the role that constitution-making played in founding the modern Philippine state and structuring subsequent Philippine political conduct.

I. BENEVOLENT IMPERIALISM

When Manuel Luis Quezon was sworn in as President of the Philippine Commonwealth, he declared, 'President McKinley's cherished hope has been fulfilled – the Filipinos look back with gratitude to the day when Destiny placed their land under the beneficent guidance of the people of the United States.'[3] Indeed, McKinley's benevolent imperialism seemed vindicated by the Filipino people's peaceful, legal transition to greater sovereignty.

McKinley's imperial construct attempted to reconcile the coercion and absolutism characterising traditional imperialism with the consent and self-imposed restraints undergirding American democracy and constitutionalism. It was devised to manage the three Spanish colonies that came as spoils of an easy

[3] Manuel Luis Quezon, 'Inaugural Address,' in Pedro de la Llana & FB Icasiano (eds), *Quezon in His Speeches* (Manila: State Publishing, 1937) 33.

victory in the Spanish-American War and which expansionist Americans viewed as a reward for intervening to save Cuba from Spanish oppression. But McKinley agonised over what to do with this 'gift of the gods.'[4]

Passing the Platt Amendment had committed the US to withdrawing from Cuba by 1901. Lack of Puerto Rican resistance to US rule rendered retention unproblematic. But when Admiral George Dewey and the Asiatic Squadron steamed into Manila Bay, Filipinos had been waging a revolution against Spain that turned into the Philippine-American War when revolutionaries led by General Emilio Aguinaldo redirected their struggle against US forces. By their revolution's outbreak in 1896, Filipinos had declared independence, adopted a constitution, and organised the Philippine Republic – actions which to Aguinaldo represented 'a people making superhuman efforts to revindicate their sovereignty and their nationality before the civilized powers.' Having chosen from among 'the governments today recognized and observed among cultured nations,' that form deemed 'most compatible with their aspirations, endeavoring to adjust their actions to the dictates of reason and of right,' Filipinos exhibited 'their aptitude for civil life.'[5] But it was precisely that aptitude that Americans contested. The first Philippine Commission, an investigative body led by Cornell University President Jacob Gould Schurman, had found in the Islands, not one people constituting a nation, but a collection of uncivilised tribes[6] disqualified by incapacity from joining the late nineteenth-century community of civilised sovereign nations. Yet neither was the Philippines a candidate for statehood. Too remote from the mainland and too inhospitable to white settlement, the Islands were also populated by inhabitants who were racially and civilisationally more similar, not to mainstream Americans, but to Native Americans and formerly enslaved African Americans. Thus, even if Filipinos had desired statehood, the bloody spectres of the Civil War and American Indian Wars made Americans wary of making a new State out of these distant islands and fellow citizens of its primitive alien peoples. Unwilling to leave the Islands vulnerable to European conquest, McKinley elected to retain them. But how would a constitutional republic justify keeping colonies without negating its identity?

At the Senate ratification hearings for the 1898 Treaty of Paris, Republican Senator Henry Teller of Colorado proposed a colonial government compatible with republican values, presaging what later took shape in the Islands. Implying that colonialism need neither be inherently despotic nor exploitative, Teller suggested that the new American possessions be administered, not in violation of, but 'in accordance with the great fundamental principles that permeate and

[4] James Rusling, 'Interview with President William McKinley' *The Christian Advocate* (New York 22 Jan 1903) 17.

[5] See Emilio Aguinaldo to Elwell Otis, 23 Jan 1899, in Maximo M Kalaw, *The Development of Philippine Politics (1872–1920)* (Manila: Oriental Commercial Company, 1926) 176.

[6] US Department of War, 'Report of a Commission Appointed to Investigate Affairs in the Philippine Islands (Manila: Government Printing Office, 1900) 182–83.

underlie republican institutions,' namely 'that the just powers of government are derived from the consent of the governed' and that it was 'our duty to secure to these people just such political rights and privileges as they are entitled to under our system,' as qualified 'by their condition.' If American principles followed her flag to the Islands, then 'there will be no harm done' if it 'floated there as an emblem of national power,' for it would symbolise American belief that their flag was 'capable of giving to those people American law, American freedom, American progress, and enabling them to share in prosperity with us as well as in American glory.'[7]

Over three organic acts, namely, McKinley's Instructions,[8] the 1902 Philippine Organic Act,[9] and the 1916 Philippine Autonomy Act,[10] McKinley's Secretary of War Elihu Root and thereafter the US Congress imposed both substantive and structural constitutional limits on the Government of the Philippine Islands, or the Insular Government, enacting most of the US Bill of Rights' provisions and distributing government functions along separation of powers theory. Designed to prepare Filipinos for sovereignty, US colonial rule was justified as temporary, with Americans gradually relinquishing responsibility to Filipinos as they acquired requisite capacity. Viewed as schooling in independence, Filipino participation in colonial governance also betokened the assent necessary to justify American colonialism within her consensual political tradition. While campaigning for President McKinley's re-election in 1900, Root reassured his audiences that 'the government of the Philippine Islands will not affect the character of our institutions, but the character of our institutions will determine and mould the government of the Philippine Islands.' Conceding that 'to govern as a despot would be fatal to the character of a republic,' Root believed that if America were 'to govern as Congress always has and always will govern in territory outside the limit of the States, in accordance with the spirit of our institutions, subject to all great rules of liberty and right, and responsible for every act to a great liberty-loving people,' then the colonial project 'can but extend and strengthen our institutions.'[11]

McKinley's benevolent imperialism ordered the Islands' political, economic, social, and cultural life following American political and constitutional categories, which, in turn, were informed by the Philippine colonial encounter. The 1935 Philippine Constitution would capture the contours and content of American constitutional democracy's Pacific incarnation.

[7] Henry M Teller, Congressional Records: Proceedings and Debates of the 55th Congress (32: Government Printing Office, 1899) 325–30, 326–27.

[8] US Department of War, 'Report of the Secretary of War to the President' (Manila: Government Printing Office, 1900) 720–26 [hereinafter McKinley's Instructions].

[9] Philippine Organic Act 1902, 32 Stat 691 c 1369 [hereinafter Organic Act].

[10] Philippine Autonomy Act 1916, 39 Stat 545 c 416 [hereinafter Jones Law].

[11] Elihu Root, 'The United States in the Philippines in 1900: Address at Canton, Ohio, 24 October 1900,' in Robert Bacon and James Brown Scott (eds), *The Military and Colonial Policy of the United States: Addresses and Reports* (Cambridge, MA: Harvard University Press, 1916) 27–64, 36, 47 [hereinafter, 'Root'].

II. CALLING THE CONVENTION

On 26 May 1934, the Philippine Legislature passed the Convention Law providing for the election of two delegates from each representative district to a Convention tasked with formulating a Constitution for the Commonwealth of the Philippine Islands.[12] Elected two months later, the 202 delegates began drafting the new Philippine charter at the hall of the House of Representatives. Major factors impacting their work were the terms of the independence package concluded between the US Congress and the Philippine Independence Missions, the doctrinal and structural precedents established by Philippine organic laws throughout American colonial rule, and the nature and dynamic of Philippine party politics.

A. The Quest for Independence Legislation

The Philippine Legislature called for convention elections pursuant to authority derived from the Tydings-McDuffie Act, or Philippine Independence Act.[13] Enacted by the US Congress on 22 March 1934 and signed two days later by President Franklin Delano Roosevelt, this law was secured following successive Independence Missions sent by the Philippine Legislature to Washington DC between 1919 to 1934. While justifying benevolent imperialism as preparing Filipinos for self-rule, Republican Presidents William McKinley, Theodore Roosevelt, and William Howard Taft remained vague as to when and how this independence would materialise. By contrast, the Democratic Party had carried an independence plank in its campaign platforms since the 1900 elections. After winning Congress and the White House in 1912, Woodrow Wilson and the Democrats followed through by enacting the Philippine Autonomy Act of 1916, or the Jones Law, which granted the Islands greater autonomy and contained the first explicit promise of independence upon the establishment of a 'stable government.' Believing that a Democratic Congress would be more receptive to independence lobbying, the Philippine Legislature began dispatching Independence Missions to Washington in 1919.

Negotiated by the 1934 Independence Mission led by Senate President Manuel L Quezon Jr, the Tydings-McDuffie Act was not the first independence law enacted by Congress. An earlier Independence Mission led by Senator Sergio Osmeña and Speaker Manuel Roxas had achieved the initial breakthrough by securing passage of the Hare-Hawes-Cutting Act.[14] Contingent upon the Philippine Legislature's acceptance, this law provided for a ten-year commonwealth period

[12] The Convention Law of 1934, Act 4125, 29 PL 243.
[13] The Philippine Independence Act, Public Law 73–127 [hereinafter, Tydings-McDuffie Act].
[14] The Hare-Hawes-Cutting Act, 47 Stat 761.

prior to the assumption by the Islands of complete sovereignty and imposed mandatory provisions regulating issues affecting US interests in the Islands, notably, trade, defence, and immigration. Partly by claiming credit for obtaining the Jones Law, Quezon had steadily supplanted Osmeña as the preeminent Filipino political leader and knew full well the electoral advantage conferred by wresting this ultimate concession from the Americans. Prevented by illness from joining the 'Os-Rox Mission,' Quezon began campaigning against the Hare-Hawes-Cutting Act even before the Mission returned and orchestrated removing Osmeña, Roxas, and their supporters from key legislative positions to ensure the law's rejection.

Osmeña and Roxas themselves conceded that the Hare-Hawes-Cutting Act was far from ideal, but believed it was the best package obtainable under the circumstances. Three features made it vulnerable to rejection: its gradually decreasing schedule for duty-free Philippine exports to the US over the ten-year commonwealth period; its cap on Filipino immigration to the US; and its stipulation allowing major US military installations throughout the Islands to counter the growing threat of Japanese invasion. Closely allied with powerful sugar interests who feared the end of free trade, Quezon also took offence at provisions restricting Filipino immigration and retaining US military bases. This led to a bruising battle between the 'Pros' led by Osmeña and Roxas and the 'Antis' under Quezon that culminated in the Act's rejection. Quezon then headed his own Independence Mission to Washington, only to discover that Congress would not reopen talks so soon after in-depth discussions about Philippine independence. Yet although the Tydings-McDuffie Act essentially re-enacted the Hare-Hawes-Cutting Act, Quezon pronounced himself 'happy to return to the Philippines the bearer of the law granting the Filipino people their complete independence.'[15] Quezon's happiness was warranted, since this success positioned him to win the Commonwealth Presidency and to become the independent Philippine Republic's presumptive first President.

B. The Delegates: 'Able Men'

To the journalist Navarro, '[n]o better collection of able men could have been gathered to draft the lasting principles of democracy that will serve as pillars of the institutions of a free Philippines.' Numbering 142 out of the 202 delegates, 'distinguished lawyers' dominated the Convention. Joining them were 'renowned professors,' 'reputable physicians,' and 'successful financiers, businessmen and farmers.'[16] Vice Governor-General Joseph Ralston Hayden took note of the delegates' political experience: with two delegates having served

[15] Navarro (n 2) at 14.
[16] Ibid. 35.

in the Revolutionary Congress and 85 in the Insular Government's central and local units,[17] the Convention was 'largely composed of practical politicians.'[18] To Navarro, this qualified them 'for whatever depends on the knowledge of mankind, on experience in mixed affairs, on a comprehensive, connected view of the various complicated, external, and internal interests which go to the creation of that multifarious thing called a free State – an Independent Philippines.'[19]

Interestingly, Navarro's glowing assessment was not shared by *New York Times* reporter Robert Aura Smith. Thanks to the exclusion as delegates of current judges and appointive civil service officials, it was 'clearly apparent that the constitutional convention, which was hailed in advance as an opportunity to bring together the ablest men in the country, is one of the weakest bodies that has been assembled here in recent years.'[20] Legislators were eligible for Convention seats, but Hayden observed that 'important politicians had declined to run … or at the last moment withdrew their candidacies.'[21] Neither Quezon nor Osmeña, the top two Filipino leaders under American rule, had vied for Convention seats – a decision Smith attributed to their desire to concentrate on the Legislature. Moreover, since many of the best men who had survived a brutal general election the month before Convention elections 'could not afford to participate in a second election,' defeated legislative candidates became delegates, allowing the minority party's numbers to almost equal that of Quezon's majority party. Finally, fresh memories of 'one of the bitterest' legislative elections led Quezon 'to allay hostility by promising equal prominence to minority men in the organization of the convention.' In combination, these various factors produced 'a group of delegates of practically no distinction and little political training.'[22]

This collective mediocrity caused 'disillusionment for all observers of the Philippine political scene.' Smith lamented, 'Disorder was apparent from the start.' Since the Tydings-McDuffie Act designated the House of Representatives as the Convention's venue, Quezon took this as the legislature's cue to organise and call the assembly into order. Resentful that Quezon, an unelected delegate, had appropriated this prerogative, Tomas Confesor of Iloilo and Eusebio Orense[23] of Batangas attempted to lead 'a filibuster before [Quezon] even swung the gavel, in protest against his usurping a power to which he had no clear right.' A month into the deliberations, more than thirty drafts had been submitted 'with little possibility that any will ever be considered' and 'long speeches' delivered

[17] Jose M Aruego, *The Framing of the Philippine Constitution*, 2 vols. (Manila: PEF 1949) 38–39 [hereinafter, 'Aruego, *Framing*'].

[18] Joseph Ralston Hayden, *The Philippines: A Study in National Development* (New York: MacMillan 1942) 35 [hereinafter 'Hayden'].

[19] Navarro (n 2) at 35.

[20] Robert Aura Smith, 'Filipinos In Snarl Over Convention' *New York Times*, 9 Sep 1934, at E8 [hereinafter 'Smith'].

[21] Hayden (n 18), at 35.

[22] Smith (n 20).

[23] Aruego (n 17) vol 1, at 47.

before rules had even been 'adopted by which a delegate could be declared out of order.'[24]

Interestingly, all three observers used 'ability' to gauge the delegates' quality, but employed different criteria. Common denominators were education and some practical political experience, but Smith and Hayden also considered whether a politician had served with 'distinction' and gained 'importance.' By their more stringent metric, delegates who made their cut 'stuck out in the convention hall like so many sore thumbs.'[25] These disparate assessments, however, obscure the homogeneity of players in a Filipino democracy that was, and still is, essentially a Schumpeterian intra-elite competition.

The American colonial regime's claims to democratic legitimacy were grounded in Filipino acceptance of American rule, which collaboration with colonial governance made most visible. But the ability to participate – and the validity of the consent that it signified – was greatly restricted, for benevolent imperialists were highly selective about whose consent counted. During the Treaty of Paris Senate ratification debates, anti-imperialists believed that the Philippine-American War meant that any American colonial government in the Islands would be sustained, not by Filipino consent, but by brute military force, thus violating a cardinal tenet of the American political faith. Root dismissed these claims saying, 'Nothing can be more misleading than a principle misapplied,' and limited the doctrine of consent's applicability to 'the conditions for which Jefferson wrote it, and the people to whom he applied it.'[26] Nonetheless, Root had encountered 'highly educated and able' and 'public-spirited and patriotic' men in both Puerto Rico and the Philippine Islands. While there were 'not enough of them to make a working government which would be anything but an oligarchy,'[27] their cooperation sanctioned American colonialism within American democracy.

Emerging in the late nineteenth century, these exceptional Filipinos consisted of *ilustrados*, or 'the enlightened ones,' who had acquired an education beyond the primary level and comprised approximately ten per cent of the Islands' population. Classifying *ilustrados* according to geographic origins, sources of wealth, educational attainment, and professions, Michael Cullinane's definitive study identifies four overlapping but internally differentiated groups, namely, municipal elites, provincial elites, urban elites, and the urban middle sector.[28]

[24] Smith, (n 20).

[25] Ibid.

[26] Root (n 11) at 47.

[27] Elihu Root, 'The Principles of Colonial Policy: Porto Rico, Cuba, and the Philippines' in Robert Bacon & James Brown Scott, *The Military and Colonial Policy of the United States: Addresses and Reports* (Cambridge, MA: Harvard University Press, 1916), 161–76, 163 [hereinafter 'Colonial Policy'].

[28] Michael Cullinane, *Ilustrado Politics: Filipino Elite Responses to American Rule, 1898–1908* (Quezon City: University of Ateneo Press, 2003) 18–22 & 331.

To Americans, only urban elites, primarily those based in Manila, and provincial elites possessed sufficient capacity. Descended from native and Spanish or Chinese *mestizo* families enriched by the agricultural export trade, especially in sugar, these *über*-elites were also the most highly educated *ilustrados*, typically holding advanced degrees in law or medicine from universities in Manila, Madrid or Paris. While urban elites usually resided in the port cities of Manila, Cebu, and Iloilo and provincial elites lived closer to their rural landholdings, they attended the same schools, read the same books, wrote for the same journals, married each other's sisters and cousins. Sharing overlapping ties and homogenous backgrounds that transcended geography, they formed what Benedict Anderson calls a cohesive 'pan-Philippine mestizo stratum.'[29]

These *über-ilustrados* appropriated the term 'Filipino' from Philippine-born Spaniards,' or *insulares*, who demanded preference to Spanish colonial administration jobs after English and American commercial houses had displaced them from the Islands' commercial life at the end of the Galleon Trade. *Insulares* invoked birth ties to the Islands to assert superior rights over recent *insulares* migrants from the newly independent American colonies and *peninsulares*, or Spaniards from Spain, who presumed to be more purely Spanish, more loyal, and more deserving of high positions in the Manila government.[30] Having earned advanced degrees and international acclaim, *über-ilustrados* also felt qualified to scale the Islands' social and political hierarchy. They began to lobby Spain for rights and opportunities and increasingly identified as Filipino. Failing in their campaign to replace Spanish regular priests with native secular priests in the Islands' parishes, *ilustrado* leaders competed for Spanish colonial administration positions against *insulares* and *peninsulares*, who coalesced to thwart them. Deeming inclusion hopeless, they began to envision separation from Spain and independent Filipino nationhood. Through the 1896 Philippine Revolution, the 1898 Spanish-American War, and the 1899 Philippine-American War, urban and provincial *ilustrados* were courted by Filipino Revolutionaries led by less educated and less wealthy *ilustrados* from the municipal elite and urban middle sectors, by Spanish Governor-General Basilio Agustin in a desperate eleventh-hour attempt to retain the Islands for Spain, and by the new American conquerors.

Although the most civilised natives, *ilustrados* remained uncivilised under the universal criteria Root espoused. Having 'merely a theoretical rather than a practical acquaintance with the processes of government,'[31] they lacked sovereign capacity by American standards, but could be civilised for sovereignty

[29] Benedict Anderson, 'Cacique Democracy in the Philippines' in Benedict Anderson (ed.), *The Spectre of Comparisons* (London: Verso 1998) 193–236, 198.

[30] Peter Stanley, *A Nation in the Making: The Philippines and the United States, 1899–1921* (Harvard, 1974) 34–35 [hereinafter 'Stanley'].

[31] Root, 'Colonial Policy' (n 27), at 163.

with American tutelage. Embracing identical civilisational standards, leading *ilustrados* were congenial to American mentoring, and their service in the Insular Government proxied for Filipino representation and consent. While couched in universal terms, literacy and property ownership as qualifications for suffrage and for appointive and elective officeholding privileged elites best positioned to qualify, thus formally institutionalising in politics their economic, social, and cultural preeminence. Forming the highest echelon of Filipino colonial officials were *ilustrados* like Philippine Commissioner Trinidad H Pardo de Tavera, Speaker and Senator Sergio Osmeña, and Resident Commissioner and Senate President Manuel L Quezon. Introducing public education and elections and multiplying the offices available to Filipinos expanded this pool of governing elites, but the education, experience, and various paths to power charted by leading Filipinos became virtual templates for insular political success that others, like the Convention delegates, replicated.

C. Safeguards

Despite his low opinion of the delegates, Smith had 'no reason to assume' that the Constitution would not be 'a well-drafted and satisfactory document.' Providing damage control were the Tydings-McDuffie Act's mandatory provisions, the organic acts that had functioned as the Islands' constitutions under US rule, and the conservatism of 'the real political leaders.' Restricting the delegates' discretion augured well to Smith 'for a final document which will meet the needs of the local case and win the entire approval of the United States.'[32]

i. Mandatory Provisions

Section 2 of the Tydings-McDuffie Act required that the Constitution establish a republican government and contain a Bill of Rights. Moreover, the Independence Law regulated US-Philippine interests with respect to their citizens, the US High Commissioner, and Commonwealth officers, legislators, and judges; protected religious liberty and provided public education; and supervised trade, defence, foreign affairs, public indebtedness and other obligations, and currency and coinage. Sections covering the transition period were to form part of the Constitution or contained in an ordinance appended thereto, while those pertaining to post-independence, embodied in a treaty subsequently to be concluded between both States.[33]

[32] Smith (n 20).

[33] Sections 2(a)(1) to (16) for Commonwealth and 2(b)(1) to (5) for Republic, Tydings-McDuffie Act.

ii. Organic Acts

Also powerfully influencing the delegates' constitutional choices were the three organic acts by which American colonial officials had calibrated the introduction of their constitutional democracy in the course of colonial governance. All colonial charters contained a territorial Bill of Rights that included all but two US Bill of Rights guarantees, namely, the right to bear arms and the right to a jury trial. Likewise, these laws also gradually separated the Insular Government's executive, legislative, and judicial branches, as Filipinos gained greater governing experience and competence. Specifically, these acts progressively increased Filipino control over the legislature while simultaneously extricating this branch from the American-controlled executive department. These internal structural shifts were reflected in the external forms assumed by the Insular Government: it resembled the American territorial government under McKinley's Instructions, followed by the British North American colonial government under the Organic Act, and, finally, the federal government under the Jones Law. Within these vehicles, Filipinos advanced from a minority role in the mixed executive-legislative Philippine Commission from 1900 to 1907, to full control, initially, over the Philippine Assembly, which served as the Insular Government's lower house to the Philippine Commission as upper house between 1907 and 1916, and, finally, over both the House of Representatives and the Philippine Senate from 1916 to 1935. The colonial political dynamic ordained by these designs shaped the delegates' understandings of executive, legislative, and judicial power as well as of the interplay between public and private spheres and informed their work.

iii. Conservatism

Increasing American confidence that the Constitution would retain the status quo was the known commitment of Quezon and Osmeña to conservatism. Osmeña was motivated by 'the desirability of reassuring the foreign community, which has been openly apprehensive about forthcoming political changes' that the 'new government will give it the same degree of protection as it has hitherto enjoyed' and that the document would be 'in no sense experimental.' Rather than radically transform prior colonial practice, the new Constitution would likely be 'based closely on American models and making little or no change in the characteristic governmental structure in the Philippines.'[34]

While neither was a delegate, Quezon and Osmeña continued to guide proceedings with an 'unseen hand,' as heads of the majority and minority parties, respectively. Hayden notes, 'party responsibility and activities openly remained as a part of Convention procedure,' despite efforts to minimise partisanship in

[34] Robert Aura Smith, 'Path of Basic Law Eased by Filipinos' *New York Times,* 23 May 1934, at E8; Robert Aura Smith, 'Turn to Right Urged by Osmeña' *New York Times,* 8 Jul 1934, at E8.

the project. For one, both were represented in the body by deputies: Quezon through Senator Claro M Recto, who became the Convention's president, and Osmeña, through his Os-Rox Mission partner Manuel Roxas. Neither Recto nor Roxas 'was merely the mouthpiece of the president of his party; yet each was the leading representative of that party in the constituent assembly.'[35]

Additionally, Quezon and Osmeña steered events through their respective party's caucuses. Hayden recounts, 'Both before and during the Convention caucuses were frequently held and important decisions were made therein,'[36] such as the assembly's organisation and officers[37] and the content of key provisions. This explains Smith's belief that 'delegates would consume some months in debate ... while leaders outside the convention draft the constitution for them and ultimately order its approval.'[38] Still, Hayden saw that party procedures and discipline 'were chiefly used not for partisan purposes, but rather to make the unwieldy assembly function and finally produce a satisfactory Constitution which would be accepted by the nation as a non-partisan charter of government.'[39]

This preoccupation with control was not misplaced, for the Convention began with inefficiency and disorganisation. Nearly a month after convening, rules had yet to be adopted and committees, fully formed and staffed; although, many florid speeches had already been delivered.[40] To discourage grandstanding, closed-door meetings were proposed, following the American Founders' strategy of insulating the Philadelphia Convention from public scrutiny, but the press balked.[41] Recognising that 'self-seekers ... might use the constitutional assembly' to enhance 'their personal popularity,' *The Philippines Herald* professed that 'the cooperation of the newspapers ... would not be impossible to obtain,' since the press already knew 'who are the solid men in our public life and who are the demagogues.'[42]

Likewise, the Convention adopted the committee system in order to expedite the drafting process and enable thorough consideration charter provisions. Forty-seven committees were created, with seven on the Convention's internal governance and operation and 40 on the Constitution itself. All provisions proposed at the plenary session would be referred to the appropriate committee, which would then submit reports to an 87-member Sponsorship Committee.

[35] Hayden (n 18) at 38.

[36] Ibid.

[37] Miguel Cuaderno, *The Framing of the Constitution of the Philippines* (Manila: Philippine Education Company, 1937) at 7–9.

[38] Smith (n 20).

[39] Hayden (n 18), at 38.

[40] See Salvador H Laurel (ed), *Proceedings of the Philippine Constitutional Convention – As Faithfully Reproduced from the Personal Records kept by Dr. Jose P Laurel*, 6 vols (Manila: Lyceum Press, 1966) [hereinafter 'Laurel'].

[41] Aruego (n 17) vol 1, at 77–78.

[42] 'The Part of the Press' *The Philippines Herald* (Manila 23 July 1934).

This mega-Committee would thereafter consider the reports, formulate the draft, and present it to the Convention for deliberation.[43] Initially confused about whether to consolidate proposals submitted by other committees or reconsider them anew, Sponsorship Committee members opted for the latter, but feared that to do so 'would unnecessarily retard the work of the convention, especially because the members of the committee were at liberty to dissent from the final report …'. Leading a bloc of younger, more 'liberal-minded' and 'independent' delegates not yet 'hardened within the moulds of narrow partisanship,' Vicente Lopez of Negros Oriental proposed forming a Sub-Committee of Seven to draft the charter, which was approved at the majority party's caucus. The Sponsorship Committee subsequently approved resolutions creating this body and another sub-committee of technical advisers to support it on 9 October 1934.[44]

Party mechanisms thus facilitated enforcing 'conservatism,' both with respect to the Convention's conduct and its output. Indeed, on the eve of final approval, the Sub-Committee of Seven managed to rush through 'a completely modified draft of the Philippine Constitution.' This leaner document 'suppressed many provisions so the final form actually contravenes the intentions of the delegates' and 'now expresses the will of a limited group.' Approval of this version was railroaded by Recto, who announced the modifications, and by Roxas, who presided over the session and refused 'to recognize opposition spokesmen after announcing that all changes had been approved by a majority of 112.'[45]

iv. Presidential Approval

One other 'safeguard' for ensuring the Filipino charter's essential conformity with American theory and practice was the prerequisite of securing the US President's approval. That delegates feared rejection is seen in protracted debates over the first major constitutional question tackled, the scope of the Philippine Constitution. From 28 August to 21 September 1934, they wrangled over whether the Convention's legal authority extended only to the Philippine Commonwealth or to the future Republic as well. On the one hand, the former faction was keen to avoid exceeding authority under the Tydings-McDuffie Act and to demonstrate accurate understanding of Philippine sovereignty's limited nature. Delegate Miguel Cuaderno of Bataan was wary of depriving 'our people, ten years from now of the liberty and opportunity to decide for themselves whether they would like to continue under the constitution … or make another one as any independent people, without any mandatory provisions …'. On the other hand, the latter faction desired economy and efficiency. Favouring one charter for both governments, La Union Delegate Camilo Osias suggested that, in order

[43] Aruego (n 17) vol 1, at 56–71.

[44] Ibid, at 79–82.

[45] 'Constitution Draft is Changed in Manila: Suggestions of Many Delegates Dropped – Final Approval by Convention Due Today' *New York Times* (New York 8 February 1935) 4.

to avoid incurring presidential disapproval, the assembly should declare a recess instead of adjourning after the draft's completion, so that it 'could be called at any time to consider' the US President's objections and 'make any such amendments as we may see fit …'.[46]

By a vote of 177 to 1, with one delegate signing his name in blood, the Philippine Constitution was adopted on 8 February 1935, then approved by President Franklin D Roosevelt on 24 March 1935 and ratified by popular vote on 14 May 1935. Commonwealth elections followed on 17 September 1935, with Quezon and Osmeña running together on the same ticket and winning on as President and Vice-President, respectively. The Philippine Commonwealth's inauguration on 15 November 1935 launched the ten-year transition to complete independence.

III. THE CONSTITUTIONAL DESIGN

When debates over the first draft commenced on 6 November 1934, Delegate Jose Laurel of Batangas reiterated Virgil's warning in the *Aeneid* to 'keep close to the shore; let others venture into the deep.' In crafting the constitutional text, the Yale-educated former Interior Secretary, Senator, and constitutional law professor advocated a 'constructive conservatism' or a 'conservative and at the same time a constructive and progressive attitude.'[47] Indeed, the 1935 Constitution built upon the past to guide the future.

A. Structure: Unitary and Departmental

Examining the Philippine government's external and internal dimensions, this part will first focus on the relationships between the central and local governing units of the Philippine state apparatus and then describe the interplay among its executive, legislative, and judicial branches.

i. Unitary State

Despite their transformative aspirations, Americans did not construct their colonial vehicle from scratch. Instead, it adapted the pre-existing Spanish administration, eschewing its theories while infusing it with their own governing principles. In turn, Filipino framers retained the Insular Government as the framework for both the Philippine Commonwealth and the Philippine Republic. It is through the Philippine government's structure, as opposed to its doctrines,

[46] Laurel (n 40) vol 1, at 521, 517–518.
[47] Aruego, *Origins* (n 1) vol 1, at 182.

that the Spanish legacy primarily endures. Consolidating authority over all government units and levels in the central government in Manila, this configuration mediated the application of American principles in the Islands.

ii. Unrivaled Sovereignty

All Philippine governments, colonial and independent, were unitary states that had no institutional competitors within Philippine territory. However, the Spanish and American colonial governments as well as the Philippine Commonwealth answered to their respective sovereigns, namely, the King of Spain for the former and the US government for the latter two. Naturally, independence would sever this tie for the Philippine Republic. Both theoretically and structurally, power was concentrated in a central government, which subordinated all other units. This differs from the federal architecture under the US Constitution, whose Article 1(8) granted Congressional authority over specific areas or activities and reserved residual sovereignty in the States through the Tenth Amendment. Outside the Union of States and incorporated territories en route to statehood, the federal government, specifically Congress, enjoyed organic, inherent, and plenary authority over unincorporated territories like the Philippine Islands. Through the *Insular Cases*, the US Supreme Court clarified that in these constitutional no-man's lands the US Constitution exerted only moral, but not legal, force, prompting Root's witty quip that 'The Constitution follows the flag, but doesn't quite catch up to it.'[48]

Although Congress controlled Philippine governance, it granted considerable autonomy to its insular agent, making the Insular Government supreme within its sphere.[49] The Philippine Commonwealth continued to exercise complete sovereignty over the Islands as Congress's agent during the ten-year transition period. Following independence, the Philippine Republic enjoyed its predecessors' vast authority, but located sovereignty in the Filipino people. Capiz Delegate Manuel Roxas, who had been Speaker and co-head of the Os-Rox Mission, explained that in a country 'with a small political sovereignty, constituted by a people expressing a whole and one sovereignty with a community of interests,' the system 'is generally unitary, one government in federated small nationalities, but one nation to govern and exercise jointly over all the territories.'[50]

[48] Philip C. Jessup, *Elihu Root*, 2 vols, vol 1 (Dodd, Mead and Company, Inc.: Archon Books, 1938; reprint, 1964), 348.

[49] See extensive discussion of US sovereignty in unincorporated territories in Leia Castañeda Anastacio, *The Foundations of the Modern Philippine State: Imperial Rule and the American Constitutional Tradition, 1898–1935* (New York: Cambridge University Press, 2016) 105–122 [hereinafter 'Castañeda Anastacio'].

[50] Aruego, *Origins* (n 1) vol 1, at 164.

iii. Administrative Centralisation

The concentrated sovereignty exercised by all four Philippine governments was complemented by a centralised administrative structure. At the onset of US rule, Americans found a sprawling Spanish colonial bureaucracy with four main divisions, but assisted by multiple advisory and consultative bodies whose interdepartmental membership performed redundant and competing functions.[51] American military and civil authorities streamlined this design by eliminating bodies with overlapping functions and reorganising and renaming its four main departments. To discourage Spanish-era patronage practices, Americans operated this bureaucracy using civil service principles of merit and fitness. The Philippine Constitution retained and expanded this insular machinery and elevated the civil service system to constitutional status, vesting oversight in an independent commission.[52]

Unified, centralised, and responsible to the colonial executive, the American colonial administration in the Islands was comparatively more developed[53] than the loosely organised 'patchwork state' that were its state and federal mainland counterparts.[54] Throughout US rule, Filipinos tried to take over this bureaucracy using whatever strategies their roles afforded. While controlling the Insular Legislature's lower house under the Organic Act, Filipino assemblymen attempted to equalise American and Filipino government salaries. After capturing both the Senate and the House under the Jones Law, legislators tried to hold the bureaucracy accountable to the Filipino people through the legislature as the Insular Government's only directly elected branch. They did so by creating combined American-Filipino executive-legislative bodies and channelling to them authority over colonial administration.[55] The Philippine and US Supreme Courts, however, later invalidated these mixed bodies for violating separation of powers.[56]

iv. Limited Local Autonomy

By default, the Philippine Constitution preserved provincial and municipal subordination to the central government. Both Spaniards and Americans placed the Manila government atop an administrative hierarchy that routed the capital's power all the way to the remotest barrios. Initially, American colonial

[51] Eliodoro Robles, *The Philippines in the Nineteenth Century* (Malaya 1969) 185–218.

[52] 1935 Phil Const, Art XII.

[53] David P Barrows, 'The Governor-General of the Philippines under Spain and the United States' (1916) 21(2) *American Historical Review* 288, at 301.

[54] Stephen Skowronek, *Building a New American State: The Expansion of National Administrative Capacity, 1877–1920* (CUP 1982; repr. 1997) 24–27.

[55] See Castañeda Anastacio (n 48), at 139–177.

[56] See *Government of the Philippine Islands v Springer*, 50 Phil. 259 (1927); *Agoncillo v Government of the Philippine Islands*, 50 Phil. 348 (1927); and *Springer v Government of the Philippine Islands; Agoncillo v Government of the Philippine Islands*, 277 US 189 (1928).

officials meant to alter this relationship. The Second Philippine Commission,[57] which was headed by William Howard Taft and became the Islands' first civilian government, had intended barrios to be incubators of democracy like New England town governments and enjoy similar autonomy. But when the Committee on Provinces and Municipalities submitted its report to the Sponsorship Committee in September 1934, its chairman Delegate Hermenegildo Villanueva of Negros Oriental lamented, 'the present system of local government has received universal criticism on account of the absence of an adequate measure of autonomy.'[58] This was because both US military and civilian officials merely adapted the Spanish framework for local governance to its purposes and basically retained and elaborated upon the channels of authority by which Manila had historically overseen local government.

During Spanish and US rule, provincial councils closely inspected and monitored municipal government work. Spanish colonial local officials answered to the Directorate General of Civil Administration, which fell under *Gobernacion y Fomento*, one of four branches overseen by the Spanish Governor-General. American colonial local officials reported first to the Executive Bureau and then to the Interior Secretary, both of whom answered to the American Governor-General, and American colonial bureaucratic offices also assigned local representatives directly responsible to them. Moreover, provinces and municipalities owed their existence to provincial and municipal government acts, so had to trace authority for measures to their incorporating statutes. Finally, Manila controlled local government revenues and finances. While originally intending to make local governments financially self-sufficient through property taxation, the Philippine Commission was impelled to allocate a greater portion of property tax revenues to Manila when it failed to pass an internal revenue law. This fiscal arrangement remained intact despite finding other central revenue sources.[59] Thus, aside from electing their own officials, local governments had 'very little control over their own local affairs.' Although their taxing power was 'supposed to be based upon a broad and general grant,' it had become 'subject to numerous exceptions provided in the statutes.' This near-complete dependence 'under the present organic laws of the Philippines' made the central government 'everything' and the local governments, 'nothing more than mere administrative units.'[60]

[57] The First Philippine Commission, which was headed by Cornell University president Jacob Gould Schurman, was an investigative body constituted in January 1899 and sent to the Islands prior to the outbreak of the Philippine-American War at the behest of Admiral George Dewey to help defuse escalating tensions between the American military government and Filipino revolutionaries. The Second Philippine Commission was sent to the Islands in April 1900 to perfect and complete the work begun by the US Army in establishing civil government in the Islands and served as the colony's highest governing body in July 1901.

[58] Report, Committee on Provincial and Municipal Governments, 25 September 1934, App G, Aruego, *Framing* (n 17) vol 2 at 866–870 & 867.

[59] Castañeda Anastacio (n 48), at 52–55.

[60] Aruego, *Framing* (n 17), vol 2, at 866–870 & 867.

To strengthen local governments for the future, the Committee submitted 'definite provisions' intended to 'give a surer and stronger protection to local autonomy than a mere general statement.' Apart from the power to elect local officials, the draft Article included the power to create their own revenue sources, levy taxes, claim a just share of central government revenues, determine the disposition and use of funds, consent to the designation of appointive officers from the central government, perform functions associated with local government administration, and control police forces.[61] These proposals, however, did not make the final document, which preserved colonial-era central-local relationships. Thus, to Roxas, post-colonial Philippine provinces remained 'only creatures of the Legislature' that exercised 'no independent sovereignty – separate and distinct from that of the nation.'[62] Delegate Jose S Reyes of Sorsogon regarded this 'absence of any provision increasing the autonomy of our municipalities and provinces' as the Constitution's 'most significant' omission.[63]

Enhancing efficient administration, structural consolidation also vested in the executive the management of government resources, which later facilitated their distribution as patronage by Quezon's Commonwealth and President Ferdinand E Marcos's Martial Law regime and enabled dictatorial control.

B. Separation of Powers

The government's main institutional checks were internal – that is, through the allocation of functions among executive, legislative, and judicial departments. Introduced to the Philippine jurisdiction by McKinley's Instructions, the separation of powers principle were among the 'certain great principles of government' that formed 'the basis of our governmental system' and were 'essential to the rule of law and the maintenance of individual freedom.'[64] Even under Spain, central government departments were already evolving towards functional differentiation, except that competition existed, not among branches enjoying varied authority, but among individuals with shared authority over identical tasks. But for both the Spanish and American colonial governments, separating powers did not create balance, for in both cases, the executive dominated: the Spanish Governor-General extended his King's absolute monarchy; the American Governor-General personified the US's organic and inherent sovereignty over the Islands. Similarly, their Filipino successor remained the Philippine government's supreme official.

[61] Ibid, at 866–870 & 868.
[62] Aruego, *Origin* (n 1) vol 1, at 163.
[63] Ibid, at 155.
[64] McKinley's Instructions.

i. Executive

The Philippine Constitution vested executive power in a directly elected President, making *him* the executive department and, as an individual, equal to and independent of the legislative and judicial branches. 'Within the orbit of his own sphere,'[65] the President virtually monopolised powers. Like Spanish and American Governors-General, he was the nation's administrative head with 'control of all executive departments, bureaus, and offices' and 'general supervision over all local governments.' Consequently, department heads could appear before the Legislature 'upon their own initiative,' but the Legislature could only request, rather than compel, their appearance, 'unless the public interest shall require otherwise and the President shall state so in writing.'[66] Along with appointment, diplomatic, and pardoning powers, the President was commander-in-chief with authority to call out the armed forces to suppress lawless violence, insurrection, or rebellion 'whenever it becomes necessary' and to suspend the writ of habeas corpus and declare martial law in case of invasion, insurrection, or rebellion, or imminent danger thereof.[67] Marcos's Martial Law proclamation was grounded on the executive's commander-in-chief powers.

Delegates like Reyes objected to this vast concentration of unchecked authority.[68] Although the Legislature could confirm appointments and ratify treaties,[69] the President could encroach upon traditional legislative prerogatives, notably, appropriations and legislation. The President initiated the appropriations process by submitting a budget, which the Legislature could not increase.[70] Moreover, the presidential veto extended, not only to entire bills, but to line items in appropriations, revenue, and tariff bills and in measures to increase public debt.[71] The President could set the legislative agenda and could, 'in times of war or other national emergency,' be empowered by the Legislature 'to promulgate rules and regulations to carry out a declared national policy.'[72] To Camarines Norte's delegate, Wenceslao Vinzons, this emergency grant was unprecedented in imposing 'absolutely no limit' except those specified by the Legislature at the onset. 'Such a power,' according to the Convention's youngest member, 'has never been exercised by even the most powerful executives in this universe;' and could 'give rise to a strong man who may, in a desire to gratify his personal ambitions, seize the reins of government.'[73]

[65] Aruego, *Origin* (n 1) vol 1, at 394.
[66] Phil. Const. Art VI§10.
[67] Phil. Const. Art VII§11.
[68] Aruego, *Origin* (n 1) vol 1, at 156.
[69] Phil. Const. Art VII§11(3) and (7).
[70] Phil. Const. Art VI§9.
[71] Phil. Const. Arts VI§11(1), (2), and (3).
[72] Phil. Const. Art VII§11(5) and Art VI§16.
[73] Aruego, *Origin* (n 1) vol 5, at 389–391.

But more delegates equated a weak executive with a weak government, so they made a powerful executive in charge of a fortified unitary state. General Douglas MacArthur traced this imperial Filipino presidency to 'the pattern of Oriental psychology to respect and follow aggressive, resolute, and dynamic leadership.'[74] Philippine Supreme Court Justice George A Malcolm agreed that, 'Filipino masses react more favorably to one-man government than to more dispersed direction.' Consequently, 'the wide array of powers lodged by the Constitution in the Filipino President – not to mention the many which are extra-constitutionally exercised by red-blooded occupants of the office – conforms to tradition, experience, and preference.'[75] But to what extent was this supposed 'nature' conditioned by 'nurture'?

Filipino experience of executive power, both under Spaniards and Americans, had always been one of tremendous strength. Specifically, powerful American Governors-General like W Cameron Forbes and Leonard Wood enfleshed this constitutional role for Filipinos. Thus, Pangasinan's delegate Jose M Aruego recounted, 'there were not so many extended debates … on the executive power principally,' since these provisions 'had been taken largely from the Jones Law and the American federal and state constitutions, which for historical reasons exercised a very dominating influence among the delegates …'.[76] Yet ought not this same historical experience have cautioned Filipinos against overweening executives and convinced them to strengthen the Legislature from which they had launched such effective resistance?[77] Instead of looking to Philippine history, however, Vinzons found his cautionary tale in Latin American countries, which, he felt, had erred in modelling their executives on the US President 'without realizing that the Latin-American people are not well prepared for such powers for the Chief Executive.'[78] But rather than fear Latin American 'instability, revolution, dictatorship' or Oriental despotism, Laguna delegate Conrado Benitez played up the positives: he took pride in inheriting 'from Occidental civilization the greatest contribution of Western culture to political institutions,' which originated 'from Latin sources' and were produced by 'the Latin temperament' and found reassurance in the Filipinos' Oriental background, since it was 'a very stable civilization,' indeed 'the second most stable' and 'the most highly developed civilization next to the Occidental civilization.'[79]

Ultimately, however, urgency may have been decisive. 'A strong executive he is intended to be,' Laurel explained, 'because a strong executive we shall need,

[74] George Arthur Malcolm, *American Colonial Careerist: Half a Century of Official Life and Personal Experience in the Philippines and Puerto Rico* (Christopher 1957) 127.

[75] Ibid.

[76] Aruego, *Framing* (n 17) vol 1, at 393.

[77] Castañeda Anastacio (n 48) at 139–177.

[78] Aruego, *Origin* (n 1) vol 1, at 168–170.

[79] Ibid, at 168–170 & 176–177.

especially in the early years of our independent or semi-independent existence.' In times of 'profound and Octavian peace,' such a leader would not become 'a "monarch" or a dictator,' but 'virtually so becomes in an extraordinary emergence.' Consequently, 'whatever may be his position, he bulwarks, normally, the fortifications of a strong constitutional government, but abnormally in extreme cases, he is suddenly ushered in as a Minerva, full-grown and in full panoply to war, to occupy the vantage ground as the ready protector and defender of the life and honor of his nation.'[80] For Laurel to say this is surprising, since he had figured centrally in contentious battles fought by Filipino leaders against Governor-General Wood. But perhaps he feared more the far from imaginary dangers threatening the viability of the nascent Filipino state. Apart from weathering the political and economic challenges of independence, the Philippine government faced both a Communist menace and a possible Japanese invasion. Unfortunately, fears of a dictatorial President proved equally real, for Marcos galvanised the office's potential using the Communist threat as pretext.

ii. Legislature

Failure to offset executive with legislative power was due neither to the delegates' ignorance nor inexperience with the legislature's ability to counterbalance executive hegemony. As previously mentioned, the legislative branch had been the institutional vessel of Filipino representation in the Insular Government. Evoking British North American colonial practice, American officials controlled the magisterial executive and judicial branches, but gradually devolved the popular legislative branch to 'the people.' Just as American colonial assemblies protected colonists' rights against British Crown officers,[81] so, too, did the Philippine Assembly under Governor-General Forbes, from 1909–1913, and the Philippine Legislature under Governors-General Francis Burton Harrison and Wood, from 1913–1928, assert Filipino rights through the Legislature and invade the executive branch through parliamentary means. But while Americans empowered their own legislatures after overthrowing the British, Filipino delegates instead enabled executive encroachment into traditional legislative prerogatives. They also resisted attempts to weaken the presidential veto and to prevent the emergency delegation of lawmaking powers to the President and rejected the proposal to shift the voting base for presidential elections from the people to the Legislature.[82] Such a handicapped Legislature mounted feeble resistance against Marcos, who shut it down soon after declaring martial law.

[80] Aruego, *Origin* (n 1) vol 1, at 183.

[81] See generally Jack P Greene, *The Quest for Power: The Lower Houses of Assembly in the Southern Royal Colonies, 1689–1776* (Chapel Hill: University of Carolina Press, 1966).

[82] Aruego, *Framing* (n 17) vol 1, at 395–397.

a. Presidentialism v Parliamentarism

To curb executive power, some delegates proposed recreating mixed parliamentary bodies like the Council of State through which Filipinos had increased their role in US colonial governance. Composed of the Governor-General, the Speaker, and the Senate President, the Council was created by Speaker Sergio Osmeña and Governor-General Harrison to replace the defunct Philippine Commission that had smoothed Filipino-American dealings within the Insular Government from 1900 to 1916. With a Filipino minority, an American majority, and the American Governor-General as President, the hybrid Commission enacted laws as the insular legislature and implemented them as the Governor-General's cabinet. Even after the Organic Act converted the Commission into the Insular Legislature's upper house from 1907–1913, its members continued to hold cabinet portfolios. When the Jones Law abolished the Commission and made the Legislature entirely Filipino, the Council of State was formed extra-constitutionally as the Commission's analogue. Justified as facilitating executive-legislative cooperation, bodies like the Council became the primary conduits for Filipino insular institutional control under the Jones Law. This was Osmeña's so-called 'quasi-parliamentary strategy,' which worked while American-Filipino/executive-legislative relations were cordial. Under the acerbic Governor-General Wood, however, these mixed bodies, notably the Board of Control charged with managing government corporations, became flashpoints of conflict and were judicially invalidated. Governor-General Henry L Stimson later revived the Council of State, but as a purely advisory body.[83] The Council's utility prompted delegates to propose one for the Philippine government, but since its main function under colonial rule had been to afford some Filipino control over a Governor-General who was appointed by and accountable only to the US President, it was deemed unnecessary, since 'there would be more cooperation in the government' when all constitutional officers were Filipino.[84]

Another parliamentary feature was the proposal to amend the prohibition barring legislators from holding other government offices or employments without forfeiting their seats. Throughout US rule, legislators had been cabinet secretaries or members of hybrid executive-legislative bodies. Amendment sponsors delegates Vinzons and Manuel Lim of Manila desired to 'make the Constitution flexible' so that the country could develop or adopt the parliamentary system without having to amend the Constitution and also to 'permit the continuance of the practice evolved under the Jones Law of appointing members of the lawmaking body to serve as heads of some of the executive departments.'[85] Yet debates over this proposal revealed a deeper rift over the presidential and parliamentary forms of government.

[83] Castañeda Anastacio (n 48) at 63, 140, 163–170, 202–205, 221–228 & 242.
[84] Aruego, *Framing* (n 17) vol 1, at 450–452.
[85] Ibid, at 302–305.

Although the Insular Government was modelled on the presidential system, its practice had been much more muddled, as seen in the Philippine Commission and the Council of State. Filipino parliamentary proclivities, however, date back to the still-born 1899 Malolos Constitution, which incorporated strong parliamentary elements into the Filipino revolutionary government. Drafted by Felipe Calderon, a Manila *ilustrado*, this charter vested in a unicameral National Assembly the right to elect and impeach the President, to direct cabinet members, and to appoint the Supreme Court Chief Justice and the *Procurador General*. It reflected his class's suspicion of the 'ignorant' military sector led by General Aguinaldo, the revolutionary government's president, and their corresponding desire to neutralise the military oligarchy with 'the oligarchy of intelligence.'[86] Filipino parliamentary inclinations resurfaced in the 1935 Constitutional Convention, which Roxas attributed to a disdain for presidentialism[87] due to difficulties diluting the American Governor-General's concentrated authority. Delegates likely also wanted legislative restraints on the executive, since Quezon, who was expected to be President, had ruled colonial politics with an iron hand.

Opponents of the Lim-Vinzons amendment believed that the Convention had reached 'the crossroads' and had to decide between presidentialism, 'with its concomitant doctrines of the separation of powers and of checks and balances,' and parliamentarism 'with its accompanying fusion of legislative or executive powers and with the legislature governing through the cabinet.' In opposition, delegate Elpidio Quirino cited the dilemma he faced when he backed laws as a Senator but opposed them as a cabinet secretary if the Governor-General found them defective. While Roxas felt that Jones Law parliamentary innovations helped 'democratize the executive department' by making the American Governor-General answerable to the people's representatives in the Legislature, they would be unnecessary when the President who was not 'a foreigner appointed by a foreign power, but a Filipino citizen directly elected by the people.' Of course, Filipinos later realized that foreigners did not monopolise autocratic predilections. Defeating the Lim-Vinzons amendment 96 to 11, delegates chose the presidential system, because supporters like Cebu Delegate Jesus M Cuenco were 'convinced that, considering the idiosyncrasies and ways of our people, a government of the parliamentary type would be the cause, the perennial source of continuous anarchy and misgovernment in this country.'[88]

b. Unicameralism v Bicameralism

Less concerned with restraining executive abuse, many delegates seemed keener to prevent hierarchies among legislators. Reacting perhaps to the long-time

[86] Cesar Adib Majul, *The Political and Constitutional Ideas of the Philippine Revolution* (Quezon City: University of the Philippines Press, 1967) reprinted in 1996, 178–182.
[87] Aruego, *Framing* (n 17) vol 1, at 159.
[88] Ibid, at 306–308 & 174.

dominance of Quezon's Nacionalista Party, the Convention's 'greatest battle'[89] was that over unicameralism and bicameralism.

The Committee on Legislative Power had recommended bicameralism, with a House elected from geographical districts and a Senate, by proportional representation nationwide. Supporters included Roxas, Laurel, and other 'able men,' who contended that a second chamber would 'serve as a check against hasty and ill-considered legislation;' 'draw more matured [sic], experienced, and able men;' 'be less susceptible to bribery and the control of big interests;' and 'provide a means for securing national views on general questions contrasted to the generally parochial views of men selected from all small geographical districts.' '[I]n vogue' worldwide, bicameralism was also familiar to Filipinos, and 'the time was not propitious' for them to 'venture in experiments, as in the adoption of the unicameral system.' Unicameralists, however, argued that a single chamber would simplify the machinery, more easily allocate responsibility, and operate more efficiently and economically, especially during the Commonwealth's 'period of stress and probation.' They feared, too, that a bicameral legislature 'would be a vestige of aristocracy, with the members of the Senate feeling that they were greater and more important than those of the lower house; whereas, under a unicameral system, all the legislators would be of equal rank.'[90]

The Organic Act had introduced bicameralism to the Islands by converting the Philippine Commission from sole legislative body to the new Insular Legislature's upper house and creating an all-Filipino Philippine Assembly as lower house. Dominated by Americans, the Commission filtered bills filed by an inexperienced Assembly. When the Jones Law established an all-Filipino bicameral Legislature, Americans controlled lawmaking via the Governor-General's extensive veto powers. Both legislative houses fell under the sway of the Nacionalista Party, which rose to power campaigning for independence during the first Assembly elections in 1907 and never yielded hegemony.[91] Legislative leaders, notably Quezon, had expressed misgivings about unicameralism[92] and tried through caucuses to steer delegates towards bicameralism. But while bicameralism enjoyed more support, advocates could not agree on the mode for senatorial elections – whether nationwide, provincial, or regional, as under the Jones Law. Thus divided, bicameralists lost to the unicameralists, who found the economy argument most persuasive. Nonetheless, the Philippine Commonwealth reverted to a bicameral legislature when the Constitution was amended in 1940.

Some delegates still believed that a body like the Senate was necessary to vet executive appointments. Wary of entrusting confirmations to an unwieldy National Assembly, a group of delegates led by Laurel proposed creating a Permanent Commission to confirm appointments, prosecute impeachment

[89] Aruego, *Origin* (n 1) vol 1, at 184.
[90] Ibid, at 184–228.
[91] Cullinane (n 28), at 258–263 & 289.
[92] Robert Aura Smith, 'Philippines Favor Unicameral Form' *New York Times*, 28 Oct 1934, E8.

cases, and formulate legislative proposals for the Assembly. He rationalised it as essential to check the executive and to serve as the Assembly's 'repository of able men.' Laurel's second rationale may have doomed the proposal, for Aruego notes that the Permanent Commission 'was opposed mainly because it was feared that it might develop into a privileged body in violation of the spirit of democratic government.' And rather than check the President, opponents thought 'it would turn out to be an agency to serve as his own instrument,' so 'it would be better to lodge the confirming power in the National Assembly than in a close group, like the Permanent Commission.'[93]

Rejecting the Permanent Commission, delegates later formed the Commission on Appointments and the Commission on Impeachment to handle two functions that would have been performed by the Permanent Commission had it been created or by the Assembly *en banc* in default of any other internal body. Likewise constituted was an Electoral Commission to adjudicate election contests. All three commissions drew its members from the Assembly's majority and minority parties and were refereed by a Justice of the Supreme Court.[94] Under US rule, the Nacionalista Party had dictated appointments, impeachments, and election contests by holding a majority in both houses of the Insular Legislature. By creating these bipartisan commissions, delegates removed these functions from a cumbersome National Assembly while impeding a majority party's ability to railroad its agenda through its viselike grip on key legislative roles.

iii. Judiciary

If the Legislature weakly restrained executive power, the Judiciary proved itself Alexander Hamilton's proverbial 'least dangerous branch.'[95] Within the inherited American constitutional system, the Judiciary was the constitutional enforcer of separation of powers, the final arbiter whose 'province and duty' it was, according to Chief Justice John Marshall's foundational *Marbury v Madison* opinion, 'to say what the law is.'[96] Unfortunately, several factors hindered the Philippine judiciary from effectively serving as constitutional gatekeeper.

Towards the end of Spanish rule, Philippine courts had only begun to emerge from the executive ambit, and their primary task of dispute resolution, only recently reclassified from an administrative to a judicial function. Bereft of their Anglo-American counterparts' political and social preeminence,

[93] Aruego, *Framing* (n 17) vol 1, at 273–280.

[94] Ibid, at 257–273 & 280–287.

[95] Clinton L Rossiter & Charles R Kessler (eds), *The Federalist Papers* (New York: Mentor, 1999) 433 (Federalist No 78).

[96] *Marbury v Madison*, Opinion, US Supreme Court, 24 Feb 1803, in Charles F Hobson, et al (eds) *The Papers of John Marshall*, (Chapel Hill: University of North Carolina Press, 1990) vol 6, 160–187, 183.

Philippine courts also lacked personnel trained in the language and tenets of the transplanted legal tradition, specifically, judicial review. Institutionally, the Philippine Supreme Court operated in a lopsided terrain tilted towards the political branches, particularly the executive. Inheriting his Spanish predecessor's commanding position in the insular institutional setting, the American Governor-General, through the Philippine Commission, controlled judicial appointments, administration, and financing. Jurisprudentially, the 'separate spheres' approach prevailing in the US mainland had inclined the Philippine judiciary to defer to the political branches' exercise of prerogatives assigned to them by the organic acts or inherent in their roles.[97] As we shall see, this translated to anaemic Bill of Rights scrutiny of legislative acts. Additionally, the Court regarded the Governor-General as personifying US sovereignty in the Islands, so categorised all his acts as official and exempted from judicial review, both substantively and procedurally.[98] Judicial deference, notably its propensity to treat executive acts as political questions, account in part for the muddled outcome of the Martial Law cases challenging Marcos's power grab, which effectively lent it judicial validity.[99]

Historically weak, the Philippine Supreme Court began buttressing its independence in the 1920s. *Borromeo v Mariano* construed an Administrative Code provision allowing the assignment of judges from one district to another as depriving the Governor-General of the power to 'force upon the judge of one district an appointment to another district against his will, thereby removing him from his district.' It later invalidated an amendment that authorised switching judicial appointments by lottery for potentially threatening judicial independence in the event that 'a judge who had, by a decision incurred the ill will of an attorney or official,' and subsequently was 'removed from one district, demoted, and transferred to another district, at possibly a loss of salary, all without the consent of the judicial officer.'[100]

Filipino framers consolidated efforts to shore up judicial independence. The Constitution abandoned the old US rule that prescribed by statute matters concerning pleading, practice, and procedure before courts and instead heeded American federal and state developments in giving rule-making power over these matters to the Supreme Court. To 'control the discretion of the appointing power,' delegates enshrined the *Borromeo* doctrine in Article VIII§7, which prevented judges 'appointed for a particular district' to be 'designated or transferred to another district without the approval of the Supreme Court.'[101]

But while shielding judicial administration from executive and legislative interference, delegates did little to strengthen the Judiciary with respect to the

[97] *Barcelon v Baker*, 5 Phil 87, 96–98 (1905).
[98] Castañeda Anastacio (n 48), at 92–96, 105–121.
[99] See *Javellana v Executive Secretary*, 50 SCRA 30 (1973).
[100] *Borromeo v Mariano*, 41 Phil. 322, 328 (1921).
[101] Aruego, *Framing* (n 17) vol 1, at 497–501, 507, & 511–516.

political branches. Seeing how the US Supreme Court had tried to thwart President Franklin D Roosevelt's New Deal response to the Great Depression, delegates resolved to allow their President to address emergencies without being shackled by their Supreme Court. Their solution was to make the grant of emergency executive authority explicit in the Constitution, thereby erasing doubt about its existence. Sponsoring the provision, Roxas explained that this extraordinary measure 'was inspired to make possible in the Philippines a delegation of legislative power in times of emergency, similar to what was being done in the United States under the administration of President Franklin D. Roosevelt.' Since New Deal measures faced constitutional challenge in the US mainland, the committee recommended the delegation so that 'the constitutionality of similar measures, in case they would be deemed necessary in the Philippines some day, would be sure.'[102]

With formidable powers and weak institutional competitors, the President was checked only by public opinion, impeachment, and the bar against re-election immediately following a single six-year term. Rejecting the efficacy of each, Vinzons argued that since Philippine public opinion was not 'well developed,' it 'cannot be relied on.' Additionally, the power of impeachment was 'a dead letter law in any constitution,' noting that throughout America's 150-year history, there was 'only a single instance of a President impeached,' but Andrew Johnson's 'impeachment failed by a single vote' at his Senate trial. Only term limits seemed promising, except that this provision, which was inspired by the experience of Latin American republics, did not go far enough, since it allowed 'reelection after the intervening term.' With the Philippines's 'Latin temperament' and 'Oriental background which always follows the predominant and powerful party,' the President who 'has a political power which he can easily use to advantage' may 'perpetuate himself in power' and 'get himself re-elected after every intervening term.'[103] Vinzons's concerns proved warranted. As Commonwealth President in 1941, Quezon engineered an amendment reducing the presidential term to four years but with no bar against re-election.

IV. SUBSTANCE: THE BILL OF RIGHTS

Substantively, the relationship between the Philippine government and individuals was regulated primarily by the Bill of Rights. Policing the boundaries between public and private, as it did those between the three great government branches, was the Judiciary. Indeed, Roxas considered the Judiciary's 'most important function' that of safeguarding 'personal or individual rights guaranteed in the Constitution,' making the Supreme Court 'the only bulwark of the people against the abuses of the Government that they establish through the

[102] Ibid, at 388–389.
[103] Aruego, *Origin* (no 1) vol 1, at 170–171.

Constitution, to defend the rights whose invasion they provide against in the Bill of Rights.'[104]

Filipino understandings of the public-private relationship formed part of their constitutional inheritance. In turn, conceptions were moulded in colonial Bill of Rights scrutiny of Insular Government activities. But rhetoric did not quite match colonial reality. Forged in the course of American colonialism's efforts to modernise the Philippine Islands, Philippine Bill of Rights jurisprudence mostly legitimated, rather than limited, the Insular Government's transformative interventions. When Filipino leaders captured the Legislature, they deployed state capacities towards their own vision of national development. Constitutional text reflected, even made explicit, this colonial incongruence between the theory of a laissez-faire state and the practice of a tropical *dirigiste*. For expressing 'the individualistic liberalism of the eighteenth and nineteenth century' while simultaneously 'providing for vast extensions in the sphere of governmental functions,' the Constitution contained no 'definite philosophy,' which constituted Reyes's 'fundamental objection to this document.'[105]

A. Progressivism

To make American-style constitutional democracy viable in the Islands, American colonialism undertook creating the material basis to support Filipino acquisition of sovereign capacity. But Americans found the Islands a terrain as undeveloped as its natives were uneducated and besieged by war and disease. It was in the course of pacifying the populace and eradicating epidemic disease that a Philippine Supreme Court institutionally conditioned to defer to political branches first defined the scope of the Insular Government's powers and adjudicated constitutional challenges against them.

As a 'creation of the United States, acting through the President and Congress,'[106] the Insular Government found in its principal's 'general,' 'plenary,' 'sovereign,' 'discretionary,' and 'supreme' powers in unincorporated territories[107] sufficient authority to carry out its civilising mandate. Included among its sovereign powers was the familiar trilogy of taxation, police power, and eminent domain. Of these three, it was police power that most frequently undergirded the Insular Government's far-reaching programmes, which were progressive in their goals, nature, and strategies. Without federalism's institutional checks and a more balanced interdepartmental configuration, only the Bill of Rights

[104] Ibid, at 161–162.
[105] Ibid, at 154.
[106] *US v Bull*, 15 Phil. 7 (1910).
[107] See, eg, *Benner v Porter*, 50 US (9 How.) 235 (1850); *National Bank v County of Yankton*, 101 US 129 (1879); *Murphy v Ramsey*, 114 US 15 (1885); *Mormon Church v US*, 136 US 1 (1890); *Boyd v Nebraska*, 143 US 135 (1892); *Simms v Simms*, 175 US 162 (1899).

mediated the Insular Government's assertions of its vast powers, and they proved to be James Madison's proverbial 'parchment barriers.'[108]

i. Police Power and Due Process

The Philippine Supreme Court articulated Philippine police power doctrine in *US v Toribio*. This public health case imported Massachusetts Chief Justice Lemuel Shaw's classic definition of police power in *Commonwealth v Alger* as that 'vested in the legislature by the constitution to make, ordain, and establish all manner of wholesome and reasonable laws, statutes, and ordinances … not repugnant to the constitution, as they shall judge to be for the good and welfare of the Commonwealth, and of the subjects of the same.'[109] Later expounding on measures contemplated by police power, the Court introduced the rubric 'public health, public safety, public morals, and general prosperity and welfare of its inhabitants.'[110] This expansive template enabled 'all kinds of restrictions and burdens in order to secure the general health, comfort, and prosperity of all,'[111] such that 'any attempt to define police power with circumstantial precision' savored 'of pedantry.'[112]

Limiting police power intrusions into personal and property rights was the due process guarantee, which all three organic acts introduced to the Islands. Article III, §1(1) of the 1935 Philippine Constitution comes from the Organic Act and the Jones Law, which combined US due process and equal protection clauses, to wit: 'No person shall be deprived of life, liberty, or property without due process of law, nor shall any person be denied the equal protection of laws.' Apart from defining Philippine police power, *US v Toribio* also established Philippine due process doctrine. Sustaining an ordinance aimed at preventing a rinderpest epidemic among carabao, the Islands' primary beast of burden, the Court required the state to justify interventions by demonstrating, 'first, that the interests of the public generally, as distinguished from those of a particular classes, require such interference' and 'second, that the means are reasonably necessary for the accomplishment of the purpose, and not unduly oppressive upon individuals.'[113] This adopted as the Philippine rule substantive, rather than procedural, due process towards which US constitutional jurisprudence was evolving. While more stringent than procedural tests, however, Philippine due process did not significantly block Insular Government interventions.

Habituated by the separate spheres approach, the Philippine Supreme Court generally subjected the political branches' activities to pro forma review.

[108] *The Federalist Papers* (n 94) at 276 (Federalist No 48).
[109] *Commonwealth v Alger*, 61 Mass (7 Cush) 53 (1851).
[110] *US v Gomez Jesus*, 31 Phil 218 (1915) and *US v Pompeya*, 31 Phil 245 (1915).
[111] *US v Gomez Jesus* 225 (1915).
[112] *US v Salaveria*, 39 Phil 102, 108 (1918).
[113] *US v Toribio*, 15 Phil 95 (1910).

Moreover, the criteria of necessity and proportionality were sufficiently broad to accommodate the progressive synthesis of science, law, and administration that typified Insular Government initiatives. Indeed, American officials felt freer in the Islands to experiment with Progressive-era policies that had met stiffer challenge in the mainland. Thus, the Islands served as a progressive laboratory for programmes spanning public health, public education, urban planning, policing, forestry, even meteorology.[114] Finally, the public purpose requirement was easily hurdled by a civilising mission aimed at modernising primitive native notions and habits, effectively making otherwise private behaviour a public preoccupation.

By essentially retaining colonial-era provisions, the Constitution preserved their colonial meanings. Delegate Salvador Araneta of Manila, a progressive businessman and lawyer, even advocated freezing jurisprudential developments in due process by allowing only deprivations of rights and property that conformed to 'reasonable law and procedure.' But Laurel opposed both transferring to courts the legislative function of determining the wisdom, reasonableness, and expediency of laws and circumscribing the scope of 'judicial statesmanship' through too much specificity. Most important, he hesitated altering the inherited text for fear that changing 'some interpretations' might entail reversing 'decisions consecrated since time immemorial, from the time of Marshall, and also decisions handed down by our tribunals of justice in this jurisdiction.' Besides, Laurel was unsure that proposed changes would improve the traditional formulation.[115]

ii. Social Justice

Maintaining the legal regime that enabled the Insular Government's progressive schemes, the 1935 Constitution also kept the colonial era's faith in Progressivism's ability to materially improve life on the Islands. This vision of progress, defined by Benitez as one that enlisted science to control nature and manage resources for social welfare,[116] was articulated in the constitutional commitment to promote scientific research and invention[117] and social justice.[118] Arguably, measures that transgressed individual and property rights to achieve social justice could fit within the capacious American-era police power rubric and lax due process scrutiny. But while loath to depart from colonial text and practice, delegates were willing to grant the Philippine government explicit authority to accomplish these objectives. Two factors appear to have impelled this move: judicial challenges to the New Deal in the US mainland that Philippine courts were replicating and a growing Communist insurgency.

[114] See Alfred W McCoy & Francisco Scarano (eds), *Colonial Crucible: Empire in the Making of the Modern American State* (Madison: University of Wisconsin Press, 2009).

[115] Aruego, *Framing* (n 17) vol 1, at 154–155.

[116] Aruego, *Origin* (n 1) vol 1, at 177–178.

[117] Phil. Const. Art XIII§4.

[118] Phil. Const. Art II§5.

Delegates feared the impending collapse of the prevailing political and socio-economic system. Since the mid-nineteenth century, the Philippines had been an agricultural export economy whose most profitable cash crop was sugar. This created a two-class society composed of feudalistic relationships between dyads of wealthy landowners and peasant masses bound together by obligations of mutual aid rendered on an individual, rather than a collective, basis. In exchange for providing cash, grain, or assistance to chronically needy peasants, the propertied received 'such intangibles as personal loyalty and obedience.'[119] According to Peter Stanley, American colonial actors aspired to 'break through traditional patterns of dependence, promote individual initiative and mobility, and reduce the economic imbalance between rich and poor'[120] by spreading skills and instilling bourgeois values in the *tao* of the fields. But while aggressively remaking natives in their image, Americans left property arrangements intact due to treaty obligations with Spain, concern for losing the cooperation of landowning *ilustrado* elites, and a philosophical aversion to redistribution.[121] Instead, they relied on capitalism to spur the economic growth necessary to transform Philippine society[122] and directed government resources towards creating a business-friendly environment.

Unfortunately, numerous entry barriers blocked the flow of American investment to the Islands. Associating exploitation with traditional imperialism, Congress restricted the ability of American corporations to own land and develop the Islands' natural resources. Filipinos themselves, however, resisted allowing yet another foreigner into an economy historically dominated by Spanish and Chinese interests and were anxious that American corporations with established Philippine concerns would lobby Congress to retain the Islands in order to protect their investments. In default of competing industries, the agricultural export trade became further entrenched, benefiting moreover from the inclusion of Philippine products within the US tariff wall and from Insular Government support.[123] This made sugar elites spectacularly wealthy and translated to vast political influence, both direct and indirect. Unfortunately, profits were not invested in modernising farming equipment and techniques, much less in launching new businesses, but in supporting their fabulous lifestyles, while government extended credit to finance production.[124] Prosperity did

[119] Carl Lande, *Leaders, Factions, and Parties: The Structure of Philippine Politics*, Monograph Series, Southeast Asia Studies (New Haven: Yale, 1964) 6 & 9.

[120] Stanley (n 30) at 84.

[121] Morton J Horwitz, *The Transformation of American Law, 1870–1960* (New York: Oxford University Press, 1992) at 9.

[122] Bonifacio S Salamanca, *The Filipino Reaction to American Rule, 1901–1913* (Quezon City: New Day 1984) 65.

[123] Stanley (n 30), at 140–144; Michael S Billig, *Barons, Brokers, and Buyers: The Institutions and Cultures of Philippine Sugar* (Honolulu: University of Hawaii Press, 2003) 32–59.

[124] John A Larkin, *Sugar and the Origins of Modern Philippine Society* (Berkeley: University of California Press, 1993) at 105.

not trickle down to their tenants. Worse, commercialisation eroded traditional patronage ties throughout Southeast Asia and fed agrarian discontent that swept the Islands in the 1930s.[125] This fuelled the rise of the radical *Sakdal* movement as a political force. Capturing national and local offices in the 1934 elections, the *Sakdalistas*' triumph was described by Frank Golay as 'short-lived,' for 'party members elected to the legislature promptly defected to [Quezon's] 'Anti' contingent of the Nacionalistas.'[126]

Against this background, delegate Jose Locsin, governor of the sugar-producing province of Negros Occidental and a sugar 'farmer' himself, declared '[o]ur present social and economic organization a real failure' and pronounced himself unsurprised by 'masses of our people' joining associations 'labeled by the government as "red",' 'the explosion of more or less bloody strikes,' and 'our prisons being filled with convicts for theft, robbery, and sedition.' As a remedy, he proposed enshrining the social justice principle as a national policy to correct a Christian culture that 'legitimizes materialism, and creates fortunes, from evening to daytime at the expense of the proletariat' and made inevitable 'the impoverishment of the masses of the people.' Leyte delegate Ruperto Kapunan backed the measure, agreeing that 'when property was only in the hands of a privileged few,' then 'the idea of social justice was born and it has developed.' Believing that Russia and Spain had fallen to Communism and Fascism, respectively, because social justice was 'completely unknown there,' he concluded, 'social justice is a necessity,' not only in the Philippines but throughout the world, 'because socialism is extending its hold.' Locsin entreated delegates to 'force yourselves to put an end [to] your conservatism, otherwise you will be showing to the aggrieved multitude the only way left for their revindication: violence with force.'[127]

What did social justice mean? For Locsin, it was 'a program of action for breaking down the dikes of selfishness, which concentrates wealth and well-being in the domain of the privileged few in order to scatter or spread them throughout the plains where the masses of people encamp themselves.' This required 'a strong government, jealous and avaricious of all its prerogatives, collectivist in its orientation,' which regarded 'the weak, because they are weak,' as deserving of 'the protection of society and of the State.' To Araneta, it meant 'sheltering the poor and the necessity of establishing a regime of property more

[125] See James C Scott, 'The Erosion of Patron-Client Bonds and Social Change in Southeast Asia' (1972) 32 *Journal of Asian Studies* 5–37; James C Scott & Benedict J Kerkvliet, 'The Politics of Survival: Peasant Responses in to 'Progress' in Southeast Asia' (1983) 4 *Journal of Southeast Asian Studies* 241–268.

[126] Frank Hindman Golay, *Face of Empire: United States-Philippine Relations, 1898–1946* (Quezon City: Ateneo de Manila University Press, 1997); reprinted 1998) at 340.

[127] Aruego, *Origin* (n 1) vol 2, at 229–231 & 233–234.

equalitarian.' Concretely, Locsin's programme bore the influence of the New Deal and Christian Democracy in including:

> diminution of landed estates (*latifundios*); extermination of usury; adoption of progressive taxation; homesteads, community property for municipalities; public works, professional unions, public welfare work which in turn includes, among other things, savings institutions, insurance, participation in benefits, cooperatives in production, hygienic homes, etc.[128]

In the end, the social justice principle found expression in constitutional provisions protecting labour and women and authorising land reform.

Constitutional challenges to the New Deal convinced delegates that an express constitutional commitment was once again necessary to ensure the Philippine government's authority to pursue similar ameliorative strategies. The need seemed especially urgent, since the Philippine Supreme Court imported substantive due process doctrine in the 1924 case *People v Pomar*. Invalidating maternity leave legislation, *Pomar* marked the Philippine debut of *Lochner v New York*, the iconic 1905 US Supreme Court decision that had voided a minimum hours law for impairing the freedom of contract and is credited with galvanising Progressivism's 'fundamental assault on the legal thought of the old order.'[129] Locsin may have been referencing *Pomar* when he lamented, 'Brilliant oratory has been used to exalt the necessity for a strong national government, so that before an emergency, a grave crisis, it can contrive the means that can discipline all the factors of the nation in the interest of public welfare and security.' Yet 'hardly had the echo of the appeal passed away, when this government surrendered itself to vested interests, instituting the sanctity of contracts and society.'[130] To override *Pomar*, delegates may have adopted the social justice and afford protection to labour principles.

Likewise, the agrarian roots of rising radicalism made addressing landholding and tenancy relations an imperative. In a speech entitled 'Large Estates and Trusts in Perpetuity' Cuaderno pleaded for the approval of his proposal authorising the break-up of large estates and prohibiting the formation of large estates and trusts in perpetuity:

> If we are to be true to our trust, if it is our purpose in drafting our constitution to insure domestic tranquility and to provide for the well-being of our people, we cannot, we must not fail to prohibit the ownership of large estates, to make it the duty of the government to break up existing large estates, and to provide for their acquisition by purchase or through expropriation and sale to their occupants, as has been provided in the Constitutions of Mexico and Jugoslavia.

[128] Ibid.
[129] Horwitz (n 120), at 33.
[130] Aruego, *Origin* (n 1) vol 2, at 230.

Since Cuaderno's programme appeared to violate the takings clause found in the organic acts and incorporated in the 1935 Constitution's Bill of Rights, Aruego explained that delegates again felt constitutional authority was necessary 'to remove all doubt' that the government had the power to expropriate landed estates and distribute them 'at cost to the tenant-dwellers thereof in the event that in the future it would deem such expropriation necessary to the solution of the agrarian problems therein.'[131]

But while delegates approved the proposal authorising land reform, landowners in the convention vigorously resisted limiting the size of landholdings. Arguing that such a policy would stymie, even destroy, private initiative that had stimulated development worldwide, they contended that the state ought not discourage men from working towards unlimited advancement, as individual success would redound to the rest of the nation. Despite strong opposition, the provision was overwhelmingly approved.[132]

Noble motivations notwithstanding, the Constitution's social justice provisions were later watered down in practice. Five years after the 1935 Constitution's ratification, former delegate and now Justice Jose Laurel expounded on social justice's meaning in *Calalang v Williams* as being 'neither communism, nor despotism, nor atomism, nor anarchy, but the humanization of laws and the equalization of social economic forces by the state so that justice in its rational and objectively secular conception may at least be approximated.'[133] In other words, social justice did not warrant redistribution. Philippine courts later clarified that social justice neither licensed the untrammelled expropriation of private land nor championed the 'division of property or equality of economic status.' Rather, it was 'intended to ameliorate the hardships of persons acting within law' and not to help 'those who trespass upon the rights of others.' Thus, mere invocation of social justice by a poor litigant did not relieve the court of its responsibility to 'dispense justice to the rich and the poor alike,' preventing it from 'giving the poor a right to which he is not entitled just because he is poor.'[134]

B. Nationalism and Nationalisation

Filipino elites had been lukewarm towards the American colonial development agenda. Generally supportive of public works, which they anticipated inheriting upon independence, they were skeptical of an economic strategy directed at attracting – and thus entrenching – private American capital. Before 1916,

[131] Aruego, *Framing* (n 17) vol 2, at 610–611.
[132] Ibid, at 608–609.
[133] *Calalang v Williams*, 70 Phil 726 (1940), 734.
[134] Aruego, *Framing* (n 17) vol 2, at 237–238.

however, Filipino political leaders had limited say over colonial policies. While controlling the Insular Legislature's lower house from 1907 to 1916, they held a minority in the cabinet and the Philippine Commission as upper house and subordinate positions in the insular bureaucracy. With the Democratic takeover of Congress and the White House, the Insular Government's structure and composition were Filipinised and, with it, colonial economic policy and the identity of the public in whose name the government justified its projects.

Speaker Sergio Osmeña identified as 'a basic obligation of Filipino political leaders to launch the Government in business and, in the process, also educate and encourage Filipinos to take an increasingly active part in the economic life of the country.'[135] Initially, the Insular Legislature pursued 'economic nationalism' by stimulating local capital investment. Anemic local response prodded the Insular Government to directly develop the economy through government enterprise. Increasingly, that government imparted a Filipino identity to the public that warranted its pursuits. Constructed by exclusion in discriminatory legislation that was either protectionist against foreign competitors or paternalistic towards 'social lepers' and the 'uncivilized,' equal protection doctrine identified this Filipino public as the Hispanicised Filipino majority.[136]

The nationalistic impulse that was suppressed when American colonial rule hijacked Philippine independence found freer expression in the 1935 Constitutional Convention. Able to imagine life as an independent polity, delegates created one with restrictive membership. They rejected *jus soli*, or place of birth, as the basis for acquiring citizenship, disqualifying from Philippine citizenship children born in the Philippines of foreign parents. At the same time, *jus sanguinis* citizenship, or citizenship by blood, was extended automatically only to children whose fathers were Filipino citizens, while those born to Filipino mothers had to elect Philippine citizenship upon reaching the age of majority. Filipino women who married foreigners lost their Philippine citizenship and risked being stateless if their husband's countries did not confer citizenship by marriage. Delegates also fixed the requirements for acquiring citizenship in the Constitution, thereby limiting the Legislature's role to regulating its loss or reacquisition.

The Philippine Constitution, like the US Constitution, limited the Presidency and Vice-Presidency to natural-born citizens.[137] More significant than restricting access to officeholding, the Constitution intended to limit to Philippine citizens the right to own or develop national resources. Aruego described the 'nationalization and conservation of the natural resources of the country' as one of the 'fixed and dominating objectives of the Convention since the

[135] Vicente Albano Pacis, *President Sergio Osmeña: A Fully-Documented Biography* (Quezon City: Philippine Constitution Association 1971), 1:235.
[136] Castañeda Anastacio (n 48) at 181–191.
[137] Aruego, *Framing* (n 17) vol 1, at 197–214; Phil. Const. Art IV and Art VIII§3.

opening days.' As this plan's 'necessary starting point,' delegates adopted the principle of state ownership of natural resources and the Regalian doctrine over mineral resources, whether found on public or private land. Delegates readily approved the latter doctrine to banish any lingering doubts over whether it had carried over from the Spanish to the American period. Since they were state-owned, natural resources, except public agricultural lands,[138] could not be alienated, but only leased for a maximum of 50 years to Philippine citizens or corporations with 60 per cent Filipino equity. Moreover, only qualified persons could own private agricultural land, unless individuals acquired the same via hereditary succession. By nationalising natural resources, delegates hoped 'to insure their conservation for Filipino posterity,' 'to prevent the extension into the country of foreign control through peaceful economic penetration;' and 'to prevent making the Philippines a source of international conflicts with the consequent danger to its internal security and independence.' While aware that 'Filipino capital had been known to be rather shy' and that 'this general apathy' might retard the development of natural resources, delegates felt that 'it was better to have such development retarded or even postponed altogether' until Filipinos were 'ready and willing to undertake it,' rather than lose natural resources to foreign ownership and control 'in order that they might be immediately developed, with the Filipinos of the future serving not as owners but at most tenants or workers under foreign masters.'[139]

Also restricted to Philippine persons was the right to hold franchises, certificates, or any other form of authorisation to operate public utilities. Like the provision on natural resources, this policy was also 'one of the earliest propositions planned to be included in the Constitution.'[140] Cuenco considered it 'very farsighted', for they 'conserve for us and posterity the common patrimony.' While Cuenco neither saw himself as 'one of those who believe with Proudhon that property is something stolen' nor thought 'that the division of properties is panacea for all social ills,' he entertained 'no doubt that one of the primordial duties of the state is to attain the welfare of the greatest number, and this welfare can be attained only with the adoption of the economic provisions in this Constitution.' Once again, the motivation for mandating the state to secure the general welfare was the radical threat. To Cuenco, 'it would not matter if in this country there would be no rich nor plutocrats as long as there would be no beggars nor mendicants.' He was convinced that 'socialism and communism will remain unknown where everyone has a house of his own and a piece of land to work,' for 'the small owner lives happily and contentedly, and there will never germinate in his mind the anarchistic, red and bloody doctrines of

[138] Phil. Const. Art XII§2 did not restrict the right to acquire, hold, or lease public agricultural lands to citizens, but limited the size of lands that could be transferred or alienated to private individuals or corporations.

[139] Aruego, *Framing* (n 17) vol 2, at 600–605; Phil. Const. Art XII§1, 2, and 5.

[140] Aruego, ibid, at 667; Phil. Const. Art XIII§8.

Marx and Stalin.'[141] Under US rule, nationalisation meant government doing business through government-owned corporations. With scarce private Filipino capital, the Filipino-controlled legislature capitalised corporations with public revenues to corner key industries, notably, sugar refining. In the Filipino people's name, the Constitution granted the Philippine state ownership or control over economic resources – a capacity fully exploited by the Marcos government 60 years later when it commandeered the sugar and coconut industries and public utilities and assigned their management to cronies.

Delegates also attempted but failed to nationalise other economic sectors, including labour; public works; retail trade; bookkeeping in commerce; and the warehousing, milling, and selling of rice, corn, and other cereals. That the Chinese monopolised the latter three sectors was, to Nueva Ecija's Florentino Chioco, a situation 'very harmful to our economic self-sufficiency and may cause grave social disorders.' So 'deeply rooted' was this evil that the delegate from 'the rice granary of the Philippines' felt it 'imperative that the same be corrected' by 'a constitutional precept reserving this field of our national economy to our nationals.'[142] Such ultra-nationalistic measures were ultimately rejected, yet Cuaderno recounts that insistence towards their adoption prodded Quezon to emphasise to his caucus 'the danger of aggressive nationalism, and called to their attention the present tendency of the nations towards internationalism.'[143]

V. CONCLUSION

The Philippine Constitution's schizophrenic philosophy was one of its most criticised features. As noted, Reyes found problematic the charter's blending of conservatism and radicalism, of elements of Enlightenment and liberal individualism with Progressive governmental activism.[144] To Manila Delegate Rafael Palma, however, this contrariety represented compromise. Nineteenth-century history taught him that untrammeled individualism spawned an economic aristocracy, for 'when you allow an individual to control the resources of a nation, you make him the ruler of the nation.' Yet the early twentieth century revealed another consequence in the chilling example of 'communism or bolshevism.' Thus, delegates had 'necessarily to try to follow the middle ground as between the two extremes.'

But perhaps the most accurate defence of the charter's nature came from Roxas. Asserting that 'government is an art; it is a practical science, not a theory, and a government can be successful only if in its structure due consideration

[141] Aruego, *Origin* (n 1) vol 1, at 180–181.
[142] Aruego, *Framing* (n 17) vol 2, at 65869.
[143] Cuaderno (n37), 27.
[144] Aruego, *Origin* (n 1) vol 1, at 154.

is given to the habits, the customs, the character, and as McKinley said, even to the idiosyncracies of the people,' Roxas explained that they 'preferred the Government established under this draft,' because 'it is the Government with which we are familiar. It is the form of government fundamentally such as it exists today; it is the only kind of government we have found to be in consonance with our experience and with the necessary modification capable of permitting a fair play of social forces and allowing the people to conduct the presidential system.'[145] For notwithstanding colonial-era rights rhetoric, the Government of the Philippine Islands had from its inception been a supple and invasive machinery with a civilising and therefore transformative mission and whose survival necessitated, even warranted, extensive and tremendous control over individual lives. Keeping 'close to the shore,' as Laurel advised, delegates did act conservatively. Yet the government model that delegates preserved was no night-watchman state, but a tropical prototype of the New Deal that they hoped would realise their vision of a modern Filipino state, while weathering economic dislocation and existential threats *sans* American trade privileges and military protection. This design, however, harboured the potential for constitutional dictatorship, which was exploited by Quezon's Commonwealth and Marcos's Martial Law regime and conceivably by strongmen like President Rodrigo Duterte.

[145] Ibid, at 179–180 & 157–158.

3

The Origins of the 1945 Indonesian Constitution

KOICHI KAWAMURA

INTRODUCTION

On 17 August 1945, Soekarno, a nationalist movement leader, together with Mohammad Hatta, declared Indonesia's independence in Jakarta. The next day, the Constitution of the Republic of Indonesia (*Undang-Undang Dasar Negara Republik Indonesia 1945*) was proclaimed as the basic law of the new nation-state. Since then, Indonesia has applied the 1945 Constitution as its basic law, except for a decade in the 1950s.[1] After the Dutch transferred sovereignty to Indonesia in 1949, the 1950 Provisional Constitution of Republic of Indonesia (*Undang-Undang Dasar Sementara Negara Republik Indonesia*), which fully adopted Western constitutionalism and a parliamentarian system, was enacted.[2] When political crisis deepened as the result of fierce competitions among political parties and the outbreak of regional separatist movements, President Soekarno issued the Presidential Decree in 1959, unilaterally proclaiming a return to the 1945 Constitution.

Under the 1945 Constitution, two authoritarian regimes – Soekarno's 'Guided Democracy' (1959–1965) and Soeharto's 'New Order' (1966–1998) – were established. When Soeharto's 32-year old government collapsed and democratisation started in 1998, the 1945 Constitution was not replaced with a new one but was instead successively reformed to adapt itself to a new democratic regime. As a result of four constitutional amendments made between 1999 and 2002, political institutions in Indonesia were greatly transformed into

[1] During the period of independence struggle against the Dutch immediately after the 1945 Constitution was enacted, a cabinet responsible to the Central National Committee (*Komite Nasional Indonesia Pusat*: KNIP) was installed contrary to the presidential scheme of the Constitution. Politics during this period was thus in practice a parliamentary system of government.

[2] When the Dutch transferred sovereignty to Indonesia at the Hague Round Table Conference, the 1945 Constitution was replaced by the 1949 Constitution of Federal Republic of Indonesia as the newly-independent state adopted a federal form of government.

a modern democratic structure, in which a separation of powers among the executive, legislative, and judicial branches was fully entrenched.

Why was the 1945 Constitution retained as the basic law for the Indonesian modern nation-state even though it was totally transformed through the four amendments during democratisation? To understand this, we need to consider the process and ideological background to the 1945 Constitution. Who drafted Indonesia's first constitution? What did the constitutional drafters discuss? What were the main arguments among constitutional founders? By analysing the drafting process of the 1945 Constitution, we can understand the characteristics of the Constitution for the newly-independent Indonesia and the reasons that Indonesia did not discard the first Constitution despite the need for fundamental changes during the democratisation process.

The first section reviews the process of drafting the 1945 Constitution before independence. The second section analyses the characteristics and origins of constitutional provisions on political institutions and human rights, arguing that there were ideological struggles by nationalist leaders to establish a new nation-state. The third section considers how those unique provisions of the 1945 Constitution led to the rise of authoritarian regimes for almost 40 years. The fourth section discusses the process and contents of the constitutional amendments after democratisation, pointing out that the 1945 Constitution has been fundamentally changed to adopt to a democratic regime without philosophical debates, but was not discarded.

I. DRAFTING OF THE 1945 CONSTITUTION

A. Deliberations at the Investigating Committee for the Preparation of Independence

The drafting of the 1945 Constitution started just two months before Indonesia's independence. The draft Constitution was discussed at the sessions of the Investigating Committee for the Preparation of Independence (*Badan Penyelidik Usaha-Usaha Persiapan Kemerdekaan Indonesia*: BPUPKI) established by the Japanese Military Administration between May and July 1945, just when Japan was about to surrender in the Pacific War. It was ratified as a formal constitution in the Committee for the Preparation of Independence (*Panitia Persiapan Kemerdekaan Indonesia*: PPKI) on 18 August 1945, following the declaration of Indonesia's independence on 17 August, two days after the Japanese surrender.

Despite the formal statement that Southeast Asian nations would be liberalised from Western imperialism, the Japanese government did not intend to admit Indonesia's independence before invading the former Dutch East Indies in 1943. However, as the fortunes of war turned against Japan and the initial confidence in the Japanese occupation declined due to political suppression and economic difficulties, the Japanese government in Tokyo had no choice but to agree to Indonesia's independence following the examples of independence given to Burma and the Philippines. On 7 September 1944, Japanese Prime Minister Kuniaki Koiso stated – in what has become known as the 'Koiso Speech' – that the Japanese government was willing to admit the independence of nations in the East Indies in the future.

In accordance with this policy, the Japanese military administration of Java set up the Investigating Committee for the Preparation of Independence (IC) in April 1945. The Committee was tasked with studying issues concerning preparations for Indonesia's independence and to report back to military headquarters. At the same time, nationalist leaders demanded the establishment of a 'preparation committee' to speed up the process towards independence. However, the military administration, especially the Japanese Armed Forces controlling Java, considered it premature to admit Indonesia's independence since there was as yet no concrete policies on the timing of independence, the form of the independent State, and the relationship between the new State and Japan. The Japanese Armed Forces also foresaw that it would take a long time to resolve the complex issues of establishing an independent State comprising of various ethnic groups, religions, and other organisations before starting independence preparations.[3]

Thus, the Japanese military administration only set up an investigating committee to unofficially study independence issues rather than one to officially prepare for independence. Indonesia's nationalist leaders, whilst disappointed with Japanese reluctance to prepare for the immediate independence, considered the setting up of the IC a good opportunity to push their agenda forward.[4] Sixty-three members, representing various strata of the East Indies – nationalist leaders, bureaucrats, Islamic leaders, academicians, women, and representatives from various ethnic groups including Chinese, Arabs, and mestizos – were appointed to the IC. They were joined by eight other special members from the Japanese military administration. The chairperson was KRT Radjiman Wediodiningrat (1879–1952), the eldest nationalist leader, and the vice-chairpersons were RP Suroso (1893–1981), a bureaucrat and Yoshio Ichibanse from the Japanese Armed Forces.

The IC held its first session from 29 May to 1 June and its second session from 10 to 17 July 1945. The IC's task was to investigate all issues concerning the preparation of the independence, to collect necessary materials, and to draw up a final report. Issues discussed at a series of meetings ranged from the principles of the nation state, the governing structure, the State organisations, religions, nations, and territory. Conclusions on these various issues were reached by the IC as follows. The Jakarta Charter (*Piagam Jakarta*), based on Soekarno's speech on 1 June 1945 to call for the coexistence of multi-religious, ethnic groups was adopted as the State principle, later known as the Five State Principle

[3] *Indonesia niokeru Nihon Gunsei no Kenkyu*, [Research on the Japanese Military Administration in Indonesia] (Tokyo: Kinokuniya Syoten, Waseda Uninversity, Okuma Memorial Institute of Social Sciences, 1959) [hereinafter 'Waseda'] at 411–417.

[4] Ibid, at 417.

(*Pancasila*) with several amendments after the independence. The unitary State and republican form of government, rather than the kingdom or a federal State was preferred. The issue of religion (Islam) and the State was discussed most intensively and the decision was that the freedom of religion would be guaranteed while Muslims would have the obligation to abide by the Islamic laws. And, the territory for independent Indonesia would cover the former Dutch East Indies, adding Malaya, North Borneo, Portuguese Timor, the whole of Papua, and the surrounding islands.

At the beginning of the second session, on 11 July 1945, the IC decided to set up three sub-committees (*Panitia*, or *Bunkakai*); the First Sub-committee to draft a constitution, comprised of 19 members and was chaired by Soekarno; the Second Sub-committee to investigate financial and economic issues, comprised of 22 members and was chaired by Mohmmad Hatta, one of the most prominent nationalist leaders trained in economics in the Netherlands and the first Vice President at the independence; and the Third Sub-committee to investigate national defence issues, comprised of 22 members and was chaired by Abikoesno Tjokrosoejono, a leader of the largest Muslim political organisation, Serakat Islam and co-founder of the Indonesian National Political Assembly (PPKI).

After the opening discussion on 11 July 1945, the First Sub-committee set up a working committee (*Panitia Kecil Perancang Undang-Undang Dasar*) to draft the constitution. This working committee, consisting of six members from the First Sub-committee and was led by Soepomo (1903–1958), a Leiden-trained lawyer. The Committee drafted a constitution of 42 articles[5] and submitted it at the IC's second session on 14 July 1945.[6] During the three-day discussions, the draft was amended twice[7] before being agreed to at the preliminary session on 16 July by all members except for Muhammad Yamin, a prominent politician who had a doctorate in law from the *Rechtshogeschool* (predecessor of the Law Faculty at the University of Indonesia).

B. Deliberations at the Committee for the Preparation of Independence

As the IC finalised its report, the Japanese government in Tokyo took a final decision to admit the independence of the East Indies at the Highest War

[5] *Risalah Sidang BPUPKI-PPKI 28 Mei 1945-22 Agustus 1945*, [The minutes of the Indonesian Investigating Committee for the Preparation of Independence and the Indonesian Committee for the Preparation of Independence. 28 May 1945 – 22 August 1945] (Jakarta: Sekretariat Negara Republik Indonesia, 1995) at 226–233 [hereinafter 'Risalah Sidang'].

[6] Another constitutional draft was submitted to the IC on 15 June by A Hoesein Djajadiningrat and six other members. Since the submission of a constitutional draft was against the procedural rules, it was not taken up for discussion. For the constitutional draft, see AB Kusuma, *Lahirnya Undang-Undang Dasar 1945: Memuat Salinan Dokumen Otentik Badan Oentoek Menyelidiki Oesaha2 Persiapan Kemerdekaan* [The Birth of the 1945 Constitution: Containing Authentic Documents of the Investigating Committee for the Preparation of Independence] (Depok: Badan Penerbit, Fakultas Hukum, Universitas Indonesia, 2004) at 191–196 [hereinafter 'Kusuma'].

[7] For the first amendment of the constitutional draft, see Kusuma, ibid, at 336–344; and for the second amendment, see Kusuma, ibid, at 446–454.

Leaders Meeting on 17 July 1945. Accordingly, the 16th Armed Forces in Java, the 25th Armed Forces in Sumatra, and the Second Southern Expeditionary Fleet proposed members for the Committee for the Preparation of Independence, and a total of 20 members were officially appointed by the Commander of the Southern Expeditionary Army Group in Saigon. They were representatives from various regions in Indonesia: 12 members from Java; 5 from Sumatra; and 1 each from Borneo, Celebes, and Lesser Sunda. On 11 August 1945, Hisaichi Terauchi, Commander of the Southern Expeditionary Army Group, called Soekarno, Hatta, and Radjiman Wediodiningrat to Saigon to appoint them to the independence preparation committee. Soekarno was nominated chairperson and Hatta as vice-chairperson.[8]

The Southern Expeditionary Army Group expected the Committee for the Preparation of Independence to be established on 18 August 1945 to prepare for the formal independence in September 1945. However, on 15 August 1945, one day after Soekarno and others returned from Saigon to Java, the Japanese government surrendered to the Allied Forces, abandoning all independence preparations. The ceremony to setup the independence preparation committee, scheduled on 18 August, was also cancelled.

Responding to abruptly changing circumstances and mounting pressures for the immediate independence from extreme young activists, Soekarno and Hatta declared Indonesia's independence on 17 August 1945 without the consent of the Japanese military administration.[9] They also held a meeting of the Committee for the Preparation of Independence unilaterally on 18 August despite a request of the Japanese military administration to cancel its first meeting. At the beginning of the meeting, Soekarno added six young leaders to the Committee.

The Independence Preparation Committee began with Hatta's proposed amendment of the draft Preamble and articles on Islam. He proposed deleting the prerequisite of the President being a Muslim and also to delete the phrase, 'Muslims have the obligation to abide by the Islamic laws.' Hatta argued that it was imperative that the constitutional draft be accepted by all the regions, especially those where non-Muslims were dominant. A day before the independence proclamation, Hatta was told by a Japanese Naval Force officer that Christians

[8] At the time of independence of Burma and the Philippines, the Japanese government called respective nationalist leaders to Tokyo, appointing the independence preparation committee members directly and conveying the order of the Japanese government directly. Yet, at the time of Indonesia's independence, since it was impossible to send its representatives to Tokyo due to the loss of maritime control in the Pacific Ocean, the Commander of the Southern Expeditionary Army Group acted for the Japanese Government to appoint the independence preparation committee members. See Waseda (n 1) at 431.

[9] The Japanese military administration of Java did not admit any activities to move forward the independence preparations on the grounds that the Japanese government owned responsibility to maintain status quo in occupied areas after agreeing the unconditional surrender to the Allied Forces. On the other hand, Tadashi Maeda at the Naval Force Office in Jakarta was sympathetic and cooperative to the independence movements, providing his house as a place to draft the proclamation of the Indonesian independence.

were deeply concerned with the provision of the Jakarta Charter referring only to the obligation of Muslims. Hatta negotiated with four representatives from various Islamic organisations before the Committee opened discussions to delete the above-mentioned provision so that the Committee unanimously passed his revisions.[10] I Gusti Ketut Pudja, the representative of Lesser Sunda further proposed that the term *Allah* in the Preamble be replaced by *Tuhan*, a more general term of God. This was also accepted without any dissent.

After Soepomo explained the basic structure of political systems in the constitutional draft, the committee discussed each draft article in turn until they were all approved on the afternoon of 18 August 1945. The committee also elected Soekarno as the first President and Hatta as the first Vice-President unanimously that same day. The next day the Committee decided regional entities, established the governmental ministries, and elected the cabinet ministers. On 21 August 1945, after a one-day recess, the Committee decided to establish the National Committee (*Komite Nasional*) in the capital as well as each region as the provisional organ to support government administration.

C. The Meanings of the Constitution

As we have seen, Indonesia's independence Constitution was drafted in a short four-month period following discussions in the IC and the Committee for the Preparation of Independence. In fact, substantial discussions on the constitutional draft occupied only four days at the IC's second session in July 1945. It was possible to draft the new constitution in such a short period because Indonesia's nationalist leaders had been preparing for its independence since the 1900s. Soepomo, one of the main drafters, had studied various aspects of constitutions since 1940 and already drafted a constitution with other nationalist leaders such as Achmad Soebardjo (1896–1978) and Alexander Andries Maramis (1897–1977) in 1942.[11] And as we shall see later, Indonesia's nationalist leaders had long been casting around for sound ideological foundations suitable for their soon-to-be independent State. They recognised a text of the Constitution as a combination of the declaration of national independence, provisions on basic State structure, and provisions on human rights. Mohammed Yamin explained at the IC's second session on 11 July 1945, 'each constitution of nations who will be independent is consisted of three parts of articles; at the opening is independence declaration and the state basic principles, followed

[10] Muneo Takahashi, 'Kokumin Togo to Pancasila' ['National Integration and Pancasila'] in Akio Yasunaka & Norio Mihira (eds), *Gendai Indonesia no Seiji to Keizai: Suharto Seiken no 30nen* [*30 Years of Soeharto Government: Its Political and Economic Performance*] (Tokyo: Institute of Developing Economies, 1995) at 53–94 and 61 [hereinafter 'Takahashi'].

[11] Kusuma (n 6) at 49.

by the statement of human rights for nations who desires independence in the world'.[12] On the other hand, Soepomo was against incorporating human rights into the third part of the constitution on the grounds that it did not fit with traditional culture of Indonesia.

It should be also pointed out that the contents of the new Constitution had great originality. Although the constitution was drafted under the supervision of the Armed Forces in Java during the Japanese occupation, the Java military administration adopted a policy of non-intervention. As Syunkichiro Miyoshi, consul of the Java military administration under the 16th Armed Forces Command to Java recalled, '[t]he Japanese authority took a stance of non-interventionism in discussions at the meeting, leaving decisions entirely to the committee'.[13]

II. CONSTITUTIONAL PROVISIONS AND ITS ORIGINS

At the time of its enactment, the 1945 Constitution consisted of only 37 articles and details were left to laws to be enacted afterwards. The constitutional drafters admitted that the 1945 Constitution was necessarily incomplete and provisional as there was an urgent need to have it approved and for Indonesia to proclaim its independence before the Dutch returned to impose colonial rule. Reading the IC proceedings and those of the Committee for the Preparation of Independence, it was clear that members who were keen on having a well-drafted constitution were overshadowed by voices of those like Soekarno who insisted that the provisional constitution first be established for early independence and that it could be amended later.

Although the 1945 Constitution was incomplete, it was not a simple imitation of Western constitutions, but rather an original, organic document with unique features such as the entrenchment of the state principle of *Pancasila* in the Preamble; the governing structure including the People's Consultative Assembly (*Majelis Permusyawaratan Rakyat*: MPR); and limited provisions on human rights.

A. The State Principle, *Pancasila*

Political institutions established by the 1945 Constitution were neither a transplant of Dutch governing structures, nor a copy of the Meiji constitutional regime of Japan, which imposed military rule for three years. They were rather

[12] Risalah Sidang (n 5) at 177.

[13] Syunkichiro Miyoshi, 'Jawa Senryogunsei Kaikoroku Rensai 13kai,' ['The Memoirs of the Occupational Military Administration in Java. Serial No 13'] (1966) 78 *Kokusai Mondai* 67.

quite unique. The Preamble includes *Pancasila* – the five State principles based on Soekarno's speech at the IC on 1 June 1945. The speech was later summarised as the Jakarta Charter (*Piagam Djakarta*) on 22 June 1945. However, the Charter specifically mentioned that Muslims should adhere to Islamic laws (*syariat Islam*). During the drafting discussions, Islamic forces pressed the adoption of the Jakarta Charter as the principle of the nascent State, but Soekarno and other nationalist leaders opposed it strongly as they sought 'unity in diversity' as the principle of the State. Soekarno replaced the words referring to Islam with 'the belief in the One, Supreme God,' making it *Pancasila*.

B. Governing Structure of the 1945 Constitution

Article 1 specifies republicanism as Indonesia's form of government. The Japanese military administration in Java considered the issue of the form of government difficult to resolve since there would be too many disputes.[14] In fact, it was reported that IC members from Central Java held a closed-door meeting, promising the establishment of a monarchy under Yogyakarta's Sultan.[15] However, contrary to Japanese expectations, almost all council members agreed to establish a republican form of government and there were no huge disputes. At the IC on 10 July 1945, 55 members voted for republicanism while six voted for a monarchy.[16]

A presidential rather than parliamentary system was also adopted. The President, as head of the state, held executive power and organises the government (Article 4). However, this presidential system was unique in that the President's term of office was not fixed. The President is elected by the People's Consultative Assembly (MPR), the highest state organ and another legislative body composed of the House of People's Representatives (*Dewan Perwakilan Rakyat* or DPR) and appointed members. Thus, the President was responsible to the MPR (Article 6) which can force him to resign. On the other hand, the President has no right to dissolve the MPR.

Under Article 1(2), the MPR is the 'incarnation' of all the people of Indonesia,[17] fully exercising sovereign power on behalf of the Indonesian people. The MPR is the highest State organ, ranking above all the other state

[14] Miyoshi, ibid, at 62.

[15] Risalah Sidang (n 5), at 120; and Waseda (n 1) at 418.

[16] Risalah Sidang (n 5), at 125–127.

[17] Indonesian laws come attached with 'Elucidations' or 'Commentaries' (*Penjelasan*) at the end. Upon the interpretation of law, this official commentary possesses quasi-biding authority as the body of law. In this chapter, (Elucidation) refers to the Elucidation of the 1945 Constitution (*Penjelasan Tentang Undang-Undang Dasar Negara Republik Indonesia Tahun 1945*) which had been drawn up by Soepomo. In 1959, it was officially declared to be part of the Constitution. This Elucidation has not, however, been updated nor augmented since the amendments were made to the Constitution in 1998.

organs, including the President, the DPR, and the Supreme Court (see Figure 1). The MPR must hold a general assembly at least once every five years (Article 2(2)) to amend the Constitution, decide on the General State Policy Guideline (*Garis Besar Haluan Negara*: GBHN) and to elect the President and Vice-President (Articles 3, 6(2) and 37). According to the MPR's General State Policy Guidelines, five high State organs operate below it: the President, the DPR, the Supreme Court, the Supreme Advisory Council (*Dewan Pertimbangan Agung*: DPA), and the Board of Audit (*Badan Pemeriksa Keuangan*: BPK) exercised respective functions.

Figure 1 Indonesia's political system before the first constitutional amendment in 1999

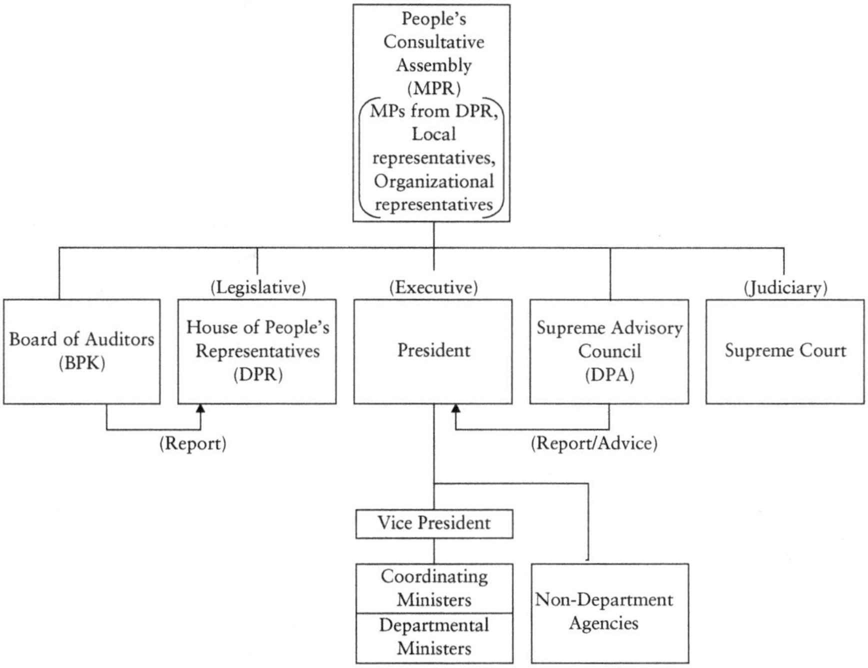

Source: The Author

Political institutions in Indonesia, therefore, did not assume a separation of three state powers and checks-and-balances between the legislature, the executive, and the judiciary. In discussions of drafting the Constitution before independence, an argument for the separation of three powers was never presented. When Muhammad Yamin proposed his personal draft of the constitution at the second meeting of the IC, he explained that there should be the separation of six powers in Indonesia, referring to the separation of five powers in the Constitution of China's Nationalist Party. According to him, the six powers included (1) the head of the state and vice-president, (2) the Representative Institution,

(3) the All Indonesia Assembly, (4) Ministers, (5) the Advisory Council, and (6) the Supreme Court.[18]

Soepomo agreed to Yamin's proposal, suggesting the separation of powers between the MPR, the DPR, the President, the Supreme Advisory Council, the Board of Audit, and the Supreme Court.[19] Soepomo explained that the reason why Indonesia should not adopt the separation of three powers was 'because in practice, a law-making institution was handed over government works, a court was handed over governmental works, and the government was given authority making laws. Because of it, the separation of three powers [*Trias Politica*] in theory did not fit with reality.' Soekarno also agreed that the separation of powers was already outdated, not guaranteeing social justice, and in any case, neither the Soviet Union nor China adopted it.[20]

In fact, IC members surveyed the constitutions of numerous countries, not only those of Western Europe but also Asian States like Japan, the Philippines, and Thailand, as well as Islamic countries like Egypt and Iraq. In the 1930s, many developed countries in Europe were facing constitutional crises: The socialists enlarged the scope of their influence after the Russian Revolution, while conservative anti-revolutionaries furiously attacked bourgeois democracy and modern constitutionalism, leading to the emergence of Fascism. In particular, when the Weimar Constitution collapsed in Germany, 'the cabinet depended on the president, rather than the representative assembly, since there were too many political parties in the representative assembly to constitute a stable majority group supporting the parliamentary system'.[21] Given such political conditions, Indonesia's founding fathers rejected the parliamentary system in favour of a presidential system. They also recognised that constitutional concepts like the traditional separation of powers between government's three branches as being outmoded and parliamentarism as dysfunctional. Instead, they drew inspiration from institutions adopted by the Chinese Nationalist Party and the 1936 Soviet Constitution.[22]

[18] See Risalah Sidang (n 5) at 176–184. The state organs of the Chinese Nationalist Party after its capitulation to Taiwan were the National Assembly, the President's Office, the Legislative Council, the Administrative Council, the Judicial Council, the Personnel Council, and the Audit Council. The five powers mentioned here are the Legislative Council as the legislative branch, the Administrative Council as the executive branch, and the Judicial Council as the judicial branch with the Personnel Council in charge of assigning bureaucrats and the Audit Council in charge of impeaching bureaucrats. The MPR in Indonesia was modelled after the Chinese National Assembly, which was supposed to elect the President as the head of the state.

[19] Soepomo opposed Yamin's proposal that the ministers be responsible to the House of People's Representatives, as it was based on the parliamentary system, and finally rejected it. See Risalah Sidang (n 5) at 302.

[20] Risalah Sidang (n 5) at 221–222.

[21] Yoichi Higuchi, *Hikaku Kenpo* [Comparative Constitutions] (Tokyo: Seirin Syoin, 1998) at 181–186 [hereinafter 'Higuchi'].

[22] The concept of the Supreme Advisory Council and the Board of Audit was possibly referred to the state organs in the Netherlands since Soepomo himself used the words, 'Raad van State' or 'Rekenkamer' respectively in the discussions at the IC. See Risalah Sidang (n 5) at 271 & 273.

Javanese intellectuals had, since the 1910s, been anti-modern and anti-Western in outlook and this partly explains the IC's rejection of Western political institutions and models. At the IC meeting, Soepomo rejected liberal democracy and individualism as part of Indonesia's founding philosophy, and accordingly rejected parliamentarism or the parliamentary cabinet system (*sistem parlementer/sistem Kabinet*) especially since this was the system of government that also gave rise to imperialism and wars all over the world. Instead, Soepomo advocated the creation of 'our own institutions' where the head of the state was given 'predominance' by concentrating power and responsibility in his hands: 'the Government has to be given confidence in order to keep permanent power, not depending on power of the DPR,' and 'the Head of the State who have the right of appointing Ministers, takes consequences from all the philosophical currents existing in the society'.[23]

The IC considered that the government, especially the head of the state, should be recognized as the Head of the Big Family (*Kepala Keluarga Besar*), ruling benignly over all the people. Soepomo assumed that while the people would 'believe policies of the head of the state', it was 'necessary to set up a system of consultative institution in order to guarantee that the Head of the State, as the supreme national leader, be always identified with spirit of the nation'.[24] Thus, while Yamin proposed the separation of six powers to prevent the rise of totalitarianism, Soepomo argued for the sharing of respective governmental functions by six institutions, rather than a separation of powers. He proposed institutions where power lay in the hands of the head of the state who was identified with the nation and who would lead it wisely while the MPR – held once in five years – would ensure the identification between the head of the state and the nation.[25] Nearly all the members of the IC or the Committee for the Preparation of Independence agreed with Soepomo's idea.

C. Philosophy of 'Family Principle'

Indonesia's founding fathers rejected individualism and liberal democracy as the basis of government, adopting instead the family principle (*kekeluargaan*) as the philosophical base for the building of original political institutions. The thinking behind the family principle arose from local intellectual efforts to derive an indigenous principle of social integration based on Indonesia's cultural traditions. Nationalists needed to formulate a legitimising principle on which to build a new nation-state while resisting Dutch colonialism. Quite naturally, the underlying sentiments saw the emergence of the idea that sovereignty of

[23] Ibid, at 274.
[24] Ibid, at 42, 274, 302–306.
[25] Ibid, at 42.

the Indonesian state should belong to 'the people' or 'the *rakyat*'. But exactly who were 'the *rakyat*'? The *Priyayi* (feudal lords), who constituted a group of nationalist intellectuals, attempted to define the *rakyat* in the context of Javanese culture.[26] Two key men were instrumental in this effort in redefining the concept of populism (*kerakyatan*): RM Soetatmo Soeriokoesoemo and Ki Hadjar Dewantoro, founding members of a private educational institution, *Taman Siswa*, an organisational base for nationalist movements. According to Tsuchiya, Soetatmo regarded that in Javanese society there should be unity of leader and followers (*Kawula-Gusti*), forged by wisdom (*wijsheid*).[27]

By redefining 'democracy' (*demokrasi*) as embedding *Kawula-Gusti*, Soetatmo argued that populism-cum-democracy would be catastrophic without a wise leader especially since it was vital to maintain peace and order (*tata-tentrem*) in a family (*keluarga*). Dewantoro supported Soetatmo's point by arguing that democracy and leadership (*democratie en leiderschap*) be practised in tandem with the family principle, and indeed putting it into practice in *Taman Siswa*. Leaders like Dewantoro looked to Eastern, and especially Indian philosophy, as an antidote to the crisis in Western democracy, and was heavily influenced by the work of Rabindranath Tagore and the Theosophists. Javanese culture which was based on that of the Indian world, had the potential to overcome the perils of modernity. Dewantoro thus argued that Western democracy, which was based on individualism, was the cause of anarchy, while Javanese democracy, which viewed the 'uniting of all individuals' as paramount, offered an attractive alternative. In this system, individuals would be less autonomous as they are united with the wider community and the whole nation, and sincerely sacrifices in the best interests of all. Thus, when 'a leader and followers are united (*manunggal ing Kaulo-Gusti*)',[28] order and peace would ensue.

The legitimising principle of the new Indonesian state, therefore, emerged from an ideology consciously derived from Javanese culture.[29] However, Dewantoro's ideas were also strongly influenced by the doctrine of the totalitarian state in Germany's Third Reich. The Nazi doctrine of the totalitarian State recognised the state as substantially the organic and the mystic, rejecting the distinction

[26] See I Sukarno, *Di Bawah Bendera Revolusi*, [*Under the Flag of Revolution*] (Jakarta: Indonesian Government Publications, 1963) [hereinafter 'Sukarno'].

[27] Kenji Tsuchiya, *Indonesia Minzokusyugi Kenkyu*, [Research on Indonesian Nationalism] (Tokyo: Sobunsya, 1982) at 72–76 [hereinafter 'Tsuchiya'].

[28] Ibid, at 334.

[29] Tsuchiya pointed out that the intellectual efforts of *Taman Siswa* was intended to establish a leading principle of Javanese *priyayi* in nationalist movements as well. Ibid, at 79. Shiraishi argues that the practice of family principle has been widely deployed inside the State structure and has nothing to do with Dewantoro's democracy and leadership. In particular, the practice was systematically deployed under the Soeharto regime. See Takashi Shiraishi, '"Kaihatsu" Kokka no Seiji Bunka: Indonesia Shinchitsujo wo Kangaeru,' [Political Culture of the 'Developmental' State: Considering the Indonesian New Order] in Kenji Tsuchiya (ed), *Koza Gendai Asia 1: Nationalism to Kokumin Kokka*, [*The Course of Modern Asia Vol. 1: Nationalism and the Nation-State*] (Tokyo: University of Tokyo Press, 1994).

between an individual, society, and the state in principle.[30] At the IC meeting on 31 May 1945, Soepomo explained that the doctrine of the integrated or totalitarian state, which emphasised the unity of leader and followers or of the State as a family, would be the most appropriate form of government for Indonesia. Drawing examples of State socialism from Germany and from the *Tenno* system in the Japanese Empire, he stated:

> … the indigenous social structure of Indonesia is the creation of Indonesian culture, the fruit of the Philosophy or inner spirit of the Indonesian people. The inner spirit and spiritual structure of the Indonesian people is characterized by the ideal of the unity of life (*persatuan hidup*), the unity of leaders and followers (*persatuan kawulo dan gusti*), that is, of the outer and the inner world, of the macro-cosmos and the micro-cosmos, of the people and their leaders. All men as individuals, every group or grouping of men in a society, and every society in the life of the entire world – each of these is considered to have its own place and its own obligations (*dharma*) according to the law of nature, the whole being aimed at achieving spiritual and physical balance. Men as an individual are not separated from other individuals or the outside world. Men, groups of men, and, indeed, all groups of creatures, all are interacting and interrelated and all have influence on each other. This is the totalitarian idea (*ide totaliter*), the integralistic idea (*ide integralistik*) of the Indonesian people which is embodied in its indigenous form of government.[31]

Certainly, all the concepts expressed by Indonesia's nationalist leaders including family principle (*kekeluargaan*), integralism, or mutual help (*gotong royong*) lack precision and concreteness. These were also concepts favoured by the Javanese *priyayi* (feudal lords).[32] In their efforts to arrive at a sound philosophical basis for the construction of the new Indonesian State, the nationalists looked both inward and out. They looked to indigenous doctrines of governance based on the family principle and mutual help but also to models like the Soviet Union and the Chinese Nationalist Party government as concrete examples.[33]

[30] Higuchi (n 21) at 192–193.

[31] Risalah Sidang (n 5) at 35. English translation was cited from Feith and Castles (1970, 190) with some modifications by the author.

[32] As to why the Javanese philosophy of the *priyayi* was accepted in the 1945 Constitution without strong opposition, we should note that the majority of the members of the IC were members of the Javanese *priyayi*. According to Benedict Anderson's estimate, among the 62 members of the Council, the *priyayi* elite including Pangre Peraja (Javanese senior colonial bureaucrats) numbered 17 or 27.4%. On the other hand, members from Islamic elites, another major group of independence movement, were 7, consisting of only 11.3%. See Benedict R O'G Anderson, *Some Aspects of Indonesian Politics under the Japanese Occupation: 1944–1945* (Ithaca, New York: Modern Indonesia Project, Southeast Asia Program, Department of Far Eastern Studies, Cornell University, 1961) at 21.

[33] Tsuchiya pointed out 9 influential intellectual movements at the time: (1) policy of 'Rich Nation, Strong Army' in Japan and the Russo-Japanese War; (2) Chinese nationalism and Three Principles of Sun Yat-sen, and overseas Chinese response to nationalism; (3) Pan-Islam and modernist Islam; (4) the Young Turks Party and modernisation in Turkey; (5) Indian nationalism especially the Suwaraji-Suwadeji movement and Gandhi's leadership; (6) 'national self-determination' after World War I, especially the independence movement in Ireland; (7) socialist democracy in the Netherlands; (8) the Russian Revolution and the birth of the Soviet, the Communist International movement; and

Thus, while the 1945 Constitution was drafted only after two weeks of discussions, its drafters had in fact been thinking through the problems of constitutionalism and democracy in the long period leading up to Indonesia's independence.

D. Philosophical Origins of 'Organisational Representatives' Doctrine

Another unique feature in the 1945 Constitution was an existence of appointed members in the MPR, the state's highest organ and those members were supposed to represent organisational interests. The 1945 Constitution institutionalised the system of the President's appointee in the legislature to elect the President. According to the Elucidation of the Constitution, organisations mean 'institutions such as cooperatives, labour unions, and other collective institutions'. When explaining the draft at the Committee for the Preparation of Independence on 18 August 1945, Soepomo described the 'organisations' as being 'like economic organisations'.[34] Since Indonesia aimed at structuring cooperative economic institutions, it would be necessary to add representatives from these economic organisations to the MPR to make it truly the 'nation's paragon'.[35]

Interestingly, Soekarno already had the idea of having 'organisational representatives' during the 1930s. In his article entitled 'I am less dynamic' (*Saja kurang dinamis*), he argued against the establishment of an Islamic state, as follows:

> Representatives from all the people assemble in the legislature (which is the national representative institution based on the principle of democracy) regardless of their belief. They are representatives from 100% Islam believers, superficially Islamic believers, Christians, non-religious believers, intellectuals, merchants, farmers, laborers, and fishermen, and in other words all components of nations, all components of the people constitute of its legislature (Sultan of Turkey did not establish such an organization. That is why the Young Turks Party movement arose).[36]

Almost the same phrase appeared 27 years later in Soekarno's speech criticising the malfunction of party politics at the time of the parliamentary democracy.[37]

(9) ideology of 'the fall of the West' and Eastern recurrence, obviously seen in philosophy of Tagore and Theosophy. See Tsuchiya (n 27) at 7.

[34] Risalah Sidang (n 5), at 425.

[35] On the contrary, Hatta argued to regulate a principle of popular vote in the constitution since the concept of 'organisations' was not clear. However, his argument was overwhelmed by voices of the committee's members to leave detailed, theoretical arguments until early independence was achieved later. See Risalah Sidang (n 5) at 218 and 425.

[36] That was the speech of 'the Soekarno Concept' (*Konsepsi*) on 21 February 1957. See, Sukarno (n 26) at 451.

[37] David Reeve, 'Sukarnoism and Indonesia's "Functional Group" State, Part One: Developing "Indonesian Democracy"' (1978) 12(2) *Review of Indonesian Malay Affairs* 43–94, at 63.

After proposing the establishment of the National Council (*Dewan Nasional*) to advise and make recommendations to the cabinet, Soekarno stated that the National Council consist of 'in the first place, representatives from functional groups in our society or individuals from this group'.[38] Examples of these functional groups were labourers, farmers, intellectuals, national enterprises, Protestants, Catholics, Islam theologians, women's associations, youth associations, the 1945 generation, and regions. It can be seen from this speech that Soekarno was highly suspicious of parliamentary politics, Western liberalism and individualism, and his belief in the traditional governing principles in Javanese society.

E. Human Rights Provisions

Another significant constitutional characteristic was a lack of human rights provisions in the 1945 Constitution. There are only six human rights articles in the 1945 Constitution: equality under the law (Article 27(1)), the nation's right to life and the right to work (Article 27(2)); the freedom of religion (Article 29); the right to participate in national defence (Article 30); the right to education (Article 31); and social welfare (Article 34).[39] Even these articles were quite incomplete in terms of protecting human rights from violations by the state. For example, Article 26(2) states that 'matters relating to citizenship shall be determined by law' which essentially leaves any form of protection up to ordinary law. The same can be said of Article 28 which states that the freedom of association, assemble, and thought and expression 'are to be determined by law'. At the same time, the right to liberty, the most basic human rights in a democratic regime, was not provided in the Constitution.

During the drafting the 1945 Constitution, arguments to include human rights provisions in the Constitution were advanced by several members. For instance, Muhammad Yamin argued for the need to guarantee human rights in the Constitution, citing the American Declaration of Independence and Bill of Rights as an example.[40] Hatta also suggested preventing arbitrary human-rights intervention of the government by guaranteeing the freedom of expression, association, and assembly in the Constitution.[41]

However, Soekarno and Soepomo rejected these views on the basis of the Family Principle. Soepomo stated:

> The constitution we are drafting, is based on the doctrine of family principle, not based on the doctrine of individualism we have rejected. Declaring the freedom

[38] Ibid.

[39] Todung Mulya Lubis, *In Search of Human Rights: Legal-Political Dilemmas of Indonesia's New Order, 1966–1990* (Jakarta: PT Gramedia Pustaka Utama, 1993) at 74–85 [hereinafter 'Lubis'].

[40] Risalah Sidang (n 5) at 177–179.

[41] Ibid, at 262–263.

> of assembly and association in the constitution is systematic from the doctrine of individualism, so that if we declare the freedom of assembly and association in our constitution, we will challenge the rationality of the family principle doctrine. … In the system of family principle, attitude of the nation (*warga negara*) is not always asking 'what is my rights', but asking "what is my duty as a member of the big family, that is, this Indonesian State".[42]

Quite clearly, Soepomo saw the embedding of human rights provisions as the adoption of individualism.[43] Thus, Article 28 (freedom of speech, assembly and association) was the result of the compromise between the Javanese-oriented group (led by Soekarno and Soepomo) and the Western-oriented group led by Hatta and Yamin.[44]

III. THE 1945 CONSTITUTION AND THE RISE OF AUTHORITARIAN REGIMES

As we have seen, the 1945 Constitution was not founded on principles of liberal democracy. Invariably, politics under political institutions established under such a constitution would operate quite differently. The executive branch, especially the President, monopolised power and this led to the arbitrary conduct of politics. Without term limits, the President was able to hold onto power for a long

[42] Ibid, at 275–276.

[43] The 1949 Constitution of Federal Republic and the 1950 Provisional Constitution, both of which referred to the Western constitutions, had detailed articles on human rights. Actually, it was Soepomo, one of the main members drafting the 1945 Constitution, who inserted human rights articles of the Universal Declaration of Human Rights into these two constitutions. However, Soepomo himself mentioned later that the constitutions recognised human rights too much. See Lubis (n 39) at 5.

[44] See Risalah Sidang (n 5), at 358–361. Since the 1945 Constitution had never been amended until the fall of the Soeharto regime, human rights provisions had never been inserted. Yet, there was a time during the early part of Soeharto's regime when an attempt was made to establish the bill of basic human rights. In July 1966, the general session of the Provisional People's Consultative Assembly (*Majelis Permusyawaratan Rakyat Sementara*: MPRS) adopted 'MPRS Decision No 14 of 1966 about the set-up of MPRS ad hoc committees to carry out duties of the survey of state institutions, the execution of a plan to separate authorities among state institutions according to the 1945 Constitution system, the preparation of a draft of a revised and enlarged edition of the Elucidation of the 1945 Constitution, and the preparation of detailed human rights.' According to this decision, four ad hoc committees (*Panitia Ad Hoc*) would be established to discuss the survey of state institutions, separation of powers, a revised and enlarged edition of the Elucidation to the Constitution and the bill of human rights. The committee finished drafting the bill of human rights itself in 1967, waiting for the deliberation at the general session of the MPRS the next year. Ismail Suny, a constitutional law professor, told Mulya Lubis in an interview that 'the first two years of the New Order were the best years for human rights' (see Lubis (n 39) at 5). However, after Soeharto was inaugurated as the Acting President in 1967 and as the President in 1968, the governmental party, Golkar (*Golongan Karya*), and the Indonesian armed forces, who supported Soeharto, withdrew their support for a bill of human rights and it was never taken up thereafter (see Lubis (n 39) at 6–7). There is a description of this in 'the Manuscript of Basic Human Rights', appendix of the MPR Decision Year 1998 No. 17. It says that the general session of the MPRS in 1968 did not discuss a draft of the bill of human rights 'since it gave priority over discussions on rehabilitation and establishment of the state (after the September 30th Movement) and … emergent problems on rebirth of nation's life.'

period and this led to the establishment of two authoritarian regimes under the first two presidents, Soekarno and Soeharto.

A. Articles of the Constitutions Supporting Authoritarianism

Let us first consider articles in the Constitution explicitly concentrating on power in the presidency. As Soepomo told the IC, the Constitution was expected to establish political institutions in which power was concentrated in the President as the State leader. They are 19 subject areas and 13 articles: Chapter III, Articles 4-15 concerning The State Administration Power; Chapter V, Article 17 about The Cabinet; and Chapter VII, Article 22(1) in which various powers are given to the President. For example, the President holds 'the highest right to command the Armed Forces, the Navy, and the Air Forces' (Article 10). The President shall declare war (with agreement of the DPR), conclude peace and a treaty (Article 11) and declare a state of emergency (Article 12). The President holds authority to appoint and accept diplomatic envoys (Article 13), to decide granting of amnesty (Article 14), and to confer decorations (Article 15) as the right of personnel. The President also appoints state ministers as the head of the cabinet (Article 17) and participates in daily administration.

The most important among the President's powers is the right to legislate. Article 5(1) states that 'the President holds the right to determine a law with the agreement of the DPR.' This gives the President and the DPR co-held rights of legislation, a clear breach of the traditional separation of powers. As head of administration (Article 4(1)) the President is also to make regulations 'to implement a law' (Article 5(2)). In addition, in times of an emergency, the President may promulgate 'government regulations in lieu of law; (Article 22(1)). On the other hand, provisions governing the DPR cover only nine subject areas in five articles while matters relating to the judiciary are covered in two articles (Articles 24 and 25) under Chapter IX 'The Judiciary'.

While Article 20(1) states that 'all laws should require the approval of the DPR', the President may refuse sanction of any bill submitted by the DPR (Article 21(2)). At the same time, the DPR has no way to override the President's right over appointment of personnel, treaty-making, and legislation. The only provision to establish the superiority of the legislative over the executive was the right to vote on budget bills (Article 23(1)) and bills of taxation (Article 23(2)). The Elucidation to the Constitution states that the DPR can monitor the President's behaviour and where the President acts against state policy, require the President to make a report of accountability by calling the MPR. However, the Elucidation does not explain further in detail about monitoring by the DPR.[45]

[45] MPR Decision No 3 of 1978 empowers the MPR to monitor the President's conduct and if necessary, request a call for the special meeting of the MPR to impeach the President. This Decision became the legal basis of Parliament's attempt to impeach the fourth President, Abdurrahman Wahid, in July 2001.

Provisions about the judiciary were scantier. Article 24(1) only states that 'the right of the judiciary is exercised by the Supreme Court and … other organizations of the judiciary' and that organizations, authority, and ways of appointing the judges are regulated by laws concerned. The Elucidation to the Constitution states that 'Indonesia is a constitutional state' (*negara yang berdasar atas hukum [rechtsstaat]*) and that the judiciary is independent power from the executive. However, details on how this works is not spelt out in the Constitution. That is why, as Mulya Lubis pointed out, the meaning of the independent judiciary ought to be unstable, depending on interpretations of what was a constitutional state.[46] Because the 1945 Constitution did not specifically mention judicial review, there is no obvious way for the judiciary to check the executive and legislative.[47]

Delineation of power for the other state organisations are equally vague. For example, the Supreme Advisory Council's function is simply stated as to 'reply to questions raised by the President'. It also has 'the right to submit recommendations to the government' (Article 16(2)). Similarly, the Board of Audit is established 'in order to inspect accountability of state finances' and to report their findings to the DPR (Article 23(5)). However, the Board of Audit has no authority to control behaviour of State organisations including the president.

B. The MPR and the Constitutional Foundations of Authoritarianism

The 1945 Constitution concentrates enormous power in the President. It thus comes as no surprise that Indonesia's subsequent political history was characterised by almost unbridled authoritarianism. The road to authoritarianism began with the composition of the MPR and with the inchoate state of the rules for the election of both MPR and DPR members. The Constitution left unresolved, precise rules for the organisation of these bodies. Indeed, Article IV of the Transitional Regulation states that 'all authority … is exercised by the president until the MPR, the DPR, and the DPA are organised according to this Constitution.' This gave the President dictatorial power immediately after independence. As long as there was no stipulation about elections, the President could, with apparent impunity, appoint members of either the MPR or the DPR. Thus, the President could appoint all members of the MPR which in turn had ultimate authority to elect the President – himself.

[46] Lubis (n 39) at 97.

[47] The majority of Indonesian constitutional scholarship argued that the system of judicial review could not adapt to the 1945 Constitution and that the power of judicial review could be exercised only by the MPR, the highest organ of the State. The Supreme Court is merely given the authority to review administrative regulations below the law (Yuzuru Shimada, 'Indonesia ni okeru Shiho Kaikaku,' ['Judicial Reform in Indonesia: Problems of the Judicial Power and Courts in the Post-Soeharto Era'] in Masayuki Kobayashi and Shinya Imaizumi, eds., *Ajia Syokoku no Shiho Kaikaku* [Judicial Reform in Asian Countries] (Chiba: Institute of Developing Economies, 2002) at 207–208).

Even if members of the DPR were elected by popular vote, it was still possible for the President to appoint representatives of regions and organisations. With the power to appoint members to the MPR, the President could entrench his position. Furthermore, there was no provision limiting the number of terms for the President. As it turned out, this allowed for the establishment of two authoritarian regimes through the neutralising of the MPR through this power of appointment.[48]

The MPR was first convened in November 1960, after Soekarno declared the return to the 1945 Constitution through the Presidential Decree of 5 July 1959.[49] At the time, the Provisional People's Consultative Assembly (MPRS) consisted of 283 DPR members, 232 organisational representatives, and 94 regional representatives. Its composition was decided by Soekarno and legally regularised by Presidential Regulation (*Peraturan Presiden*) No 12 of 1959.[50] There were 326 organisational and regional representatives out of the 609 MPRS members. They were all appointed by the President.[51] Earlier that year, on 5 March 1960,

[48] Tasuo Umezawa, *Soeharto Taisei no Kozo to Henyo*, [The Structure and Change of the Soeharto Regime] (Tokyo: Institute of Developing Economies, 1992) at 10 [hereinafter 'Umezawa'].

[49] For four years between independence in 1945 and the creation of the Constitution of the Federal Republic of Indonesia in 1949, the MPR was not established because of a chaotic state of independence struggle with the Dutch. As Article IV of the Transitional Clause of the 1945 Constitution States, State power is concentrated on the President immediately after independence, while the Central National Committee (KNIP) supports him until the MPR and the DPR are officially institutionalised. The KNIP grew out of the Committee for the Preparation of Independence on 29 August 1945. However, the KNIP decided to give itself the power of legislation and additionally to establish the Working Committee (Badan Pekerja), which carried out daily administration. On the same day, the first Vice-President Hatta made a Proclamation (Proclamation of Vice-President No 10) to vest the Central National Committee with legislative power and the right of participation in decisions of the General State Policy Guideline. As such, the Working Committee virtually held the legislative power. According to Kahin, the organisation of the Working Committee was set up after the model of organisations of the National Congress in India. See George McTurnan Kahin, *Nationalism and Revolution in Indonesia* (Ithaca, New York: Cornell University Press, 1952). On 14 November, a new cabinet with Sjahrir as the head was organised with the support of the KNIP and was in fact a responsible cabinet government. From then till 1949, there had continued to be responsible cabinet governments under the 1945 Constitution regime. These series of events were spearheaded by Sjahrir and Hatta who considered that the problem of winning independence should have been resolved through cooperation and negotiation with the Dutch and by excluding Japanese collaborators. They intended to exclude Soekarno and others who had authoritarian thinking and claimed armed struggle against the Dutch (Kahin, ibid, at 153). Bit by bit, they modified the political institutions in the 1945 Constitution and created what was in fact a parliamentary cabinet system. See Kenichi Goto and Isao Yamazaki, *Soekarno: Indonesia 'Kenkoku no Chichi' to Nihon*, [*Soekarno: 'The Founding Father' of Indonesia and Japan*] (Tokyo: Yoshikawa Kobunkan, 2001), at 130–132.

[50] This Presidential Regulation provided that the MPRS consisted of 200 organisational representatives and 94 regional representatives in addition to DPR members. Its composition was different from the number of representatives appointed in September 1960 (see Shigenobu Nagai, *Indonesia Gendai Seijishi* [*The Modern History of Indonesia*] (Tokyo: Keiso Syobo, 1986 at 260). Members were added to the MPR before it convened since the President had power to do so. Although the number of MPRS members and the Mutual Help Parliament increased a little, its composition did not change drastically. See Umezawa (n 47), at 51.

[51] Presidential Decree No 2 of 1959.

Soekarno suspended the DPR – who were critical of his arbitrary behaviour – by presidential decree and replaced it with the Mutual Help (*Gotong Royong*) Parliament, all of whose members he appointed. This Parliament consisted of 130 political party representatives, 152 organisational representatives (including 35 armed forces representatives), and one representative from West Irian. Thus, there were 384 organisational representatives from the DPR in the MPRS. With 95 regional representatives (including a DPR member from West Irian), over three-quarters of the MPRS membership was chosen by the President.

A few months before, on 31 December 1959, Soekarno gave himself unilateral authority to decide rules on the establishment, registration and ban of political parties.[52] Parties that oppose the basic principles and objectives of the state or were involved in a rebellion would thus be banned. This power was further bolstered when on 5 July 1960 another Presidential Regulation empowered the President to approve and supervise activities of all political parties.[53] Soekarno invoked this authority and banned the modernist Islam party of *Masyumi*, which had been involved in a regional rebellion in West Sumatra in 1967 and the Indonesian Socialist Party (*Partai Sosialis Indonesia*: PSI).

During the period of Soekarno's Guided Democracy (*Demokrasi Terpimpin*) most organisational representatives were affiliated with certain political parties.[54] At the same time, the armed forces (*Angkatan Bersenjata Republik Indonesia*: ABRI) capitalised on their mandate as organisational representatives to push aggressively for a bigger role in parliamentary politics. This proved a major challenge to Soekarno who decided to rely less on organisational representatives for support and instead to regulate the existing political parties in the MPR which he used to continually secure the legitimacy of his government.

Soeharto, who inherited the Soekarno's authoritarian regime, made aggressive use of his power to appoint additional members of organisational and regional representatives to secure his power base. After the 30th September Movement in 1965, Soekarno transferred presidential authority to Soeharto through the Letter of Order (*Surat Perintah Sebelas Maret: Supersemer*) on 11 March 1966. One year later, on 12 March 1967, Soeharto was appointed Acting President at the special session (*Sidang Istimewa*) of the MPRS,[55] and on 27 March 1968, Soeharto was officially inaugurated as President at the MPRS.[56] By this time, he had already utilised the appointment system in the MPR and the DPR and expelled pro-Soekarno and communist members from both legislatures, replacing them with his appointees.[57]

[52] Presidential Decree No 7 of 1959.
[53] Presidential Regulation No 13 of 1960.
[54] See Umezawa (n 47), at 51.
[55] MPRS Decree No 64 of 1967.
[56] MPRS Decree No 64 of 1968.
[57] See Umezawa (n 47), at 51–52).

Thereafter, Soeharto was re-elected by the MPR on 23 March 1973 after he successfully got through the general elections in 1971 by constraining political parties on the one hand and strengthening a political base by propping up the Functional Group (*Golongan Karya*: Golkar) on the other. The composition of the MPR, which was formally convened for the first time, was stipulated in the Law No 16 of 1969 about Compositions and Positions of the MPR, the DPR, and the Regional Parliament (DPRD) (hereinafter the 'Law on Legislative Composition'). It was established through a compromise between Soeharto and the various political parties in 1969.[58] According to this law, there were 100 organisational representatives (including 75 armed forces representatives) among the 460 DPR members. The MPR was supposed to consist of DPR members and the same number of additional members. Among the 460 additional members, 207 were organisational representatives (including 155 armed forces representatives) and 130 regional representatives. The remainder were allotted to political parties in proportion to results of the general elections. Thus, Soeharto secured a little less than a half among the total number of 920 MPR members.[59]

The Law on Legislative Composition was revised to increase the total number of legislative seats and to change their composition, first in 1975 with a few modifications (the Law No 5 of 1975) and the second in 1985 with further revisions when the so-called five political laws were enacted (the Law No 2 of 1985). The total members of the DPR were increased to 500, while the appointed members were reduced to 100 armed forces representatives. The total members of the MPR were changed to 1,000 and this included 500 DPR members and 500 additional members. Among the 500 additional members, 253 seats were allotted to political parties in proportion to the seats held in the DPR (including 51 armed forces representatives), while 100 seats were reserved for organisational representatives and 147 seats were reserved for regional representatives. This new allocation decreased the proportion of appointees from organisational, regional, and armed forces representatives to 40 per cent of the seats in the MPR. Yet, by this time, the ruling Golkar had already put its vote-gathering function on a firm footing. Political parties and other societal groupings were completely marginalised and this allowed the Soeharto regime to secure a strong foothold in the MPR, thus ensuring his re-election as President.

The number of appointees in the DPR and the MPR was manipulated with great skill so that the 1945 Constitution need not be amended. This made it all the more conducive to the maintenance of an authoritarian regime. The Constitution can only be amended with the consent of two-thirds of the total

[58] Ibid, at 26–27.

[59] Furthermore, since the 1971 general elections, Soeharto propped up Golkar, which embodied the concept of 'organizational (golongan) representatives', against political parties. In the result, the Golkar had a great victory in the general elections (see Masashi Nishihara, 1972. *Golkar and the Indonesian Elections of 1971* (Ithaca, New York: Modern Indonesia Project, Cornell University, 1972); and David Reeve, *Golkar of Indonesia: An Alternative to the Party System* (Singapore: Oxford University Press, 1985).

membership of the MPR (Article 37(1)). Furthermore, any decision on a constitutional amendment must be taken with the approval of not less than two-thirds the number of members in attendance (Article 37(2)). For example, according to the composition decided in the 1969 Law on Legislative Composition, a motion to amend the Constitution can commence in the MPR where 614 of the 920 members are present. If Soeharto wanted to scuttle such a motion, he need only secure more than one-third the total of MPR members to do so. In this case, that would be 307 members, a figure that coincides exactly with the total of 100 organisational representatives in the DPR and 207 additional organisational representatives in the MPR. According to the 1985 Law on Legislative Composition, the sum of armed forces, organisational, and regional representatives was 398, more than the 334 members to disrupt any attempt to amend the Constitution.

This is not at all a coincidence. Soeharto mentioned the importance of this figure in the Pekanbaru speech (*Pidato Pekanbaru*) before the staff conference of the armed forces on 27 March 1980:

> Because the Armed Forces itself does not want to amend (the 1945 Constitution), we have to use guns if the amendment is enacted. If we do not want to use guns, then I will explain to all political parties as follows: When facing amendment of the 1945 Constitution and *Pancasila*, it would be better for us to kidnap one from the two third who want to amend than to use guns. Because taking one from the two third is no longer effective according to the 1945 Constitution.[60]

Thus, Soeharto clearly recognised that the number of appointees in the legislature was crucial for maintaining his government. As we can see, the 1945 Constitution legitimised the establishment of authoritarianism by concentrating authority in the President while having minimal provisions on human rights. This enabled both Soekarno and Soeharto to successfully maintained their positions by exploiting the incomplete draft by manipulating the appointing bodies and capitalising on the widespread anti-Western, anti-colonial sentiments and making use of the 'Family Principle' to secure their dominance.

Interestingly, anti-government groups also made use of the 1945 Constitution or *Pancasila* to criticise the government. One significant example was the Petition of 50, a prominent group that submitted a document criticising Soeharto to the DPR in May 1980.[61] Among the prominent political elites opposing Soeharto's dictatorial leadership by Soeharto were former chief commander of the military Nasution, former Chief of Police Hoegen Imam Santoso, former

[60] Fatwa, ibid, at 214.

[61] After the Pekanbaru speech, the Petition of 50 group (Petisi 50) submitted 'the Statement of Concern' (Pernyataan Keprihatinan) to the DPR. Regarding a series of incidents, see AM Fatwa, *Demi Sebuah Rezim: Demokrasi dan Keyakinan Beragama Diadili [For a Regime: Democracy and Religious Convictions Are Tried]* (Jakarta: PT Gramedia Pustaka Utama, 2000) at 200–229; and David Jenkins 1984. *Suharto and His Generals: Indonesian Military Politics 1975–1983* (Ithaca, New York: Cornell Modern Indonesia Project, Southeast Asia Program, Cornell University, 1984) at 157–173.

Jakarta Governor Ali Sadikin, former Prime Minister Burhanuddin Harahap, and Muhammad Natsir. They argued that Soeharto had misused *Pancasila* to attack his political opponents instead of using it to unite the nation.[62]

IV. THE 1945 CONSTITUTION AFTER DEMOCRATISATION

Before 1998, no one imagined amending the 1945 Constitution as it was a product of the nationalist fight for independence and of the new Indonesian nation. As such, it was almost sacrosanct. Even so, both Soekarno and Soeharto has used it to legitimise their authoritarian rule. However, with a breakdown of authoritarian rule in 1998–1999, the myth of a sacred and inviolable constitution disappeared. A new theme discourse emerged: How can the 1945 Constitution be adapted for a new democratic regime in Indonesia?

A. Limits on the Presidential Powers

One of the most important issues during the amendment process was the need to institutionalise the separation of powers. In the first and second amendments of 1999 and 2000, one key objective was to transfer political power from the President to the legislature, to transform it from an executive-centric presidency to a legislative-centric presidency.

This change resulted in political instability since the President's position was directly affected by political maneuvering within the MPR, whose membership was dominated by members of the DPR. Political instability was exacerbated by the fact that the President cannot maintain a stable political base within the legislature due to the polarised pluralism of the party system. In July 2001, things came to a head and President Abdurrahman Wahid was impeached by the MPR because of severe conflicts between the President and the legislature.

Quite clearly, more reforms were needed. In the third and fourth constitutional amendments of 2001 and 2002, attempts were made to institutionalise a more equal balance of powers, with heightened legitimacy being given to the President who would now be elected by the people and not by the MPR. An impeachment of the President required the consent of the judiciary to prevent undue influence from partisan interests in Parliament. The legislative institutions were also reformed to prune the MPR's substantial powers. A Constitutional Court was created not only to provide authoritative interpretations of the Constitution but also to correspondingly constrain the executive and the legislative branches.

[62] Hiroyuki Tosa, 'Globalka to Atarashii Aliran: Indonesia no Minsyukakatei ni tsuiteno Kaisyaku,' ['The Globalization and the New Aliran: Interpretation about Democratization in Indonesia'] *Ajia Keizai* 41(12) (2000) 62–74, at 71; and Douglas E Ramage, *Politics in Indonesia: Democracy, Islam and the Ideology of Tolerance* (New York: Routledge, 1995) at 184–202.

Indonesia's current political system dates from 2004 as a result of the four sets of amendments (see Figure 2). Insofar as it employs the separation of three powers – executive, legislative and judicial, it resembles the American–style presidentialism. The President, holding the executive power, is elected directly by the people for a five-year term. The legislature is composed of the DPR, whose members are elected by the proportional representation system, and the House of Local Representatives (*Dewan Perwakilan Daerah*: DPD),[63] whose members are elected by the people to represent 34 provinces (each province has four representatives). The MPR, once the highest organ of state, was transformed into a consultative forum of the two chambers.[64] The judiciary consists of the Supreme Court, whose jurisdiction covers the general courts, and the Constitutional Court, whose functions are judicial review, settlement of disputes between state institutions, and reviews of election results.

Figure 2 Indonesia's political system after the fourth constitutional amendment in 2002

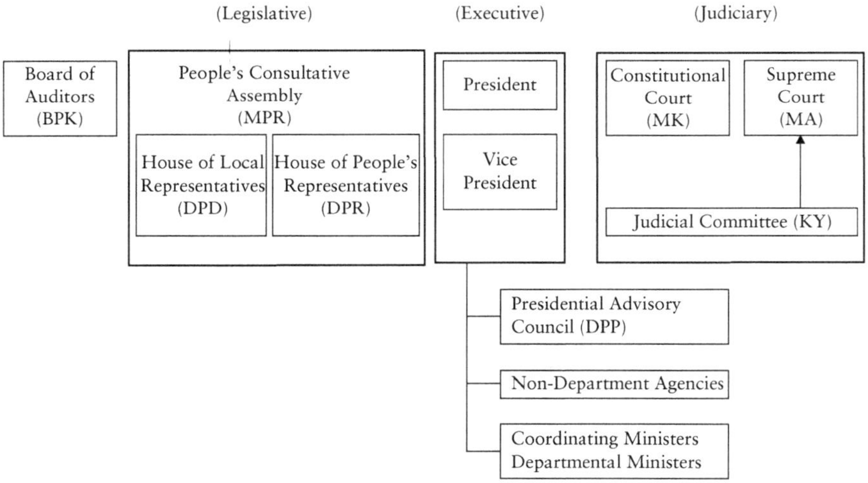

Source: The Author.

[63] The House of Local Representatives (DPD) was newly constituted in the third constitutional amendment of 2001, and came into being after the 2004 general elections. Although membership of functional organisations' representatives in the MPR were abolished after democratisation, representatives of local governments were organised into a single chamber with members directly elected by the people. The DPD has the authority to propose bills concerning issues of regional autonomy and can participate in the deliberations on such legislation, but it does not have powers of approval.

[64] When the DPD was newly institutionalised, the MPR lost its status as the highest state organ in the political system and has since been regarded as a combined chamber with the DPR as the lower chamber and the DPD as the upper chamber and itself as a consultative forum. Yet, as noted above (n 63), insofar as it has no legislative power, the DPD has limited authority. Some Indonesian analysts call this type of political institution 'soft' bicameralism. See, eg, Jimly Asshiddiqie, *Format kelembagaan negara dan pergeseran kekuasaan dalam UUD 1945* [*The Structure of the State Institutions and the Transformation of Powers in the 1945 Constitution*] (Yogyakarta: TH UII Press, 2004)

The president is elected directly by the people every five years and in the same year as the general elections for the DPR and DPD. Presidential candidates run as a team, with a candidate for the vice presidency, with both candidates having political party affiliation and a certain share of parliamentary seats. Thus, independent candidates are excluded. A candidate wins by securing a majority vote at the national level,[65] but where no candidate secures a majority, the top two candidates proceed to face-off in a second round of voting. The incumbent President can only be re-elected once.

The process for the impeachment of the President was also amended. In the event that the DPR finds the President engaging in any unlawful activity, including corruption and criminal acts, it can, with two-thirds approval, send a request of impeachment to the Constitutional Court. If the Constitutional Court considers the request valid, the MPR discusses the matter and the President may be impeached by the approval of two-thirds of those attending the relevant MPR session. The President may not dissolve the DPR.[66]

B. Provisions Relating to Human Rights

Another important constitutional defect that had to be addressed after democratisation was the lack of human rights provisions in the Constitution. Newly-introduced provisions about fundamental human rights were based on the Bill of Basic Human Rights in the MPR Decision No 17 of 1998 and finally incorporated in Articles 28A through 28J in the new Chapter XA of the Constitution in 2000. First, the rights of equality and freedom were proclaimed. Equality of all citizens under the law (Article 28D) and prohibition of discrimination (Article 28I) were proclaimed along with the freedom of thought and

at 52–56. Asshiddiqie was one of the drafters of the constitutional amendments. He has since changed his position and his recent work interprets Indonesian legislative institutions in terms of tricameralism, made up of the MPR, the DPR, and the DPD (see, eg, Jimly Asshiddiqie *Pokok-pokok hukum tata negara Indonesia: pasca reformasi* [*Basics of the Indonesian State Law: Post-Reformation*] (Jakarta: Bhuana Ilmu Populer, 2007) at 159). His reasoning is that the MPR has the right to appoint and dismiss the President (the formal right to appoint the president and the right to dismiss the president following a decision by the Constitutional Court on a proposal of impeachment by the DPR) and the right to establish and revise the Constitution.

65 But a presidential candidate must fulfil other conditions to win the election: he or she must win more than 20% of votes in more than a half the provinces and come first in more than half of the provinces as well as winning a majority vote at the national level.

66 Once in 1960, President Soekarno issued a Presidential Declaration (*Maklumat Presiden*) to suspend the DPR after he abrogated the 1950 Provisional Constitution and announced a return to the 1945 Constitution the previous year, marking the beginning of the period of so-called Guided Democracy. After democratisation, President Wahid, who faced a fierce conflict with Parliament, issued a Presidential Declaration to suspend the DPR on 22 July 2001. On this occasion, the political parties and the military refused to accept the President's decision, and instead proceeded to commence his impeachment through the MPR.

conscience, freedom of religion, freedom of assembly and association, and freedom of expression (Article 28E). Second, in order not to repeat the rampant state abuses of human rights in the past, the revised Constitution contains new provisions on the freedom of the human body. These provide for protection of children (Article 28B), the protection by laws (Article 28D), the prohibition of use of threat or torture (Article 28G), any kinds of bondage, and retroactive punishment (Article 28I).[67] New stipulations were also adopted to guarantee freedom of economic activities, including freedom to choose one's occupation, freedom to choose and change one's residence (Article 28E(1)), and property rights (Article 28H(4)). The right to work and to get good value for it is provided in Article 28D.

Further, a few clauses were introduced to guarantee social rights. Beginning with the guarantee of the right to life in Article 28A, these articles provide for a broad range of social rights, such as children's right to grow (Article 28B) and receive education, the right to benefit from development of scientific technology and culture (Article 28C), the right to disseminate and receive information (Article 28F), and the right to receive health and medical services and social security benefits (Article 28H). Finally, the revised Constitution declares that these fundamental human rights 'shall not be restricted under any circumstances' and 'guaranteeing, developing, maintaining, and enriching the basic human rights shall be the duty of the state' (Article 28I).

These amendments represented a major step toward the substantiation of constitutional democracy. The 1945 Constitution, which had not been revised between 1945 and 1998, experienced four major sets of amendments in the four-year period of democratic transition between 1998 and 2002. The post-amendment 1945 Constitution has almost no trace of its original form. The governing political institutions have drastically changed, compared with those stipulated in the original 1945 Constitution.

In the deliberations of constitutional amendments, no argument was ever raised that traditional cultural values be protected or entrenched in the Constitution. In contrast to the debates surrounding the 1945 constitutional drafting exercise, the constitutional amendment debates did not touch upon the philosophical aspects of the constitution. This may reflect the difference in the ideological competitions between the period of the constitutional drafting and

[67] Article 28I on the prohibition of 'retroactive punishment' (*hak untuk tidak dituntut atas dasar hukum yang berlaku surut*) aroused controversy among lawyers and human right activists, however. Questions about this principle were raised because there were concerns that a clause might preclude the bringing to court of past human rights violations committed by the military and other government agencies. Suspicion was intensified as the military actively lobbied for the insertion of this clause. The clause had not in fact been discussed in the Ad Hoc Committee I before the 2000 MPR annual session. However, the addition of its clause was decided by political manoeuvring of the military against other MPR members during the annual session. Neither did the Committee A of the MPR discuss it. It was also procedurally questionable.

that of the amendments; the former was a period of intense ideological competition between liberalism and socialism, capitalism and communism, and the East and the West, while the latter occurred in the post-Cold War period and was part of the third wave of democratisation. Uniquely, Indonesia did not discard its old constitution which supported the former authoritarian regime, but revised it to accommodate the country's transition to democracy.

V. CONCLUSION

In this chapter, we have considered the process of constitution-drafting at Indonesia's independence and seen how the 1945 Constitution reflected a strong nationalist, anti-West philosophy that favoured the incorporation of indigenous culture and philosophies in the foundational document. That explains why the 1945 Constitution, having acquired the patina of history, continued to be maintained as Indonesia's basic law even after more than 70 years. However, in its original form, the Indonesian Constitution gave rise to two long periods of authoritarian government, led by two successive Presidents, Soekarno and Soeharto. It would have been thought that in 1998, the logical and natural thing to do was to scuttle the 1945 document in totality to facilitate Indonesia's transition from authoritarianism to democracy. However, that was not what happened. Instead, reformers determined that the 1945 Constitution be retained as Indonesia's foundational nationalist document but instead to totally renovate it through the four major amendments that followed. This makes Indonesia's 1945 Constitution not only a historical but also a living document.

4

Timor-Leste's Post-Revolutionary Constitution: From Foundations to Practice

LEIGH-ASHLEY LIPSCOMB

INTRODUCTION

On 20 May 2002, Timor-Leste's Constitution came into effect on the same day its sovereignty was recognised by the whole of the international community. For many, the birth of the Constitution in 2002 marked the end of centuries of resistance: resistance to colonial rule by the Portuguese; resistance to a 24-year Indonesian occupation and, in different ways, resistance to more than two years of administration by the United Nations (UN). Accordingly, the Constitution provided the principles and structures to establish a new order of independent governance by and for the people of Timor-Leste, the East Timorese. The timing of this Constitution as the breakpoint between the past and the future took precedence over many aspects of its inception and its subsequent analysis.

More than 15 years later, this Constitution remains unchanged. It has survived a period of internal violent conflict in 2006, which recalled the UN to the country for administration of policing and security. It steered the country through a state of emergency after simultaneous assassination attempts on the President and Prime Minister in 2008. It carried on when the UN peacekeeping presence withdrew in 2012, and when the vestiges of the UN judicial presence were ousted in 2014. It guided the formation of seven constitutional governments during periods of crisis and uncertainty, and is frequently referenced and discussed when the East Timorese went to the polls in May 2018 to elect its second government in less than one year.[1] This Constitution has exceeded

[1] See Giacomo Tagnini, 'Early elections test East Timor's hard earned stability' (*Asia Times*, 3 March 2018) www.atimes.com/early-elections-test-timor-lestes-hard-earned-stability/ accessed 14 March 2018; Judicial Systems Monitoring Programme (JSMP), 'Dissolution of the National Parliament and the effect on the political legitimacy of the current Government' (Dili,

the average life span of Constitutions in Southeast Asia, which one scholar has calculated as 13 years.[2] Due to its adherence to its constitutional order, in 2017 Timor-Leste was declared the most democratic nation in Southeast Asia.[3]

Yet, to portray Timor-Leste's 2002 Constitution as the end step in the path to revolution and the starting point of democracy would not adequately capture its foundations, transitional effects or the challenges that persist to its practice. For decades defining Timor-Leste's constitutionalism has been at the heart of political tensions between entrenched revolutionary, 'resistance' elite, power structures and a populist need for a complete transition to multi-party, liberal democratic modes of governance. The Constitution has served as a common path for continuity at the same time as it has been the foundational document for intensifying, democratic change.

This chapter extends the scholarship on Timor-Leste's 2002 Constitution to examine its predecessors and the early days of its practice.[4] Discussion will illustrate the universal and dynamic nature of Timor-Leste's constitutionalism by mapping areas where there has been significant adherence and divergence from the principles and rules governing the institutional order founded by constitutional processes. It analyses some of the key factors and players driving this practice, versus those that contributed to its conception. It will question the degree to which the Constitution's durability is a sign of strength, or an indication of a fragile façade. This chapter will show how the 2002 Constitution is embedded in a series of foundational constitutional moments, which have

7 February 2018); Damien Kingsbury, 'Timor-Leste's "government of national disunity"' (East Asia Forum, 30 December 2017) www.eastasiaforum.org/2017/12/30/timor-lestes-government-of-national-disunity/ accessed 15 March 2018.

[2] The average life span for constitutions in Southeast Asia promulgated under authoritarian regimes was calculated at 13.5 years and 10.5 years for those promulgated under democratic regimes. See Aurel Croissant 'Ways of constitution-making in Southeast Asia: Actors, interests, dynamics' in Marco Bünte and Björn Dressel (eds), Politics and Constitutions in Southeast Asia (Kindle edition, New York, 2017) location 815–827.

[3] The Economist Intelligence Unit 'The Democracy Index 2016' (*The Economist*, 25 January 2017) https://infographics.economist.com/2017/DemocracyIndex/ accessed 25 September 2017.

[4] For examples of this scholarship see: L Aucoin and M Brandt 'East Timor Constitutional Passage to Independence' in LE Miller and L Aucoin (eds), *Framing the State in Terms of Transition: Case Studies in Constitution-making* (United States Institute of Peace, 2010) 245–274; Alipio Baltazar 'An Overview of the Constitutional Drafting Process in East Timor' [2004] *East Timor Law Journal* http://easttimorlahournal.wordpress.com/2012/05/1 (accessed 7 Sep 2017); Jamal Benomar 'Constitution-Making and Peace Building: Lessons Learned from the Constitution-Making Processes of Post-Conflict Countries' (New York: United Nations Development Programme, August 2003) 9; JM Carey 'Does it Matter How a Constitution is Created' in Z Barany and RG Moser (eds) *Is Democracy Exportable?* (Cambridge University Press, 2009) 155–178; H Charlesworth 'The Constitution of East Timor, May 20, 2002' (2003) 1 (2) *International Journal of Constitutional Law* 325–344; Philipp Dann and Zaid Al-Ali 'The Internationalized *Pouvoir Constituant* – Constitution-making Under External Influence in Iraq, Sudan and East Timor' (2006) 10 *Max Plank Yearbook of United Nations Law* 423–463; Annemarie Devereux Timor-Leste's Bill of Rights: A Preliminary History (Australian National University Press, 2015); Rui Graça Feijó 'Constitutionalism Old and New in the "UN Kingdom of Timor-Leste"' in Bünte (n 2); Wallis, J. Constitution-making during State Building (Cambridge University Press, 2014).

balanced the consolidation and progressive 'disentrenchment' of Timor-Leste's revolutionary political order in the process of forging a new State.

I. RELEVANCE

This chapter examines Timor-Leste's constitutional processes on their own terms and makes them accessible to a wider audience. At the same time, I consider how the case of Timor-Leste may be relevant to the study of the region of Southeast Asia and other comparative frameworks.

Timor-Leste's constitution in 2002 is notable among the Southeast Asian Constitutions discussed in this volume because of its relatively recent drafting and external influences. Commonalities exist with other Southeast Asian countries in the role that colonial pasts and cosmopolitan, anti-colonial alliances played in early constitutionalism. However, when considering the 2002 Constitution, foremost among external influences is the United Nations and international law. Consequently, Timor-Leste's constitutionalism can be analysed alongside other countries where supra-national organisations or occupying powers have played a significant role in constitutional processes since the 1990s, including Cambodia, Iraq and Afghanistan.[5] These studies, and the case of Timor-Leste, can help us to understand the role of non-domestic law, international advisors and human rights norms in shaping national constitutions through transnational legal processes.

This chapter will highlight the transnational nature of constitution-making and its effects in Timor-Leste, demonstrating how its universal orientation and construction of new political spaces began before the UN administration's and Dili-based international advisors' involvement.[6] It will map an evolutionary, internationalised constitutional process, softening some of the scholarly assertions about the immensity of impact of the UN,[7] which can arise from examining East Timor's constitutional founding only from the perspective of 2002. While the UN's role was formative, this chapter may add to those that express caution about viewing post-conflict constitutions emerging from 'blank slates', which may unwittingly distort the formal role of short-term, international

[5] Eg, Markus Bockenforde and Daniel Sabsay 'Supranational Organisations and Their Impact on National Constitutions' in Mark Tushnet, Thomas Fleiner and Cheryl Saunders (eds) *Routledge Handbook of Constitutional Law* (Kindle edition, Routledge, 2013); Simon Chesterman, 'Imposed Constitutions, Imposed Constitutionalism and Ownership' (2004–2005) 37 *Connecticut Law Review* 947–954.

[6] For a definition and discussion of transnational constitutionalism see Peer Zumbansen, 'Carving Out Typologies and Accounting for Differences Across Systems: Towards a Methodology of Transnational Constitutionalism' in Michel Rosenfeld and András Sajó (eds) The Oxford Handbook of Comparative Constitutional Law (Kindle edn, Oxford University Press, 2012) location 2067–2094.

[7] Bockenforde (n 5) location 14162–14174.

advisors and governments compared to domestic elites and the experiences of the local population.[8] Indeed, if Timor-Leste's Constitution is to be evaluated or compared, then the longer-term, discursive and often less formal practices that comprise transnational constitutionalism must be delineated alongside the 2002 text.

Consequently, one of the aims of this discussion is to provoke further thought on how constitutions woven from both international and domestic threads and formal and informal constitutional processes may factor into the 'dis-entrenchment' of the makers of revolutions who installed 'first' Constitutions in Southeast Asia. How can imperfect or incomplete foundational moments foment new episodes of constitutional change? To that end, this case study stresses the dynamic nature of Constitutions in Southeast Asia and raises questions about how to identify legitimacy and the effects of these Constitutions over time. To this aim, I employ a historical and political view of constitutionalism, rather than a legalistic one.[9]

In the case of Timor-Leste, if its persistent constitutional principles are put fully into practice they will inevitably raise the past and dismantle it without discrimination between internal and external parts of the former political order in motion since 1975. If the Constitution is to function with legitimacy, the revolutionary past carefully crafted and captured in the 2002 Constitution and the state's foundations cannot survive unexamined or untouched. As we shall observe, shifting the internal political patterns of the past is an area where constitutional practice has progressed and faced challenges, particularly when building institutions. This process has unfurled episodically; not in a single foundational moment.

II. PRECURSORS TO THE 2002 CONSTITUTION

A. 1975 Constitution

Although it is rarely acknowledged, the first Constitution of 'East Timor' was promulgated in 1975, not 2002.[10] The 1975 Constitution is the founding document that christens the nation the 'Democratic Republic of Timor-Leste' – the

[8] Chesterman (n 5) 950 (reference to Feldman). See also, Kim Lane Scheppele, 'A Constitution Between Past and Future' (2008) 49 (4) *William and Mary Law Review* 1405–1407.

[9] For legal analysis of the text and practice of the 2002 Constitution see Patricia Jeronimo 'Os Direitos Fundamentais na Constituição da República Democrática de Timor-Leste e na jurisprudência do Tribunal de Recurso' (Year unknown, on file with author) and Pedro Bacelar de Vasconcelos, Constituição Anotada República Democrática do Timor-Leste (Braga: Direitos Humanos – Centro do Investigação Interdisciplinar, Escola de Direito da Universidade do Minho, 2011).

[10] For the original text of the Constitution see FRETILIN, 'Timor-Leste: uma Luta Heróica' (Lisbon: CasaComum.org) http://hdl.handle.net/11002/fms_dc_130466 accessed 25 September 2017.

official name of the country that constitutional drafters in 2002 retained without referring to its origins in the 1975 text. Consequently, this chapter and the associated website translation uses 'Timor-Leste' to refer to the country from the 1975 Constitution's promulgation.

On 28 November 1975, the FRETILIN[11] political party rushed to establish a government in East Timor in the vacuum left by the Portuguese authorities that fled the island in August 1975 at the outbreak of internal armed conflict. The colonial officials had not completed the scheduled decolonisation process. The subsequent FRETILIN military victory over the UDT[12] and other East Timorese political parties led to FRETILIN's default administration of the territory. With some areas already occupied by Indonesian troops and a full-scale invasion imminent, FRETILIN party members felt that it was imperative to issue the Constitution along with a Declaration of Independence as evidence of their ability to govern East Timor as an independent nation.[13] The declaration by the FRETILIN appointed President, Francisco Xavier do Amaral, and a reading of the Constitution by the FRETILIN appointed Defence Minister, Rogério Lobato, were broadcast by radio to reach the broadest possible audience of East Timorese and international observers. Members of FRETILIN reportedly drafted the text several days before the 28 November ceremony, and approved the first Constitution hurriedly. Further information about its drafting and authorship has not yet been made a matter of public record. While the declaration of independence in 1975 is heralded, the first Constitution is seldom mentioned.

The Constitution in 1975 was written and read in Portuguese. Later, a few hard copies circulated in the capital of Dili.[14] Consequently, it was a document accessible only to the handful of elite within Timor-Leste who could read Portuguese. Members of the FRETILIN party at that time included some of the first generation of East Timorese elite who studied and obtained higher degrees in Portugal or its colonies where they were exposed to entrenched anti-colonial movements and their proponents, such as those from Angola and Mozambique. Brazilian philosopher and educator Paulo Freire's works published in Portuguese from 1968 were also reportedly influential on this revolutionary group's thinking, drawing on anti-colonial and Marxist theories. The language choice for this first Constitution signalled that the founding of the nation was orchestrated to send a message primarily to an external audience, particularly Lisbon, which held the powers to recognise and support their independence. Further, the language of the Constitution expressed solidarity with other Portuguese speaking nations from whom it hoped to garner support. Ironically, the language and anti-Portuguese rhetoric of this first Constitution may be contributing factors to its present-day obscurity.

[11] FRETILIN stands for Frente Revolucionária do Timor Leste Independente (Revolutionary Front of Independent East Timor).

[12] UDT stands for União Democrática Timorense (Timorese Democratic Union).

[13] Interviews with Fracisco Xavier do Amaral (Dili, Timor-Leste, July–August 2009).

[14] Ibid.

The highlights of this first Constitution need to be outlined as a prelude to our subsequent discussion on constitutionalism and practice. The Constitution of 1975 was organised into six chapters and 55 articles, which stated the general principles of government; established a 'bill of rights' for citizens; outlined the political organs of the state and administrative organisation and established powers for constitutional amendment.

Part of the reluctance to attribute drafting and authorship of the document may be due to its content, which displays characteristics of militarism, one-party rule and communist government structures. For example, the organs of the Popular Assembly and the state were: (1) The Central Committee of FRETILIN; (2) Ministers and Vice-Ministers of the government; (3) Regional Administrators; (4) Representatives of Military Units; (5) Two Representatives from each regional sub-committee of the FRETILIN party. A date for the Popular Assembly elections was to be set one year after the first meeting of the first party congress of FRETILIN, but no deadline was stipulated for when the first congress must be held. There was to be both a Prime Minister and a President, as is the case today and as was proposed for Portugal's new Constitution under draft in 1975. However, unlike today, the President was not directly elected. The President was the Head of the FRETILIN party. The President would have presided over the Popular Assembly and would have also been Commander of the military. The Prime Minister (also a FRETILIN party member) would have presided over the Council of Ministers. Legislative power was vested equally in the Central Committee of FRETILIN, the Popular Assembly and the Council of Ministers (consisting of all FRETILIN members). Only the Central Committee of FRETILIN had the power to amend the Constitution. There were no provisions for consultation or approval of the Constitution by the population. The Constitution was written as final, without interim status. This governance structure reflects the rhetoric that the FRETILIN party had pursued since its founding – that it was the only true representative of the people of Timor-Leste.[15]

A number of provisions in the first Constitution foreshadowed the human rights principles and Bill of Rights that would appear in later, more broadly recognised constitutional documents, including the 2002 Constitution. There was a non-discrimination clause, which prohibited discrimination on the basis of race, colour, ethnicity, sex, place of birth, religion, socio-economic status or occupation. Rights explicitly guaranteed included freedom of expression, freedom of thought, freedom of assembly; health, education, work and privacy. The first Constitution guaranteed social protection for the elderly, persons with disabilities, and veterans and their families. In the judicial sphere, the right to representation was guaranteed and a person could only be tried and convicted

[15] For more information on this rhetoric see CAVR, Chega!: Final Report of the Commission for Reception, Truth and Reconciliation of Timor-Leste (CAVR), Vol I, Pt III (Dili, Timor-Leste: 2005) 168.

on charges under the law. Significant for later developments, there were provisions declaring the complete separation of church and state, and there was no reference to a specific religion. On the other hand, undercutting these rights, the Constitution allowed for the removal of political rights of anyone that by 'action, omission or conduct favour colonialism, imperialism, racism or regionalism' (Article 21).

The recognition of the Declaration of Independence and the FRETILIN government by a handful of Asian and Lusophone African countries in 1975 conferred only limited international legitimacy to the first Constitution, which was not considered sufficient to sustain the broad-based, political backing needed to resist the subsequent Indonesian occupation and restore independence.[16] Even so, a number of the principles and basic governance structures in this Constitution were incrementally adapted and put into force internally during the Indonesian occupation in areas in the bush controlled by FRETILIN and its armed wing, *Forças Armadas para a Liberação Nacional do Timor Leste* (FALINTIL).[17] The most significant break from the principles and concepts for governance in the 1975 Constitution occurred in 1987, when Xanana Gusmão resigned from FRETILIN and declared that the resistance armed forces (FALINTIL) would not be aligned with any political party and founded an alternative to FRETILIN – the National Council of Timorese Resistance (CNRT). The shift towards a more complex, multi-party resistance movement and governance structure began.

The content, timing and practice of the first revolutionary Constitution is not surprising given the political changes underway in Portugal, Africa and Southeast Asia. The year 1975 marked a wave of constitutional activity in Portugal and its former colonies and in Southeast Asia. The FRETILIN unilateral, impromptu declaration of independence and constitution was reminiscent of the strategy used in Guinea–Bissau, where the *Partido Africano da Independência da Guiné e Cabo Verde* (PAIGC) party unilaterally declared independence in 1974 at a similar ceremony, and was granted independence one year later. The structure of Timor-Leste's 1975 Constitution is nearly identical to the Constitution of Mozambique promulgated by the *Frente de Libertação de Moçambique* (FRELIMO) party months earlier in June 1975.[18] There also appear to be significant structural and rhetorical influences from the constitution of Angola, which was promulgated just weeks earlier on 11 November 1975. In Southeast Asia,

[16] The countries that recognised Timor-Leste as an independent nation were Mozambique, Angola, Guinea – Bissau, San Tomé and Príncipe, Cape Verde, China and Vietnam.

[17] For further information, see CAVR (n 16) 'Structure and Strategy of the Resistance' 423, 432–434.

[18] Senior members of the FRETILIN political party attended the independence ceremony of Mozambique in June 1975 (ibid, 180). The uniforms worn by Xavier do Amaral and the FRETILIN leader Nicolau Lobato for the declaration and constitutional reading ceremony were presents to the FRETILIN leaders from Samora Michel, the leader of the FRELIMO party of Mozambique (Constancio Pinto and Mathew Jardine, Inside the East Timorese Resistance (Toronto: James Lorimer and Company, Publishers, 1997) 39).

a regime change in Laos in 1975 led to the abrogation of its Constitution and a call for the drafting of a new socialist Constitution.[19] In Cambodia drafting of a new Constitution began in April 1975, which was adopted by a self-appointed group of leftist military commanders only weeks after Timor-Leste in December 1975. In Portugal a Constituent Assembly was elected and it proceeded to draft a substantive part of a new Constitution by December 1975. It was promulgated in early 1976. There was a significant lobby to adopt a revolutionary, socialist text for this new Portuguese Constitution, which coincided with a movement to install a leftist regime in Lisbon. On 25 November 1975, there was a leftist, military coup attempt to overthrow the government in Lisbon. It is not clear if the East Timorese revolutionary leaders heard that this coup attempt failed before the inaugural ceremony and first constitutional reading began.

The primary impetus behind the timing of the first Constitution was the military campaign by the Indonesians, but the 1975 Constitution was not an ad-hoc document penned in isolation. It is abbreviated compared to its 1975 counterparts. However, it demonstrates deliberate influences, alliances and strategies that were meant to place it on par with its contemporary revolutionary constitutions, which were recognised by other nations that had broken free of colonial powers in Africa and Asia at that time.

The Indonesian occupation prevented the full implementation of the first Constitution of Timor-Leste, but this fact alone does not explain its lack of acknowledgement by the international community and the East Timorese in recent years. From the legal perspective, there is no reference to the 1975 Constitution in the 2002 Constitution or UNTAET Regulation No 2001/2 on the guidelines for the election of the Constituent Assembly and the 2002 Constitution. It was also not referenced in the FRETILIN political party's draft constitution created at a conference in August 1998, which became the basis for its 2002 proposed draft Constitution. Interestingly, the constitutional chronology featured in Timor-Leste's Museum of Resistance archives website, makes no mention of it. The official government website also fails to refer to this Constitution in its narrative of nation building and constitution-making.[20] It might well be that the first Constitution's single-party rule, the leftist organisation of its government, the elite drafting process and lack of popular consultation and concomitant lack of transparency and accessibility to the Timorese public has, over time, undermined its legacy. Nonetheless, it is critical to trace the consistent and divergent understandings of constitutionalism that emanate from it: its absence in the historical and legal narrative indicates the rejection of some, but not all, of its core principles and their replacement with new ones.

[19] The drafting of a new Laos Constitution was not completed until 1991, leaving the country functioning without a constitution for a number of years.

[20] Government of Timor-Leste, 'Official website of the Government of Timor-Leste: History' http://timor-leste.gov.tl/?p=29&lang=en accessed 15 September 2017. See also the section, 'Constitution'.

B. The 1998 Magna Carta

The next pivotal moment in Timor-Leste's constitution-making process occurred in Peniche, Portugal from 23–27 April 1998. A conference of the East Timorese diaspora that represented most political parties resisting the Indonesian occupation drafted and approved the 'Magna Carta of Liberty, Rights, Duties and Guarantees of the People of Timor-Leste'.[21] There were 218 East Timorese delegates comprising the two largest East Timorese political parties – FRETILIN and UDT. These parties, who had been locked in armed conflict with each other in 1975, had reconciled and were united at this conference under an umbrella framework (the National Council of Timorese Resistance, CNRT) to resist the Indonesian occupation. Representatives of the Catholic Church and some other smaller parties such as *Klibur Oan Timor Asuwain* (KOTA) and Associação Popular Democrática Timorense (APODETI) were also represented among those who approved the Magna Carta.

Unfortunately, there are not yet accessible records on the drafting process of the Magna Carta. Some sources say the then FRETILIN member, former Prime Minister of Timor-Leste, Mari Alkatiri, drafted the main text of the document with draft inputs from at least two other representatives.[22] It is not clear if it was debated or amendments were made based on feedback from the delegation. The original text indicates it was adopted by acclamation of the representatives at the conference.

The Magna Carta was considered the core document to guide the drafting of a new constitution for Timor-Leste. Unlike the Constitution proclaimed in 1975, this Constitution involved multiple political parties and civil society organisations in its approval process. Milena Pires, an East Timorese researcher on the diaspora at that time, explained its significance:

> The Magna Carta provides a comprehensive basis for the future constitution and political direction of an independent East Timor, pledges adherence to the rule of law and guarantees civil and political rights for East Timor's citizens.[23]

A set of principles to guide the drafting of a new, multi-party, democratic East Timorese constitution existed in the Magna Carta from 1998, which was successfully drafted completely outside the auspices of the United Nations or its corps of associated, professional, post-conflict constitutional advisors.

The Magna Carta shows drastic changes since 1975 in constitutional principles. In terms of theoretical foundations, there is a stronger emphasis in the Magna Carta on the 'people' or '*povo*' (a populist term in Portuguese) as the

[21] My translation from Portuguese text. For original text see: CNRT, 'Carta Magna' (1998) http://hdl.handle.net/11002/fms_dc_137516 accessed 24 September 2017.

[22] George Aditjondro, 'From Colony to Global Prize' (Arena Magazine, date unknown) https://arena.org.au/from-colony-to-global-prize/ accessed 18 September 2017.

[23] Milena Pires, 'East Timorese National Convention in the Diaspora' (Estafeta, Summer 1998) www.etan.org/estafeta/98/summer/7nationa.htm accessed 18 September 2017.

agents of constitutionalism whereas in 1975 the rhetoric of the Constitution stresses the party acting on behalf of the people. For example, in the preamble of the Magna Carta, the list of core principles is predicated with the heading: '*Nos, o Povo de Timor-Leste*' (We, the People of Timor-Leste). There is also the introduction of frequent references to the centrality of rule of law or 'a state of law' (*estado do direito*). In contrast to 1975, the Magna Carta makes explicit reference to the Timorese people as primarily Judeo-Christian in identity and culture. This deliberate mention may have been for the purpose of contrasting the national identity to stereotypes about Indonesian Islamic culture. It may also reflect the fact that churches (primarily the Catholic Church) played an important political role in the revolutionary movement. While there still is a commitment to secularism in the Magna Carta, this reference is radically different from the 1975 Constitution's separation of the state and people from a particular religion. In terms of governance, the biggest change from 1975 was a new, explicit commitment to a multi-party, pluralist democracy.

One of the continuities from the 1975 Constitution was a clear commitment to social justice, encompassing political, social and economic rights. However, the language of human rights is much more sophisticated and specific in the Magna Carta compared to that of the 1975 Constitution, reflecting the internationalisation of the resistance movement that had culminated in the award of the Nobel Peace Prize to José Ramos-Horta and Bishop Carlos Filipe Ximenes Belo in 1996. The Preamble of the Magna Carta shifted the focus from breaking the chains of colonialism in the Constitution of 1975 to the global fight for human rights in the 1990s. The 'right to self-determination' replaced anti-colonialism. The second section of the Magna Carta includes a list of the international human rights treaties that would be recognised by Timor-Leste, which encompassed all the core human rights treaties applicable in 1998. This list is significant to understand as an expansion of the principles in the first Constitution from 1975. The Magna Carta demonstrated that East Timorese constitutionalism increasingly embraced technical and legal tools for implementing human rights; the overall goals were the same as in 1975 but they had found new language and methods. The adoption of this language has textual continuities with 1975, such as the anti-discrimination article that is similar in both texts. Political continuity exists because this language appears tailored to attract the support of an international political audience, as much as an East Timorese one. Finally, it should be noted that the East Timorese had decided before the UN administration ever existed to incorporate a broad range of human rights protections into their post-revolutionary Constitution's legal framework. Accounts of the 2002 constitution-making process can leave the impression that the international involvement in the 2002 Constitution yielded the universalist text and human rights protections, when in fact they were internalised as a fundamental part of Timor-Leste's constitutionalism earlier.

The position of language in Timor-Leste's post-revolutionary constitutional order took on new significance with the Magna Carta. Like the Constitution in 1975, the Magna Carta was written in Portuguese by educated elites and was not translated into local languages: an English translation of the Magna Carta appeared in 2000 after the CNRT Congress was held in Dili and was later published in an academic journal. In 1975 Portuguese was the presumed language of governance with no specific status declared. By 1998 the status of the Portuguese language was no longer certain and the drafters of the Magna Carta felt the need to declare Portuguese as the official language of the future nation. This shift responded to changes in the composition of and influences on the revolutionary elite. The resistance movement in the 1990s included a younger generation of East Timorese who identified with Indonesian-speaking human rights movements. It also included an English-speaking diaspora who had settled in Australia and other places outside the Lusophone world. Finally, as an international human rights issue, the resistance included people who were not East Timorese or Lusophone. English and Indonesian vocabularies of resistance were becoming as important as the Portuguese anti-colonial ones. Although this linguistic diversity was evident at the conference, the older guard of revolutionaries who spoke Portuguese led the party delegations. As we will see, the Magna Carta declaration of an official language was a matter of significant political importance for subsequent constitutional debates and drafting processes.

The Magna Carta of 1998 forged the multi-party consensus on the principles of East Timorese constitutionalism that would be finalised with the adoption of the 2002 Constitution. It was an important part of the constitution-making process, even though it occurred before the formal processes put in place by the UN after 2001. Months after its approval, the Magna Carta was used as the basis for composing a full draft Constitution at a FRETILIN conference held by the diaspora in Sydney, Australia. This FRETILIN draft became the lead document the Constitutional Assembly used to debate and draft the 2002 Constitution. The Magna Carta also reportedly influenced the draft Constitutions submitted for consideration by other parties in 2002, including UDT. In addition, the Magna Carta was the basis for discussions at the next CNRT Congress held after Peniche in August 2000 in Timor-Leste. At this conference, all East Timorese resistance parties were present. The discussion of the Magna Carta was not limited to the diaspora. It also encompassed the viewpoints of people who had remained in Timor-Leste throughout the resistance struggle. If one wants to locate the foundational site of political bargaining and space for constitutional discourse and practice, it must be with the Magna Carta.

Despite their roles in constitutional discourse, the 1975 Constitution and the Magna Carta received limited attention because they fell outside of the formal timeline published for the 2002 constitution-making process and because they required a deeper look into the state's revolutionary past.[24] Records of the

[24] Michael Leach's recent publication covers the highlights of the Peniche conference and the first Constitution. See Michael Leach, *Nation Building and National Identity in Timor-Leste* (New York: Routledge, 2017).

drafting processes have not been publicly available, further compromising their historical legacy and legitimacy when formal constitutional discussions began under UN transitional authorities after 1999.

III. THE 2002 CONSTITUTION

A. Drafting of Constitution

As the drafting process of the 2002 Constitution has received detailed scholarly analysis, I will only summarise its most critical aspects for the purposes of our later discussions. The UN Security Council gave the UN Transitional Administration in East Timor (UNTAET) authority to administer all aspects of governance in East Timor after the vast majority of the East Timorese voting population chose independence from Indonesia in a 1999 UN-sponsored referendum.[25] In the lead up and aftermath of the referendum there was devastating violence resulting in gross human rights violations and the destruction of much of Timor-Leste's infrastructure, precipitating a humanitarian crisis. This meant that the UN did not only administer the government but was also physically building it. The Security Council Resolution endowed the UN with the full range of legislative and administrative powers, including the administration of justice.[26] The head of the UN Mission, referred to as the Transitional Administrator, had executive and legislative authority,[27] with power to make all laws and appointments to office.

The adoption of a constitution and popular elections were the keystones for handover of full governing authority from the UN transitional administration to the East Timorese. Although drafting a constitution was not required by the Security Council mandate for East Timor, UNTAET determined, early in its mission, that without achieving these two aims, political transition would be delayed and independence stalled. Hence, there was enormous pressure on the East Timorese and the UNTAET administration to achieve these goals as quickly as possible. The fast- track solution that emerged was to do both at the same time.

Following discussions between the UN Transitional Administrator and 34 appointed members of a consultative East Timorese National Council, a timetable for the political process of transition was adopted that included the creation of an elected, constitutional assembly. According to the proposal favoured by the UN, this assembly would draft and adopt the Constitution, and then by default become the legislative assembly of East Timor following the

[25] UN Security Council Resolution 1272 (25 October 1999) S/RES/1272 (1999). East Timor, rather than Timor-Leste, was adopted by the UN as the name of the mission and country during its period of governance.

[26] Ibid para 1.

[27] UNTAET Regulation 1999/1, s 1.

Constitution's entry into force. This solution was cost effective and fast because it meant holding only one popular election or consultation as opposed to two. It was also surmised that this solution would minimise conflict between the East Timorese political parties, particularly at the local level during elections. The political parties who expected to do well in hasty elections favoured this option, primarily FRETILIN. Smaller and newer political parties as well as the head of the National Consultative Council (Xanana Gusmão) wanted to separate the constitution-making process from popular elections and favoured a broader popular consultation or popular referendum for the approval of the Constitution. There was significant debate and disagreement among international and East Timorese political actors about the best modality to produce a legitimate and durable Constitution. On 16 March 2001, UNTAET issued a law to implement the election of a Constituent Assembly (UNTAET Regulation 2001/2). The law deferred the issue of whether the Constituent Assembly would become the legislative assembly, allowing it to be decided during the drafting of the Constitution.

On 30 August 2001, the East Timorese Constituent Assembly was democratically elected. The elections were free and fair. The assembly consisted of 88 members, who represented 12 out of the 16 political parties who participated in the election. Seats were allotted by geographic area (one representative per district), complemented by 75 national representatives who were allocated to parties by proportional representation. As expected, the historical political party of the resistance, FRETILIN, won the majority of seats with 55 representatives. However, they did not win enough votes to be able to adopt the Constitution on their own. The UNTAET regulation stipulated that the Constituent Assembly must draft, debate, consult and adopt the Constitution with a minimum of 60 votes in favour. On 15 September 2001, the Constituent Assembly convened.

To appease some of the discontent with the choice of the Constituent Assembly as the method for drafting, UNTAET created district-level Constitutional Commissions to gather the populace's views on the Constitution. Prior to the election of the Constituent Assembly, from 18 June–14 July 2001, UNTAET held 205 public meetings on the Constitution with an estimated total of 38,000 people participating.[28] UNTAET presented the outcomes on the initial day of the assembly's meetings, which resulted in 45 suggested amendments to the draft Constitution that were later considered by the Constituent Assembly thematic committees. Only eight recommendations derived from public meetings and 13 derived from consultations with civil society were considered at plenary level.[29] Of these, only four were adopted in the final draft of the Constitution, reportedly from the civil society recommendations rather than concerns raised in the district-level commissions.[30] There was further consultation at the

[28] Graça (n 4) location 2220 and Baltazar (n 4) 3.
[29] Baltazar (n 4) 4.
[30] Ibid.

sub-committee level but the Constitutional Commissions were the most significant aspect of popular participation. Most analysts of the process conclude that the consultations did not provide sufficient opportunity for popular input into the drafting of the Constitution.

The UNTAET regulation stipulated that the Constituent Assembly had 90 days to draft and adopt the Constitution. By all accounts, this was a foolish timeline. After being granted an extension, the Constituent Assembly continued to operate at lightening pace because many members wanted to adopt the Constitution in time for the 20 May anniversary of the founding of the precursor of the FRETILIN political party. To meet this deadline, the space for popular consultation and plenary date was compressed; in fact, the majority of the first 90 days of deliberation was spent on procedural issues rather than substantive debate. In the end, the draft adopted at plenary by the Constituent Assembly in early March was distributed and consulted with the public for less than two weeks. Nevertheless, on 22 March 2002, the Constituent Assembly adopted the Constitution with 72 votes in favour, 14 against, 1 abstention, 1 absentee. The Constitution provided that it would enter into force on 20 May 2002, appropriate given this key paragraph adopted for the Constitution's preamble:

> The preparation and adoption of the Constitution of the Democratic Republic of Timor-Leste is the culmination of the historical resistance of the Timorese People intensified following the invasion of the 7th of December 1975.

The past and the future of Timor-Leste as a nation converged at this watershed moment.

B. Key features of the 2002 Constitution

Despite its speedy drafting, the 2002 Constitution is comprehensive. Set out in seven parts with multiple chapters and 170 articles, it demonstrates the extent of constitutionalism's development since 1975. It lays out the Fundamental Principles for governance; contains an extensive Bill of Rights (Part II, 'Fundamental Rights, Duties, Liberties and Guarantees'); determines the Organisation of Political Power, Economic and Financial Organisation, National Defence and Security; and lays out the process for revision of the Constitution and its enforcement.

In the Preamble there are echoes of the 1975 Constitution and the Magna Carta. For example, the first paragraph recalls the revolutionary rhetoric from the early days of the FRETILIN party's self-proclaimed rule:

> Following the liberation of the Timorese People from colonization and illegal occupation of the Maubere Motherland by foreign powers ….

References to colonisation had dropped out of the Magna Carta due to the focus on Indonesian occupation at the time, and the use of 'Maubere' as the

FRETILIN symbol of the Timorese people had been eschewed in 1998 in the spirit of consensus (the term 'Maubere' had a long history of contention between FRETILIN and UDT). This language, which appeared in the first article of the 1975 Constitution, was revived in the 2002 Constitution, no doubt influenced by FRETILIN's majority representation in the assembly. Another example of FRETILIN's strong influence over the rhetoric and symbolism in the 2002 Constitution is the choice of the date of proclamation (20 May). This date coincides with the founding of the political party ASDT, the predecessor to the FRETILIN political party. Despite the heavy FRETILIN tones in the language of the Constitution, the commitment to a multi-party system that first appeared in the Magna Carta is clear and is enshrined in Part I, Section 7(2) of the Fundamental Principles.[31]

References to the 'rule of law' that appeared first in the Magna Carta are eminent, appearing in the Preamble and the first Provision of the 2002 Constitution (section 1, paragraph 1), as well as being defined as one of the purposes of the State.[32] The Bill of Rights is significant and provides a comprehensive range of guarantees. It includes the rights to access courts and the right to representation, providing a stronger basis to protect these guarantees made in the 1975 Constitution and the Magna Carta. Like the Magna Carta and the 1975 Constitution, there is a strong emphasis on socio-economic rights as well as political rights. For example, the 2002 Constitution specifies one of the purposes of the state is to 'promote the building of a society based on social justice, by establishing material and spiritual welfare of the citizens'.

Unlike the 1975 Constitution, there is a substantive section on the courts. This section outlines the principles, powers and organisational structure for a national justice system to give substance to the administration of all aspects of justice – political and social. As we will examine, there have been differing views on where the emphasis in implementation of the Constitution's principles of justice and the rule of law should lie.

However, some principles in the 2002 Constitution, including the 'rule of law', were not universally accepted. The first article of the Constitution reads: 'the Democratic Republic of East Timor is a democratic state ruled by law, sovereign, independent and unitary, based upon the popular will and respect for the dignity of the human being.' The majority of the assembly approved the text. However, there were still four persons opposed and 11 abstentions to this article. This dissent among the Constituent Assembly members demonstrates that there was not absolute acceptance of this new generation of globalised, constitutional language.

[31] It reads, 'The State shall value the contribution of political parties for the organized expression of the popular will and for the democratic participation of the citizen in the governance of the country.'

[32] The English translation of the text reads 'The Democratic Republic of East Timor is a democratic, sovereign, independent and unitary State based on the rule of law, the will of the people and the respect for the dignity of the human person.'

In terms of principles for the administration of government, there is a strong commitment to the separation of powers. They adopted a semi-presidential system, with a President elected by direct popular vote and a legislature popularly elected on a different time frame by a proportional representation system. The government is formed by the party that wins the largest proportion of the popular vote in the legislative elections, at times through a coalition with other parties. The Prime Minister heads the government and the Cabinet comprises the Council of Ministers, with significant legislative powers over some administrative areas of governance. The judiciary is independent and comprised of a professional corps of officers selected on the basis of competitive examinations and merit with life tenures. The structures of government largely mirror those in a number of Lusophone and Latin American countries.

The separation of powers is markedly different in principle from that of 1975, but this is an area of practice that has raised questions about the degree to which there has been a break from earlier visions of governance. For example, not surprising given the vested interests of its authors, the 2002 Constitution determined that the elected members of the Constituent Assembly who drafted the Constitution would become the members of Parliament for an initial term of five years. The lack of veiling procedures in the drafting process of the Constitution to give effect to the separation of powers in determining this crucial decision of governance is noticeable.

The role of the military significantly shifted in the 2002 Constitution from the prominent and partisan role it played in the 1975 Constitution. In the Magna Carta, the military's role is absent. In the 2002 Constitution, the role of the military arm of the resistance is celebrated in the Preamble and in the special recognition and status afforded to veterans in Section 11, 'Valorisation of Resistance', among others. At the same time, in accordance with the rule of law and democratic principles of the Constitution, the military's powers are limited to providing military defence. They must be non-partisan and 'shall not intervene in political matters.'[33] The military is 'obedient' to the organs of government; not above it. The Constitution provides for a military court and justice system to further enhance accountability of members of the armed forces. At the same time as there are substantive limits on the military's role, the Constitution also provides that every citizen has a 'right' and a 'duty' to defend the state's sovereignty. It is unclear if this part of the Constitution was meant to lead to a system of national conscription. As will be discussed, giving meaning to the role of the military in the 2002 Constitution has been one of the most dynamic areas of constitutional practice and challenge.

As was the case with the Magna Carta, the role of the Catholic Church is pronounced in the 2002 Constitution, while still committing East Timor to a secular state and freedom of religion. For example, the Preamble states: 'In its

[33] Part V, s 146(3).

cultural and humane perspective, the Catholic Church in East Timor has always been able to take on the suffering of all the People with dignity, placing itself at their side in the defence of their most fundamental rights.' Along with veterans, the Catholic Church is explicitly acknowledged in Section 11 of the Constitution that requires the 'Valorisation of the Resistance.' The Constitution does not mention any other religion.

One of the biggest departures from the previous constitutional documents was language. Portuguese was kept as a national language as designated in the Magna Carta and the FRETILIN draft constitution. However, following debate in the assembly, the most dominant local language in Timor-Leste, Tetum, was also made an official language of equal standing in the Constitution. English and Indonesian languages were declared working languages. This language choice reflected the growing diversity in the composition of the East Timorese elite who drafted the Constitution, but also a desire to make the Constitution and governance accessible to a broader audience of East Timorese.

The 2002 Constitution is relatively unique among constitutions in that it provides directly for the criminal liability for and prosecution of 'crimes against humanity of genocide [sic] or of war'.[34] In many other countries, this is a matter dealt with in other forms of legislation. The 2002 Constitution incorporates the national prosecution of these crimes by the structures installed by the UN before the 2002 Constitution was adopted. It also makes transitional arrangements for international personnel to participate in the administration of the justice system. These provisions are in line with the more specific references to justice in the Magna Carta, which included a commitment to pursue justice at the international level for war crimes and crimes against humanity committed against the East Timorese. This unusual level of specificity about international law and international justice mechanisms in the Constitution underscores the dual role the Constitution played as an instrument of transitional justice, as well as a product of a pursuit for not only a 'forward looking' revolution; but also, a globalised movement to address the human rights violations of the past.

Another unique feature of the Constitution is a prohibition against its amendment during a state of siege or state of emergency (Section 157). This provision has served East Timor well in its first decade where there have already been several periods of state of siege or emergency and a government has been maintained in accordance with the Constitution throughout the turmoil. Another complementary provision on Constitutional revision places limits on the subject matters of revision. There is an absolute prohibition against amendments that threaten the current Constitution's protections of independence and the unity of the State; rights, freedoms and guarantees of citizens, and the 'republican' form of government. Other provisions that can only be amended

[34] Section 160 (Serious Crimes).

through a popular referendum include: the separation of powers, the independence of courts, a multi-party system with the right of democratic opposition, and the national flag. Further, there were special rules in place to delay revision of the Constitution for a period of six years. It was possible to amend the Constitution within its first six years (of provisions other than those in the special subject areas), but such an amendment would require a vote of four-fifths of the total membership of Parliament. Constitutional revisions that do not fall within the purview of these topics and that were to be made after the period of the initial six years (ie after 2008) can be amended by the Parliament by a vote of two-thirds of its members. By placing a number of limitations on the revision process, the drafters sought to use the Constitution as a source of stability and consistent, predictable rules during the period of transition (six years) which coincided with the installation of the first Parliament elected for that explicit purpose in 2007. In this way, the Constitution was created as a tool for transition from the Constituent Assembly to the first elected Parliament. However, the Constitution has continued to serve as a tool for stability beyond the six-year period. Although many revisions could have been made by parliamentary vote, there have not been any attempts to revise it since its adoption.

According to observer reports, some of the most active constitutional drafting debates were not on the substantive issues of structures and governance, but rather over rhetoric and symbolism that defined the new nation's relationship with its past. For example, the first article of the Constitution includes a statement on the official date of the first independence proclamation on 28 November 1975 (and the Constitution). Although the text passed, there were six persons opposed and eight abstained. The thematic committee that recommended the provisions on the national anthem, symbol and flag presided over some of the most polemic debates.[35] The Popular Consultations held by the UN before the assembly also spent significant time debating the symbols of the State. The Preamble of the Constitution that describes the different fronts of the resistance and valorises the resistance is written as a historical narrative as much as it serves as a legal document. Like the date, the flag, and the anthem, the Constitution was conceived as a symbol of the past and of the East Timorese future. The 2002 Constitution was an emblem of and a constituent of transition.

IV. REFLECTIONS ON PRACTICE

In this section we reflect briefly on the practice of the 2002 Constitution with a focus on three themes: (a) the role of the military; (b) the role of the courts; and (c) economic and financial organisation. This discussion will analyse

[35] Baltazar (n 4) 5. Leach (n 24) also discusses the debate over the flag related to the Constituent Assembly elections and in the Constitution.

those aspects of East Timorese constitutionalism that have persisted, as well as those that have been side-lined, and also consider those aspects with transformative potential for state-building in the future.

A. Role of Military

As outlined in the previous section, the role of the military significantly changed in the conception of East Timorese constitutionalism from 1975 to 2002. In 1975 the military was party-aligned and received designated seats in governing bodies. After 1975, the experience of occupation when the Indonesian military played a dual political and military role undoubtedly contributed to the conceptual shift in what constitutes the appropriate role of the military in governance. The negative experience of the Indonesian military exercising direct authority over internal security also contributed to the limitation of the role of the East Timorese military in 2002. The politicisation of the Portuguese military in its final days in Dili in 1975 could have been another historical influence in this shift. By 2002, drafters agreed that all security forces should be non-partisan and the military should focus on the external defence of the country (Part V, Section 146 (2)), while the Police and other security forces should be responsible for the 'internal security' of the citizens (Part V, Section 147(1).

The 2002 Constitution provides further protections against military rule or usurpation by placing the military under the authority of an elected civilian government. The separation of powers in the command and control structures for the military prevents one branch of the government or a single leader exercising authority over it: the President is the Commander of the Armed Forces, but the government maintains control over the administration of the armed forces through the Ministry of Defence, the budget, and the law making powers that further defines the powers of the military in accordance with the Constitution. This system addresses the experience of the Indonesian past, where the dictator and military general Suharto served as the Executive while exercising authority over the military and the government. It also affirms the 1987 internal rejection of the 1975 Constitution's alignment of the military with a single, political party (FRETILIN). The 2002 Constitution reflects the international 'best practices' of separation of powers and civilian control over the military, but it is perhaps better understood as an internal corrective reaction to their direct experience of human rights violations under previous regimes and the 1975 revolutionary structures.

While there is a circumscribed role for the military in the 2002 Constitution, the expansive concept of 'Defence of Sovereignty' is prominent. National defence is clearly deemed important to protect the borders and people of this small, island nation from the incursions that led to its occupation in the past. This was the role of the revolutionary, East Timorese armed resistance members who are valorised as veterans in the Constitution in Section 11. The 2002

Constitution's treatment of the military's role is meant to address wrongs of the authoritarian government systems that ruled it in the past, but at the same time be transformative, building an independent East Timorese military force out of the corps of former armed revolutionaries, who hold a privileged place amongst the political leadership and in society. The 'Defence of Sovereignty' provisions in the Constitution provide a tool for the expansion of military purposes and powers. The tension between the intentions to simultaneously limit and expand the East Timorese military was evident at the time of the Constitution's drafting and continues in practice.

For example, when the 2002 Constitution was drafted, the name of the national defence forces that would appear in the document was reportedly hotly debated. The 'Defence Forces of Timor-Leste' was not accepted as a valid designation for the armed forces because of concerns about a lack of valorisation and uncertainty about the role of former armed resistance fighters under a national defence force that was newly defined by the 2002 Constitution. To reach consensus the drafters had to append the name of the resistance armed forces, FALINTIL, to the post-revolutionary Defence Forces, creating the FALINTIL – Defence Forces of Timor-Leste (F-FDTL).[36] There was reluctance to separate the future defence force from its entrenched, revolutionary role in the past.

This reluctance found expression throughout the past 15 years in debates about the extent to which the Constitution restricts the F-FDTL's operations. Consistently and increasingly, the F-FDTL has been unable to restrict its activities to external defence as required by a strict interpretation of the Constitution. It has frequently participated in policing activities, although usually couched in more constitutionally-acceptable language of performing a 'support' role to the East Timorese national police force. Furthermore, East Timor has not been able to effectively distinguish between the symbolic role in defence of demobilised former Resistance fighters recognised by the Constitution, and the tangible and limited powers the Constitution grants the post-revolutionary professional defence force.

The experience of the 2006 Crisis, which resulted in 38 deaths and the internal displacement of 150,000 people,[37] shows the need for the constitutional limits on the military to be monitored closely. A series of political events and dismissals of 594 F-FDTL members who had abandoned their posts triggered protests that led to armed confrontations in the streets of the capital, killing security forces and civilians. At this time, F-FDTL and police began to conduct joint operations to control internal security. Factional politics within the military further escalated into armed conflicts between different groups aligned with police and military,

[36] International Crisis Group, 'Timor-Leste's Veterans: An Unfinished Struggle?' Asia Briefing No 129, (Dili/Jakarta/Brussels: Dec 2011) 4.

[37] Office of the High Commissioner of Human Rights, 'Report of the United Nations Independent Special Commission of Inquiry for Timor-Leste' (2 Oct 2006). www.ohchr.org/Documents/Countries/COITimorLeste.pdf accessed 5 Oct 2017, para 100–101.

which then spread into an armed rebellion by a former F-FDTL military police officer (Alfredo Reinado) and inter-ethnic communal violence. As part of the violence, some key political leaders allegedly participated in the unauthorised and illegal giving of weapons to former Resistance, FALINTIL fighters and civilians.[38] They reportedly armed the veterans and their other civilian followers to play a role in internal security and defence. Some observers described the arming of the former FALINTIL fighters as an unconstitutional, failed coup attempt, while others saw it as a legitimate act of 'Defence of Sovereignty' when the national defence and police forces could no longer be trusted.

In line with the Constitution, UN and judicial investigations were conducted into the violence and arming of the former FALINTIL members directly by unauthorised political leaders.[39] A series of indictments were issued and trials were held but some of the most senior leaders implicated in the violence were not prosecuted, which led to some civil society critiques of the transparency and strength of the justice system. The speed with which the 2002 constitutional limits on military and government power were overlooked in 2006 to return to a 1975 mode of defence, demonstrates the challenges in maintaining the new constitutional order in Timor-Leste. Given these events and some of the institutional responses, there are reasons to question a definitive, foundational reading of the 2002 Constitution. When it comes to implementing constitutional requirements with regard to former revolutionary leaders and security actors, East Timor's constitutionalism is a work in progress.

In another example, following the assassination attempts on the President and Prime Minister in 2008 a state of emergency was declared. Parliament adopted laws that again formalised arrangements to allow domestic, joint security operations between the F-FDTL and police. These activities had occurred formally and informally before the state of emergency. Indeed, there are accounts of the Military Police acting alone in a policing role apprehending civilians since 2006.[40] Although the state of emergency subsided within several months, the joint operations continued to be renewed even though the

[38] An East Timorese court convicted the former Minister of Interior (Rogerio Lobato) on charges of manslaughter and illegal distribution of weapons. The UN Commission of Inquiry report (cited above) stated: 'there was reasonable suspicion that the former Prime Minister at least had knowledge about the distribution of PNTL weapons to civilians' (p 40) The same report held that 'The evidence before the Commission establishes that the F-FDTL began to arm civilians on 24 May 2006. This was done on the order of Brigadier General Ruak and with the knowledge of the Minister of Defence [...] Brigadier General Ruak told the Commission that he was aware that there was no specific law allowing for the arming of "reservists." He stated he was authorised to do so by the Minister of Defence after he made the proposal. It was a political decision for which the Minister was responsible.' (p.40) Allegations against the former Prime Minister (Mari Alkatiri), former Minister of Defence (Roque Rodrigues) and former F-FDTL Commander (Taur Matan Ruak, current Prime Minister as of 22 June 2018) were investigated by East Timor's prosecution service, but did not result in prosecution due to their determination that there was insufficient evidence.

[39] Ibid.

[40] Eg, see Fundasaun Mahein, 'Polísia Militár: Suporta ka Hakat Liu PNTL?' (Mahein Nia Lian, No 22, 18 Aug 2011).

security threat diminished to negligible levels. A recent survey by a civil society organisation in 2017 documented negative public perceptions about the security forces' compliance with the rule of law and alleged human rights violations by F-FDTL acting in joint internal security operations with police.[41] There has not been a case brought to the courts to clarify the constitutionality of these operations yet. There appears to be room for interpretation of the Constitution to allow for limited F-FDTL involvement in the 'defence of sovereignty' when for example the Executive institution was under direct physical threat and when these activities followed a formal process of request and approval through civilian authorities. The problem has been the military's willingness to act in an internal security role in response to requests for protection of communities or at the behest of former FALINTIL commanders or individual political leaders, in the style of revolutionary fighters, without formal processes being observed.

Another tangible example of this tension between constriction and expansion of the role of the military can be seen in the practice of the constitutional structures outlined for the accountability of the military. The Constitution, Section 130 on Military Courts requires the establishment of military courts to judge in the first instance crimes of a military nature. This court system has never been established. Moreover, there has not been any significant discussion on its establishment, despite a host of international consultants who have created plans for the development of the East Timorese military as well as the judiciary. *Força 2020*, the national plan for the development of the national military, never mentions a military justice system or provides for its creation or use. There is also no specific plan for its enactment as part of the country's Strategic Development Plan, or in previous government's programmes. While there have been basic laws passed on rules and disciplinary measures for the military forces (F-FDTL), there has been no legislation that establishes or even foresees military courts, or a professional, military legal corps. The result has been highly discretionary enforcement of the disciplinary system by commanders, and a system of military prison(s) that are outside of civilian monitoring. Since 2014, there has been review and recommendations for reforms to the legal system, but the establishment of a military justice system has not been considered as part of these reforms despite its requirement in the Constitution.

There appears to be a lack of interest in implementing a strong accountability system in line with constitutional requirements for the East Timorese military. This reluctance stems from the hallowed status veterans and the armed resistance has in the historical past, which is venerated in the 1975 and 2002 Constitutions. It also demonstrates the difficulty of dislodging entrenched practices of the resistance when the military had broad governing powers and operated outside of government or other forms of oversight. Despite the limitations

[41] See Belun, 'From Kindergarten to High School: Perceptions of Timor-Leste's Military and Police Ten Years after the 2006 Crisis' (Sep 2017) www.belun.tl/wp-content/uploads/2017/09/Belun_ALTSS_Tetun_low-compressed-for-web.pdf accessed 8 Oct 2017.

determined by the 2002 Constitution, in practice the military's role has crept back into matters of politics and internal security without systems to effectively monitor, manage and report on its actions.

What remains to be seen is whether the constrained principles for the military enshrined in the 2002 Constitution are accepted by a younger, post-revolutionary, generation of East Timorese leaders. If there is commitment to these ideals then the 2002 Constitution will continue to serve as a tool for incremental improvements and state building, ensuring an effective, transparent system of military justice and F-FDTL's security role remains within legitimate bounds. On the other hand, if the limits placed on the military in the 2002 Constitution were mere 'window dressing' to win consensus among rival parties, veterans and international observers for its passage for the 20 May 2002 deadline, then the military will increasingly undermine the police and become a client to political leaders or parties. Those parties or leaders who support expansive interpretations of the military's role will justify their policies in defence of national sovereignty, rather than advocate more restrictive interpretations of the Constitution that prioritise the rule of law and address violations of the past.

B. Role of Judiciary

The role of the judiciary as an organ of sovereignty and the enforcer of the rule of law are powerful components of the 2002 Constitution, which primarily derive from the 1998 Magna Carta. The principle of the independence of the judiciary is enshrined in Section 119 of the Constitution: 'courts are independent and subject only to the Constitution and the law'. The principle of independence is further underscored in Section 121 that defines the role of judges: 'judges are independent and owe obedience only to the Constitution, the law and their own conscience.' This independence is made operational through a system of security of tenure for judges, which prohibits their arbitrary removal and excludes them from liability for their judgments and decisions (except in circumstances provided by law). To ensure independence and separation of powers, judges are not permitted to perform any other functions outside of their legal duties, which means they are not permitted to hold political office or exercise other political functions. A complex system of checks and balances is constructed between the judiciary and other organs of government by allowing each organ to appoint key positions within the judiciary, such as the President appointing the Chief Justice of the Supreme Court and the Legislature electing a member of the Supreme Court. These checks and balances are further enhanced by each organ of state choosing a member of the Superior Council for the Judiciary. This council is responsible for administration and discipline for the judicial organ. In principle, the 2002 Constitution constructed a judicial system with the independence and powers to be effective.

Structurally, the Constitution puts into place a civil law system for the judiciary with three main categories of courts: (a) The Supreme Court of Justice and other lower courts of law; (b) the High Administrative, Tax and Audit Court and other administrative courts of first instance; and (c) Military Courts. Maritime and Arbitration Courts may be added to supplement this system. Although the widely practiced 'traditional' forms of justice, or *adat*, are not directly acknowledged in the Constitution, it allows for subsequent law to 'institutionalise means and ways for the non-jurisdictional resolution of disputes.' Transitional measures are written into the 2002 Constitution for the courts operating under the UNTAET administration to continue to do so until the full structure of the judiciary could be put into place. These transitional measures included a means for the highest functioning court at the time, the Court of Appeal, to perform the functions of the Supreme Court until it is established. These transitional measures show there was an understanding among the drafters that the judicial system envisioned in the Constitution would be developed incrementally.

However, the drafters may not have anticipated that the judicial structure would not be realised for decades, if ever. The Court of Appeal has continued to function as the Supreme Court and for appeals, which is the system that was anticipated in the original 1975 Constitution. As of 2018, there has not been any legislation proposed to establish the Supreme Court, despite a number of legal challenges that have arisen from its absence. Further, as referenced above, the Military Courts have not been established and there does not appear to be any initiative to do so in the near future. The Tax and Audit Court was established in 2013, with considerable push and funding from key donors including Portugal, the EU and the US. The support for the establishment of this court among donors has been linked to anti-corruption efforts; but there has not been the same interest in establishing the Supreme Court, which has the critical functions of constitutional review; determining eligibility and legality of elections as well as operating as a body for appeal. Although the 2002 Constitution created a judiciary with substantive and comparable powers to the other organs of governance, in practice it has been assigned a lower priority and is weaker in its ability to exercise the powers the Constitution envisions for it.

A unique feature of the 2002 Constitution is the transitional justice arrangements for the judiciary, which have been partially implemented. The Constitution provided for the continued use of international judges in the court system to complete the prosecution of Serious Crimes – crimes against humanity, war crimes, genocide, torture, murder and sexual offences – under the hybrid international/domestic tribunal established by UNTAET to adjudicate these crimes that occurred from 1 January 1999–25 October 1999. The 2002 Constitution further stipulated that national or international courts could prosecute crimes against humanity (including in the form of genocide) committed in East Timor from 24 April 1974 (Carnation Revolution in Portugal) until 25 October 1999, in the spirit of the principles proposed in the Magna Carta in 1998. No time constraints were placed on the prosecution of this latter category of crimes from 1974, although according to the 2002 Constitution prosecutions by the UNTAET hybrid court were to remain operational only as 'strictly necessary' to conclude the cases already under investigation when the Constitution entered into force. The UN-backed prosecutions continued until 2005 and were re-initiated in limited form from 2007 to 2013. The 2002 Constitution also designated the National Truth and Reconciliation Commission, an indispensable body for transitional justice, and required it to complete its functions under law. This Commission concluded its work in 2005. Although these powers have not been exercised, national courts continue to have the authority to prosecute some of the most serious crimes committed from 1974. As with the structure of the judiciary, the Constitution provided for a system of incremental application of transitional justice, including language that would allow for temporary UN-backed initiatives and more permanent options for transitional justice prosecutions by Timor-Leste's judiciary or another international body.

i. The Armando dos Santos *Case*

Putting the constitutional principles, structures and powers of the judiciary into practice has been one of the most contentious endeavours of the post-revolutionary state, as was illustrated early on in the case of *Public Prosecutor v Armando dos Santos*.[42] Armando dos Santos was an East Timorese militia member convicted of three counts of murder by the hybrid Special Panels for Serious Crimes, established by the governing UN administration (UNTAET) in 2000 within the Dili District Court of East Timor. The Prosecutor appealed the case, submitting the conviction should have been for the crimes charged in the indictment, which were three counts of murder as crimes against humanity. The Appeals Court heard the case in July 2003 and the decision written by the international, Head of the Appeals Court (a Portuguese judge of East Timorese origin) shocked nearly everyone for its erroneous interpretations of the 2002 Constitution. In a 2-1 decision by the three-person panel of judges, the head of the Appeals Court determined:

(1) Portuguese law was the applicable law in East Timor, rather than Indonesian law (as established by UNTAET regulations and subsequently verified in the 2002 Constitution).
(2) The Special Panels for Serious Crimes operating within the Dili District Courts of East Timor (as provided for by the Constitution) were unconstitutional.
(3) Armando dos Santos was guilty of murder in the form of genocide under Portuguese law and was sentenced to 22 years of imprisonment, although he had not been charged with the act of genocide, nor under Portuguese law, and did not have an opportunity to defend himself on those charges.

[42] UN-ETTA CA, Judgment (15 Jul 2003).

Under the 2002 Constitution, in the absence of the Supreme Court, the Appeals Court was the highest court in the country and according to Section 118, 'court decisions shall be binding and shall prevail over the decisions of any other authority'. Thus, this decision threw the entire legal basis for the country into upheaval, rendering all previous court decisions open to appeal, all transitional justice convictions by the Special Panels unconstitutional, and any commercial or legal transaction conducted since 1975 null and void. The judges of the lower courts refused to recognise the Appeals Court decision, issuing a decision in another Special Panels case explaining:

> … this panel is unable to follow that decision [Armando dos Santos], because it would not be following its understanding of the applicable law in East Timor and the oath "to faithfully apply the Constitution of the republic and other laws in force". Also, if this were the case, the Special Panel judges would not be adjudicating "in accordance with their conscience."

The judicial organ of the State was brought to paralysis, with higher and lower courts each citing and applying different parts of the 2002 Constitution and different bodies of law. To break the stalemate, in accordance with the powers granted to him by the Constitution, Timor-Leste's Prosecutor-General filed an application for the Supreme Court to review the constitutionality of the decision and the UNTAET law on the Special Panels for Serious Crimes. However, the Appeals Court, with only three judges (one international judge and two East Timorese), was also acting as the Supreme Court, and would simply review their own decision, returning the same conclusion.

Ultimately, the judicial impasse was breached through the intervention of Parliament. Lobbied by the UN and civil society, the Parliament passed a new law that consisted of one sentence, reaffirming that Indonesian law was the applicable legal framework in accordance with the previous UNTAET regulations (and Constitution). This legislation left little doubt as to what the applicable law was but left open the question as to whether the Appeals Court decision on the unconstitutionality of the Special Panels was binding. The lower courts, including the Special Panels, operated on the presumption that the Appeals Court's decision was not binding. For Armando dos Santos, there was no solution, but nearly one year later in the appeal of another Serious Crimes case, *Paulino de Jesus*, the Court of Appeal (with the same judge presiding) found a defendant guilty under the UNTAET provision establishing the Special Panels that they had deemed unconstitutional previously. At this point, the courts again moved forward without revisiting the *Armando dos Santos* decision and its impact.

The *Armando dos Santos* case is significant because it demonstrates how key players have used incremental and selective application of the 2002 Constitution and borrowing of laws from other countries as a mechanism to reconstitute the state, either in an atavistic way or in a progressive manner to enact a transition to a new political paradigm. The Head of the Appeals Court cherry-picked parts of the Constitution to re-instate the vision of Timor-Leste before the civil war, the Indonesian invasion and the UN administration. Through these leaps of time, the judge not only ignored the UNTAET and Indonesian legal regimes but also the 1975 Constitution and the 1975 Declaration of Independence by the East Timorese, to legally revert Timor-Leste to the period of Portuguese colonial law. This judge used the powers of the Court as a means of pursuing a different, partisan and historical vision of the East Timorese state, at odds with what had been decided by consensus for the Constitution in 2002. In addition to this selective interpretation of the Constitution's provisions of applicable law, he also chose to ignore the human rights protections afforded to defendants in the 2002 Constitution, the Magna Carta and the 1975 Constitution, which all stipulate the right to representation for defendants on charges that are clearly put to them in a court of law. In his eagerness to convict the accused of 'genocide' – that encompassed the political and historical dimensions of the suffering of the East Timorese people captured in the language of the 2002 Constitution and Magna Carta – the judge chose to implement some parts of the law that were convenient (acknowledging the judicial system that brought the defendant to trial), and ignored those constitutional protections that were not convenient to the overarching political and historical purpose. At the same time, by rejecting the Appeals Court decision, the lower Courts also selectively applied the Constitution on the assumed logic that they had to decide according to 'conscience' rather than on legal precedent. Parliament intervened through its law-making powers, but no doubt created questions about the degree of intervention other sovereign organs can make if they disagreed with a judicial decision. This case illustrates the court's resistance in accepting the Constitution as a whole, with the new globalised, multi-party, mixed legal system, hodgepodge of consensus and pluralism it represents. The symbolism and rhetoric of the 2002 Constitution often appear to play a stronger role than its state-building functions.

The dissenting appeals judge in *Armando dos Santos* explained the erroneous reasoning of the majority decision stating: 'in interpreting any law or provision from an Article, one must also look at other provisions of the same Article [the relationship] between one clause and another'. Eventually, the original intent of the 2002 Constitution's text in its entirety prevailed through the constitutional battles over the *Armando dos Santos* case, which may be yet again a significant foundational constitutional moment. It shows that the creation of the 2002 Constitution cannot be interpreted as the final text of constitutionalism, where it established a sharp break with the past that goes unchallenged and charges forward. Rather, this case shows that constitutional practice works in a two-steps-forward-one-step-back manner in Timor-Leste. Even the judiciary, the guardians of the Constitution, applied the Constitution in an incremental, selective and chaotic manner to transition the state to a new legal order.

ii. The Maternus Bere *Case*

The *Armando dos Santos* case highlights one of the first transitions in constitutional practice that occurred only a year after the installation of the new Constitution. The case of *Maternus Bere* is worth examining to highlight how the principles of judicial independence and separation of powers were interpreted midway into the life of the 2002 Constitution.

Maternus Bere, a former East Timorese militia commander, was indicted in 2003 by the Special Panels for Serious Crimes in East Timor for multiple counts of crimes against humanity in the form of murder, extermination, forced disappearances, torture and rape, among other offences. He was well-known to have commanded the militia group who massacred a group of civilians, including three priests, inside a Suai church following the referendum in East Timor in 1999. He fled East Timor to Indonesia following these alleged acts. Although there was an INTERPOL arrest warrant for him since 2003, he remained free in Indonesia until he crossed the border back into Timor-Leste to visit his family in Suai in 2009. Community members in Suai recognised him and reported him to police, even though an angry mob attacked him before the police could arrive. Suai police arrested him and brought him before the Suai district court for a detention hearing in accordance with the law. Given the nature of his alleged crimes and protection concerns, the Suai court transferred him to a detention centre in the capital of Dili to await trial by the Dili District Court that continues to have jurisdiction over the serious crimes for which Bere had been indicted.

Following a political agenda of reconciliation with Indonesia, soon after Bere's arrest, Prime Minister Xanana Gusmão and President José Ramos-Horta allegedly met with Indonesian officials who insisted on Bere's handover to them. Without following legal process, Gusmão ordered Bere's release from executive detention and his transfer to the Indonesian Embassy. The Ministry of Justice and prisons complied with the Prime Minister's orders. Bere was later transferred from the Indonesian Embassy out of the country, reportedly to seek medical treatment for hypertension. He never returned to East Timor and was never prosecuted in Indonesia.

As the scandal unfolded in the following months, the international community, Parliament, the judiciary and civil society protested against the actions of the Prime Minister and President. Multiple UN agencies, including the UN High Commissioner for Human Rights, contacted the President and Prime Minister to try to prevent or reverse Bere's release. International and domestic civil society actors further explained the East Timorese officials' obligations under domestic and international law. The lobby failed. Next, the Parliament reacted. Under the 2002 Constitution the Parliament must approve international travel by the President. In protest to the President's alleged collaborative role in the release of Bere, the Parliament voted against the President's planned travel to attend the UN General Assembly. The President then threatened to resign, and the Parliament granted the travel permission. The following day, the President of the Court of Appeal called a press conference and correctly stated that any person who effects the release of a lawfully detained prisoner without a judicial order commits a crime, punishable by law. He refrained from stating who had broken the law, although it was obvious. One week later, two political parties in the Parliament (FRETILIN and KOTA) initiated a Motion of Censure on

9 September 2009 arguing that Bere's release by the government was unlawful. The motion failed (25 for and 39 against) and the ruling party and Prime Minister remained in government. Two weeks later a civil society organisation filed a petition with the Court of Appeal acting in the role of the Supreme Court to seek a formal constitutional review of the legality of Bere's release based on Article 48 of the Constitution which grants 'every citizen the right to submit, individually or jointly with others, petition and claims to organs of sovereignty or any authority for the purpose of defending his or her rights, the Constitution, the law or general interests.' The petition to the Court was simultaneously sent to the Prime Minister, the President and Parliament. A month later, in an about face, the Court of Appeal declared the petition invalid without responding to the legal arguments raised in the petition. In the end, the protests did not impact on either the release of Bere or the organs of sovereignty that threatened the independence of the judiciary (Section 119) and the separation of powers (Section 69) as stated in the Constitution. The violations of law and the Constitution were overlooked.

iii. Expulsion of International Judicial Actors

In October 2014, another critical incident of interference in the judiciary occurred which challenged East Timor's constitutionalism. In a closed session, Parliament passed a resolution to terminate the contracts of all international judicial personnel. They also called for a complete review, or 'audit', of the judiciary. The government followed immediately by issuing a resolution to confirm and enact the parliamentary resolution. Several days later the government issued an order revoking the visas of all international judicial personnel and gave them 48 hours to leave the country. The President of the Appeals Court, who serves simultaneously as Chief Justice of the Supreme Court, issued a letter to all judicial officers stating that the resolutions from the Parliament and government were not legally binding under the Constitution. He instructed all judicial officers to continue to serve in their positions. The Prime Minister went on national television and made a presentation about alleged errors judges made in deciding a high-profile petroleum tax case against the government, and accused the judiciary of being weak. Civil society rallied around the courts and lobbied the international community to support the principle of judicial independence. Nevertheless, seven international judges and four prosecutors who were actively involved in court cases were effectively expelled from the country after the government intervened with the resolution and requested through diplomatic channels that their countries recall them. As a result, critical trials and corruption investigations were brought to an abrupt halt and the legal training centre that was preparing a corps of East Timorese judges, public defenders and prosecutors ceased to function. The fact that it is highly questionable as to whether Parliament or the government had the constitutional powers to take these actions did not stop the removal of the final vestiges of international presence in the

East Timorese judiciary. The interference in the judiciary over the presence of international judges also created the basis for a Legal Reform Commission with a broad mandate to access records and review the entire legal system.

In early 2015, the Parliament and Prime Minister began to challenge the validity of the appointment of the Head of the Appeals Court/Chief Justice and attempted to remove him from the position. While their initial attempts did not succeed, in 2016 he resigned from his position. The shakedown of the judiciary from 2014–2015 had all the hallmarks of a revolutionary coup.

Following on from the wake of these dramatic events, the Prime Minister, Xanana Gusmão, resigned in February 2015. He hand-picked his successor from the opposition FRETILIN party and they formed the government of National Unity, or the sixth constitutional government. As a result, in actual terms from 2015–2017 East Timor operated without an Opposition in the Parliament. While this form of governance was certainly legal, it resembled the vision of a single party government in the 1975 Constitution rather than the 2002 Constitution. However, during this period the President, Taur Matan Ruak, became active and exercised his role to the fullest extent possible to provide a measure of accountability for the organs of the government and the Parliament. Whether these events that began with the dismissal of international judges are interpreted as politically motivated attacks or strategic reform, this period marked a transition within the judiciary and for constitutionalism.

In the past 15 years, Timor-Leste has struggled to put the judiciary in place that it envisioned in the 2002 Constitution and Magna Carta. There has been slow, incremental and selective implementation of the judicial structures and principles established in the 2002 Constitution. The other state organs have trampled on the judiciary when it was politically expedient without significant, negative repercussions. At the same time, in each of these instances the 2002 Constitution has provided civil society and other organs of sovereignty with tools and powers to resist, if not stop, violations of the rule of law. In the process, the public and the judiciary has been made more aware of the values the Constitution protects, and in each instance has become more sophisticated in their efforts to prevent reverting to systems that could allow human rights violations or elite dominance that occurred in the past.

C. Economic and Financial Organisation

Part IV of the 2002 Constitution establishes principles and structures to conduct the finances of the state, a fundamental aspect of state-building. It makes clear that control over East Timor's land and resources is an issue of national sovereignty and should be regulated and administered in accordance with the rule of law. The Constitution establishes systems to enact these principles: it requires the State Budget be prepared by the government and approved by the National Parliament, which is then monitored in its execution by the courts and the National Parliament. This system brings into play checks and balances and separation of powers. As observed with the judicial system, putting the Constitution into practice in the economic realm has been a selective and transitional process.

i. Economic Stabilisation Fund case

On 5 August 2008, the National Parliament passed an annual State Budget that included an Economic Stabilisation Fund, which would be used among other things to subsidise rice imports. On 29 August, 16 members of Parliament referred the State Budget to the Appeals Court for review of the budget's legality. The Appeals Court was also acting in the capacity of the High Court for Audit because it had not been established yet (in addition to acting as the Supreme Court, which had also not been established). The Appeals Court ruled unanimously that the Economic Stabilisation Fund was illegal, violating the 2005 Petroleum Fund Law and it was unconstitutional, violating the Constitution's requirements to preclude secret appropriations and funds (among other provisions). The Fund had been established by Decree Law by the government (without parliamentary consultation or approval) and was executed by transferring US $396 million from the national Petroleum Fund. Upon receipt of this decision from the court, the President of the Parliament appealed the decision of the Appeals Court again. The Appeals Court (which was the same panel of judges that heard the case in the first instance because the lack of a Supreme Court) returned the decision confirming that the Economic Stabilisation was illegal and unconstitutional. After the rulings, the Parliament continued to debate, calling into question the qualifications and judgment of the Court and threatening to remove judges. An independent, East Timorese civil society organisation evaluated the decision of the Court and deemed its reasoning in the case valid.[43] The government tried to implement the Economic Stabilisation Fund despite the Court's ruling that it was unconstitutional and illegal, but ultimately difficulties with executing the budget forced the government to comply with the Court ruling.[44]

The Petroleum Fund accounts for 97 per cent of East Timor's state revenues. Yet, according to the World Bank's October 2017 Timor-Leste Economic Update:

> … the petroleum fields that have fuelled government spending to date are fast-depleting, and the uncertain prospect of new revenues will only offer, at best,

[43] JSMP, 'Legitimacy of the Court's decision in the case of the Economic Stabilisation Fund' (Justice Update, Jan 2009).

[44] Lao Hamutuk, 'Revising the Petroleum Fund Law', (Dili, 13 Jul 2012) www.laohamutuk.org/Oil/PetFund/revision/10PFRevision.htm accessed 8 Oct 2017.

> temporary respite from the difficult tasks of diversifying the economy and improving public services that are needed in order to bring down the alarmingly high levels of poverty.[45]

The ability to implement the Constitution's protections for these resources is critical to ensuring the rule of law, but also for state-building to guarantee the economic and political survival of the people of Timor-Leste. Subsequent to the Economic Stabilisation Fund case, there have not been further referrals to the courts to rule on the constitutionality or legality of government management and budgets that have exceeded the Petroleum Fund law's proposed limits on government spending on an annual basis. In the Economic Stabilisation Fund case, the Court and the Constitution prevailed, exhibiting a healthy exercise of the balance of powers. However, it remains to be seen if a full and permanent transition to constitutional management of financial resources has been established.

Since the 1975 Constitution (Article 8), there has been a conscious recognition of the need to guarantee the nation's economic rights and sovereignty over natural resources as part of the revolutionary movement and state-building. This area of constitutional principles and practice has become increasingly important in Timor-Leste's domestic debate and policy, and this has led to a global campaign to re-negotiate its boundaries with Australia to allow it a more equitable share of oil revenues. In March 2018, Timor-Leste claimed victory when it became the first nation to initiate and settle a dispute through a conciliation process under the United Nations Convention on the Law of the Sea (UNCLOS).[46] While the concrete economic impact of the new boundaries remains uncertain, the East Timorese leaders (primarily Gusmão) have utilised international legal instruments and rhetoric to enhance both their international and domestic powers and position. Once the spoils of those powers are received, it will require strict adherence to the 2002 constitutional rules to administer the state's finances in a way that fulfils the socio-economic promises of the constitutional texts since 1975. In the coming decade, economic stewardship is likely to be the determinant measure of the success and durability of East Timor's constitutionalism.

V. CONCLUSION

This chapter sketched the development of East Timor's constitutional principles, structures and practice from 1975 to present. It illustrated Timor-Leste's

[45] See http://pubdocs.worldbank.org/en/287641507869111074/Oct2017-TimorLeste-EconUpdate.pdf at p 152.

[46] United Nations, 'Secretary-General's remarks at Signing Ceremony of a New Maritime Boundary Agreement between Australia and Timor-Leste [as delivered]' (UN News, 6 March 2018) www.un.org/sg/en/content/sg/statement/2018-03-06/secretary-generals-remarks-signing-ceremony-new-maritime-boundary accessed 31 Mar 2018; Oki Raimundos, 'Hero's welcome for Timor border negotiator', (Australian Associated Press, 12 March 2018) www.westernadvocate.com.au/story/5277236/heros-welcome-for-timor-border-negotiator/?cs=5 accessed 31 Mar 2018.

constitutional links in the 1970s in Southeast Asia and in the Lusophone world; human rights movements in the 1990s; post-conflict constitution-making in the 2000s; and current international legal movements for transitional justice and responsible management of state resources. Timor-Leste's constitutional foundations and future are inextricably linked to international law and practice.

Timor-Leste's constitutionalism has been consistently sensitive to external political changes, adopting or applying international norms and incorporating different political ideas and groups in its formulation and practice even when the United Nations or other international advisors were not present. This conscious adoption of universalist approaches to constitutionalism has contributed to the nation's political survival on the global stage, allowing it to move from political isolation in the 1970s to attract sufficient international support for international intervention for independence, reconstruction and most recently, increased control over its natural resources. While in the 1970s Timor-Leste was a follower on the coat tails of its contemporary revolutionaries in Africa and Southeast Asia, in this century it has become known as a leader of the G7+ post-conflict countries and even within Southeast Asia for its perceived liberal constitutionalism.

Thus the 2002 Constitution, which is in force today, stands out among a series of foundational moments as the product of the revolutionary, resistance movement that liberated East Timor from Portuguese colonialism and Indonesian occupation. It continues to guide and transform the East Timorese state because it contains principles and practices that can address the root causes of past human rights violations experienced by the population of Timor-Leste, with language and symbols that meaningfully bridge the constitutional past and the future for its internal and external audiences. However, maintaining constitutionalism over the long term will require that the traces of some illiberal aspects of the revolutionary regime and convenient, political, amnesia when it comes to the Constitution must be addressed. When this can be done, institution-building and governance will become as important as the Constitution's revered symbolic and historic functions.

Some of the areas of state-building where the process of constitutional change has been most contentious is in defining the role of the military, constructing a robust judiciary and managing the State's natural and economic resources. In these three areas, some of the inspiring, revolutionary leaders who helped to construct the first Constitution in 1975, the Magna Carta in 1998 and the new state in 2002 have diverged from the strict requirements of the 2002 Constitution in their positions within organs of state. While there have been sporadic legal consequences for these actions, there has been persistent political responses from the populace and from other organs of sovereignty which have challenged them, using the 2002 Constitution as a tool. Constitutional practice has gradually moved from a handful of Portuguese speaking, political elites concentrated in a few political parties in 1975 to a broader array of actors, generations and institutions in multiple languages. No doubt the Constitution and applying it has transformed these leaders themselves and the future generation of East Timorese leaders who are gradually taking the reins of the state.

By moving beyond the previous scholarship that has focused on the legitimacy derived mostly from the design of the 2002 Constitution, this chapter raises new questions, which I do not propose I am able to answer here. How and why do measurements of constitutional legitimacy change with practice and gradual shifts in power structures and players? Further, how will East Timor's constitutional principles and practice position it in the regional and international arena for the next 15 years? The exploratory nature of this analysis has only begun to outline the background and issues that can contribute to answering those questions.

5

The Making of Myanmar's 1947 Constitution: Geography, Ethnicity, and Law

MAITRII AUNG-THWIN

INTRODUCTION

MYANMAR'S 1947 CONSTITUTION was composed and ratified during a period of transition and uncertainty.[1] The destruction and displacement caused by World War II since 1942 left the country's pre-war infrastructure in ruins, its economy shattered, and the administrative functions of the colonial State essentially incapacitated. Millions of acres of rice land were devastated, transportation networks were rendered inoperable, and cities were bombed to their foundations.[2] British prestige suffered due to their initial defeat by the Japanese, while the shared suffering and hardship across community lines provided the basis for a growing national solidarity. With the surrender of the Japanese in 1945, officers of the Burma Defence Army, armed communists, nationalists (*Thakins*), various political parties, militias, minority groups, exiled government officials, and returning British colonial administrators jockeyed to fill the political vacuum. Without an agreed blueprint to guide the transition, an armed post-war struggle was imminent.

At stake was the future of the country: would Burma return to British rule or would power and sovereignty be transferred to a domestic leadership?[3] If the former, which British vision would be implemented – the plan to prepare Burma gradually towards independence or the plan to prepare it for eventual membership into the Commonwealth? If the latter, would a Burmese leadership consist

[1] See generally, Maung Maung, *Burma's Constitution*, 2 ed (The Hague: Martinus Nijhoff, 1961) [hereinafter '*Burma's Constitution*'].

[2] John F Cady, *A History of Modern Burma* (Ithaca: Cornell University Press, 1958) at 485 [hereinafter 'Cady'].

[3] This chapter will use the term 'Burma' in the context of British Burma and the immediate post-World War period. It is important to remember that Burmese language sources regularly used the term 'Myanmar' well before the usage of the term was politicized in the early 1990s.

of General Aung San and the *Thakin* nationalists or would pro-British elites, communists, or socialists claim the state? To what extent would ethnically-defined minorities have a place in the new national community and would their expectations be met by state managers? The 1947 Constitution was forged out of this difficult, post-War context, deepening and entrenching pre-World War II divisions over the future of the country.

It is worth mentioning that the Constitution was also hewn out of a longer, more layered history of ideological rivalry, class difference, cultural diversity, economic stratification and racial tensions that characterised Myanmar's political landscape during its time under British colonial rule. The issues that shaped the post-World War II context were a continuation of older debates that dominated domestic politics and the growing nationalist movement in the 1920s and 1930s.[4] Colonial legal legacies, especially those that conflated territory with ethnicity and ethnicity with identity, created almost insurmountable political hurdles for post-independence leaders as they attempted to draft a new Constitution that addressed the concerns of communities who had different ideas about what the shape of the new nation might look like and their place within it.[5] Questions of representation, equity, access, belonging, and governance were the key issues for stakeholders before the war, and they would continue to be relevant after the war as well. The story behind the making of the Constitution reveals the special role of law, ethnicity, and space in the historical construction of Myanmar.

I. THE PRE-WAR CONTEXT: 1885–1942[6]

Pre-World War II Myanmar was characterised by a period of confusion, uncertainty, and opportunity for Myanmar's many communities. Prior to the third Anglo-Burmese War in 1885, the country had been divided into 'two Burmas', Lower and Upper, representing the territory controlled by the British and the remaining area ruled by the Burmese court in Mandalay. Lower Burma had been under direct colonial rule since the 1850s and was therefore exposed to British administrative law, education, and economic structures for nearly four decades before communities in Upper Burma were assimilated into the system. This difference in exposure to colonial rule meant that elites and minorities

[4] Albert D Moscotti, *British Policy and the National Movement in Burma, 1917–1937* (Honolulu: University of Hawaii Press, 1974).

[5] Robert H Taylor, *The State in Myanmar*, (Singapore: NUS Press, 2009).

[6] See generally, DGE Hall, *Burma*, 3 ed (London: Hutchinson University Library, 1960); Cady (n 2); Michael & Maitrii Aung-Thwin, *A History of Myanmar Since Ancient Times: Traditions and Transformations* (London: Reaktion Books, 2013); Frank N Trager, *Burma from Kingdom to Republic: A Historical and Political Analysis* (Pall Mall Press, 1966); U Htin Aung, *A History of Burma* (New York: Columbia University Press, 1967); and Than Tun, *A Modern History of Myanmar, 1752–1948* (Yangon: Myonwe Sarpay, 2010).

in Lower Burma had greater access to political and economic opportunities offered by the British than those attached to the monarchy, creating an important constituency for the British but creating two groups of political elites. After the conquest of Upper Burma and the banishment of the monarchy to the west coast of India in late November 1885, a unified British Burma would bring these two elite groups into contact with another, each with different experiences with British law and different ideas about the future of the country.[7]

Spatially, there was a 'third Burma' made up of the hill communities that had traditionally been less connected to the lowlands. Under the Burmese monarchy, there was a long history of connection via religious culture, trade, and nominal tribute, but for the most part, the communities in the mountain ranges of North and Northeast Burma had a looser history of integration than groups living in the lowland river-valleys. Under British rule, these groups were also less critical to the colonial economy given that the priority was then more about the development of British Burma's rich natural resources than finding a road to China. Hill community experiences with the British were less disruptive than for those living in the lowland zones. Local leaders were allowed to maintain nominal autonomy while the elites among them were given opportunities to join the British army, attend university, and for some, attain a lucrative civil service position.[8]

Chin men, for example, were incorporated into the colonial security apparatus due to their ability to navigate the highland forestry areas with relative ease. Many of these troops were deployed against armed resistance movements which created no shortage of animosity between groups.[9] Many Karen men and women were provided educational opportunities through missionary schools, creating not only a sense of status relative to other ethnic groups in the colony, but also a sense of shared experience that came along with British patronage and protection. Access to economic and political positions within the colonial system as a result of this educational background became a source of pride for these ethnic minority groups, but it also generated frustration and envy amongst majority Burmese who did not enjoy the same privileges. Minority groups' access to the English language world also exposed them to different models of governance, including British Indian law and other political principles of the West. The opportunities provided by the British colonial state contributed to the development of different ideas about the future of the colony, its relationship with the British, and the place of minorities within the colony.

Divided by administrative policies and topographical diversity, these communities would later attempt to connect ethnic identities with territorial

[7] See generally, Robert H Taylor, 'Perceptions of Ethnicity in the Politics of Burma' (1982) 10(1) *Southeast Asian Journal of Social Science* 7–22; and Matthew J Walton, 'Ethnicity, Conflict, and History in Burma: The Myths of Panglong' ((2008) 48(6) *Asian Survey* 889–910.

[8] Mandy Sadan, *Being and Becoming Kachin: Histories Beyond the State in the Borderworlds of Burma*, (Oxford: Oxford University Press, 2013).

[9] Mary P. Callahan, *Making Enemies: War and State Building in Burma*, (Ithaca: Cornell University Press, 2004).

expressions of belonging to distinguish themselves from the lowland Burmans, who were regarded by many with considerable suspicion. These spatially peripheral groups, living in what we now call borderland areas, would be less inclined to accept central authority over them by the new Independence government precisely because they had enjoyed relative political freedom, privacy, and economic opportunities under the British. Their representatives in the constitutional process were considerably different from later nationalists who came from different socio-economic backgrounds and who thus held different political positions. Minority groups regarded their culture, histories, and identities as distinct from lowland Burmese, so the prospect of a single constitution and membership into a nation defined by lowland leaders was, for many in the highlands, worth fighting against in the years to come.

This early generation of elites would eventually encounter a later generation of reformers who were not from traditional locales of authority. Whereas early elites came from more traditional sources of power and from a generation of British sympathisers, a new group of social activists, drawn from university student ranks, provided a different take on the future of the country. Many were student leaders, such as Aung San, who would soon forge new bonds of political affiliation that were based on different political objectives than the generation before them. While traditional elites had, for the most part, sought to initiate reform through mechanisms provided by the colonial state, this new group of reformers called themselves nationalists and sought to change the system upon which the colony was run. These student groups would appear to be the most radical to British administrators, as the rhetoric they used and the measures they took were drawn from Scottish nationalists, Indian nationalists, Socialists, and Communists. It was from this latter group that the core of the Burma Independence Army leadership would emerge.

Thus, British Burma was established unevenly over time and space, affecting the degree to which elites and commoners alike were exposed to the rhythms and mechanisms of the colonial state. These differences in exposure to colonial law, education, business, and culture would shape British Burma's communities in different ways; some groups would be more comfortable working with the colonial administration, others would remain more distant from it, affecting in turn their attitudes towards the British and their place in Burma. Those affiliated more closely to the colonial government, either by geographical or political proximity, had particular expectations about their role in the country – sentiments that continued well after World War II.

Highland communities in the northeast, northwest, and the western edges of the colony had little exposure to the British and therefore had little stake in lowland Burmese political movements. Crucially, these territories were delineated as different legal spaces from Ministerial Burma or the lowland, river-valley, plains areas. These 'Frontier' spaces were considered 'Excluded' from the central administration and given more political autonomy. The legal construction of spaces in colonial Burma was not consistent. Lowland territories were more directly under British legal authority than the highlands, probably due to the differences in economic importance and the lack of infrastructure to connect these areas with Rangoon.[10] While it is true that coastal communities were perhaps more aligned with the international rhythms of trade and commerce than interior communities, there was still considerable differences amongst those groups living on the coast. Chinese and overseas Indian communities tended to prosper under the British, but dock workers from Upper Burma did not. Lowland communities and those based in urban zones tended to be more involved in the various strands of the nationalist movement. Rural rice and other agriculturalists had their own priorities and concerns even as urban elites and intellectuals seemed to speak for them. British Burma's varied landscapes produced different experiences under colonialism that in turn affected their relationships with both the British and home-grown nationalist groups.

Early political expression emerged at the turn of the twentieth century with the arrival of young local elites into the English language school system that enabled them to enter the civil service. However, this first generation of Western-educated elites were less inclined to involve itself in political affairs, not only for fear of reprisal but also because these groups benefitted from their colonial patrons and the system at large. Rather, they focused on social and cultural issues that did not pose a threat to the political establishment. Exposed to a range of literature at the time, these reformers formed book clubs, literary associations, and newspapers, commenting on Burmese society since the fall of the monarchy and endeavoured to improve society both through secular and religious terms. The formation of the Young Men's Buddhist Association (YMBA) in 1906 was an example of such organisations. The YMBA was dedicated to uplifting the state of Buddhism in society through new platforms of communication and organisation.[11] This generation of reformers were decidedly more apolitical than those who would follow, and thus, they tended to choose carefully the topics they would discuss publicly.

Out of the YMBA emerged a more politically motivated faction of reformers much more eager to immerse itself in the issues of the day. Forming the General Council of Buddhist Associations (GCBA), the group led by men such as Chit Hlaing, U Pu, and U Kyaw Dun sought greater self-rule and began to take more public positions on political issues of the time. Whereas Buddhism was used as a shared bond that tied various smaller associations within the political landscape

[10] Mandy Sadan, *Being and Becoming Kachin: Histories Beyond the State in The Borderworlds of Burma*, (Oxford: Oxford University Press, 2013).

[11] See, E Michael Mendelssohn, *Sangha and State in Burma: A Study of Monastic Sectarianism and Leadership* (Ithaca: Cornell University Press, 1975); Manuel Sarkisyanz, *Buddhist Backgrounds of the Burmese Revolution* (The Hague: Martinus Nijhoff, 1965); Donald Eugene Smith, *Religion and Politics in Burma* (Princeton, New Jersey: Princeton University Press, 1965), Alicia Turner, *Saving Buddhism: The Impermanence of Religion in Colonial Burma* (Honolulu: Hawaii University Press, 2014) and Mathew J Walton, *Buddhism, Politics and Political Thought in Burma* (Cambridge: Cambridge University Press, 2017).

to the GCBA, issues concerning education, budget expenditure, the allocation of resources, representation in government, and taxes were some of the topics that the GCBA began to engage through rallies, newspaper articles, and lobbying of politicians. Constitutional reform and the granting of more powers of self-rule to India became divisive issues for the GCBA, who began referring to themselves as the General Council of *Burmese* Associations. At stake was whether British Burma would be granted similar powers of self-rule as those being granted to India, given that British Burma was a formal province under British Indian authority.

Some within the GCBA believed that staying attached to India would ensure that these reform measures would extend to British Burma. In other cases, stakeholders preferred a different trajectory to that of India and felt that Burma was in a different political phase of development, a position held by the colonial authorities and business interests in Rangoon. For those stakeholders who generally benefited from British rule, they were naturally inclined to vote for separation while those who sought a faster trajectory to home rule and independence opted to vote against separation. This 'Separation' issue dominated political debate in the 1920s–1930s and defined political affiliation for many stakeholders and the political parties to which they pledged their loyalty. Political parties took variant positions on the Separation issue which caused deep rifts between groups calling themselves 'nationalists'.[12]

This question of whether British India and British Burma would remain legally and administratively connected illustrates the way in which concepts of law and territory were at the very heart of understanding what constituted 'British Burma' in spatial terms. Law was a language through which the territories of British Burma and British India were combined into a single, spatial entity. It would be through the enactment of laws that British India would separate from British Burma to form two separate colonial states. The challenge ahead would lie in how different stakeholders and minority interests understood and applied these two concepts during the founding of the first Constitution.

II. POLITICAL FACTIONALISM IN PRE-WAR BRITISH BURMA[13]

Political parties were divided over constitutional reforms that were first raised in 1917 and later over the issue of whether Burma should be included in the

[12] See Cecil Hobbs, 'Nationalism in British Colonial Burma' (1947) 6(2) *The Far Eastern Quarterly* 113–121; BK Drake, *Burma: Nationalist Movements and Independence* (Kuala Lumpur: Longman, 1979); U Maung Maung, *From Sangha to Laity: Nationalist Movements of Burma 1920–1940* (New Delhi: Manohar, 1980); U Maung Maung, *Burmese Nationalist Movements 1940–1948* (Edinburgh, Kiscadale Publications, 1989); and Surendra Prasad Singh, *Growth of Nationalism in Burma 1900–1942* (Calcutta: Firma KLM, 1980).

[13] See generally, Tun Thwin, *The Impact of Political Thought on Burma's Struggle for Independence (1930–1948)* (Ann Arbor, Michigan: Centre for South and Southeast Asian Studies, 1989).

formation of a self-ruling government being proposed for India. The issue of 'Separation' split nationalist groups with some favouring reforms that catered to Burma's unique socio-political development and others who felt that change should occur alongside India in case it would be withheld if separated. Beyond the 'Separation' issue, policies on education, taxes, representation, and leadership in the government divided Burmese politicians and their political parties, rifts that would carry on well into the post-World War II era.

The challenges facing the Independence government's attempt to construct a new constitution stemmed from deep divisions that began well before the onset of World War II. Ideological, class, educational, cultural, racial, and personal differences defined the development of party politics in British Burma and these dynamics continued into the post-war era. Differences over representation, governance, and policy in the immediate post-war era reflected socio-political fractures that characterised both grass roots and elite politics in the 1920s and 1930s.[14] Many of these differences evolved as a result of access to resources and authority provided by the colonial administration. Opportunities for communities to acquire wealth, power, and influence varied according to one's support of and political proximity to the colonial administration. These differences in access and equity produced commensurate political platforms that reflected these respective positions. These varying experiences under colonial rule resulted in different attitudes towards how politics, law, and governance should be pursued once independence was attained. Not everyone was a nationalist promoting independence.

As mentioned earlier, supporters of the British included those traditional elites who were co-opted into the administration became the first clerks, lawyers and barristers in the colonial administration. Sometimes these were lower ranking officials or ministers who maintained some influence over local networks despite the dismantling of the monarchy. These groups were the first to have access to British education and English-language instruction that would benefit them economically and politically so long as the colonial state remained in place.

The descendants of these groups often formed associations and eventually political parties that sought social reform through the colonial system, choosing to use the administrative, commercial, and legal apparatus that was available to them rather than advocate for a change in the system. Their campaigns for social reform focused on less confrontational issues in the first decades of the twentieth century. For example, the YMBA, formed in 1906, focused on cultural and religious topics that would draw attention to recognition of the country's traditions. Men such as Ba Pe, U Kin, Ba Yin, Sein Hla Pe and May Oung, founded the Association on the premise of maintaining apolitical objectives. The 'shoe-wearing' controversy, a campaign to prohibit Europeans from wearing shoes in Buddhist religious sites, was one such example of these efforts.

[14] Robert H Taylor, *The State in Myanmar* (Singapore: NUS Press, 2009).

Following a national education strike in the 1920s, a nationalist faction of the YMBA broke off and formed the GCBA to engage the colonial government on political issues of the day.[15] The communist party, formed in 1939 by Thakin Aung San and his brother-in-law Thakin Soe, would become a significant political influence before and after World War II. For these radical nationalists, a major grievance was lack of access to the institutions of governance and what they saw as the inequitable distribution of economic and social power in the country.

For instance, Eurasians, Indian and Chinese business communities, and ethnic minority groups (such as the Karen) were given special access to educational, economic, and political opportunities that enabled them to rise in influence in British colonial society over traditional elites and precolonial power networks. These groups benefited from the colonial encounter and thus had a different orientation to both the British and their system of governance. They had the advantage of learning English – the language of political authority in British Burma – and they developed an appreciation for the legal, economic, and social policies that were promoted by the colonial administration. Their privileged status resulted in appointments within the government and in the economic sector that further entrenched their acceptance of British rule.[16] For the majority of the population, especially those communities in the rural countryside, these experiences were as alien to them as the British; peasant loyalties and bonds of affiliation would be towards elites that seemed to understand their priorities and concerns. Until the rise of more grass-roots political groups that emphasised the needs and concerns of the countryside, 'local' representation in government would consist of primarily those who benefited from and wished to continue the privileges attained under the British. The seeds for post-colonial conflict were a direct product of colonial policy and practice from the beginning.

Yet the differences lay far deeper than the opportunity to rise in status and prestige under the British. For some of these stakeholders, the future of their very existence as a community was at stake; whether or not independence from the British would address this concern was at the heart of their political platform. The shape and direction of the country (and the Constitution that would articulate this vision) was predicated on the preservation of their world-views, priorities, and identity within this new system. For some, this future lay with the continuation of British rule, dominion status, and a close relationship with the Empire. Ethnic minorities would eventually adopt this position given their access to missionary education, English language, and jobs in the administration. After all, it was the colonial authorities who were the first to provide patronage and support to these communities, who otherwise did not have as much access to resources as the majority Burmese.

[15] Alicia Turner, *Saving Buddhism: The Impermanence of Religion in Colonial Burma* (Honolulu: Hawaii University Press, 2014).

[16] Cady (n 2) at 293.

As a result, minority communities began to express their sense of belonging through a more standardised ethnic, linguistic, and religious vocabulary that was designed to differentiate themselves from the British on the one hand and from the Burmese (Burman) majority on the other. Notions of where one's ethnic group 'lived' began to attain a more fixed character as well, based primarily on the internal district boundaries that were mapped, marked, and authorised by colonial cartographers. Finally, minority communities were provided a way of expressing how they were different from Burman majorities through their conversion to Christianity via the many British (and American) missionaries who had been operating within the kingdom since the mid-1850s. It was through these missionaries and missionary education that minority Karen, for instance, were exposed to British social norms and values, British culture, and of course, politics. Karen elites were often affiliated to various Baptist and Anglican churches, further distinguishing themselves from the majority Buddhist population, especially when Buddhism was becoming an important attribute associated with being from 'Burma' or being 'Burmese'. Thus, the range of ways one could express one's identity during this period emerged as a result of colonial administrative practices. These multiple means of expression complicated efforts by nationalists to bridge internal divisions in order to attain their political objectives.

While the conflation of ethnicity, language, and religion with political identity served as a platform for nationalist groups to unite against colonial rule, these same ingredients also created heated rivalries amongst various stakeholders. The 'nationalist' movement in pre-World War II British Burma was a loose conglomeration of multiple interests held together by the allure of political independence. Beyond ethnicity and class, factions within the nationalist movement were divided over ideology, political strategy, and leadership. Within the GCBA, by far the largest nationalist party, there were different factions that debated over what sort of political action was acceptable under the umbrella organisation. Some advocated for direct confrontation through a series of sit-ins, marches, and boycotts in order to embarrass the government. These groups also suggested that the forming of village defence units (*wunthanu athins*), local militias, and other forms of grass-root mobilisation would enable rural communities to connect with their urban counterparts while protecting their immediate interests.

Another political community that became prominent were the Communists, who at the time enjoyed status as one of the more innovative, modern, ideologies circulating amongst colonised intellectuals.[17] Many saw in Communist ideology an answer to the problem of colonialism. At the same time many

[17] See Virginia Thompson, 'Burma's Communists' (1948) 17(9) *Far Eastern Survey* 103–105; and Bertil Lintner, *The Rise and Fall of the Communist Party of Burma (CPB)* (Ithaca: Southeast Asia Programme, Cornell University, 1990).

were attracted to its class explanations and blueprint for framing a vision for the future. Others saw the role of religion needing to play an important role in promoting reform, with many of these advocates coming from the monkshood (*sangha*). *Dhammakatikas* or 'political' monks who were not tied to any particular monastery, began touring the countryside distributing leaflets and other literature condemning social policy in the colony and urging villagers and other rural communities to become more politically active. More activists than ascetics, these 'political monks' became increasingly active in connecting politics to religion, using the latter to translate concepts in a language and grammar more accessible to many Buddhists. These figures, some of them the first grassroots organisers to venture into the countryside, focused on rural issues and concerns that were not always aligned with urban, elite groups and their strategies. Finally, there were radical actors who supported a more confrontational, violent approach advocating for rural peasants and cultivators to rise up against the British. One such group, the *Dobama Asyione* (We Burmans)[18] organised boycotts, distributed literature, and held political rallies. Not only were these groups often separated by differences over means and objectives within the nationalist movement, they were often divided over the boundaries of personal networks and relations.

Within the Burmese nationalist camp were a range of factions, a spectrum of reformists, revolutionaries, and rebels with different ideas about how to comprehend, no less address, the socio-economic changes that had been occurring since the 1890s. By the 1920s, a second generation of students prepared to take their place at universities to study law, medicine, engineering and a range of topics that might provide opportunity to join the civil service or to start a lucrative business in the growing economy. The government's attempt to raise the standards of university entrance exams drove students into the streets in protest of the new educational proposals. These students would join unions and newspapers that began to agitate for greater political participation in the colony's affairs. The implementation of Dyarchy government[19] provided some space for participation in Parliament, with many of the seats taken up by an older generation of reformers who were trained barristers, businessmen, and other mainly urban notables who had worked closely with the colonial government. Most students of this generation were less patient with the colonial government than the local

[18] See Khin Yi, *The Dobama Movement in Burma (1930–1938)* (Ithaca: Southeast Asian Programme, Cornell University, 1988); and Kei Nemoto, 'The Concepts of *Dobama* ("Our Burma") and *Thudo-Bama* ("Their Burma") in Burmese Nationalism, 1930–1948' (2000) 5 *Journal of Burma Studies* 1–16.

[19] 'Dyarchy government' refers to the system of 'double government' introduced in 1919 in British India. Under this system of government, the executive branch of each provincial government was divided into two sections. The first was made up of councillors appointed by the Governor while the second was made up of ministers chosen by the Governor from among the elected members of each provincial legislature; and the latter were invariably Indian. This paved the way for limited self-government within the colonial state. Dyarchy was introduced into Burma in 1923 and the first election of the Legislative Council was held that year.

MPs who were voted into Parliament. These differences would widen in the coming years over what political platforms to adopt in connection with reform: should reformers work through the colonial apparatus or should they campaign for a complete replacement of the system?

By the mid- to late-1920s, economic conditions began to worsen, and monks began to agitate for political change, which was a departure from the norms that governed the sangha (Buddhist monastic community). The spread of print technology and the growth of newspapers provided the means for new groups of social reformers to emerge and share their ideological visions for British Burma. Different factions of the most influential nationalist organisation, the GCBA, began to take shape around charismatic leaders who disagreed with the main leadership on particular issues. These issues tended to be over what the GCBA represented, who belonged, and what sort of strategic direction should the organisation take on issues of elections, access to education, taxation, rice prices and land reform. The 'U Chit Hlaing GCBA' and the 'Soe Thein GCBA' were known for their particularly more confrontational approaches to British policy. Like the political monks, these groups were inclined to advocate boycotts, sit-ins, and other forms of public display of disobedience over policies that were deemed detrimental to Burmese society and its political future.

Given their similar strategies, colonial officials long suspected collaboration between 'political' monks and these more radical factions of the GCBA. The Saya San Rebellion of 1930–1932, a collection of rural uprisings that spread across the colony, was thought to be the brainchild of an ex-monk who had become a member of the Soe Thein GCBA. Saya San, allegedly a *se saya* or traditional healer, was thought to have used traditional symbols and medicinal practices to attract potential rural cultivators to help him rid the country of the British. By December 1930, thousands of rural farmers and labourers had started an uprising that began in Tharrawaddy District and quickly spread to neighbouring districts.[20] Although it took a few years to suppress the violence, the rebellion was a clear sign to urban leaders that rural cultivators and labourers were important constituents in the population. The recognition of peasants, as yet another stakeholder in the contest for the State, demonstrates the uneven situation within Burmese society. The world-wide depression, rapid immigration of labour, and rising agricultural rental prices were likely the immediate causes of the rebellion, while long-term socio-economic policies that exposed the colonial economy to fluctuations in commodity prices along with broader social dislocation contributed to the sense of anxiety and distrust of the colonial government.

While Rangoon experienced racial riots between communal groups, the countryside was afflicted with disorder, violence, and poverty, which created the

[20] Maitrii Aung-Thwin, *The Return of the Galon King: History, Law, and Rebellion in Colonial Burma* (Athens: Ohio University Press, 2011).

conditions that prompted radicals, such as the *Thakins*, to seek options from foreign patrons. For example, while fleeing arrest from the British, Aung San and his comrades attempted to contact the Communist Chinese but were instead intercepted by the Japanese. As a result, Aung San and the Thirty Comrades aligned themselves with the Japanese, which led to their rise in political prominence, and consequently, to their writing of the country's first Constitution.

III. WAR-TIME PLANNING[21]

Planning for post-War Burma was conducted by a range of stakeholders. Politicians and civil service officials in London and Simla (the city in Northeast India that served as the capital of Burma's government-in-exile) represented one arm of British civilian interests while Lord Mountbatten's military command and the Civil Affairs Service of the military reflected British views on the ground. The civil service and the military did not always see eye to eye on post-War policy nor was there consistent consensus *within* these two groups. The civil service was divided over whether to gradually pass power over to the Burmese or to focus on re-establishing the colonial system. The military was also divided between the army's leadership and the civilian affairs service (CAS) of the army who disagreed over the role of the Burmese in the future of the country. Mountbatten wanted to honour agreements made during the heat of war; the CAS wanted Burmese nationalists who benefited from the Japanese invasion to pay for their alleged sins. British plans for post-war Burma was therefore somewhat divided along civil service-military lines, a tension that had escalated during the war, if not earlier.[22] London viewed the situation in Burma from afar and struggled to understand local power dynamics that characterised the situation during wartime. Due to the varying experiences during the war, civil servants and their military counterparts had very different ideas about post-war reconciliation and retribution.

Much of these differences concerning the future of Burma stemmed from civil servants who fled to northeast India after the Japanese attacked. In general, many were resentful of the fact that Aung San had turned his loyalties away from the British when he decided to connect the BIA to the Japanese. Pro-British Burmese who accompanied Governor Reginald Dorman-Smith to Simla were also wary of Aung San given that his political stance on a number of issues had been far more radical and confrontational than they were prepared to accept. Whereas Aung San's *Thakins* had called for independence from Britain,

[21] See Nicholas Tarling, '"A New and Better Cunning": British Wartime Planning for Post-War Burma, 1942–43' (1982) 13(1) *Journal of Southeast Asian Studies* 33–59; and Nicholas Tarling '"An Empire Gem": British Wartime Planning for Post-War Burma, 1943–44' (1982) 13(2) *Journal of Southeast Asian Studies* 310–348.

[22] Cady (n 2) at 485.

reformers like Sir Paw Tun relied on the British as patrons and saw the future of Burma led by political moderates, not radicals. The Simla government in-exile had little intention of installing a government led by Aung San and his post-War coalition, the Anti-Fascist People's Freedom League. Instead, London gave the government at Simla authority to establish a new government in Burma under the leadership of British administrators who had fled to Simla during the war. The Simla Reconstruction Department, led by Secretary Amery and Governor Dormon-Smith, decided that a key component of this planning would require an extension of the governor's emergency authority for up to seven years in order to reconstruct the country, an approach that was in direct contrast with the aspirations of Aung San and the Burma Independence Army.

Back in Rangoon, the Japanese established their own constitution and installed their own government, made up of mainly *Dobama Asiayone* nationalists who were allied with Aung San.[23] The war-time government in Rangoon was declared 'Independent', and figures like Dr Ba Maw (a barrister by training) began to work towards building a new government. The Constitution the Japanese enacted in August 1943 was based on the 1889 Meiji constitution of Japan, that called for both a head of state and an equally-empowered head of the army.[24] The Japanese Constitution also called for a Planning Board, an embassy in Tokyo, a supreme court, and a cabinet. While this Constitution's role did not last long, the crucial point here is that the Burmese who did serve under the Japanese became another stakeholder competing for state power at the end of the war. Under this scheme, Aung San was named head of the Burma National Army. Those Burmese who served under the Japanese government would be at political odds with both the British and their Burmese colleagues who had fled to Simla under British protection.

To complicate matters further, even the Simla Reconstruction Department struggled at times to achieve a consensus on its approach to post-War Burma. Secretary for the Colonies, Leopold Amery focused on the return of British business, the development of new enterprises, and the recovery of assets lost in the war. Dormon-Smith was less concerned with the business sector because he had to face a growing and emboldened group of nationalists who had yet to achieve a sense of compromise on the issue of independence. Placing an emphasis on returning British business interests would make securing cooperation from Burmese politicians that much harder, given that the Japanese had already declared Burma 'Independent' and installed their own group of nationalist Burmese to run the country.[25] Managing these Burmese officials would be a

[23] See *Burma's Constitution* (n 1) at 57–59; and Jan Becka, *The National Liberation Movement in Burma During the Japanese Occupation Period 1941–1945* (Prague: Oriental Institute in Academia, 1983).

[24] See App II of *Burma's Constitution* (n 1) at 223–228; and Robert H Taylor, *Dr Maung Maung: Gentleman, Scholar, Patriot* (Singapore: Institute of Southeast Asian Studies, 2008) at 228.

[25] Cady (n 2) at 491.

difficult task for they would not want to vacate their seats of power even though that is what the British would expect them to do. Worse, Dorman-Smith had to deal with an unsympathetic British Prime Minister, Winston Churchill, who regarded the idea of handing power over to the Burmese as being incongruent with his views on the colonies and the future of the Empire. The Simla Plan was thus doomed to failure because it failed to recognise the determination of Burmese nationalists to achieve political progress following the war. In the end, the Simla Reconstruction Department faced a question that defined all others: should it focus on preparing the Burmese for self-government or reinvigorating the economy and British businesses?

By 1944, a report of the Commons Committee on Burma Policy was published detailing a time-line for the transfer of power to not exceed six years. Provisions were made so that the Burmese would be trained in governance and business administration in order to push both the political and the economic reconstruction ahead. It stipulated that a Burmese representative assembly would be able to 'review' a constitution, presumably written by the British and that land reform would need to be enacted in order to alleviate the ownership of land by Chettyar moneylenders. The release of the report antagonised Burmese stakeholders, especially nationalists who expected an immediate transfer of power and a more direct role in writing a new constitution. This position clashed with conservative civil servants who were unconvinced that the Burmese had the capacity for self-governance and they felt that a six-year transition period was too *short* a period of time for a proper hand-over. As a result, the final Simla policy in 1945 called for the restoration of law and order and the re-establishment of economic operations that would essentially restore British control over the country.[26]

Lord Mountbatten, Supreme Allied Commander for Southeast Asia, had somewhat different ideas about post-War Burma. Southeast Asia Command took seriously the war-time agreement made with Aung San and his growing political party, the Anti-Fascist People's Freedom League (AFPFL), to consider their aims for the reconstruction of both a new government and army in return for joining the Allies. This position contrasted with the military's own CAS, which was led by Major General DFB Pearce, a former Burma Civil Servant who had little sympathy for Burmese political aspirations. Pearce and other generals were concerned that supporting the Burma Independence Army would place the future of the country in jeopardy. The involvement of the BIA (at this period called the Burma National Army, BNA) was significant in that they were able to disrupt the Japanese army's lines of communication and supplies in lower Burma[27] which led to the recapture of Rangoon. While this coordination with the BNA was key to Allied operations, CAS officials felt that members of Aung San's AFPFL would not be exempt from being tried as war criminals.

[26] Cady (n 2) at 498.
[27] Ibid, at 503.

When Mountbatten over-ruled the CAS for fear of causing a civil war, the CAS leadership resigned and returned to Simla.

This infighting amongst the British complicated the development of a coherent policy for post-war Burma. To make matters worse, London did not place a high priority on Burma, which left competing elements in Simla and in Rangoon to sort out their differences over the future of the country. London's lack of interest in the post-War situation suggests that officials were unable to understand the fractured nature of post-War Burmese society and the equally dire socio-economic situation that survivors of the War faced. The political vacuum left by the Japanese provided an opening for the British to return, but questions remained over the conditions and the objectives. While some advocated a gradual transition to self-government along the lines of India, bitter groups within the former civil service and military sought retribution for certain Burmese nationalists who they regarded to be traitors. Perhaps the biggest misconception the British held was that they anticipated to be welcomed back by the majority of former colonial subjects. Instead, they faced a Burmese population that had been devastated by the War, a countryside filled with armed militias, a fractured nationalist movement, a small group of capable Burmese leaders who were only loosely aligned, and an annihilated infrastructure.

By the end of the War, these differences were so entangled that the British were unable to present a consistent policy for their equally divided Burmese colleagues to choose. The release of the White Paper of 1945, detailing the British intention to determine the pace and nature of political-economic reconstruction was met with frustration on the part of AFPFL nationalists who regarded the report as having turned back the clock of political progress by 20 years. It stated that the Burmese would have to endure the restoration of the 1935 Constitution and that London would continue to hold considerable power over the future of the country. Crucially, territories such as the Shan states would continue to be under the jurisdiction of the Governor, and if they desired to join with 'Burma', this would need to be discussed by all parties at some future time. For all intents and purposes, the 1945 White Paper was a reassertion of British rule in Burma. It would be up to Burmese nationalists to assert their independence and write their own constitution.

Thus, the AFPFL sought to draft their own constitution while the war raged. The drafting of the 1944 Anti-Fascist People's Freedom League Constitution emerged in the process of holding secret meetings on whether the BNA would join the Allies against Japan in return for political concessions in reference to self-rule. Thakin Aung San and Than Tun, related by marriage, had also formed the Communist Party of Burma in 1939. By 1943, they had already made contact with other anti-Japanese groups, such as the delta Karens in the hope of convincing them to join. The detailed programme included provisions to ensure the economic, social and political interests of the Kayin, Shan, Paluang, Taungthu, Chin, Kachin, Chinese and Indian nationals. The Constitution would outline the following features: a bicameral legislature with a Chamber of Deputies and a Chamber of Nationalities that would represent the minority groups in equal proportion to the number of Burmese. The cabinet would guarantee a minister from each of the major ethnic groups and be subject to oversight by the legislature. Rakhine, Kayin, Chin, Kachin, and Shan State representatives would all be organised into a federal system with the right of secession. Early meetings of the AFPFL, which are not clearly discussed within the historical records, were held from 1 to 3 March 1945.[28]

IV. POST-WORLD WAR II CONTEXT: 1945–1947[29]

The British government and Burmese political stakeholders had divergent views about the reconstruction of Burma and these differences affected the trajectory of post-War events preceding independence in 1948. Although the end of the war saw British forces and the Burmese Independence Army working together to defeat the Japanese, their war-time alliance did not prevent them from forgetting how they felt about each other before the War. Not only was there a lack of trust and shared vision during the immediate post-War years, there was a considerable amount of vengeance and retribution simmering on both sides. Not only were pre-War tensions rekindled, they grew far more serious considering that everyone was now armed. To complicate matters further, both Burmese and British stakeholders were deeply divided amongst themselves about the future of the country. Competition ensued over who spoke 'for' the British government or 'on behalf' of the Burmese people. Following the retreat of the Japanese, pre-war rivalries began to resurface within the AFPFL, the organisation that had unified different political and military interests against the Japanese. Fissures also developed amongst British civilian and military personnel over the future of their ex-colony, divisions that influenced how communities who had traditionally aligned themselves with the colonial authorities positioned themselves in this period of political ambiguity.

In broad terms, there were divisions between groups who served in or benefited from the colonial administration and those who were part of the anticolonial nationalist movement. The former favoured the return of British rule for they had prospered during the colonial period and were uncertain of their status under the leadership of former activists and radicals who were competing for control of the State. The latter regarded themselves as more legitimate having fought and died for their country during what they regarded as a war for self-rule and independence from the British. Yet there were also differences amongst stakeholders over how independence should be achieved: some sought

[28] Universities Historical Research Centre, *The 1947 Constitution and the Nationalities* (2 Vols.) (Yangon: Innwa Publishing House, 1999).

[29] See Hugh Tinker, 'Burma's Struggle for Independence: The Transfer of Power Thesis Re-examined' (1986) 20(3) *Modern Asian Studies* 461–481.

to work in dialogue with the British government while there were others, including Aung San, who did not dismiss the possibility that it would take armed revolution against the British to secure self-rule. Finally, there were strong ideological differences over how the future nation (if achieved) would be governed and the type of principles that would guide the new state's structure, development, and policies. Within the AFPFL itself, there were socialists, communists, capitalists, and democrats of varying degrees and persuasions – each attached to different political factions that were themselves defined by personal relations, class, occupation, language, ethnicity, genealogy, and place. Overcoming these social and cultural differences that were politicised in the colonial and postcolonial eras was a key challenge for stakeholders at the time.[30]

London gave the exiled Simla government the authority to establish a new administration under the leadership of British administrators who had fled to Simla during the War. To the dismay of Aung San and his trusted advisors, the White Paper directives enabled the return of Sir Paw Tun to the powerful post of home-minister, a position he held before the War and one that he had used to imprison many of the nationalist *Thakins*. Dorman Smith's circle of older, pro-British Burmese advisors likely coloured his impression of the nationalist *Thakins* and the AFPFL as radical activists with little qualifications or legitimacy. The governor did not accept the claim by the AFPFL that it spoke on behalf of the Burmese people, especially for religious and ethnic minorities. Nor did they see eye to eye on economic policy given that there were stark differences between the priorities of British businesses and the socialist-oriented policies sought on behalf of peasants and workers by the AFPFL. Setting aside the role of Dorman-Smith for the moment, what evolved was a contest for the postcolonial State between two political communities in Burma. While both groups – older Burmese statesmen and younger, more radical *Thakins* – shared aspirations of self-rule for Burma, their differences lay in whether that goal would be achieved under British management or autonomously. The means of achieving independence would, in turn, affect their own role in the future of the country. In no uncertain terms, the return of Dorman-Smith signalled the return of direct colonial rule in the eyes of the AFPFL, and negotiations broke down two months later in November 1945.[31]

Dorman-Smith's re-appointment as Governor was deemed a significant setback for the AFPFL because the White Paper stipulated that any changes to the 1935 Constitution were contingent upon reviving the economic and financial position of the country and only possible after proposals to change the Constitution had reached a 'sufficient measure of agreement' by various stakeholders.[32] Furthermore, it stipulated that constitutional changes would only come about

[30] Robert H Taylor, *The State in Myanmar* (Singapore: NUS Press, 2009) at 230.
[31] Cady (n 2) at 521.
[32] Ibid, at 507.

after Parliament had granted its approval, that the Shan States would remain under British rule, and full self-government would only be established within the context of the British Commonwealth.[33] In Burmese nationalist eyes, the 'White Paper' would set Burma's political progress back to the 1920s, in effect re-establishing colonial rule. At this point, nothing short of independence and the writing of a new constitution by a constituent assembly would be considered acceptable to the AFPLF.[34]

In 1946, the AFPFL's challenges came from within, rather than from abroad. Members of the League who called themselves Communist began to split over disagreements concerning their own specific priorities and interests. Again, the issue was over the method of achieving independence and self-rule: would political autonomy be secured through cooperation with the British or through mass mobilisation and revolution? Younger members of the communist party sought to use more radical means to achieve their political goals by staging demonstrations, boycotts, and sit-ins to disrupt the already fragile ties that were holding together post-War Burmese society. Their more aggressive vision for achieving Communist ends under the banner of the AFPFL would be a key factor in the eventual expulsion of the Communists from the League. This division amongst the communists led to a split in their ranks, with the younger, more radical members choosing to follow Thakin Soe, who created his own 'Red Flag' Communist Party and went underground. The departure of Thakin Soe and his supporters relieved the AFPFL of some of its more extremist voices, leaving more 'moderate' communists in the AFPFL to pursue their goals.

A second challenge to the AFPFL came from political opponents within the Burmese political scene. Home Minister Sir Paw Tun, a close advisor to Governor Dorman-Smith, had always regarded the *Thakins* as rivals and incapable of governance, perhaps the result of class and ideological differences that had divided reformists since the early days of colonialism. He revived the attempt to have Aung San arrested on the grounds that the BIA leader had murdered a village headman during the fighting of 1942. The AFPFL leader was placed before a court-martial tribunal where evidence was collected and eventually sent to London for evaluation. Initially, London told Rangoon to go ahead with the arrest, especially after Aung San admitted that he did kill the village headman but it was under orders. At the last minute, London changed its mind and rescinded its order. Aung San's release thwarted the attempt by Sir Paw Tun to rid himself of his old rival and the vision of Burma that the AFPFL represented. Even attempts by Governor Dorman-Smith to engineer a 'third option' by resuscitating old rivalries within the AFPFL to lead a campaign against Aung San lost momentum. Though these were important victories for the AFPFL, critical

[33] Ibid.
[34] Ibid, at 510.

fractures still separated Burma's political elite, a key dynamic that would influence the writing of the 1947 Constitution.[35]

By mid-1946, it was clear that the British government was losing its grip on the post-war recovery process. Not only had the nationalists lost all confidence in the Governor, but London was also beginning to realise that Dormon-Smith was losing control of the task at hand: to restore order so as to enable British business to re-establish itself. The countryside was lawless, with armed militias controlling the roads, which forced a visible security presence on all public forms of transportation and official state travel. Industry, trade, and agriculture were also affected by the instability, leaving little space for state or private sector investors to rebuild vital infrastructure that had been destroyed by the War. Criticism in the Burmese and London press attacked the Governor for his policies while the AFPFL held public meetings to highlight the government's shortcomings. Although Dormon-Smith attempted to placate the AFPFL by raising the issue of holding Constituent Assembly elections and including Aung San in the government's executive council, it was too little too late. Prime Minister Attlee requested that the Governor return to London for consultation amidst heavy criticism from Parliament. He resigned in August 1946 and was replaced by Sir Hubert Rance, a former chief of the CAS who had continued to engage Aung San and the AFPFL.[36]

Rance's appointment triggered a general strike in September 1946 and added to the growing instability in the country. In response, the Governor reached out to the leadership within the AFPFL to help take control of the situation by inviting them to join the executive council; Aung San was made deputy chairman under Rance. With the presence of Aung San and other AFPFL leaders in the council, the government was able to suppress the strike. However, in doing so, Aung San alienated his allies in the communist party who favoured a more revolutionary approach to securing their objectives. After their lone representative was forced to resign from the Council, the communist party refused to acknowledge the authority of the government's executive council and was soon excluded from the AFPFL. Following their expulsion from the League, the Communists began to oppose the government and the AFPFL on ideological and socio-economic grounds. When warrants for their arrests were issued, the Communists went underground. The Communists retreated to the countryside and began preparing for what would become one of the longest insurgencies in Southeast Asian history.[37]

With the AFPFL finally positioned within the post-War government, Aung San made four demands to London that they (1) agree to the election of a Constituent Assembly Election, (2) guarantee that the Constituent Assembly will include

[35] Ibid, at 528.

[36] *Burma's Constitution* (n 1) at 76.

[37] Robert H Taylor, *The State in Myanmar* (Singapore: NUS Press, 2009) at 244.

'Frontier peoples', (3) announce Burma's independence within a year's time, and (4) agree to re-evaluate the economic recovery plan that was inherited from the previous government. The Constituent Assembly would prepare for Burmese independence by constructing a new constitution and consulting with communities in the Frontier Areas. The Labour government under Prime Minister Attlee agreed and even invited a Burmese delegation to London to formalise the arrangement. The Attlee-Aung San Agreement of January 1947 established the legal mechanisms and framework for initiating the writing of the new constitution and the transfer of power. Predictably, members of the executive committee – Aung San's political rivals U Saw and Thakin Ba Sein – refused to sign the agreement and eventually resigned from the council in March 1947. Their exit and formation of a rival political party (a pattern that was already quite the norm) did little to fluster Aung San as his main concern was now focused on connecting the peoples of the Frontier Areas to his transition government.[38]

The context within which the 1947 Constitution was written was very much shaped by the ability of Burmese and British stakeholders to negotiate a settlement following the end of World War II. This was not an easy task as political objectives were fluid and often contested from within their respective constituencies. If negotiating the transfer of power with the British was Aung San's first major hurdle, the second was convincing 'Frontier Area' communities that joining the government was in everyone's interests. These groups were historically separated by language, religion, custom, lifestyles, and environment from the majority of lowland communities who spoke Burmese, practiced Buddhism/animism, and whose worldviews were shaped by wet-rice agricultural cycles, urbanisation, and coastal maritime rhythms. Although connected to lowland communities via trade, migration, inter-marriage and religion, the peoples of the highlands had relatively looser ties to the pre-colonial or colonial states that claimed nominal authority over them. The colonial boundaries and administrative circuits that linked these people spatially to the province of Burma were often not enough to bind these groups emotionally, psychologically or politically to their lowland neighbours. Convincing them that they were all part of a single national community, let alone participate in the forthcoming Constituent Assembly elections in 1947, was a monumental task for Aung San and the AFPFL.

Aung San toured the Frontier Areas, consisting of the northern upland regions of the country, in order to convince the communities there to join the constitutional process. Shan, Kachin, and Chin communities were promised separate political status with full autonomy within the Union, active participation in central governance, protection of minority rights, and the privilege of secession. The key challenge was how to translate their relationship under the British (which involved coercion) into a voluntary relationship under the new Burmese

[38] Cady (n 2) at 543.

government. In April 1947, Aung San proceeded to Panglong in the Shan States to convene a conference with representatives from ethnic groups to decide on how best to achieve unification. The ethnic groups wanted representation on the executive council, democratic rights for all citizens, regular financial aid to the Frontier Areas, local autonomy and consultation on developing the borders of a new Kachin State. The real challenge to all involved was that these ethnically designated 'States' were being constructed via notions of law, ethnicity, and territory to represent spaces that were not ethnically homogenous, monolingual, or even historically embedded in the experiences of these groups.[39] Nonetheless, representatives from the different ethnic groups – with the exceptions of the mainstream Karens – pledged their commitment to the constituent assembly elections in April 1947.

The AFPFL won the majority of seats in the constituent assembly elections, giving them the authority to draft a new constitution and formulate the structure of the country, a project they had in fact been working on since 1944. Although the Karen National Union (a political party representing ethnic Karens) boycotted the elections, a younger group of Karen politicians participated in the election and took their elected seats. The Karens, a community who had benefited from cooperation with the British, were deeply concerned about a nation being led by the majority Burmans and thus campaigned for a separate Karen State under *British* authority, a position that was untenable for Aung San's government. Attending to the demands of the Karens and other ethnically-designated minorities was a significant hurdle for Aung San's government and it became a foundational issue in the drafting of the 1947 Constitution. These challenges were compounded with the assassination of Aung San and the majority of his cabinet on 10 June 1947, a little over a week after his interim government officially withdrew from the Commonwealth. Although the Constituent Assembly managed to continue their work and complete the Constitution by September, the loss of Aung San's unifying voice severely hampered the ability of the future government to maintain the political coalition and vision he had established.

The struggle for the post-War state in Myanmar was in many ways a continuation of older dynamics that predated World War II. Young, university-educated activists had clashed with an older generation of western-educated elites over issues of reform, ideology, and governance since the 1930s. Personal rivalries and factionalism weakened each of these groups from within, affecting the ability of political leaders to form strong, unified, movements that could bridge vertical bonds of allegiance and patronage. In the absence of strong state institutions, bridging these gaps often relied on the charisma of particular leaders, coercion, and their ability to utilise the mechanisms of colonial law in order to meet the expectations of those with whom they hoped to build alliances.

[39] Robert H Taylor, 'Ethnicity, Federalism, Citizenship, and Politics in Myanmar', *ISEAS Perspective*, No 31, (Singapore: Institute of Southeast Asian Studies, 2015).

In many respects, the differences between groups concerned with reform in colonial Burma were based on the same criterion that characterised the post-War situation: would stakeholders work with the British or work to remove them?

At the same time, post-War dynamics brought new challenges for groups contesting for the state. The circumstances surrounding the invasion by Japan and the retreat by the British changed the political landscape in several ways. First, many radical *Thakins* who had been imprisoned or marginalised under the British were released by the Japanese and installed into positions of influence, replacing pro-British elites who had served under the British. Although these two groups would compete for the state in the post-War years, the *Thakins* would be in a greater position of strength due to their leadership role in the AFPFL. Second, collaboration with the Japanese provided the means for nationalists to form a national army that was capable of resisting the British war-machine, levelling to some extent the political playing field and providing the Burmese with the only unifying secular institution that survived the war. Aung San's People's Volunteer Organization (PVO), a loosely tied conglomeration of armed village militias, were an additional force to be reckoned with. It enabled the AFPFL to make demands that, in theory, represented the will of the countryside. Probably the most significant post-War development that affected the legal rendering of the nation was the weakened position of the British; a situation that effectively left the defining of the nation, via the Constitution, to the radical and moderate mishmash of reformers, intellectuals, activists, journalists, educators, businessmen, politicians, soldiers, civil servants, and thugs who represented the AFPFL membership. While the original mission of the AFPFL was originally expressed as a unifying campaign against the Japanese during the War and against the British following the War, the story of the AFPFL and the making of the 1947 Constitution marks its role in attempting to channel its unifying campaign towards the legal rendering of the new nation.

V. DRAFTING THE CONSTITUTION, 1944–1947

The origins of the 1947 Constitution stemmed from the legacies of colonial law in Burma, the administrative connections to British India, and the circumstances surrounding the process of decolonisation discussed earlier. The very idea of a constitution serving as a charter for the state was a direct legacy of the 1923 and 1935 Constitutions that had been written under the 'Dyarchy' government that divided the tasks of governance between the British and Burmese administrators. The Constitution and the processes associated with producing one were also representative of modern political practice at the time, acknowledged by the Burmese in their referencing of constitutional models found in Sweden, the United States, Australia, Ireland, the Soviet Union, and Yugoslavia. Forming a new government that met the standards of the day required an electoral format that could produce a constituent assembly to write a constitution. These ideas were known to the AFPFL at the time and they began anticipating the need for such procedures well before the Japanese surrendered.[40]

In fact, in 1944, the AFPFL began drafting a constitution in anticipation that they would require a plan to initiate a constitutional convention once independence was achieved. Discussions began within the AFPFL leadership and involved turning towards India, which had always been an important reference during the early years of nationalism. Communication between various nationalist groups, intellectuals, and activists from the two colonies had been strong since the 1920s, with India providing many of the models and direction for political stakeholders in British Burma. Aung San's decision to refer to the procedures of the Indian Constituent Assembly and consult with the Constitutional Advisor to India, Sir Benegal Narasinga (BN) Rao, represented a continuing connection between the two countries that remained active in the post-War years despite 'Separation' in 1937. Aung San appointed U Chan Htoon to serve as Constitutional Advisor in 1947 and invited Sir (BN) Rao to provide suggestions in the drafting. Many of the procedures and practices were adopted and put into place when the elections for the Constituent Assembly were convened in April 1947.

Following the elections, a draft Constitution consisting of 14 basic principles was completed on 23 May 1947 by a preliminary committee led by Thakin Mya, one of the AFPFL's key leaders, and U Chan Htoon. The draft delineated the territorial composition of the new Union, highlighting the continuities between the colonial and postcolonial state. Burma would include 'ministerial' Burma (the core areas of direct administration governed by Rangoon), specific districts and subdivisions, and the federated Shan States, Kayah States, Kachin Hills, and the Chin Hills. The draft outlined that the new Union would consist of five 'states' and that each state would be defined by a demarcated geographical area, a single language different from Burmese, a single culture, a community of a single tradition, a community of economic interests, a measure of self-sufficiency, a fairly large population and a desire to maintain a distinct identity as a separate unit of the Union. Though in 1944 the objective was to create an independent sovereign state, in substance the form of the territory that emerged was a near clone of British Burma. The AFPFL draft nonetheless established a template for the Constituent Assembly that would form over a year later, and it contained the basic principles surrounding the formation of the state, the relationship between Burma (proper) and the Frontier Areas, and an idea of how the influential Karens would fit into the mix.[41]

Despite internal quibbling from marginal AFPFL members about the inherent problems of a multi-national union and the fact that the drafting committee had

[40] Maung Maung, 'The Search for Constitutionalism in Burma' in RN Spann, *Constitutionalism in Asia* (London: Asia Publishing House, 1963).

[41] Universities Historical Research Centre, *The 1947 Constitution and the Nationalities,* 2 vols (Yangon: Innwa Publishing House, 1999) at 80 [hereinafter 'UHRC'].

relied on the Indian and Soviet Union versions of the Constitution, Aung San and the AFPFL leadership accepted the draft. But in doing so, Aung San risked losing the political capital he had gained from his discussions with ethnic leaders who pointed out that the draft did not adopt measures that had been raised in the important Panglong Agreement nor did it reflect the concerns outlined by the Frontier Area Committee of Enquiry, which represented the priorities of the major hill communities living in those territories. Representatives from the Shan States were particularly concerned that the draft had not addressed the issue of autonomy, but Aung San decided to convene the first session of the Constituent Assembly anyway on 9 June 1947, where other equally fundamental issues addressing both the spatial construction and the ethnic constitution of the nation were raised.[42]

U Nu – one of Aung San's oldest and closest allies – was elected as Chairman of the first meeting of the Constituent Assembly where he faced considerable differences over how the future of the nation would be legally rendered. The main purpose of the session was to establish the framing of the Constitution and to appoint a Constitution Committee to produce a draft. On 18 June, a resolution to appoint a Constitution Committee of not less than 75 members 'to study and finalise the draft' was passed.[43] Key questions concerning the lack of specificity in the AFPFL draft of 1944[44] were raised. In particular, spatial categories such as 'union state', 'autonomous state', and 'national area' were not understood in the same way by members of the committee. Other members found the lack of reference to the rights of the Union Assembly and the rights and powers of the Union States to be a serious deficiency, given what had been stated and promised through the Panglong Agreement.[45] More crucially, the draft had not stated what was meant by 'national minority' and how it was legally different from the category of 'minority'. Finally, the Shan were keen to ensure that the right of secession would be reflected in the Constitution, a clause that would be of crucial importance in the coming decades. In response, Aung San gave a 90-minute speech where he explained that the draft was intentionally ambiguous in order to ensure that the Constituent Assembly was provided with enough legal space to customise it according to the needs of the nation.[46]

The Constitution Committee met on 20 June 1947 and formed four sub-committees to facilitate the drafting of the document's different sections: (1) powers of the Union and the State, (2) Judiciary, (3), Fundamental Rights, and (4) Minorities. A separate sub-committee would later be formed in order to deal with the specific issue of the Shan States.[47] One of the most pressing

[42] Ibid, at 81.
[43] See *Burma's Constitution* (n 1) at 82.
[44] For the text of the AFPFL Draft, see App IV of *Burma's Constitution* (n 1) at 231–253.
[45] *Burma's Constitution*, ibid, at 79–80.
[46] UHRC (n 28) at 90.
[47] See *Burma's Constitution* (n 1) at 82.

issues faced by the Constitutional Committee had to do with the demands of the Karens, who despite boycotting the constituent assembly elections, petitioned to have a separate autonomous state established in order to ensure their place within the new nation. Since the Karens were dispersed throughout Burma and lacked a specific territory, their case for establishing a state was fairly weak. Nonetheless, their representatives suggested that several districts, subdivisions and areas would be combined to form a 'Karen region', adopting colonial forms of place-making that they inherited from the British. In general, they argued that the sub-regions of Taninthayi and the entire Delta area should be designated a Karen area in order to meet the population criteria for 'making' a national state. Specific districts such as the Toungoo, Thanlwin, Pyinamma Hill Tracts, and Thaton Hill Tracts were all included into this vision of their new state. Where there was some overlap with other populations, they suggested that such spaces, such as the Salween River and the city of Moulmein be designated as 'inter-state' areas. Needless to say, Aung San found the Karen proposal problematic since it was only in the Thanlwin District that the Karens were in the majority with an estimated population of 1.5 million while the rest of them were dispersed throughout many other regions.[48]

After months of deliberation of the original AFPFL draft, the various sub-committees amended sections pertaining to issues of secession, religion, definitions, the judiciary, the composition of the various chambers within the legislative branch, citizenship and the form of the government in relation to the states. The draft Constitution was then submitted to the general Constituent Assembly in the form of a Preamble, twelve chapters, and four schedules. The second meeting of the Constituent Assembly on 7 July 1947 was focused on revisions to the draft and the important inclusion of the Karenni States into the national fold. During this period, Aung San was assassinated, and U Nu was chosen to replace him. The work of the Constituent Assembly continued, and it formally enacted the Constitution on 24 September 1947. In general, the final document resembled most of what the AFPFL draft had entailed and therefore represented a vision of Burma that was forged in the context of war, decolonisation, and reconstruction. It was a document that was influenced by anti-colonial nationalists, soldiers, and politicians who were themselves shaped by a strain of British colonialism that was perhaps more analogous to post-Mutiny India than the colonialism experienced in the Straits Settlements.

VI. LEGACIES

The 1947 Constitution[49] was a distinct product of the AFPFL and the times – a political organ that had been established by nationalists calling themselves

[48] UHRC (n 28), at 94.

[49] For the text of the 1947 Constitution, see App VII of *Burma's Constitution* (n 1) at 260–308.

'communists' and 'socialists' who had found in these ideologies both a rationale to contest the ideas often associated with the market economy and a blueprint for a modern state. Although Aung San served as the first president due to his affiliation (both ideologically and personally) with the Communist Party of Burma, he would eventually break from those ideological and political constraints in order to achieve his broader political objectives. The final document contained references to his socialist leanings that no doubt framed the original AFPFL draft. Private property was guaranteed but with some provisions to prevent monopolies and price dictation; the possibility of nationalising either single enterprises or entire sectors of the economy for acquisition by the state were also inscribed into the Constitution. Although later scholars would presume that the turn towards socialism was due to the military takeover in 1962, in fact the Constitution specifically established protections for the welfare of peasants and workers while prohibiting large landholding, which had been a source of grievance during the late 1920s and 1930s.[50] Scaled up, the Constitution can be read as a document that emerged out of the colonial situation and the dislocation created by the chaos of World War II in Asia.

Scaling down, the making of the 1947 Constitution reveals the anxieties and uncertainties that emerged involving the many communities who were part of the broader decolonisation process. From a domestic perspective, the Constitution represented an attempt to legally render an arrangement between the central government and peoples of the Frontier Areas. Deliberations contained in the minutes of the constitutional committee, the debates within the Constituent Assembly, and the discussions of the sub-committees reveal that inherited notions of territoriality, ethnicity, and law were employed to create the spaces that would constitute the geo-body of Burma.[51] If 'social spaces, lived places, and landscapes are inscribed with legal significance', then the formation of the Union of Burma and the Union/Ethnic States in 1947 are also imbued with the legal forms of meanings that were borne out of colonial law.[52]

This period between 1942 and 1962 in Myanmar history has been hotly contested, especially after the collapse of the Soviet Union and the end of the Cold War. As a result of current discourses and assumptions of democratic change since *Glasnost* and 'People Power' in the Philippines, much of Myanmar's history since 1948 has been framed within the context of democratic struggle, producing a lens of analysis that has problematically been applied to understanding this era. Within this stream of scholarship, the events leading to 'Independence' from Britain and the nation that emerged in the 1950s have been interpreted as a period of democratic awakening, with a constitution that

[50] Michael Adas, *The Burma Delta* (Madison: University of Wisconsin Press, 1974).

[51] Thongchai Winichakul, *Siam Mapped: A History of the Geo-Body of a Nation* (Honolulu: University of Hawaii Press, 1994).

[52] Irus Braverman, Nicholas Blomley, David Delaney & Alexander Kedar (eds), *The Expanding spaces of Law* (Palo Alto: Stanford University Press, 2014).

was forged with those ideals as its guiding principles.[53] That momentum was unfortunately stalled, subscribers hold, by the military coup of 1962 which kept Burma isolated by military rule until the 'unfinished revolution' erupted again in 1988.[54] Viewed from a legal perspective and the context in which the document was produced, the government that formed in 1948 through the efforts of Aung San and the AFPFL was more a continuation of the colonial structures that provided reference to state managers, an argument that has been made through cultural perspectives as well. While the language of liberal-democratic ideals certainly framed and were featured within the 1947 Constitution, issues concerning decolonisation, territorial consolidation, and administrative integration of the former colony were more likely the over-riding factors behind its construction.

[53] Michael A Aung-Thwin, '1948 and Burma's Myth of Independence: Order Without Meaning' in Josef Silverstein (ed), *Independent Burma at Forty Years: Six Assessments* (Ithaca: SEAP Publications, 1989) 19–34.

[54] Ibid.

6

A Foreign Commission for Domestic Needs: The Constitutional Founding of Malaysia

H KUMARASINGHAM

INTRODUCTION

'THE CALIBRE OF the Commission will have to be very high, since the problems will be unusual and of great complexity'.[1] Thus stated the last British colonial High Commissioner in Malaya, Sir Donald McGillivray, when assessing the needs and demands a constitutional commission would be tasked with drawing up the constitutional foundations for an independent Malaysia. The constitutional founding of Malaysia is one of the more unique in British and Imperial constitutional history and McGillivray was not exaggerating in describing the situation as 'unusual'. Not only was this the first major transfer of power in British Asia since the end of the Indian Empire a decade before, but it also confronted the constitution-makers with a complex polity enmeshed in rebellion, racial divisions, peculiar legal relations with Britain, esoteric governing structures, indigenous rulers with varying privileges, precarious geo-political position and pronounced religious and ethnic sensitivities. Far from being a dry, pro forma and incidental body, the Federation of Malaya Constitutional Commission, better known as the Reid Commission, and its Report, were unquestionably critical and conspicuous in the constitutional founding of independent Malaysia. While it would be another eight years before modern Malaysia would appear – with the incorporation of North Borneo and Sarawak, and the exclusion of Singapore – the Reid Commission's report laid the constitutional foundation for Malaysia when published in 1957. This chapter examines the constitutional context that led to the founding of

[1] 'Letter from Sir D MacGillivray to A M MacKintosh on the views of Tunku Abdul Rahman', 5 January 1956, CO 1030/132 no. 3, in AJ Stockwell (ed), *British Documents on the End of Empire – Malaya*, Pt III – The Alliance Route to Independence, 1953–1957, Series B, vol 3 (London: Her Majesty's Stationary Office, 1995) at 227 [hereinafter 'BDEEP'].

independent Malaya. Malaya stands out in British colonial constitutional history as one of the most complex and unique constitutional founding moments, let alone in Southeast Asia.

The leading local actors were the indigenous rulers across the Federation jealous of their prerogatives and a pragmatic coalition between the major communal parties: United Malays National Organisation (UMNO), Malayan Chinese Association (MCA) and the Malayan Indian Congress (MIC). Despite this, Malaya sought an entirely non-local Commission to establish the constitutional identity for an independent state. As Lauren Benton and Lisa Ford noted in their work on international law and the nineteenth century British Empire, colonial commissions of inquiry have been largely eschewed by academics and have thus become a 'grossly understudied constitutional moment'.[2] This essentially remains the case for the following century when the Southeast Asian states' constitutions covered in this volume were framed. The Reid Commission provides for Malaysia this critical 'constitutional moment' that ushered in the constitutional character and complexion of the country.

I. MALAYAN CONTEXT

The Malay Archipelago since early times has been a region of deeply rooted governing traditions and experience of diversity in every sense. Melaka, especially, became the centre of the Malay world and had a rich cosmopolitan culture and a flourishing trading network and historically controlled most of the modern Malaysian peninsular and islands. The Sultanate of Melaka, as a commercial and cultural entrepôt, attracted significant migration not just from the Malay world, but also from across Asia. When the Sultanate fell to the Portuguese in 1511 the centre of the Malay world may have been lost, but its example, even if romanticised, remained as a template of kingship and governance. The *Sejarah Melayu* or *Malay Annals*, though written well after the fall of Melaka details a founding story of Malay kingship that successor regimes, both colonial and local, would try and emulate. As Harper states, they served as a 'source of instruction' and 'enshrined the sanctity and authority, the *daulat*, of the Ruler', which in turn help give cohesiveness to the state and foster Malay nationalist thought and their authority and fitness in government.[3] This narrative remains critical to traditional authority in contemporary Malaysia and was openly prominent in the foundation of the state when Rulers' position and prerogatives were at the forefront of debate. European colonialism did not dismantle

[2] Lauren Benton and Lisa Ford, *Rage for Order – The British Empire and the Origins of International Law 1800–1850* (Cambridge, Massachusetts: Harvard University Press, 2016) at 59.

[3] TN Harper, *The End of Empire and the Making of Malaya* (Cambridge: Cambridge University Press, 1999) at 15 [hereinafter 'Harper'].

traditional rule. Instead, as will be discussed further below, the British were in favour of keeping traditional Malay governance roles and styles in place. As Harper argues 'the hallmark of colonial rule was the reinvention of traditional forms'.[4] Unlike some other traditional societies affected by colonialism the local Malay rulers largely not only retained their position, but also their influence on their subject culturally and constitutionally. However, while the Sultans were accepted as sovereign rulers, they had to admit – through a series of treaties – an on-the-spot British resident who had substantial powers. This was formalised in the 1874 Pangkor agreements that ensured British indirect rule in the Malay states. The Straits Settlements, which did not have Rulers, was administered directly by the British. Nonetheless Malay culture and practices permeated throughout. Even before it was formalised in 1957, the Malayan polity and constitutional culture contained what former Lord President of the Supreme Court, Salleh bin Abas, described as 'traditional elements': (a) the Sultanate or Rulership; (b) the Islamic religion; (c) the Malay language; and (d) Malay privileges.[5] The need for such constitutional and cultural considerations in the Malaysian founding was due to major demographic changes, the Malays were far from being the only community in the archipelago and sought protection of their status.

Migration caused a tremendous impact upon the composition of Malaya that would consequently affect the political bargaining surrounding the state's constitutional foundation. Colonialism accelerated the migration of various communities to the region. In particular, Chinese and Indian immigrants came to Malaya particularly from the nineteenth century as the British encouraged labourers specially to work on the plantations that were critical to the region's substantial commercial contribution to the imperial economy. The growth in economic power of non-Malays and formation of political groups based on identity made many Malays fear for their position. So many of the colonial era confrontations were associated with tensions and violence between the Malays and non-Malays. The Malays were fearful of the growing permanence of the Chinese and Indian communities. While all had originally seen the migrant labour as being temporary, greater settlement in fact occurred due to economic and geopolitical reasons. In 1947 over 60 per cent of the so-called 'immigrants' had actually been born in Malaya.[6] This had major repercussions. With little inclination or capability of moving, this large non-Malay population would seek not only rights for their respective communities, but also participation and recognition in the foundation of the state.

[4] Ibid at 19.

[5] Mohd Salleh bin Abas, 'Traditional Elements of the Malaysian Constitution' in FA Trindade and HP Lee (eds), *The Constitution of Malaysia: Further Perspectives and Developments – Essays in Honour of Tun Mohamed Suffian* (Singapore: Oxford University Press, 1986) 1–17.

[6] Harper (n 3), at 41.

II. COLONIAL AND CONSTITUTIONAL PRECURSORS

The founding of independent Malaya could have gone very differently. As the Japanese Occupation drew to its close, there were many ideas from Malays like Ibrahim Yaacob and Mustapha Hussain to craft a Malay constitutional polity before the British restored colonial rule. There was even vigorous support from certain Malay quarters to join an 'Indonesia Raya' or Greater Indonesia under Sukarno's leadership of this pan-Muslim Southeast Asian creation. As the Japanese surrendered on 15 August 1945, plans were also afoot to announce a Malayan Democratic Republic with the Sultan Abdul Aziz of Pahang as its figurehead. However, Sukarno went ahead with Indonesian plans that did not include Malaya and British colonial rule re-emerged that scuppered these alternate ideas for Malaya's constitutional founding.[7] Instead the British, in a secret planning session in Wimbledon, which CA Bayly and Tim Harper label one of the most thorough colonial documents for future constitutional reform in the Empire[8], prepared the way for a Malayan Union, which would be more centralised and uniform than had been the case previously.

Sir Harold MacMichael, fresh from Palestine, was the His Majesty's Government's Special Representative in 1944. He determined that his mission would modernise governance in Malaya, and this involved each traditional ruler effectively surrendering his powers to the British Crown and then being offered direct and centralised British rule. Rather than help facilitate the path to self-government, MacMichael's strategy had the effect of alienating the Rulers as traditional allies and giving a spur to Malay and Malayan nationalism and this seeming reinvigorated attempt in British imperialism.[9] Sir Edward Gent, the first Governor of the Malayan Union, decided that the constitutional path lay in conciliation with Malayan interests rather than in diminishing them, especially considering their need of allies against the Malayan Communists. Nonetheless the Rulers were not appeased and boycotted his installation as Union Governor while senior Malay politician Dato Onn Jaafar and others in consequence of the so-called MacMichael treaties, formed the United Malays National Organisation (UMNO) in May 1946. That same month, Malcolm MacDonald was sworn in as Governor-General of Southeast Asia and made immediate overtures to the Rulers and Dato Onn to restore the sovereignty of the Malay Rulers and eventually create the Federation of Malaya in 1948.

As MacDonald reported to the Secretary of State, Malay opposition was not just from the Rulers, but 'comes strongly from Malayan democratic opinion as

[7] Christopher Bayly & Tim Harper, *Forgotten Armies: The Fall of British Asia 1941–1945* (London: Allen Lane, 2004), at 453–455.

[8] Ibid.

[9] Appointment of Special Commissioner in SE Asia, 13 Feb 1946, CAB 21/1954 and Local Reactions to the White Paper, 23 Feb 1946, CO 537/1581, BDEEP (n 1), vol 1, docs 71 and 72.

a whole'.[10] Malayan constitutional consciousness was very alive. New parties emerged and eventually, and crucially, Tunku Abdul Rahman took over the UMNO leadership in 1951 from Dato Onn who left to form his own party that same year. Both of these distinguished Malays hailed from aristocratic backgrounds. The Tunku's father was Sultan of Kedah while Dato Onn came from a long line of high officials in Johore. Dato Onn was the more complex and intellectual of the two. He had thought deeply about Malays and their place in a new Malaya. At times he could be pro-monarchy and an eloquent proponent of Malay nationalism while at other turned a fierce critic of the Sultans and prophet of the need to abolish communal feels and craft a united Malayan identity drawn from all communities. He also advocated that UMNO be open to non-Malays. The rejection of this idea caused him to leave the party. He also, unfashionably, was not convinced by the demand for independence. Between 1945 and 1948 he repeatedly said *belum layak* (not yet ready) demonstrating his anxieties over the constitutional and political direction the Federation was heading.[11] His views also caused consternation with the Rulers, particularly with the Sultan Ibrahim of the State of Johore where he served on multiple occasions as Chief Minister. The Rulers effectively scuttled a British proposal to have a Malay as deputy high commissioner who most likely would have been Onn. Telling the UMNO youth wing in August 1949 that 'the days of feudal rule are over' and that we 'are in the age of democratic and constitutional rule' was unlikely to find favour with the Malay monarchs some of whom had already expressed contempt for the idea of popular democracy and elections.[12] While wanting to promote the Malays he also strived to broaden the movement to reach out to the non-Malays. As Bayly and Harper argue, Onn was moving too far ahead of Malay opinion.[13] These points and others caused him to split from UMNO and leave its leadership to the more relaxed Cambridge-educated Tunku who not only was more sensitive to the position of the Rulers, but accepted the special place of Malays in any constitutional structure albeit while in *alliance* with the other communities.

Many from the British side sought to dampen expectations of rapid self-government. Lord Killearn, Special Commissioner to South East-Asia since 1946, believed too much had been determined by the need to provide a regulation map for the path to independence. This, he argued, only made local 'irresponsibles' think that constitutional advancement was 'the panacea for all ills'. A few years later in 1949 officials in the Foreign and Colonial Offices believed that Malaya could only expect self-government in up to 20 years and not the eight

[10] Clyde Sanger, *Malcom MacDonald – Bringing an End to Empire* (Montreal: McGill-Queen's University Press, 1995), at 273–276.

[11] Stockwell, BDEEP (n 1), Pt I, at lxxix.

[12] Joseph M Fernando, *The Making of the Malayan Constitution* (Kuala Lumpur: MBRAS, 2002), at 12.

[13] Christopher Bayly and Tim Harper, *Forgotten Wars – The End of Britain's Asian Empire* (London: Penguin, 2007), at 502.

that eventually occurred.[14] Nonetheless, Labour ministers like James Griffiths and John Strachey and their Conservative successors like Oliver Lyttelton and Alan Lennox-Boyd came to see the lessons from India and the need to ensure a swifter and more co-operative style self-government to maintain not only peace and order, but also protect British interests through cooperation with a local leadership they could work with, as opposed to the potential of a Communist or Nationalist regime who would surely break down crucial defence and economic edifices that Britain relied upon.[15] Malaya accounted in 1951 for just under 10 per cent of Britain's world exports and a valuable defence pivot in its Asian ambitions.[16] For the traditional Malay leadership there was also interest to maintain good relations since the very Communists and Nationalists the British wanted excluded were also keen to throw off the feudal government and society of the region, which the British had enabled, and replace with 'true democracy'.

The Pusat Tenaga Rakyat (or PUTERA) sought the end of class and communal division and instead the unity of all Malayans.

> The People's Constitution of PUTERA is based on election, *kedaulatan rakyat* [sovereignty of the people], and moves towards social justice, and egalitarianism, without upper and lower classes in the *bangsa* [nation] except according to the capability, intelligence and industry of the individual. We hope in this matter the *rakyat* no longer have any doubts, but instead have more faith in the struggle and loyalty to their respective movements. Because of this we appeal once more, struggle onwards with a fiery spirit, but cool head until the sacred aims that we aspire to are achieved. Remember, comrades, that the world is changing fast and we cannot live with the understandings and feelings that we had in the year 1941. We are now in the year 1947 in the atomic age, the old era has passed.[17]

The All-Malayan Council of Joint Action founded in 1946–47 which brought together Malay radicals, Chinese Kuomintang, Communists, Leftists, Businessmen, Englishmen and others proposed a 'People's Constitution'. For many in this disparate group the goal was to create a constitution founded on common citizenship, but without individual conformity and to wrest power away from the British and their interlocutors in the Malay leadership. The British and UMNO under the Tunku largely ignored this constitutional populism and the organisation became riddled with division and was unable to provide a realistic constitutional alternative for a sovereign Malaya.[18]

The Tunku's UMNO eventually joined with the MCA in 1952 and later the MIC to form the Alliance party to contest elections and demonstrate

[14] Frank Heinlein, *British Government Policy and Decolonisation 1945–1963 – Scrutinising the Official Mind*, (London: Routledge, 2002), at 51–53.

[15] See, eg, Ronald Hyam, *Britain's Declining Empire – The Road to Decolonisation 1918–1968*, (Cambridge: Cambridge University Press, 2006), at 156–160 and 198–201.

[16] Bayly and Harper, *Forgotten Wars* (n 13), at 408.

[17] Ibid, at 517.

[18] Bayly and Harper, *Forgotten Wars* (n 13), at 361–371

inter-communal cooperation. The British had made it clear, perhaps with a mind to other parts of Asia, that political cooperation and accommodation between the three main communities was a necessity to achieve independence.[19] The Alliance fitted this requirement and its ethnic components, by and large proved practical and sensitive to their separate needs, while keeping the common goal of *merdeka* to the fore. The 1955 federal elections were the first real test for this constitutional concert party. The level of success of the Alliance coalition in the 1955 general elections surprised even the Tunku. The Alliance won every single elected seat except in Krian, Perak, – which was almost entirely populated by Malays – went to the Pan Malayan Islamic Party. The Alliance's great rival Dato Onn and his Party Negara were prevented from providing any opposition to the Alliance vision since they were unable to gain any representation in the legislature. With 51 of the 52 elected seats, the *Straits Times*, previously a critic, predicted that the Alliance's victory 'probably unparalleled outside the totalitarian countries' will allay 'doubts and fears' and produce 'a wholesome effect in that a strong, stable government can be formed, which can be sustained solely by its electoral strength'.[20] A point that would clearly reinforce the Tunku's independence objectives. The victory also served to achieve, electorally at the least, evidence of cooperation among the Malay, Chinese and Indian communities, which was a critical condition for the British to transfer power. Though, as with all elections, the results could be deceiving. Malays constituted 84 per cent of eligible voters despite their population being nowhere near that amount numerically in the Federation. The Chinese for example while comprising about 40 per cent of the population only made up 11 per cent of eligible voters of which only an estimated eighth voted. Only 5 per cent of registered voters were Indian. Nonetheless the Alliance came away with 79.6 per cent of the popular vote.[21]

The British and Malayan leadership resolved early in 1956 at the London conference that 'self-government and independence within the Commonwealth should be proclaimed by August 1957, if possible'.[22] As Stockwell recounts the constitutional and political hurdles to surmount in just over a year from those talks were formidable to forge an independent state.

> The mass of business to complete before that included the following: drawing up the independence constitution and defining citizenship and nationality; negotiating the defence agreement; working out financial provisions; settling the peculiar problems of Penang and Malacca; reaching a decision on the question of appeals to the Judicial Committee of the Privy Council; reaching terms for expatriates, pushing ahead with Malayanisation and establishing the public services commission; selecting Malaya's head of state and designating Malayan governors for Penang and Malacca; submitting

[19] Fernando, *Making* (n 12), at 37.

[20] Joseph M Fernando, *The Alliance Road to Independence* (Kuala Lumpur: University of Malays Press, 2009) at 101.

[21] Francis G Carnell, 'The Malayan Elections' (1955) 28(4) *Pacific Affairs* 316.

[22] *Report by the Federation of Malaya Constitutional Conference,* Cmnd 9174, London: 1956.

> an application for Commonwealth membership; and preparing for independence celebrations. The pace of business was breathtaking.[23]

To this bewildering array of issues and objectives Stockwell adds that with such needs in so short a time there was, inevitably, 'controversy, tension and dispute'.[24] To this context arrived a constitutional commission full of ethnic diversity, legal expertise, jurisdictional breadth, and slight, if any, knowledge of the country they were tasked to prepare a constitution for.

III. CONSTITUTIONAL COMMISSION

Less than a month after his landslide victory, the Tunku wrote to Lennox-Boyd arguing the need for the appointment of a constitutional commission whose overseas members would come 'preferably from the Commonwealth countries'. The Tunku then outlined the some of his reasons.

> In our opinion, only such a Commission would be able to exercise complete impartiality in the inquiry into the Constitution. We feel confident that the Commission composed of members, rich in experience of constitutional and political matters, would be able to bring a fresh approach to the problems of our country. They would be able to produce an unbiased report on the constitutional reforms which will fit this country for full responsible self-government and independence in the shortest time possible.[25]

The Alliance had said as much in their 1955 election manifesto. This would be mean that unlike India Pakistan, Burma, Ceylon and Ghana, all recent cases of States that had gained independence from Britain, the Alliance preferred to wholly place their constitution framing in the Commission composed entirely of those drawn from outside their land. The Rulers did not initially share the Alliance's opinion as they expressed preferment for a Malayan body with possibly a British chair.[26]

The Alliance had already contacted the governments of Australia and Canada about their participation in the Commission; even outlining the possibility of an Australian chair.[27] In Britain various names were mentioned for two members from Britain, one of whom would be the chair. The Colonial Office originally wanted the former Lord Chancellor, Lord Simonds, but eventually the former Solicitor-General for Scotland and Lord Advocate, Lord Reid, was selected. Australian justice Michael Kirby, in an analysis of 50 years of Malaysia's Constitution, said that Reid was 'one of the greatest jurists of the

[23] Stockwell, BDEEP (n 1), s Pt I, p lxxvii.
[24] Ibid.
[25] Ibid, Pt III, p 154.
[26] Fernando (n 12), at 103.
[27] Ibid, at 104.

century in the English-speaking world'.[28] Sir Kenneth Wheare and Nicholas Mansergh, Commonwealth constitutional scholars in Oxford and Cambridge respectively, were considered, but eventually the Tunku's old friend from his days as a student in St Catharine's, Cambridge, Sir Ivor Jennings, was selected in spite of certain Colonial and Commonwealth Relations Office opposition to a man who had long troubled them since his days in Ceylon.[29] Australia drew many different names, but in the end Robert Menzies recommended his former political rival Sir William McKell to the Commission.[30] The former boilermaker and Australian governor-general had served as Labour premier of New South Wales who had trained as a barrister. Canada's nomination fell through due to personal circumstances and was not replaced.[31] India provided Bidhubusan Malik, a former Chief Justice of Allahabad. Pakistan recommended Justice Abdul Hamid who had once served as Secretary to the Law Ministry in West Pakistan, and who knew Jennings from his time advising in Karachi. Upon hearing of Hamid's appointment, Jennings wrote to the Colonial Office official Sir john Martin:

> I am glad that Pakistan has at last appointed Abdul Hamid: indeed, it is not easy to understand why it took so long. He is a cautious and precise lawyer, a little conservative and sometimes very obstinate. He can draft but not write. His great advantage, for present purposes, is that his only grievance against H[er] M[ajesty's] G[overnment] is that it walked out in 1947. Like many of the Pathans, he prefers the Queen-Empress to the Punjabi politicians. I hope India does us equally well, though since Hamid is a very orthodox Muslim it would be best to have a Hindu – two Muslims might frighten the Chinese.[32]

The Terms of Reference for the commission provided key institutional and political parameters that shaped the intentions and realities of Malaysia's constitutional independence.

> To examine the present constitutional arrangements throughout the Federation of Malaya, taking into account the positions and dignities of Her Majesty The Queen and of Their Highnesses the Rulers: and To make recommendations for a federal form of constitution for the whole country as a single, self-governing unit within the Commonwealth based on Parliamentary democracy with a bicameral legislature, which would include provision for: (i) the establishment of a strong central government with the States and Settlements enjoying a measure of autonomy (the question of the residual legislative power to be examined by, and to the subject of recommendations by the Commission) and with machinery for consultation between

[28] Kirby quoted in HP Lee, *Constitutional Conflicts in Contemporary Malaysia* (Kuala Lumpur: Oxford University Press, 1995), at viii.

[29] H Kumarasingham (ed), 'Introduction', *Constitution-Maker – Selected Writings of Sir Ivor Jennings* (Cambridge: Cambridge University Press, 2015).

[30] Australian legal experts that were discussed to be on the Reid Commission included the Solicitor-General Sir Kenneth Bailey, law professor Zelman Cowen, and judges Sir John Latham, Sir Owen Dixon, Sir Alan Taylor, Sir Wilfred Fullagar, Sir Ned Herring, and Sir Reginald Sholl.

[31] Kumarasingham (n 29).

[32] Jennings to Martin, 1 June 1956, CO 1030/130.

the central Government and the States and Settlements on certain financial matters to be specified in the Constitution; (ii) the safeguarding of the position and prestige of Their Highnesses as constitutional Rulers of their respective States; (iii) a constitutional Yang di-Pertuan Besar (Head of State) for the Federation to be chosen from among Their Highnesses the Rulers; (iv) a common nationality for the whole of the Federation; (v) the safeguarding of the special position of the Malays and the legitimate interests of other communities.[33]

As the above indicates and along with the discussions emanating from the London Conference previously, the Commission's objectives were relatively clear. As Harding argues 'Its task was perceived therefore not so much as a political exercise as the translation into legal and practical terms of that which was already politically settled'. As such the members were chosen for their political and constitutional expertise instead of experience of Malaya, which with the exception of Jennings' university work there, was almost entirely absent.[34]

Another side to the unusual nature of having a Commonwealth constitutional commission without local participation is that Malaya did not feel the need to follow the precedent of India or Pakistan a decade earlier and convene a constituent assembly for local representatives to debate, research and prepare a constitution. Andrew Harding believes this constitutional evasion was a mistake.

> Although this enabled independence to be reached probably sooner than otherwise have been possible, and although the Commission consulted widely and sympathetically and the Reid Constitution was accepted by all the relevant institutions in Malaya, the Malaysian Constitution has probably suffered from the fact that it was not drafted by the representatives of the people. It has often been seen or presented as a foreign document rather than an indigenous one. A more democratically chosen body would, undoubtedly, have come up with radically different recommendations.[35]

This perspective opens the charge that the constitution was not, in KC Wheare's famous characterisation autochthonous, 'sprung from the land itself'.[36] However, the involvement, preferment and sanction of the Alliance, drawing as they did from not only a massive legislative dominance, but also representing the three main communities of Malaya with the active distinction that the Commission formally derived its authority from the Malay Rulers (as well as the Queen) did illustrate not insubstantial indigenous influence and conditions in its creation and context. Whatever else, as Sir David Watherspoon, Chief Secretary of Malaya put it, the Commission's actions and plans seemed to 'be singularly fluid'.[37]

[33] The Colonial Office, *Report of the Federation of Malaya Constitutional Commission 1957, no. 330* (Reid Report).

[34] Andrew Harding, *The Constitution of Malaysia – A Contextual Analysis* (Oxford: Hart, 2012) p 31.

[35] Andrew Harding, *Law, Government and the Constitution in Malaysia* (London: Kluwer Law International, 1996), at 29.

[36] KC Wheare, *The Constitutional Structure of the Commonwealth* (London: Oxford University Press, 1960), p 89.

[37] CO 1030/132, 3 August 1956.

IV. COMMISSION DELIBERATIONS

The Commission held 118 meetings and considered 131 memoranda and took evidence from diverse groups and individuals across the breadth of Malaya. Nonetheless the style and saunter of the Commission raised questions. Lord Reid and his wife, 'the eminence grise', as Jennings called her, did not always endear themselves to the Commissioners with Lady Reid's insistence on remorseless protocol and leisurely pace of travel and work. As Jennings remarked 'What the deuce is the good of our sitting in our chalets reading papers, when the Malayans are all around us?'[38] Reid, Hamid and Jennings in particular were the most influential members of the Commission with Jennings alone preparing most of the working papers on subjects such as federal-state relations, elections, the monarchy and economic development.[39] He was also often caustic about the deficiencies of his fellow members – at one point commenting that Reid was 'using the tricks of a small-town lawyer' or that 'There is no doubt that Malik is out of his intellectual environment. He is rather a stupid fellow, third class in ability and fourth in imagination' while McKell was out 'lunching with Australians'.[40] Occasionally, however, Jennings recognised the value of the Commonwealth crew.

> Lord Reid himself has done a lot of work on the drafts and his criticisms are always acute. He is unfortunately prejudiced by an emotional sympathy with the Rulers; but he might not unreasonably complain that McKell and I have an emotional antipathy to the Rulers. I must confess that I have no very high opinion [of] Tunkus, except Abdul Rahman, who is noteworthy for his plain common sense. On these matters McKell supports me and I support him. Nevertheless, Lord Reid has been a most effective critic of my drafts, which have generally been improved by him. His draft Report, too, is very sensible, and I have not found much in it to criticise – though I have not done very much on the Report, because my main job has been to produce the Draft Constitution.[41]

The real tension, however, was between Justice Hamid and the others. Hamid saw himself as a defender of the Malays and protector of their faith. Hamid argued to his fellow Commissioners:

> The new Constitution confers citizenship rights on a very large number of non-Malays and in the course of a very short time non-Malays will outnumber the Malays on the electoral roll and will be in majority in the legislature. The protection which a majority in a legislature enjoys will not be available to them for long.[42]

[38] Kumarasingham (n 29), at 59.

[39] Joseph M Fernando, 'Constitutionalism and the Politics of Constitution-Making in Malaya, 1956–1957 in Kumarasingham (ed), *Constitution-Making in Asia: Decolonisation and State-Building in the Aftermath of the British Empire* (London: Routledge, 2016), at 142–143.

[40] Kumarasingham (n 29), at 69–72.

[41] Ibid, at 70.

[42] B10/6, Sir Ivor Jennings Papers, ICS 125, Institute of Commonwealth Studies, University of London (henceforth Jennings Papers).

He wanted stronger wording of the already agreed provisions for Malays including the provision of 15 years of protection be extended indefinitely and that the Yang di-Pertuan Besar as head of state have discretionary responsibility to safeguard the privileges of Malays, especially if future demographics placed the Malay people as a minority within the legislature. The Commission members mostly recoiled at this proposal since many saw that this could transform a constitutional head of state into something more powerful and one that could act without advice or support from the government.[43] The Commission members were particularly incensed that Hamid was returning to issues that not only had they thought settled, but in many cases, such as Articles 82 and 157, where Hamid had actually drafted the special position of Malays. Jennings eventually had a showdown with Hamid.

> At dinner I told Hamid that I was going to draft a violent attack on him as our draft reply to his Note, and that I was going to do it in defence of the people of Malaya, of the Federation Government, and in particular of my friend Tunku Abdul Rahman…This morning at 9.30 a.m. (2nd Feb) Hamid said that he saw the force of my argument. If anything said by him were to prevent the people of Malaya from living and working together as a band of brothers he would be a very great sinner. He wanted to do everything he could to help, but he feared that it might not work, so he wanted some protection for the Malays, who have been very generous and deserved protection… I then asked Hamid if he was prepared to risk a riot by inserting all this political dynamite merely for a few quotas. Lord Reid broke in and said: "Hamid, do you realise that if this goes in, the blood of thousands of people may be on your hands? Will you not remove all this and merely express your dissent on Quotas on the simple basis that you do not think the protection goes far enough?"[44]

Hamid was able to include his note of dissent, but largely the issue of the Malay special position was settled by the Alliance when they had a chance to respond to the report. The Tunku was able to ensure through his personal sincerity and relationships with the MCA and MIC leadership compromises that upheld the special Malay position with clear undertaking that their languages and schools could continue to operate.

Interestingly the Assistant Secretary to the Commission, K J Henderson, believed that personal dynamics rather than pure intellectual differences had bedevilled the Commission's outcome and unfortunate dissent. It was reported to the Colonial Office that 'The Commission's report reflects the disharmony which prevailed throughout, and which I think we cannot but ascribe to the absence of real leadership. I think we must be profoundly grateful that the report is as good as it is'.[45] The minute continued that it was Henderson's impression that:

> the Commission had finished up completely at loggerheads with each other, largely because of the extraordinary behaviour of the Reids who had set an example of

[43] Ibid, at B 10-7-3, Jennings Papers.
[44] Kumarasingham (n. 29) at 74.
[45] 'Minute by J B Johnston on the behaviour of Lord and Lady Reid while in Malaya and Rome', 18 February 1957, CO 1030/518, in BDEEP (n 1), vol 3, 443 doc.

> self-concern and had been utterly and consistently inconsiderate not only of the staff of the Commission but of the other members. Mr. Henderson was quite certain that Mr. Justice Hamid's insistence at the last minute on producing a minority report was little more than an attempt to assert himself after his opinions and views had been consistently brushed aside by Lord Reid during the Commission's time in Malaya. The rudeness with which the Reids visited almost everyone with whom they came in contact is scarcely credible.[46]

V. RULING AND REIGNING

In many ways, the Reid Commission's report not merely preserved, but enhanced the status and powers of the Malay Rulers. As such the power of people and power of the Rulers at independence arguably muddied a clear sense of who truly safeguarded the representation of Malays. Were the Rulers with their religious and cultural significance the traditional defenders of the Malay people or was it the newly elected government with electoral backing? The Reid Commission and the independence settlement, as Simon C Smith contends, by 'consolidating the position of the Rulers…ensured that the issue of where sovereignty resides has remained contentious' ever since.[47] Some submissions to the Commission were deeply concerned about the potential for Sultanic aggrandisement that might arise with the entrenchment of the Rulers into the Constitution. The Labour Party of Malaya, which contained Chinese and Indians, for example, believed that the Alliance as the 'Party of Privilege' had by 'skilful propaganda' convinced the Malays that their own fortunes were identical to the Malay Royals. Labour therefore believed that in deference to the Malays the Sultans would be able to become constitutional monarchs, but on their death, a 'referendum' would occur among the entire population to gauge whether the monarchy should remain. Even more radically they believed the country should have a head of state elected from the federal and state legislatures called a President (though they did not explicitly state that this would mean a republic). The Alliance idea of election among the Rulers for the top post would be 'retrograde' serving only the interests of the 'ruling clique' and 'not compatible with present democratic trends in South-East Asia.[48]

As discussed earlier, many groups, including in the Colonial Office, felt the British Crown should maintain a presence not only to protect the 'Queen's Chinese' for example, but especially in the Straits Settlements, where no Malay ruler presided. Ideas included having the Queen represented in Penang and Malacca by a Governor or Lieutenant-Governor, who in turn would hold a

[46] Ibid.

[47] Simon C Smith, 'Moving a Little with the Tide': Malay Monarchy and the Development of Modern Malay Nationalism', (2006) 34(1) *Journal of Imperial and Commonwealth History* 133.

[48] B 10-7-3, Jennings Papers.

position similar to Rulers in the states. The Federal monarch, it was suggested, would not only be Yang di-Pertuan Besar, but also Governor-General as in the Dominions. Even the high imperial title of Viceroy was mooted by the Colonial Office.[49] The High Commissioner, Sir Donald MacGillivray, while acknowledging that groups like the Chinese may prefer to keep the British Crown in some capacity in the Straits Settlements, overall felt this idea a dangerous one. Aside from the difficulty of finding a constitutional formula that would could work where the Queen would at one level share sovereignty with the Malay monarch at the centre, but also be subordinate at the state level, there would be major presentational and political concerns that would render the Queen as part of the Constitution of independent Malaya problematic. Malaya would become the first state to begin independence within the Commonwealth and not be a Dominion thus eschewing a constitutional place for the Queen. It was also the first indigenous and independent monarchy within the Commonwealth. MacGillivray believed however nominal the Crown's role would be it would lay the charge that Britain was still engaged in colonialism and that the sovereignty of the state would be in question by being thought of as still being 'governed' by the British. Not only would there be speculation about British 'intrigue and interfering', but those Malays with 'jealous nationalism' would potentially recoil at the thought of a British Governor in Malacca since that area was 'the seat of the original kingdom of the Malays' and centre of symbolically pre-European Malay culture and history.[50] The Reid Commission came to see this view too after meeting groups around the Federation. Indeed they supported this position despite senior officials on the Colonial Office saying explicitly that they 'excluded' the 'possibility of advising the Queen to cede her rights and abandon her sovereignty in the two Settlements' and 'hope[d] the Commission will seriously recommending this'.[51] The Queen of the Straits Settlement in post 1957 Malaya was to be in a position not unlike the residual constitutional extensions she maintained following independence in South Asia.[52]

VI. RIGHTS FOR THE INDIVIDUAL OR RIGHTS OF THE COMMUNITY

Malaya had always been a place where different cultures and communities lived. The Malayan Chinese leader Tan Cheng Lock and others saw themselves just as much 'sons of the land', as the Malays called themselves. For Tan Cheng Lock, for example, who traced his family's roots in Malaya from 1771, he was a 'true

[49] Memorandum, CO 1030/132, 21 Mar 1956.
[50] MacGillivray, CO 1030/132, 19 Jul 1956.
[51] JB Johnston CO 1030/132, 20 Jun 1956.
[52] See H Kumarasingham, 'The 'Tropical Dominions' The Appeal of Dominion Status in the Decolonisation of India, Pakistan and Ceylon (2013) 23 *Transactions of the Royal Historical Society* 223–245.

anak Malaka [son of Malacca]'. This major political figure spoke of Malaya's need to craft a moderate nationalism with democratic and ethnic unity.

> We in Malaya have adopted and want to apply the dynamic conception of nationalism and democracy. Nationalism, if it is to be unifying force, requires the elimination of communalism from political life. Democracy demands for it free operation an understanding of the conflicting claims of race and language and a willingness to compromise on major political issues after full and free discussion.[53]

Tan Cheng Lock grew increasingly frustrated at the Chinese not being viewed as full and valued members of Malayan society. Nonetheless he recognised that only 'when the Chinese acknowledge the same sovereigns as the Malays do, can they demonstrate their wish to the equals of the Malays'.[54] This in some ways was discussed earlier and would see constitutional light. A proposal in 1949 began to emerge based on technical provision in the Nationality Bill of Johore whereby a subject of the ruler automatically became a federal citizen. Could this, it was suggested, see the Chinese included?[55] At the time there were reservations, but the new state would see a new sense of loyalties and responsibilities emerge for all the political actors. The relationship between Malays and non-Malays lay at the heart of the predicament of the Commission. The Malay leadership felt that their historic position warranted constitutional protection and promotion.

UMNO in their memorandum produced the following guidance on the need for special 'privileges' for Malays.

> While we accept that in independent Malaysia, all nationals should be accorded equal rights, privileges and opportunities and there must not be discrimination on grounds of race or creed, we recognize the fact that the Malays are the original sons of the soil and that they have a special position arising from this fact, and also by virtue of the treaties made between the British Government and the various sovereign Malay States. The Constitution should, therefore, provide that the Yang di-Pertuan Besar should have special responsibility of safeguarding the special position of the Malays. In pursuance of this, the Constitution should give him powers to reserve for Malays a reasonable proportion of lands, posts in the public service, permits to engage in business or trade, where such permits are restricted and controlled by law, Government scholarships and such similar privileges accorded by the Government; but in pursuance of his further responsibility of safeguarding legitimate interests of the other communities, the Constitution should also provide that any exercise of such powers should not in any infringe the legitimate interests of the other communities or adversely affect or diminish the rights and opportunities at present enjoyed by them.[56]

Abdul Razak was questioned on the position of Malays in the future Constitution and the UMNO's policy that the language and position of the

[53] Bayly and Harper, *Forgotten Wars* (n 13), at 365.
[54] Ibid, at 503.
[55] Ibid, at 501–502.
[56] CO 889/6.

Malays be protected. Reid was especially interested in how this would affect non-Malays. Razak replied that 'We do not want to reduce the legitimate interests of the others. What we have in mind is not to give Malay special rights by taking away the legitimate rights of other people'. While Reid accepted this argument he pointedly qualified it by stating that 'every additional privilege is, to some extent, prejudicing the others because it is limiting the amount of land or the number of jobs they could get and so on'.[57]

Intentionally or not, mention of a 'large alien population' threatening the 'interests of national unity' was unlikely to find favour with the wider Chinese and Indian community across the Federation.[58] On being pressed on why dual nationality was a problem for UMNO the Tunku stated that:

> For a new nation, it will be rather troublesome later. It is all right for an established or old nation; it can make all sorts of laws. But, at this moment, our main interest is to try and bring these people towards one common nationality and that is the reason why we have provided in our terms of reference that that be a common loyalty, so that loyalty of the people shall not be divided. They shall be Malaya alone.[59]

For these communities not only was recognition of their right to reside important, but also the right to publicly express their language. Language, of course, proved to be a major issue. Proposals to instil qualifications for Malayan nationality based on proficiency of English or Malay, which would in turn determine languages accepted in the legislature, raised concerns particularly among the Chinese community who feared that this would 'mean depriving a large number of these Chinese nationals of the right to stand as candidates.' Lord Reid's response that the 'Chinese are pretty able people' who could learn English or Malay 'pretty easily' did not placate them. Justice Malik, however, with his experience of polyglot and republican India's legislative acknowledgement and parliamentary procedure that recognised other languages beyond English and Hindi, which he argued could work in Malaya was more 'acceptable' as well as understanding of the linguistic pluralism.[60] UMNO appreciated this too and did not press a 'Malay Only' condition as their majority community Sinhalese counterparts were doing in Ceylon with the Sinhala Only Act that same year, which made Sinhalese the sole official language sowing the seeds for the ethnic conflict that would consume Sri Lanka.[61]

Interestingly the Sinhalese and Tamil communities in Malaya submitted memoranda to the Commission, which argued for the special protection of their own languages and community. Perhaps the recent developments that very

[57] Ibid.
[58] Ibid.
[59] Ibid.
[60] Ibid.
[61] Officially the Act was the Official Language Act No 33 of 1956. See Neil DeVotta, *Blowback – Linguistic Nationalism, Institutional Decay, and Ethnic Conflict in Sri Lanka* (Stanford CA, Stanford University Press, 2004).

year in Sri Lanka that removed the Tamil language from being officially recognised throughout the country motivated the Malayan Tamil Pannai to record its service and history of the Tamil people in Malaya and passed on the resolution of its members that:

> The New Constitution of the Federation of Malaya should guarantee the preservation of the respective racial languages and cultures which is a cardinal right.[62]

The reality meant that as the Rulers' counsel, Neil Lawson, put it 'There is only one cake, and they all want a bit of it, and the bigger the slice of cake one has, the less is left to the others'.[63]

VII. A MALAYAN EASTMINSTER

As that early constitutional writer of independent Malaysia, RH Hickling, observed in 1991, the 1957 Constitution:

> sought to reflect the basic principles of a Westminster-style parliamentary democracy. A Western lawyer reading that Constitution would suppose the reflection to be reasonably accurate; but further investigation would reveal that the reality is different from the appearance.[64]

Malaya was set, and determined, to be an *Eastminster*. This entailed forging a state 'that consciously had clear institutional and political resemblances to Britain's system, but with cultural and constitutional deviations from Westminster'.[65] The Malaya Eastminster case would display the all five of the key 'deviations' that an Eastminster regime holds – having an indigenous political elite often educated in Britain; heads of states in the for form of Sultans that routinely interfered in political matters despite being constitutional non-executive heads; the legislature dominated by an overwhelming party in the Alliance with little parliamentary opposition and exclusive control of the executive; critical misgivings and issues regarding the rights of minority groups, especially vis-à-vis the privileged position of Malays; and finally critical continuities from the colonial period in the exercise of executive and emergency powers enabling the Tunku and his UMNO successors near unassailable authority over the state.[66]

Charles Parkinson contends that the 'minimalist bill of rights in the Malayan independence constitution stands as a failed experiment in producing bespoke

[62] B-10-5, Jennings Papers.

[63] CO 889/1.

[64] Hugh Hickling, 'Malaysia' in David Butler and DA Low (eds.), *Sovereigns and Surrogates – Constitutional Heads of State in the Commonwealth* (London: Macmillan, 1991), at 206.

[65] H Kumarasingham, 'Eastminster – Decolonisation and State-Building in British Asia' in H Kumarasingham (ed.), *Constitution-Making in Asia: Decolonisation and State-Building in the Aftermath of the British Empire* (London: Routledge, 2016) 1–35.

[66] Ibid.

bills of rights in countries with minorities problems'.[67] Nonetheless it was a considerable 'innovation' for English trained Commonwealth constitutional authorities like Jennings to recommend a Bill of Rights. Malaya was the first Colonial Office dependency to have a Bill of Rights, even though it was not the idea of the department. In common with many English legal scholars of the time Jennings saw bills of rights as restrictive and unnecessary devices. In 1952 Jennings provided a famous criticism of India's constitutionally mandated fundamental rights.[68] However, by the time Jennings joined the Reid Commission his opinion was changing, especially with the perspective of watching the collapse of his constitutional progeny in Ceylon and Pakistan. The Bill of Rights that became Malaya's own, as Jennings acknowledged, was greatly influenced by Malik's experience in India and Hamid's in Pakistan, and perhaps spoke of Jennings' own patchy record on the device.[69] Jennings who had been constitutional adviser to the first Prime Minister of Ceylon and who effectively single-handedly framed that Constitution, was destined to witness, only a few years later, the failure of his broad non-discrimination clause in preventing the enactment of the Sinhala Only Act 1956, which made Sinhalese the sole official language and consequently catalysed ethnic riots.[70]

In Pakistan where Jennings had been constitutional adviser to the Constituent Assembly and later to the Governor-General in the mid 1950s, arguably contributed to the ease with which rights and democracy could be suspended.[71] These experiences contributed to Jennings' different approach in Malaya where he constructively framed a Bill of Rights that openly drew on India's. Just prior to his death in 1965 he noted that his 1952 'criticisms were misconceived' towards India's Bill of Rights.[72] While the Malayan Bill of Rights was not as strong as scholars such as Parkinson and Harding would understandably prefer it to be, it was nevertheless an improvement on Jennings' previous attitude and approach. It was also an advance on contemporary legal mechanisms in practice across the British Empire and Commonwealth. This included open

[67] Charles OH Parkinson, *Bills of Rights and Decolonization – The Emergence of Domestic Human Rights Instruments in Britain's Overseas Territories* (Oxford: Oxford University Press, 2007) at 201.

[68] See Sir Ivor Jennings, *Some Characteristics of the Indian Constitution – Being Lectures given in the University of Madras during March 1952 under the Sir Alladi Krishnaswami Aiyer Shashitaahdapoothi Endowment* (Madras: Oxford University Press, 1953).

[69] B-10-7-3, Jennings Papers.

[70] See H Kumarasingham, *A Political Legacy of the British Empire – Power and the Parliamentary System in Post-Colonial India and Sri Lanka* (London: IB Tauris, 2013) 171–201; and for Jennings' role in Ceylon see H Kumarasingham, *The Road to Temple Trees – Sir Ivor Jennings and the Constitutional Development of Ceylon: Selected Writings* (Colombo: CPA, 2015).

[71] H Kumarasingham, 'A Transnational Actor on a Dramatic Stage – Sir Ivor Jennings and the Manipulation of Westminster Style Democracy: The Case of Pakistan' (2017) 2 *UC Irvine Journal of International, Transnational and Comparative Law* 33–56.

[72] Kumarasingham (n 29), at 280–281.

cross-Commonwealth borrowing from India, Pakistan, Ceylon, Burma, Ghana, South Africa, Newfoundland, Canada, Australia, New Zealand and Ireland.[73]

As Fernando argues, the publication of the Reid Commission's report on 20 February 1957 was greeted with attention surrounding the communal issues. Whereas, like many such experiences across the decolonising world, there 'was hardly any public discussion of the structure and function of government, the powers of the executive, the independence of the judiciary the "limited" functions of the Conference of Rulers or the merits or demerits of the Federal concept outlined in the Reid Report'.[74] The special status of Malays within the federation and Constitution was the issue that generated the most notice. For many Malays the Constitution needed to protect and promote their position and religion. While for the non-Malays like the Chinese and Indian communities there was critical concern that their language and communities would be reduced to a second-class rank. The predicament, therefore, facing the Reid Commissioners was to balance, what for most of them was the uncomfortable objective of providing special privileges for Malays, with the need to still create a democracy that did not diminish the rights of non-Malays. Malaya's constitutional history showed that at times, its constitutional development had been stunted under the British because of fears of excessive centralisation at the cost of the state interests and potential increased power for non-Malays.[75]

Responsible government par excellence was contained within the Alliance memorandum and its presentation to the Commission.[76] The preference for the flexibility an Eastminster provided was seen as a virtue. During the Alliance's meeting in late 1956 with the Commission, the MCA representative Ng Ek Teong ended the meeting by stating he 'wished the new Constitution be flexible as possible to encourage the growth of conventions'.[77] In a characteristic utterance Lord Reid on hearing a proposal pronounced: 'I would like to know how this would work because one does not want to recommend anything unless it can be worked'.[78]

The left-leaning and multi-cultural Labour Party in its memorandum to the Commission advocated a traditional Westminster state arguing for an independent judiciary and civil service, bicameral legislature, popularly elected lower house and a 'strong central government'. It even went so far as to recommend not only for Malaya the classic Westminster concept of parliamentary supremacy, but also wished to avoid, like the UK, the rigidities of a written constitution seen

[73] H Kumarasingham, 'Eastminster – Decolonisation and State-Building in British Asia', p 10.

[74] Fernando (n 12), at 144.

[75] LA Sheridan, *Malaya and Singapore, The Borneo Territories – The Development of their Laws and Constitutions*, London: Stevens and Sons, 1961, pp 11–13.

[76] CO 889/2.

[77] CO 889/1.

[78] CO 889/6.

nowhere else in the world bar New Zealand and Israel. Their recommendation on this issue bears repeating to illustrate the concerns and puzzles constitutional founding can evoke for those beyond the political and effective majority and, perhaps, lay out why constitutions are often discarded or replaced.

> The Labour Party does not believe that a written Constitution for Malaya at this juncture can be anything but a temporary measure. While recognizing that a Federal form of Government has the sanction and approval of those allied with State interests and of those who are at the moment in political ascendency, the Labour Party is of the opinion that a written Constitution must, to be effective in the flux of Malayan history, possess the elasticity and flexibility to meet the demands of economic developments, political progress and social change. A written Constitution must therefore be an instrument and a means for the building-up of a peaceful, progressive and democratic nation. To this end, the Labour Party cannot too strongly emphasise the need to avoid the rigidity that is characteristic of all written constitutions. The creators of a written constitution nearly always tend to obstruct, hamper, and restrict the aspirations of future generations. The Labour Party therefore submits that in its present stage of development, Malaya should not be unduly subject to such constitutional fetters as a written Constitution must necessarily create.[79]

The Reid Commission presented its report on 20 February 1957. The Colonial Office tried to see the report in advance, but the Commissioners insisted on their independence, which played to their reason of deliberating in, and then printing their report from Rome. The Commission also found themselves being criticised by the Colonial Office in their official response. Jennings was not impressed:

> The statement in paragraph 3 (of the White Paper) was at best maladroit, and in paragraph 53 the writer tries to teach his grandmother to suck eggs. I have drafted too many constitutional documents to care two hoots; but it is most unfortunate that such statements should be made by Her Majesty's Government about very distinguished lawyers in other parts of the Commonwealth.[80]

Lord Reid insisted to the Press that the Commission was not the creature of His Majesty's government, but jointly responsible to the Queen and Rulers:

> We have never consulted Whitehall. One reason that we are to meet in Rome to draft our report is to avoid the impression that we would consult the British government. It will be our report and nobody else's.[81]

The tripartite negotiations followed where representatives of the Alliance, the Rulers, and the High Commissioner met 23 times between 22 February and 27 April 1957. Once again it was the special position of the Malays and the prerogatives of the Rulers, which caused the most discussion. However, largely, while there was strengthening of Malay privileges and some attempts from

[79] B-10-5, Jennings Papers.
[80] Jennings to Reid, 6 July 1957 in Fernando (n 12), at 180.
[81] *Straits Times*, 26 Oct 1956 in Fernando, ibid, at 115.

members within the MCA and MIC to derail the process as well as elements of disapproval of the communal bargain in Britain, the Malayan Independence Bill went forward in the British Houses of Parliament unchanged and ready for the anointed day of 31 August 1957.[82]

VIII. CONCLUSION

The Colonial Secretary, Alan Lennox-Boyd, assured Reid, who was worried that people might blame him or the Commission for any shortcomings of the last version of the Constitution after being amended by the Alliance:

> If therefore anyone should feel that the final form of the Constitution falls short of perfection, responsibility for that lies not at the door of the legal draughtsmen but with the Malayans who, for political reasons, felt that they had to force the pace. But you will know as well as I do that I could not say that in public.[83]

John Darwin argues that independence in 1957 caused 'barely a ripple' since through the Anglo-Malayan Defence Agreement of the same year the new government could call upon British military assistance against 'internal subversion and external attack'. In addition, Malaya remained in the Sterling Area and agreed to maintain its commodities earnings in London's dollar pool.[84] Colonial rule continued in North Borneo and Sarawak, while Singapore remained a critical defence base for British interests. It was not so much the end of empire as a 'new phase of cooperation'.[85] Legally, the Privy Council remained a fixture in the Malaysian judicial hierarchy in part until 1985 despite, uniquely, not having the Queen as head of state. Harding believes that too much power was placed with the Executive and there were not enough innovations to deal with Malaya's conditions and needs:

> Jurisprudentially, this all smacks of a rather too executive-minded approach, arguable and no doubt fashionable at a time when communist insurgency was an ever-present threat (British legal advisers agreed with the Alliance view); but in the light of international opinion at the time and subsequent developments in Malaysia and elsewhere in the Commonwealth, outmoded, discredited and unsatisfactory as a blueprint for government in the advanced and sophisticated society Malaysia was to become.[86]

Whatever else, the demands on those tasked with the constitutional founding of the Malays were tremendous. The Tunku was critical to this founding and

[82] See Fernando, ibid, at 143–188.

[83] Secretary of State to Lord Reid, 26 Sep 1957 in Fernando, ibid, at 182.

[84] John Darwin, 'British Decolonization since 1945: A Pattern or a Puzzle?' in RF Holland and G. Rizvi (eds.), *Perspectives on Imperialism and Decolonization – Essays in Honour of A.F. Madden*, London: Frank Cass, 1984, p 201.

[85] Ibid.

[86] Harding (n 35), at 38.

his faith in the British system. For Tunku Abdul Rahman the granting of an honorary doctorate in Law from Cambridge in 1960 despite 'scraping through' with his degree as a young student many years before, was a major honour for this man who nostalgically appreciated his time in Cambridge and his learning of English principles of law.[87] Far from being just nostalgia this had a critical impact on Malaysia. HP Lee reflecting on 50 years of independence said that for Malaysia it was a 'blessing' to have 'a leader who obtained his legal education in the homeland of the common law, who imbibed notions of the rule of law, the independence of the judiciary and the separation of powers'.[88] Lee argues that in many ways:

> The lowering of the Union Jack and the raising of the flag of the new Federation 50 years ago on 31 August 1957 symbolised a change of constitutional order but not a change of that underpinning.[89]

Turning to its founding, Jennings observed in hindsight that the work of this unique Commission showed '...that, in the opinion of five lawyers trained in five different environments, it was possible to produce an agreed solution of the constitutional problems of a complex country... Our scheme, being quite original, is constitutionally very interesting, and the only expert who has so far commented on it in my presence went so far as to call it "ingenious"'.[90] This is debatable, but at the least it provided an extraordinarily influential Commission that framed the constitutional founding of the country, despite changes that the Alliance and later governments would make. As an editorial in the *Manchester Guardian* described after as *Merdeka* approached:

> Whatever the criticisms which will be made in Malaya during the next few days, the Constitution looks, in final shape, an ingenious document for bringing democracy to a plural society. The three main communities can at least see the possibilities of a tolerable life under the system now offered to them.[91]

As with all Constitutions, the true test would be if it worked in practice.

[87] Chandran Jeshurun, 'Tunku Abdul Rahman Putra and His Links with the Universities of Cambridge and Malaya, 1960–1962' (2009) 82(1) *Journal of the Malaysian Branch of the Royal Asiatic Society* 1–15.

[88] HP Lee, 'The Malaysian Constitution after 50 Years – Retrospective, Prospective and Comparative Perspectives' (2008) 9(2) *Australian Journal of Asian Law* 301.

[89] Ibid.

[90] B-10-7-3, Jennings Papers.

[91] *Manchester Guardian*, 4 Jul 1957.

7

Foundational Moments: The 'Singapore Constitution'

KEVIN YL TAN

INTRODUCTION

BECAUSE OF THE way in which Singapore lurched and spluttered its way to independence between 1955 and 1965, it is impossible to identify a single document as its foundational constitution. Indeed, when Singapore finally became an independent unitary State on 9 August 1965, it had no real constitution to call its own. It had a State Constitution from 1963, but that Constitution contained no provisions dealing with matters which had been covered in the Federal Constitution of 1963, including the judiciary and fundamental rights and liberties. A new Constitution was promised and there was talk about a drafting commission being established but in the end, Parliament simply augmented the state Constitution with provisions from the Malaysian Constitution. This chapter describes the tentative moves made by the Singapore State towards the forging of its post-independence Constitution.

I. A MESSY 'FOUNDING' CONSTITUTION

Singapore's independence as a unitary State in 1965 was effected through a series of legal documents – the Constitution and Malaysia (Singapore Amendment) Act;[1] and the Independence of Singapore Agreement[2] – but no new Constitution was drafted. The first document transferred all legislative and executive powers previously possessed by the Federal government to the new government of Singapore. Under section 4 of this Act, the Singapore government retained its executive authority and legislative powers to make laws while the Parliament of Malaysia relinquished all powers to make laws for Singapore under section 5.

[1] Act No 53 of 1965 (Malaysia).
[2] GN No 1824 of 9 August 1965.

Section 6 transferred the sovereignty and jurisdiction of the Yang di-Pertuan Agong (King of Malaysia) over the island and vested them in the Yang di-Pertuan Negara (Singapore's head of state). Finally, section 7 provided that all laws in force in Singapore immediately before Singapore Day 'shall continue to have effect according to their tenor … subject however to amendment or repeal by the Legislature of Singapore.'

The Parliament of Singapore did not convene until 22 December 1965 to put things in order. In the meantime, a brand new Constitution was promised. Immediately after independence from Malaysia, Prime Minister Lee Kuan Yew promised Singaporeans that a new Constitution would be drafted. He announced that though the Constitution would not 'be radically changed', the Singapore government's ideal of a multi-racial society would be perpetuated in the new document. Lee further stated that Chief Justice Wee Chong Jin would leave for Sydney to invite 'eminent international jurists and chief justices to help draw up this constitution.'[3] Wee was tasked with gathering a group of Commonwealth justices and local legal luminaries to 'recommend to the Government a constitution which would ensure that democratic practices prevail, that everybody has got his rights guaranteed.' Lee further stated that he hoped to secure the assistance of Indian Chief Justice PB Gajendragadkar, and Australian Chief Justice Garfield Barwick to help.[4] By early September 1965, Law Minister EW Barker stated that he had secured promises from Australia and New Zealand to help Singapore in drafting the new Constitution[5] while Chief Justice Wee Chong Jin, back from the Commonwealth Law Conference in Sydney, indicated that the Australian, New Zealand and Indian Chief Justices were willing to help out in the Constitution's drafting.[6] A Commission of legal experts, assisted by foreign specialists was to be convened to draft this new Constitution.[7] Barker told the press that the ideas for the new Constitution had yet to be crystallised and that it would take a few months before the draft was ready. Nonetheless, it would include clauses to entrench minority rights and democracy:

> As you know, the PAP is a multi-racial party and Singapore is a multi-racial city. We want every citizen to know that he has a place in the sun at least in Singapore. We want to write in a clause in the Constitution for the protection of the minorities. One man, one vote. We will have another entrenched clause to safeguard democracy. We don't want any totalitarian regime to take over.[8]

However, there came no further news of this Commission and on 3 October 1965, Barker – speaking to the Law Society of the University of Singapore – announced that the State Advocate-General, Ahmad Ibrahim 'had written

[3] Jackie Sam, 'Safeguards for the minorities' *Straits Times* 13 Aug 1965, at 1.
[4] Ibid.
[5] 'Australian, NZ, India to help Singapore' *Straits Times* 8 Sep 1965, at 7.
[6] See 'Three CJs may aid drafting' *Straits Times* 5 Sep 1965, at 1.
[7] 'A team of experts to draft S'pore Charter' *Straits Times*, 11 Sep 1965, at 20.
[8] Ibid.

an entirely new constitution'. Strangely enough the State Advocate General himself issued a statement on 25 November 1965 that the government did 'not intend to introduce any Bill setting out a new Constitution for Singapore'[9] at the next parliamentary sitting. Instead, a constitutional commission to be established under the chairmanship of the Chief Justice would be established to 'draw up constitutional safeguards for minorities'. Only 'after the commission's recommendations have been decided upon by Parliament' will 'a comprehensive Bill' be introduced. Ahmad stated:

> I have the authority of the Government to state that the Government does not intend to introduce any Bill setting out a new constitution for Singapore in the coming sitting of Parliament. What will be introduced is a Bill to complete the formal assumption of sovereignty by the Government and the legislature of Singapore and to allocate the powers which were exercised by the Malaysian Yang di-Pertuan Agong, the Malaysian Prime Minister, Ministers and other authorities to the their counterparts in Singapore. But what is exercising the minds of the Minister for Law and my chambers is a draft of the provisions to ensure that minority rights shall always be respected and that nobody shall be penalised or victimised by reason of race, language or religion.[10]

The Constitution which Singapore ended up with is a composite document, containing most of the State of Singapore Constitution of 1963, the Republic of Singapore Independence Act ('RSIA', an ordinary Act of Parliament),[11] amendments made by the Constitution (Amendment) Act 1965,[12] and provisions of the Federation of Malaysia Constitution 'imported' by the RSIA. It was, as former Chief Minister David Marshall opined, the 'untidiest and most confusing constitution that any country has started life with'.[13]

A brief word about these various enactments. The Constitution of Singapore Amendment Act[14] was passed by Parliament on the 22 December 1965, but made retrospective to 9 August 1965. This Act amended the State of Singapore Constitution 1963 and changed the procedure required for constitutional amendment. The two-thirds majority was abolished and only a simple majority was required for an amendment to the Constitution. In addition, this Act also changed the relevant nomenclatures to bring the Constitution in line with Singapore's independence status. The RSIA, which was passed immediately after the Constitution Amendment Act, was also passed retrospectively and provided, inter alia, that certain provisions of the Malaysian Federal Constitution were to be made applicable to Singapore. The RSIA also vested the powers relinquished by the Constitution and Malaysia Singapore Amendment Act in the executive and

[9] 'Singapore's Constitution: A full debate' *Straits Times*, 25 Nov 1965, at 10.
[10] Ibid.
[11] Act 9 of 1965.
[12] Act 8 of 1965.
[13] 'Singapore's Untidy Constitution' *Straits Times* 21 Dec 1965.
[14] Act No 8 of 1965.

legislative branch of government.[15] A unique provision in the RSIA is contained in section 13 which empowers the President to make 'such modifications in any written law as appear to him to be necessary or expedient in any written law as appear to him to be necessary consequence of the enactment of this Act and in consequence of the independence of Singapore upon separation from Malaysia.' This power was to last for three years after the RSIA came into operation. This untidy state of affairs lasted until 1979 when a constitutional amendment was passed authorising the Attorney-General to print and publish a consolidated *Reprint* of the Constitution of Singapore amalgamating such 'provisions of the Constitution of Malaysia as are applicable to Singapore, into a single composite document.' But as to how all that happened, we need to go back to the beginning – to 1945, when World War II ended – to understand the reasons why Singapore's constitutional development occurred as it did.

II. MAKING THE STATE OF SINGAPORE CONSTITUTION

A. Constitutional and Political Developments 1946–1955

Singapore had been a British colony since 1824 and was, from 1824 to 1946 governed as part of the Straits Settlements (which also included Penang and Malacca). During World War II, the British Colonial Office and War Office were already making plans to integrate Penang and Malacca into the soon-to-be-formed Malayan Union – that included the Federated and the Unfederated Malay States. The British decided that Singapore would be excluded from the Malayan Union because its population was overwhelmingly Chinese and thus feared that this could jeopardise its negotiations with the Malay Sultans. The Straits Settlements was dissolved in 1946 and Penang and Malacca joined the states of Perak, Pahang, Selangor and Negeri Sembilan (the former Federated Malay States); Perlis, Kedah, Kelantan, Terengganu and Johore (the former Unfederated Malay States) to form the Malayan Union. Singapore was constituted as a separate colony with the view that at some time in the future, it would be reintegrated into Malaya. As history has shown, this eventually happened in 1963, but the union was short-lived.

A new colonial Constitution was promulgated by the Singapore Order-in-Council 1946.[16] It preserved the Governor's veto and reserved powers over legislation and set up an advisory Executive Council of six officials and four nominated unofficials. The Legislative Council, consisting of four ex-officio

[15] For a controversial discussion of the significance of the Constitution (Amendment) Act and the RSIA, see AJ Harding, 'Parliament and the Grundnorm in Singapore', (1983) 25 *Malaya Law Review* 351.

[16] Order-in-Council dated 27 Mar 1946, Statutory Rules and Orders 1946, No 462.

members, seven officials and at least two, but not more than four nominated Unofficials, and nine elected members was therefore without an unofficial majority. This epitomised the Colonial Office's desire for a gradual transition to self-government and the new Constitution was heavily criticised as failing to permit local people to play an effective role in public affairs.[17]

In order to work out the number of nominated and elected unofficials and the manner in which the seats will be filled, a Reconstitution Committee comprising official and local representatives was convened by Governor Sir Franklin Gimson in 1946. The Committee presented its report[18] that year and all but two of their recommendations were accepted. The government increased the number of nominated Unofficials from two to four to safeguard minority interests. Of the nine elected seats, three were allotted to the Singapore Chamber of Commerce, the Chinese Chamber of Commerce and the Indian Chamber of Commerce which represented European, Chinese and Indian economic interests respectively. The other six seats would be filled by democratic elections based on universal suffrage. The revamped Legislative Council comprised:

(a) four ex-officio members;
(b) five Officials;
(c) four nominated Unofficials;
(d) three Chamber of Commerce representatives; and
(e) six popularly elected members.

These reforms were significant for three reasons. First, there was an unofficial majority of between 13 and 9 members in the Council; second, democratic elections were being introduced for the first time;[19] and third, the idea of reserved seats for minority representation was introduced formally for the first time. The new Constitution came into effect on the 1 March 1948[20] and elections were held for the first time on the 20 March 1948.[21]

Originally, the Colonial Office had visualised a Legislative Council in which representation would be based on race. However, this was vehemently opposed by the Malayan Democratic Union (MDU), the only organised political group at the time and this was unanimously supported by the Advisory Council which insisted that elections be based along territorial lines.[22] Most of the seats in the first election were won by the Progressive Party which dominated Singapore politics till the late 1950s. The judicial structure and hierarchy of courts was not

[17] See Yeo Kim Wah, *Political Development in Singapore, 1945–1955* (Singapore: Singapore University Press, 1973) at 55 [hereinafter 'Yeo'].

[18] See 'Report of the Committee for the Reconstitution of the Singapore Legislative Council', as reproduced in App A of *Annual Report on Singapore for 1st April to 31st December 1946*, pp 17–25.

[19] Yeo, n 17 above, at 55–56.

[20] Singapore Colony Order in Council, 1946, SR & O 1946, I, p 1539.

[21] See Order-in-Council dated 24 Feb 1948, Statutory Instruments, 1948, No 341.

[22] CM Turnbull, *A History of Singapore, 1819–1988*, 2 ed (Singapore: Oxford University Press, 1989) at 235 [hereinafter 'Turnbull'].

changed by the new Constitution and the Chief Justice and the Judges of the Supreme Court of Singapore were 'appointed by His Majesty by Letters Patent, or by the Governor by Letters Patent under the Public Seal in accordance with such instructions as he may receive from His Majesty through a Secretary of State.'[23]

Singapore's constitutional development between 1946 and 1953 was slow and leisurely, with the government being pre-occupied with communist front activities which held up constitutional change both in Singapore and the Federation.[24] In 1950, the British government acceded to the Progressive Party's demand for three additional elected seats in the Legislative Council and this was effected by an Order-in-Council dated 21 of December 1950.[25] This change was made and it was implemented in early April 1951 in time for the triennial elections. This amendment left the basic constitutional structure intact, with the 13 ex-officio and nominated members retaining their majority. In the second general election of 22 March 1951, 22 candidates contested the nine available seats with the Progressive Party winning six of them. Only 52 per cent of the population voted.

In 1953, the Progressive Party set a 10-year target date for achieving self-government, to be followed by full independence through merger with the Federation. In the meantime, it advocated introducing a predominantly elected Legislative Council, with a Member system comparable to that in the Federation. This proposal was greeted enthusiastically by the Colonial authorities since they regarded the Progressives as a reliable and responsible group who could be counted on to ensure the smooth and peaceful transfer of power. All through this period, the general public was apathetic towards the new political situation and this was regarded by the British as the major impediment to the development of a democratic government in Singapore.[26] Changes in the constitutional system was necessary to increase widespread participation in central and local government and to this end, a Constitutional Commission headed by Sir George Rendel was set up in 1953. The Commission was charged with 'a comprehensive review of the constitution of the Colony of Singapore, including the relationship between the Government and the City Council, and to make such recommendations for changes as are deemed desirable at the present time.'[27]

The Rendel Commission issued its report in February 1954 and most of its recommendations were accepted by the government.[28] There would be an automatic system of voter registration since only about 25 per cent of the citizens had taken the initiative to register themselves as voters; the Legislative

[23] See Art 14.

[24] Yeo, n 17 above, at 56.

[25] Statutory Instruments, 1950, No 2099.

[26] Turnbull, n 22 above, at 241.

[27] See letter from Governor Sir John Nicoll to Sir George Rendel, as reproduced in the Annex to Report of the Constitutional Commission, Singapore, 1954.

[28] *Singapore Constitutional Commission* (Singapore: Government Printing Office, 1954).

Council would be transformed into a mainly elected Assembly of 32 Members comprising:

(a) 25 Elected Unofficial Members;
(b) 3 Ex-Officio Official Members holding Ministerial posts;[29] and
(c) 4 Nominated Unofficial Members.

The Commission also recommended the creation of a Council of Ministers consisting of three ex-officio Official Members and six Elected Members appointed by the Governor on the recommendation of the 'Leader of the House', who would be the leader of the largest Party in the Assembly or of a coalition of Parties assured of majority support. English was to be retained as the sole official language of the Legislative Assembly and the Commission considered that the functions of local and central government should be carried out by separate bodies. Although outside the scope of their terms of the reference, the Commission saw fit to comment on the relations between Singapore and the Federation of Malaya feeling that 'a closer association of the two territories will … be necessary in order to justify the removal of … reserved and veto powers'[30]. The Commission also recommended the removal of the Chamber of Commerce representation.

The above recommendations were, as a whole implemented by the Singapore Colony Order-in-Council of 1955.[31] Despite criticisms against the new Constitution for not being sufficiently progressive – colloquially referred to as the 'Rendel Constitution' – it proved to be just the catalyst Singapore politics needed. The run-up to the 1955 elections marked a significant departure from the past. There emerged numerous nationalist leaders and issues which affected the masses were finally being debated in public. A total of 79 candidates contested the 25 seats and the Labour Front, led by David Marshall won ten seats; the Progressives, four seats; the UMNO-MCA Alliance, three seats; the People's Action Party three seats and the Democratic Party, two seats.

While the Labour Front won the most seats, it did not have a sufficient majority to form the government. Governor Sir John Nicol invited Marshall to form the government and this he did by forming a coalition with the UMNO-MCA Alliance. He thus became Singapore's first Chief Minister. One problem with the Rendel Constitution was that the powers of the ministers, especially those of the Chief Minister, were not well-defined. Furthermore, the retention of the portfolios of Finance, Administration and Internal Security and Law in the hands of the official ministers proved to be a major impediment to the development of self-government in Singapore.

[29] These are the Secretary of Finance, the Secretary of Administration and Internal Security, and the Attorney-General.

[30] Para 141 of the Report.

[31] Statutory Instruments, 1955, No 187.

Marshall was determined to wield real power and dramatise the change from a colonial to an elected government. He saw his task as one of co-ordinating policy in particular and governing the country in general and he saw himself as a Prime Minister. Governor Nicoll was of a diametrically opposite view, expecting Marshall to concentrate on the Ministry of Commerce and Industry and to initiate legislation in the assembly. The crucial decisions and policies should, thought Nicoll, reside in the Governor and the Official ministers.[32]

In July 1955, Marshall – under pressure from his party members to appoint more ministers – demanded the appointment of four Assistant Ministers. This demand was refused by Sir Robert Black, the new Governor who succeeded Sir John Nicoll and Marshall immediately threatened to resign unless Singapore was given immediate self-government. The issue, Marshall claimed, was 'whether the Governor governs or we govern'. It is important to note that these were turbulent times, with the communist-infiltrated Opposition urging extremist views and political back-stabbing and rivalry was white hot in its intensity. The Colonial Office was appalled by Marshall's demands but feared that his resignation would pave the way for more radical and irresponsible government. The Governor was therefore instructed to act on the Chief Minister's advice and agreed to hold constitutional talks after the assembly had been in existence for one year, instead of allowing it to run its full term.[33]

B. Constitutional Talks 1956

Speaking at the Legislative Assembly on 4 April 1956, Marshall explained that the purpose of the constitutional talks was to 'seek full legislative autonomy and equality in status with other independent members of the Commonwealth'.[34] The agenda for the April meeting would include the following items:[35]

(a) A definition of 'internal self-government';
(b) A date for the introduction of internal self-government;
(c) Structure of the Legislative Assembly;
(d) Future of the public service;
(e) External relations and external defence; and
(f) Any Other Business.

Over the next few months, Marshall expanded this objective to seeking full independence from Britain. This changing position was no doubt encouraged by his constitutional advisors and fuelled by his own brinksmanship.

[32] Yeo, n 17 above, at 62.
[33] Turnbull, n 22 above, at 262.
[34] Chief Minister David Marshall, 'Constitutional Talks in London' *Singapore Legislative Assembly, Official Debates*, vol 1, 4 Apr 1956, col 1785.
[35] See Chief Minister's Statement on 'London Talks and Commonwealth Visit', *Singapore Legislative Assembly Debates*, 8 Feb 1956, at cols 1439–1440.

Three constitutional advisors had been engaged to help the Singapore delegation with their negotiations. The first was Walter Raeburn QC, who had been Marshall's pupil master in London; the second was Stanley Alexander de Smith, then Reader of Public Law at the London School of Economics, and Sir Ivor Jennings, then Master of Trinity College, University of Cambridge. The three of them met in London on 25 March 1956 to discuss the line to be taken and Jennings recorded that both Raeburn and de Smith 'seemed to agree' with his line, which was that they 'should ask for independence subject to emergency powers' to be exercised by the Commissioner-General or Commander-in-Chief under the control of the British government.[36] If they failed with this plan, the fall-back plan was to seek 'independence with a cession of foreign affairs + defence'.[37] Jennings arrived in Singapore on 28 March 1956 and quickly got down to work. By the next day, he had completed a draft agreement and memorandum as well as a note on tactics and submitted them to Marshall.[38] Marshall made some amendments which were incorporated but more significantly, Hamid Jumat the Malay Minister for Local Government, Lands and Housing and leader of the UMNO-MCA Alliance approached Jennings asking if he could 'write in some provision for raising the standard of the Malay minority'. Jennings agreed.[39] This was most probably Article 8(8) of the 'Heads of Agreement between the government of the UK and the government of Singapore, reproduced in Appendix B to *The Constitutional Conference, London*. Article 8(8) reads:

> 8(8)— That it shall be the duty of the Government of Singapore at all times to protect the political, economic, social and cultural interests of Malays, Eurasians, and other minorities domiciled in Singapore. It should also be the deliberate and conscious policy of the Government of Singapore at all times to recognize the special position of the Malays, who are the indigenous people of the Island and are most in need of assistance, and, within the framework of the general good of Singapore, to foster and promote their political, economic, social and cultural interests, and the Malay language.

It is significant that this clause was inserted as part of the Heads of Agreement as it would form the basis for the present Article 152.

The All-Party's main concerns for the talks was to secure as much autonomy as possible without surrendering control over internal security. While these matters were certainly of great importance and urgency at the time, we will not be examining them in detail since they are largely transitory provisions and have no place in Singapore's independence Constitution. Between 23 April and 15 May 1956, the Constitutional Mission, comprising 13 Assemblymen representing all the parties in the Assembly held discussions in London with officials of

[36] H Kumarasingham (ed), *Constitution-Maker: Selected Writings of Sir Ivor Jennings* (London: Cambridge University Press for the Royal Historical Society, 2014) at 173–174 [hereinafter 'Jennings'].

[37] Ibid, at 174.

[38] Ibid, at 175. The Memorandum appears as App 4 of the draft agreement.

[39] Ibid, at 176.

the Colonial Office.[40] The demand for independence, or 'Merdeka' was quickly dropped as it was clear that the Colonial Office, and in particular, the Secretary of State for the Colonies, Sir Alan Lennox-Boyd, was against independence.[41]

At the Conference, Marshall demanded full internal self-government by 1 April 1957, leaving foreign policy and external defence in British hands but allowing Singapore a veto on defence and rights of consultation on foreign affairs. This proposal was rejected although the British government was prepared to grant a great deal. There would be a fully-elected assembly and the ex-officio members would be removed. Under the terms, Singapore would also have its own special citizenship and complete control over trade and commerce. The only major demand of the Colonial Office was that in the proposed Defence Council, on which Britain and Singapore should have equal representation, the casting vote should be in the hands of the British High Commissioner who would only use it in an emergency. Marshall refused to concede on this point, proposing instead that the casting vote be placed in the hands of a representative of the government of the soon-to-be independent Federation of Malaysia. At this point, the talks broke down.[42] Marshall's 'independence or resign' gambit had come home to roost and he had to resign upon his return to Singapore, in June 1956.[43] Lim Yew Hock, hitherto Minister for Labour and Welfare, succeeded Marshall as Chief Minister.

C. Constitutional Talks 1957 and Self-Government

Lim knew that unless he could control the constant rioting and the strikes in Singapore, his hopes of persuading the British to give Singapore self-government were illusory. As John Drysdale observed:

> Clearly, the Secretary of State for the Colonies must have impressed upon Lim Yew Hock during his visit to London [in December 1956] that, if he (Lennox-Boyd) were to persuade his ministerial colleagues in the cabinet that Singapore should be given internal self-government, it was axiomatic that the internal security situation, on which the previous Constitutional Conference foundered, should be seen to be under control. In other words, the government had to govern with the wide powers at its disposal … This is precisely what Lim Yew Hock did, receiving the support of all the parties, other than the People's Action Party.[44]

[40] See *The Constitutional Conference, London*, 1956, Cmnd 9777 at 9. The members were: David Marshall, Lim Yew Hock, Abdul Hamid bin Haji Jumat, AJ Braga, JM Jumabhoy, Seah Peng Chuan, Wong Foo Nam, Lim Cher Kheng, Lim Choon Mong, Lim Koon Teck, William Tan, Lee Kuan Yew, and Lim Chin Siong.

[41] Jennings, n 36 above, at 179.

[42] See statement of Sir Alan Lennox-Boyd, Secretary of State for the Colonies, *Hansard*, Vol 552 no 155, 15 May 1956, cols 2017–2020.

[43] Turnbull, n 22 above, at 263.

[44] John Drysdale, *Singapore: Struggle of Success* (Singapore: Times Books International, 1984) at 152 [hereinafter 'Drysdale'].

Lim, who was Marshall's deputy in the LF was a very different character from the former Chief Minister. Milne and Mauzy described Lim as 'a tough, action-oriented, hard-drinking, white-collar trade unionist, allegedly with some triad associations; bold and resolute but also relaxed and pragmatic' who 'could communicate with most local people in their native language.'[45] Unlike Marshall before him, Lim was prepared to use the full arsenal of security measures against the communists. In the next few months, Lim Yew Hock mounted a series of purges and operations against the communists. He dissolved seven communist-front organisations, including the communist-infiltrated Singapore Chinese Middle Schools Students' Union (SCMSSU),[46] detained Chia Ek Tian, a member of the PAP's Central Executive Committee, and Soon Loh Boon, the former President of the SCMSSU.

Lim worked out a new internal security plan with the Commissioner of Police and the General Officer Commanding Singapore Base District known as *Operation Photo* and was prepared to confront any trouble-maker. In October, following dissatisfaction over the expulsion of 142 students for subversion, riots involving more than 4,000 militant students broke out outside the Chinese high school and soon spread all over the rest of Singapore.[47] This was followed by a sympathy strike by more than 7,000 busmen and other workers. The Duke of Edinburgh, who was scheduled for a visit was advised to cancel his visit, and his plane was diverted to Kuala Lumpur instead.[48] The rioting, which was even worse than the Hock Lee Bus riots, began on 25 October 1956 when police charged into the Chinese middle schools after Lim's ultimatum to disband expired, and spread rapidly throughout the island, with crowds of several thousand gathering in key points mapped out by the communist leaders. Six infantry battalions and their armoured vehicles were brought in from the Malayan jungles to restore order, and by 28 October 1956, the riots had all but dissipated. On the night of 26 October, the Special Branch made several raids and arrested almost the entire open front leadership, including Lim Chin Siong, Fong Swee Suan, Devan Nair, James Puthucheary, Sandra Woodhull and Chan Chiaw Thor. The responsibility for the riots – which left 13 dead, 123 injured, and millions of dollars of property damaged – was pinned on the PAP.

In the Assembly, Lee mounted a scathing attack on Lim's government, calling them stooges of the British, and accused them of attempting to remove all forms of opposition for the next elections. Lee's was a lonely voice in the Assembly. All the other politicians in the Assembly, and the colonial authorities, praised Lim for his sterling performance. In a sense, the riots could not have come at a better

[45] See RS Milne & Diane K Mauzy, *Singapore: The Legacy of Lee Kuan Yew* (Boulder, San Francisco & Oxford: Westview Press, 1990) at 49 [hereinafter 'Milne & Mauzy'].

[46] See Yeo Kim Wah & Albert Lau, 'From Colonialism to Independence, 1945–1965' in Ernest CT Chew & Edwin Lee (eds), *A History of Singapore* (Singapore: Oxford University Press, 1991) 117–153 at 148 [hereinafter 'Yeo & Lau'].

[47] For a detailed account of the riots, see Richard Clutterbuck, *Conflict and Violence in Singapore* and Malaya, 1945–1983 (Singapore: Graham Brash, 1984) at 120–138.

[48] Drysdale, n 44 above, at 156.

time for Lim. In December 1956, he was due to be in London for preliminary discussions with Lennox-Boyd on re-opening constitutional talks the following year. Clearly, Lim's stern action demonstrated his resolve to deal effectively with the communists and strengthened his bargaining position vis-a-vis the British government. While Lim may have ingratiated himself with the British and strengthened Singapore's chances of obtaining self-governing status, he also committed political suicide, since the Chinese masses were convinced that he was nothing more than a British lackey out to destroy Chinese culture. This was compounded by the fact that equal force had been used against protesting Chinese middle school students as against rowdy unionists.[49]

On 9 January 1957, Lim Yew Hock made a statement in the Legislative Assembly confirming the agenda for the new constitutional talks set to open in March that same year. The agenda read as follows:[50]

(1) To take note of the items in the Constitutional Proposal by the United Kingdom Government which have already been agreed to in principle;
(2) Internal Security;
(3) External Relations and External Defence;
(4) Designation of Her Majesty's Representative in Singapore;
(5) Date of coming into force of the new Constitution;
(6) Position of civilian employees in the Armed Forces; and
(7) Any other business.

On 7 March 1957, Lim tabled a motion in the Assembly, asking the Assembly to approve the recommendations of the All-Party Conference, and instruct the 'All-Party Mission to secure from Her Majesty's Government for the people of Singapore the status of a self-governing state with all the rights, powers, and privileges thereto appurtenant in all internal affairs and the control of trade, commerce and cultural relations in external affairs.'[51] After a brief debate, the motion was unanimously approved. Lim's All-Party delegation was considerably smaller than Marshall's had been. It comprised Abdul Hamid bin Haji Jumat (Alliance), Chew Swee Kee (LF), Lim Choon Mong (Liberal-Socialist), Lee Kuan Yew (PAP), and of course Lim himself.[52]

Having showed his mettle in dealing with the communist menace at home, Lim Yew Hock was confident of securing self-government. The only nagging question was, of course, the problem of the chairmanship of the Defence and Security Council. Lim was prepared to try re-presenting Marshall's late proposal that the chairman be a Malayan nominated by the government of the Federation of Malaya. In the run up to this, Lim went secretly to Kuala Lumpur to

[49] Milne & Mauzy, n 46 above, at 49.

[50] *Singapore Legislative Assembly Debates*, 9 Jan 1957, at col 1202.

[51] *Singapore Legislative Assembly Debates*, 5 Mar 1957, at col 1457.

[52] See App A to *Report of the Singapore Constitutional Conference Held in March and April, 1957*, Cmnd 147, at 18 [hereafter *Constitutional Conference 1957*].

confer with his good friend the Tunku. He explained why he needed a Malayan on the council and the political implications for Malaya if the Tunku did not consent. The Tunku agreed. In December 1956, when Lim was in London finalising arrangements for the new constitutional talks, the Tunku joined him and together they met up with Lennox-Boyd. Drysdale suggests that it was at this meeting that the Federation's participation in the Defence and Security Council was finalised.[53] Lim Yew Hock's personal account is slightly different. He figured that the British Secretary of State 'would firm up when one started thumping the table' but would 'respect good reasoning and would be prepared to concede if he were convinced' of your argument.[54] Lim's own account of his meeting with Lennox-Boyd and his strategy is as follows:

> On my arrival in London I took the first opportunity to pay him [Lennox-Boyd] a courtesy call. We welcomed each other like long-lost brothers. We were Alan and Andrew (my early Christian name) to each other. I told him: "Alan, I can appreciate your British tradition of hastening slowly. If you could delay giving a new constitution to Singapore you would try to do so. Let me tell you this. I am not keen for a new constitution for Singapore, but if you and I do not hammer out a new relationship between Britain and Singapore, you will bring trouble for the British and I will be in bad odour and will be forced by circumstance to stir up trouble." He response was most prompt: "Let us try our best to reach agreement."[55]

The meetings were held over a period of four weeks, with Lennox-Boyd being called away unexpectedly to deal with a crisis which developed in Cyprus. By the end of the conference, the Singapore delegation accepted essentially the same terms which Marshall's team rejected a year ago. On the surface, it seems ironic that the British were now prepared to accept terms they turned down only the previous year, but by then, a number of things had changed. In an interview in 1980, Lennox-Boyd gave four main reasons for this change of heart. First he felt that having been in the job for four years, he was better able to persuade cabinet colleagues as to the rightfulness of his decisions and choices, something that may not have been possible the year before. Secondly, the independence of the Federation under the Tunku's leadership bolstered the British cabinet's confidence in the new nation and in its leaders. Third, Lennox-Boyd was convinced that Lee and his PAP would win the next elections and that he had the capacity to control the communists, and finally, he felt that 'it was much easier to persuade cabinet colleagues to agree when the defence appreciation of Singapore showed a smaller role than what it had been before … the fact that defence considerations had diminished made it more easy for the cabinet as a whole to accept it.'[56]

[53] Drysdale, n 44 above at 165.

[54] See Lim Yew Hock, *Reflections* (Kuala Lumpur: Pustaka Antara, 1986) at 86 [hereinafter 'Lim Yew Hock'].

[55] Ibid, at 89–87.

[56] Drysdale, n 44 above, at 199.

There would be a fully elected 51-member legislature with the British controlling external defence and foreign affairs.[57] The main differences were in the appointment of the Head of State and the composition of the Internal Security Council. Instead of appointing a Governor as the Queen's representative, the conference adopted Marshall's belated suggestion that the Head of State be a Malayan-born representative – in this case, the Yang di-Pertuan Negara – who would be appointed for a term of four years by the Queen on the advice of Her Majesty's government.[58] To represent the British government, a High Commissioner would be appointed to 'discharge Her Majesty's Government's responsibilities' as set out in the Constitution.[59] It was also proposed that a Singapore Internal Security Council be established to:[60]

(a) consult on all questions of policy relating to the maintenance of public safety and public order;
(b) maintain the efficiency of all organs of the Singapore government concerned with internal security; and
(c) ensure equal access by both the Singaporean and British governments to the services of these organs and to all information at their disposal.

The Council would comprise the Prime Minister and two other Ministers of the Singapore government, the UK Commissioner and two other UK members and (subject to a formal agreement with the government of the Federation of Malaya), a Minister from the Federation of Malaya nominated by his government.[61] The UK Commissioner would be chairman of the Council but would have no extra vote. Lim Yew Hock explained how he argued his case for this composition which was rejected by the British in the 1956 talks:

> The British administration had always treated the internal security as a Malayan-wide problem (that is to say, Malaya plus Singapore). It was therefore proper and fitting that Malaya should have a seat in the Internal Security Council. The composition of the Internal Security Council should therefore be British three, Singapore, three and Malaya one. With this composition Singapore would be willing to concede the Chairmanship to the British representative. Came the quick rejoinder: This would mean that the deciding vote would be in the hands of the Malayan representative. My answer to this was equally prompt. Why not? Any deterioration in the internal security in Singapore would immediately and directly affect the internal security situation in Malaya. Its reverberations would only be heard, but not felt, in Britain, after a short lapse of time despite the speed of sound. In such an eventuality, would the British think that Malaya would join hands with Singapore for just the ridiculous pleasure of spiting the British side in the Internal Security Council? Surely, Malaya would take

[57] See *Constitutional Conference 1957*, para 22, at p 8.
[58] Ibid, paras 16–17 at 6.
[59] Ibid para 19, at 7.
[60] Ibid para 26, at 8.
[61] Ibid para 27, at 8.

> prompt and stern action in the interests of her own internal security. Tunku Abdul Rahman was not a Nero who fiddled while Rome burned. If Singapore had to be slapped, we would accept the slap of a good neighbour and respected friend but we would not and could not accept it from the British for obvious political reasons.[62]

An independent judiciary was established with the Chief Justice being appointed by the Yang di-Pertuan Negara on the advice of the Prime Minister while all other Supreme Court judges would be appointed by the Yang di-Pertuan Negara 'on the advice of a Council consisting of the Chief Justice, all other Judges of the Supreme Court, and the State Advocate General'. Judges of the Supreme Court could not be removed except by the Yang di-Pertuan Negara on grounds of 'inability or misbehaviour'. Before the Yang di-Pertuan Negara can remove the Judge, he must establish a tribunal of judges for the purpose of determining whether the Judge ought to be removed, and the Yang di-Pertuan Negara is bound to establish this tribunal upon the advice of the Prime Minister or the advice of the Chief Justice in consultation with the Prime Minister. Finally, the Yang di-Pertuan Negara must refer the matter to the Judicial Committee of the Privy Council who will advise the Queen on the desirability of removing the said Judge.[63] At the 1956 talks, the British agreed to the creation of a separate Singapore citizenship within the Commonwealth, and details were worked out on the requirements to be incorporated in a Singapore Citizenship Bill to be passed by the Singapore legislature.[64]

The only spanner in the wheel during the entire proceedings was the British insistence on preventing those persons known to have engaged in subversive activities from participating in the elections to the State of Singapore's first Legislative Assembly. This requirement was imposed as a pre-condition to the grant of the new Constitution,[65] a non-negotiable requirement. Lennox-Boyd was adamant on this point:

> I am not prepared to vary my decision at all. It was arrived at after a great deal of consideration. I am convinced that if we are to give privileges to democratic communities in the Far East or anywhere else, we should see that they are provided with the means of defence against those who are contriving their subversion.[66]

The Singapore delegation opposed this 'departure from normal democratic practice protested at the unilateral imposition of this condition', but was left

[62] Lim Yew Hock, n 54 above at 87–88.

[63] *Constitutional Conference, 1957* at paras 45–46, at pp 13–14.

[64] Ibid para 50, at 15–16.

[65] Ibid at para 30 which states:

> At the final Plenary Session of the Conference Her Majesty's Government made it clear that their agreement to the internal security arrangements in particular, and to the new Constitution as a whole, was dependent upon provision being made to ensure that persons known to have been engaged in subversive activity should not be eligible for election to the first Legislative Assembly of the new State of Singapore…

[66] *Debates of the United Kingdom Legislative Assembly*, 17 Jun 1958 at col 878.

with no other option. However, unlike the Marshall delegation, the 1957 negotiating team did not reject the terms *in toto* for there was too much going for them. Instead, they 'took note with regret of the intention of Her Majesty's Government'[67] without accepting it, offering to table the condition before the Legislative Assembly back in Singapore.[68]

On 26 April 1957, Chief Minister Lim Yew Hock tabled a motion before the Legislative Assembly to 'take note of the Report of the Singapore Constitutional Conference' and to approve 'the stand of the All-Party Delegation in not accepting the condition stipulated in paragraph 30 of the Report.' The debate raged for four days, with a very agitated and bitter David Marshall slinging mud at the entire delegation. Marshall spoke for almost four hours and was in turn lambasted by the delegation members. On 30 April, a decision was taken and the Assembly voted overwhelmingly in favour of the motion.[69] A third All-Party delegation – comprising the same members as the 1957 All-Party team – left for London in May 1958 to finalise the terms of the new Constitution. Agreement was reached in London after six plenary sessions and 11 working party meetings between 13 May and 28 May.[70] On 1 August 1958, the UK Parliament passed an Act 'to provide for the establishment of the State of Singapore and for the peace, order and good government'.[71] In November that year, the Singapore (Constitution) Order in Council, 1958[72] was passed.

III. THE 1958 ORDER IN COUNCIL

The new Singapore Constitution was unique. It granted Singapore all the trappings of self-government just short of independence. To represent the British monarch, a local-born head of state called the Yang di-Pertuan Negara, was to be appointed by the Queen, holding office at her 'pleasure'.[73] Under the Constitution, the Yang di-Pertuan Agong had the power to grant pardons,[74] appoint and dismiss public officials,[75] and dispose of land in the name of Her Majesty.[76] In addition, he was empowered to declare the office of Prime Minister vacant

[67] Ibid.

[68] Drysdale, n 44 above at 168. In fact, Lim Yew Hock was at pains to point out that the Report of the conference, was precisely that, a report, and 'not an agreement signed by both parties.' See *Singapore Legislative Assembly Debates*, 26 Apr 1957 at col 1667.

[69] There were a total of 23 Ayes, 2 Noes, 5 Abstentions and 2 Absentees (Lim Chin Siong and Francis Thomas). See *ibid* 30 Apr 1957 at col 1868.

[70] *Singapore Annual Report 1958* (Singapore: Government Printing Office) at 3–4.

[71] See State of Singapore Act, 1958, 6 & 7 Eliz 2 Ch 59.

[72] No 1956 of 1958.

[73] Art 4, Singapore (Constitution) Order in Council 1958 [hereinafter 1958 Constitution].

[74] Art 9.

[75] Art 10.

[76] Art 8.

in certain circumstances,[77] prorogue and dissolve the legislative Assembly on the advice of the Prime Minister,[78] and appoint ministers,[79] assistant ministers[80] and permanent secretaries of the various government ministries.[81] A UK High Commissioner would be appointed by the Queen to represent the British government.[82] His functions would be protect British interests and responsibilities on the island. As a transitionary procedure, the UK High Commissioner would assume the office of Yang di-Pertuan Negara for the first six months.[83] There would be a fully elected Legislative Assembly of 51 members[84] presided over by a Speaker.[85] A Cabinet consisting of the Prime Minister and such other Ministers as may be appointed would constitute the executive. The Yang di-Pertuan Negara, acting in his discretion, would appoint the member of the Legislative Assembly who, in his judgment, was likely to command the confidence of the majority of the members of the Assembly.[86]

The Constitution also established the Supreme Court of Singapore with such jurisdiction and powers as may be provided by any law in force.[87] The Court comprised the Chief Justice and such Puisne Judges as may be appointed from time to time.[88] The Yang di-Pertuan Negara appoints the Chief Justice on the advice of the Prime Minister;[89] he appoints the Puisne Judges on the advice of a Council consisting of the Chief Justice, the substantive Puisne Judges and the State Advocate-General.[90] Security of tenure for the Chief Justice and all judges of the Supreme Court are guaranteed by section 91(1) which provides that a Judge of the Supreme Court shall hold office until he attains the age of 62 years. The office of a Supreme Court Judge may not be abolished during his tenure without his consent,[91] nor will the terms of his office be altered to his disadvantage during his continuance in office.[92]

Control over defence and foreign affairs was in the hands of the British government[93] and was exercised through their representative the British High

[77] Art 22.
[78] Art 62.
[79] Art 21.
[80] Art 28.
[81] Art 29.
[82] Art 15.
[83] Art 107. The outgoing Governor, Sir William Goode became the first Yang di-Pertuan Negara and UK High Commissioner in Singapore.
[84] Art 34.
[85] See s 50, ibid.
[86] Art 21.
[87] Art 87.
[88] Ibid.
[89] Art 89.
[90] Art 90.
[91] Art 87(1).
[92] Art 92(3).
[93] Pt VIII.

Commissioner. And through the mechanics of the Internal Security Council (ISC),[94] internal security was a shared responsibility between representatives of the Singapore, British and Malayan governments, with the Malayan government having the casting vote.[95] The main functions of the ISC were:[96]

(a) to consult together on all questions of policy relating to the maintenance of public safety and public order in Singapore;
(b) to maintain the efficiency of all organs of the government of Singapore which are concerned with internal security; and
(c) to ensure equal access by the government of the UK and of Singapore to services of the said organs and to all information at the disposal of those organs.

The 1958 Constitution also contained numerous transitionary provisions to smoothen the transfer of power and to ensure minimal disruptions to the workings of government. At the same time, some of these transitionary provisions were necessary to bring the status of Singapore's constitutional development up to date. As such, certain changes to the existing body of laws were necessary, and provisions empowering the Yang di-Pertuan Negara to 'make such adaptations and modifications in any [existing] law. ... as appear to him to be necessary or expedient'.[97]

IV. THE ROAD TO MERGER: 1958–1961

A. Local Government?

Between 1951 and 1956, three separate commissions investigated the question of local government[98] in Singapore. All of them considered it essential for Singapore to have two levels of government – a central government and local government. Developments in local government were however, overshadowed by the implementation of the Rendel Commission and the attempt by Marshall and Lim Yew Hock to secure self-governing status for the island. In any case, the

[94] Pt VII.
[95] The Malayan government's agreement to participate in the Internal Security Council was formalised by an Exchange of Letters in November 1958 between the government of the Federation of Malaya and the UK. These letters were published for general circulation in *Gazette* Notification No 4351 of 1958.
[96] Art 65.
[97] Art 21(4)(a).
[98] The first was a one-man commission under Dr LC Hill, a local government expert from Britain in 1951 (see LC Hill, *Report on the Reform of Local Government* (Singapore: Government Printing Office, 1952); the second was the Rendel Commission which also considered local government within the framework of its constitutional proposals (see *Constitutional Commission, Singapore* (Singapore: Government Printing Office, 1954); and the final one was a committee under Sir Percy McNeice, the President of the Municipal Commission (see *Report on the Committee on Local Government* (Singapore: Government Printing Office, 1956).

colonial government was anxious to revitalise local government in Singapore for two main reasons. First, it was part and parcel of their plan to guide Singapore towards independence. The local government institutions would function as nurseries for democracy, with elections for local officials, and where greater political consciousness could be raised through the citizenry's increased participation in the political processes. Secondly, the central government was not equipped to handle many of the more mundane aspects of local administration such as market stall licensing, car parks etc. The recommendations of the Committee on Local Government[99] were finally adopted in 1957, with the passing of the Local Government Ordinance.[100] Essentially, the Local Government Ordinance divided Singapore geographically and administratively into one City Council and various District Councils. In 1957, the four District Councils were Katong, Serangoon, Bukit Panjang and Jurong. Their main functions were to administer such matters as rates and taxes, water, gas and electrical supplies, street cleaning, garbage collection, public health and to maintain fire services.

The first City Council was to comprise 32 fully elected members[101] presided over by a Mayor and assisted by a Deputy Mayor.[102] The District Councils comprised 12 elected members[103] presided over by a Chairman and assisted by a Deputy Chairman, both of whom were nominated by the Governor during the first four years of the operation of the Ordinance.[104] Elections[105] for the first City Council were held in December 1957 with 81 persons vying for the 32 seats. Under the Local Government Elections Ordinance, voter registration and voting were not compulsory.[106] As a result, only 165,526 voters or 32 per cent of the City's more than 500,000 eligible voters actually cast their votes.[107] The City Council elections attracted the main political parties, with the Liberal-Socialists contesting all 32 seats. The PAP, still reeling from the Lim Yew Hock government's detentions, was in no condition to contest all the seats, but nonetheless fielded 14 candidates. The Workers' Party (WP) fielded five candidates, the Labour Front (LF – 16 candidates) and the United Malays Nationalist Organisation (UNMNO – three candidates) also contested the seats, the latter two having agreed with the PAP not to fight each other and split the left-wing votes. There were 11 independents.[108]

[99] Singapore Legislative Council, *Report of the Committee on Local Government* (Singapore, 1956).

[100] Local Government Ordinance 1957, No 24 of 1957 passed on 9 Aug 1957.

[101] Section 6, ibid.

[102] Sections 8–9, ibid.

[103] Section 16, ibid.

[104] Section 17, ibid.

[105] See generally, Local Government Elections Ordinance 1957, No 23 of 1957.

[106] See Pts II and III, ibid.

[107] See Then Lian Mee, *The Singapore Municipality 1946–1959* (Academic Exercise, Department of History, University of Malaya in Singapore, 1960) at 48.

[108] Drysdale, n 44 above, 187.

When the results were announced, the PAP's anti-corruption election platform was vindicated when it captured 13 seats, the WP secured four seats, UMNO two seats, LF four seats and the Liberal Socialists seven seats. Among the PAP councillors who took office were the Party's Organising Secretary, Ong Pang Boon and the Party Treasurer, Ong Eng Guan. They are unrelated. Ong Eng Guan was educated both in English and Mandarin and spoke Malay and Hokkien fluently. Because of his fluency in the Hokkien dialect, Ong had been built up by the PAP as the moderates' answer to 'that rhetorical firebrand, Lim Chin Siong.'[109]

The PAP's 13 seats were insufficient to give them a working majority in the City Council, and even after including the two UMNO seats, the loose PAP-UMNO coalition still only commanded 15 seats out of 32. Nonetheless, due to inter-party squabbles, Ong Eng Guan was elected Mayor at the first meeting of the Council, and Ong Pang Boon, Deputy Mayor. The PAP's minority position in the Council did not stop Ong Eng Guan from personalising the office of Mayor. As Drysdale put it, Ong 'exhibited an unexpected talent for unconventional behaviour, drawing enormous (and not unpopular) attention to himself, and, by definition, to his not entirely happy Party leadership.'[110] Ong's first few days in office was fraught with controversy. He ended up in jail momentarily by openly defying a police ban on fire-crackers, when he and his colleagues went to the City Hall to take over officially as Mayor. During his inauguration as Mayor, Ong took a snap vote of the Council and got rid of the $15,000 Mace which he called 'a relic of colonialism.'[111] The public lapped up Ong's antics with relish. His open and often audacious confrontation with the colonial authorities made him a folk hero, and his popularity rose accordingly. As Drydale so accurately observed:

> The political advantage of this opening gambit – an attack on colonial institutions – was that it established for Ong in the minds of his followers the reputation of a firm and uncompromising politician on the extreme left of the anti-colonial spectrum: further left even than the pro-Communists, Lim Chin Siong and Fong Swee Suan, had portrayed for themselves in speech and action. Indeed, in terms of histrionics, there was nothing more electrifying for mass consumption that the open front leaders of the Malayan Communist Party could have conjured out of the air. Lim Chin Siong and Fong Swee Suan had used their evocative tongues, and the example of their selfless lifestyles, to command a following which could be led with heroic fervour into violent action when required. But neither of them had come anywhere near to a prop of such majestic symbolism which, in the full glare of public acclamation, could be thrown into the dustbin of colonialism.[112]

[109] Ibid at 188.
[110] Ibid.
[111] Ibid at 190.
[112] Ibid at 191.

Ong was clearly ambitious, and made no secret of eyeing the top position in the PAP itself. Using the City Council and later his Hokkien-speaking Hong Lim constituency as a base, he prepared his assault on the PAP leadership. However, his actions in the City Council soon became intolerable to the other parties. Ong was said to have abused officials, hired and fired officials at will, and generally abused his enormous powers as Mayor. After a time, the other parties decided that they had enough of Ong's abrasive style. Formally or informally, they conspired to bring down the Mayor.

On 26 March 1959, the Lim Yew Hock government stepped in to stop Ong. Abdul Hamid, Lim Yew Hock's Minister for Local Government transferred to himself, certain functions relating to the appointment of officers, the making of Provident Fund rules, disciplinary action, the delegation of powers to employees, the emergency powers of the Mayor and supplemental budgets.[113] The Minister stated that this was an interim measure adopted in the public's interest since he was establishing a Commission of Inquiry to investigate staff matters and the overall workings of the City Council. His draconian actions were prompted by numerous complaints from the public, Council employees and even Councillors themselves, many of whom had lost confidence in the management of the Council.[114] The following month, Ong Eng Guan and the other PAP councillors resigned. The Commission of Inquiry headed by District Judge JF McWilliam commenced hearings on 12 May 1959, but six days later, McWilliam decided to suspend the proceedings for fear that with impending general elections on 30 May, the Inquiry could be turned into a political forum.[115]

B. The 1959 General Elections

The new Singapore (Constitution) Order in Council was passed on 21 November 1958 and whispers of impending general elections floated all over the city. The 1958 City Council elections effectively became a rehearsal for the actual general elections which were slated to be held in 1959. The general elections had already been postponed once before to facilitate the registration of the 'alien Chinese' on the electoral rolls required by the new Singapore Citizenship Ordinance.[116] This time, Chief Minister Lim Yew Hock pointed out that elections had to be delayed again because time was needed to prepare the necessary constitutional

[113] City Council ((Transfer of Powers) Order, 1959.

[114] See Then Lian Mee, n 107 above, at 49.

[115] Ibid at 57.

[116] The Singapore Citizenship Ordinance, 1957, No 35 of 1957, was passed by the Singapore Legislative Council on 16 October 1957. Under the Ordinance, 4 groups of residents qualified for automatic citizenship, while naturalisation was offered to those who had resided in Singapore for 10 years of more and were prepared to pledge allegiance to Singapore and renounce all foreign ties.

instruments and legislation to improve the electoral procedure, especially since compulsory voting was being introduced for the first time. Nonetheless, Lim assured the Legislative Assembly that the life of his government would not extend beyond that of the Rendel Constitution.[117]

A record 194 candidates contested the 51 seats, and to everyone's surprise, the PAP contested all the available seats. The 1959 election was epoch-making in several ways. First, this was the first time that no nominated or official seats were reserved in the Legislative Assembly, and the increase of elected seats from the 1955 elections, from 25 to 51 was more than double. Secondly, a record 13 political parties took part in the elections. Finally, for the first time, voting was compulsory and the voter population increased from 300,292 in 1955 to 587,797 in 1959.[118] After a blistering campaign, full of mud-slinging and rhetorical duels, the PAP won a landslide victory, claiming 43 seats. The remaining eight seats went to the Lim Yew Hock's new party, the Singapore People's Alliance (SPA) (four seats), three to the UMNO-MCA Alliance and one to an independent, AP Rajah.

V. THE TERMS OF MERGER

The new PAP government sought a merger with the Federation of Malaya as a matter of urgency for two main reasons: first, to achieve political independence and secondly, to guarantee Singapore's economic survival. This was denounced by the pro-communist elements in the PAP as an imperialist plot who were defeated on a motion of confidence on this issue in the legislature. As there were then no anti-hopping laws, the dissident factions proceeded to form an opposition party, the Barisan Sosialis with Lim Chin Siong as its Secretary-General. All the defectors thus continued to sit in the Legislative Assemblies as representatives of their constituencies but now with a completely different party affiliation.[119]

At a meeting of the Commonwealth Parliamentary Association held in Singapore in July 1961, the principle of merger was approved by representatives from Malaya, Singapore, North Borneo, Brunei and Sarawak. This constitutional development was considered necessary because Singapore and the Federation were 'inextricably bound by common racial, historical, cultural, economic and political ties'.[120] On 15 November 1961, a *Memorandum Setting Out Heads of Agreement for a Merger Between the Federation of Malaya and Singapore*[121] was published and presented to the Singapore Legislative Assembly.

[117] Drysdale, n 44 above, at 197.

[118] See Ong Chit Chung, 'The 1959 Singapore General Election' (1975) *Journal of Southeast Asian History* 41 at 62.

[119] See Turnbull, n 22 above, at 279.

[120] See *Memorandum Setting Out Head of Agreement for a Merger between the Federation of Malaya and Singapore*, Singapore Parliament, Cmd. 33 of 1961, para 1.

[121] See Cmd 33 of 1961.

This important document detailed the terms for merger as agreed upon between the two governments. From the outset, Singapore was treated differently from the other Malay States. The two governments agreed that:

> Singapore will be a State within the Federation but on special conditions and with a larger measure of local autonomy than the other States forming the Federation. Defence, External Affairs and Security will be the responsibility of the Federation Government; Education and Labour that of the Singapore Government.[122]

As a constituent state within a federation, the head of state would be the Yang di-Pertuan Negara appointed by the Yang di-Pertuan Agong in consultation with the Prime Minister of Singapore. As the head of the executive branch, he would be empowered to assent to legislation passed by the State Legislative Assembly and to exercise the prerogative of mercy on the advice of a Pardons Board.[123] The Legislature Assembly would continue as the State Assembly, but will lose its competence to legislate on matters relating to defence, external affairs, security and matters agreed to be Federal matters.[124] Representation in the Federation Parliament was restricted to 15 seats in the Federal House of Representatives, with two members in the Senate.[125] The administration of justice was a Federal responsibility, but it was agreed that in view of 'the special conditions in Singapore', there would 'be a separate branch of the Federal Judicial and Legal Service in Singapore, with opportunities for secondment or voluntary transfer to the other branches of the service.'[126] At the same time, provisions would be made for a joint court of appeal and for final appeals to go to the Judicial Committee of the Privy Council which will advise the Yang di-Pertuan Agong on appeals from Singapore.[127]

The protection of fundamental liberties would be entrenched in the Constitution[128] as would the special position of the Malays of Singapore.[129] As for citizenship and nationality, the Memorandum stated that all 'Singapore citizens will keep their citizenship and automatically become nationals of the larger Federation.' However, these nationals can only vote in their respective states.[130] The finance provisions divided responsibilities between the two governments. The Federal government would have legislative competence over all fiscal policy and taxes provided that the free port of status cannot be changed without the prior consent of both parties. The Singapore government would have 'wider powers of raising domestic loans, subject to the approval of

[122] Ibid at para 5.
[123] Ibid at para 8.
[124] Ibid at para 9.
[125] Ibid at para 15.
[126] Ibid at para 13.
[127] Ibid.
[128] Ibid at para 6.
[129] Ibid at para 7.
[130] Ibid at para 14.

the Federal Government.'[131] Finally, it was agreed that 'a working party be set up to go into the overall financial and other implications arising out of the arrangements.'[132]

Among the many 'special provisions' granted to Singapore, two require further elaboration and discussion. The first pertains to the issue of 'citizenship' and 'nationality.' Under the *Heads of Agreement*, Singapore citizens will retain their *state* citizenship, but do not automatically become citizens of the Federation. Instead, they were considered 'nationals' of the Federation, which will:

> have equal rights, carry the same passport, enjoy the same protection and be subject to the equal duties and responsibilities under the Constitution of the larger Federation.

This proposal is consonant with the Tunku's concern that an enlarged Chinese citizenry would upset the fine racial balance in the Federation which favours the Malays. This provision differs significantly from the citizenship provisions of other states, notably Penang and Malacca – which up to 1946 formed part of the Straits Settlements with Singapore – where citizens were given automatic Federal citizenship. This issue of citizenship subsequently became the focus of the tussle between the PAP and the break-away Barisan Socialis faction in the Referendum of 1962.

The second special provision of note is the agreement that the 'special position of the Malays who are Singapore citizens will be safeguarded in the Constitution of the larger Federation [and that as] in Malacca and Penang that the Yang di-Pertuan Agong will be the head of the Muslim religion in the State.'[133] The interpretation of this particular provision also subsequently became a sore point in the relationship between Singapore and the Federation.

Finally, the proposals relating to the finances of Singapore gave exemption from the Federation Constitution's financial provisions which applied to the other states. Instead, the Federal government would be given jurisdiction over all national monetary policy and power of taxation on all taxes of national character. These proposals marked a significant departure from terms subscribed to by the other states in the Federation. Singapore was given greater latitude in financial matters and greater state reserve powers because of its autonomy over labour and education issues. These provisions also eventually generated a great deal of controversy, and in many ways, led to the break-up of the union.

[131] Ibid at para 17.

[132] Ibid at para 2. The Working Party comprised Dato Abdul Aziz bin Haji Abdul Majid (Permanent Secretary, Prime Minister's Department), Abdul Jamil bin Abdul Rais (Secretary to the Treasury) Nik Daud bin Jahi Nik Mat (Deputy Secretary of the Ministry of Internal Security) & Abdul Kadir bin Shamsudin (Acting Secretary for Defence), Ali bin Hassan, (Senior Federal Counsel), Muhammad Ghazali bin Shafie (Acting Permanent Secretary, Ministry of External Affairs) and Ismail bin Mohamed Ali (Deputy Governor, Bank Negera) from the Federation; and Ahmad bin Mohamed Ibrahim (State Advocate-General), ST Stewart (Permanent Secretary, Ministry of Home Affairs) and Hon Sui Sen (Chairman, Economic Development Board) from Singapore.

[133] Cmd 33 of 1961 at para 7.

The proposals for the new Federation were accepted by the British government provided she retained control over the military bases in Singapore and provided also that the people of the territories involved were in favour of the merger.[134] The Referendum for Merger with Malaya was treated as an election issue and 71 per cent of the population voted for the government's proposals.

VI. CREATING MALAYSIA

Having secured the people's endorsement for merger on PAP terms, it was still necessary for the British, the Federation and Singapore to iron out the legal and constitutional issues of constituting the new Federation. Singapore working party officials[135] began negotiations with their Federation counterparts on 5 December 1962, four months after the Referendum. The delay was due to the fact that Federation officials were pre-occupied with negotiations with Sabah and Sarawak and wanted to complete these negotiations before meeting up with the Singapore officials. A total of 22 meetings were held between 5 December 1962 and 14 February 1963 and the officials submitted joint recommendations on most of the provisions to be incorporated into the new Constitution of the Federation of Malaysia and the State of Singapore.[136]

A number of issues were referred to the Ministers of Singapore and the Federation for resolution since an agreement could not be reached. These points involved issues in banking, insurance, shipping, navigation, broadcasting, television, constitutional guarantees and finance. During the three ministerial plenary meetings held on 21 and 22 March 1963 and 2 April 1963, all of these issues, except for finance had been agreed on.[137] There are two main points which merit discussion on the agreements reached thus far. The first relates to the Singapore State government's constitutional duty to advance the interests of Malays in Singapore, and the second concerns the troublesome finance provisions.

Under the new Constitution, Article 153 of the Federal Constitution which imposes upon the state a duty to safeguard and advance the language, culture and interests of the indigenous people applies to Singapore. Prime Minister Lee Kuan Yew explained that:

> … it was agreed that on application of Article 153 to Singapore after merger, the following conditions will apply. In other words, first, no proportion of posts in a Federal Public Service in Singapore will be reserved for Malays; second, recruitment

[134] See *Federation of Malaysia: Joint Statement by the Governments of the United Kingdom and of the Federation of Malaya*, UK Cmnd 1563.

[135] The Singapore Working Party Officials consisted of Encik Ahmad Ibrahim (State Advocate-General), Mr Steward (Permanent Secretary, Home Affairs), Mr Howe Yoon Chong (Permanent Secretary, Finance Division), Mr Sim Kee Boon (Ag Permanent Secretary, Ministry of National Development) and Mr Wong Chooi Sen (Cabinet Secretary).

[136] See speech of Prime Minister Lee Kuan Yew, *Singapore Legislative Assembly Official Reports* 5 Apr 1963 at col 24.

[137] Ibid.

> in Singapore to Federal Public Services will be open to all citizens of Malaysia; and three, no proportion of permits or licences for the operation of any trade or business in Singapore will be reserved for Malays; and four, the definition of 'Malays' for the purposes of Article 153 will be amended to include Singapore Malays.[138]

Lee also pointed out that Article 8(2) of the Federal Constitution, which guarantees equality before the law and equal protection of the law had to be amended to allow Singapore to carry on its education policy of favouring Malays with free education right up to university level. In response to a question by Dato Abdul Hamid bin Haji Jumat as to what privileges Singapore Malays would get by being citizens of the Federation, Lee responded:

> … It means that in Singapore, Malays will enjoy their special rights as at present, with particular reference to free education from primary school to university and if they choose to go to the other States, will enjoy special rights as for Malays there. In this way, we have been able to maintain the principle of free competition in Singapore for employment in the Public Service and for businesses like taxi licences, bus licences, trade licences and so on.[139]

The main financial provisions problems arose from the collection of taxes and the administration of taxed monies and the extent of Singapore's contribution to federal finance. In respect of the first issue, the Singapore government's view was that Singapore should have autonomy over the collection of taxes and the revenues should be kept in Singapore, with the Federal government having a first charge on the revenues collected in respect of Singapore's contribution to federal services in Singapore. The Federal Finance Ministry 'envisaged an arrangement whereby they would take over the functions of the Singapore Finance Ministry in respect of all taxes, and year by year make such payments to the State Government as is necessary for its discharge of its other duties.'[140] The more difficult problem was the price of Singapore's entry in Malaysia. This difficulty was succinctly described by Sopiee as follows:

> In the protracted March to July 1963 negotiations over the economic terms of Singapore's entry into Malaysia, the Federation quite naturally wanted as substantial a financial contribution to federal finance and the development of Sabah and Sarawak as it could get from Singapore; the smaller Singapore's contribution, the greater would be the overall financial burden to Malaya. Singapore's great emphasis on its industrialization programme understandably led it to strongly advocate a common market. The Federation, apprehensive about the capacity of its industrial sector to compete against Singapore (with its free-port status) was naturally not as keen on a common market. These three issues were constitutionally resolved only (after rounds of always tough and often biter talks) in early June 1963, four months after the talks commenced.[141]

[138] Ibid at cols 31–32.
[139] Ibid at col 38.
[140] Ibid at col 33.
[141] Mohd Nordin Sopiee, *From Malayan Union to Singapore Separation: Political Unification in the Malaysia Region 1945–65* (Kuala Lumpur: Penerbit Universiti Malaya, 1976) at 184.

The eventual resolution of these issues in June 1963 was achieved after a series of meetings in London but they were never fully resolved. Time and again they were reopened, and it was essentially these economic issues which led to the unravelling of Singapore's merger with Malaysia.[142]

The *Agreement Relating to Malaysia* was finally prepared and circulated, together with the Malaysia Bill on 9 July 1963.[143] All the key negotiators, were in London at this time to iron out the final details of the Bill and the new Federal and State Constitutions. Representing Singapore were Lee Kuan Yew and Goh Keng Swee. Under the *Agreement*, the government of the Federation of Malaya would take the appropriate steps to enact the Malaysia Bill and ensure that it was brought into operation on 31 August. At the same time the UK government would take such steps to secure the enactment of an Act 'providing for the relinquishment, as from Malaysia Day, of Her Britannic Majesty's sovereignty and jurisdiction in respect of North Borneo, Sarawak and Singapore so that the said sovereignty and jurisdiction shall on such relinquishment vest' in the Federation.[144] On 19 July 1963, the British government took the Malaysia Bill through its Second Reading in the House of Commons and it was passed without amendment.[145]

Under the Malaysia Agreement, which was concluded on the 9 July 1963,[146] it was agreed that the Colonies of North Borneo and Sarawak and the State of Singapore would be federated within the existing States of the Federation of Malaya to form the Federation of Malaysia.[147] Singapore left control over foreign affairs, defence and internal security to the central government but maintained considerable powers over finance, labour and education. It was also allocated 15 of the 127 seats in the Dewan Rakyat (federal legislature) and retain her own executive government and legislative assembly. The day-to-day administration of Singapore was the responsibility of the executive government and Singapore was to pay 40 per cent of her income from taxes to the Federal government.[148] A new State Constitution was granted to Singapore to effect this change in status.[149]

It should be noted that though most of the provisions relating to the legislative and executive bodies remained very much the same as those of the 1958

[142] For a detailed account of the tough negotiations regarding the financial provisions see Milton Osborne, *Singapore and Malaysia* (Ithaca: Cornell University Southeast Asia Program, July 1964) at 50–61.

[143] Cmd 22 of 1963, Singapore Legislative Assembly.

[144] Ibid, Art IV.

[145] *Hansard*, House of Commons, 19 Jul 1963, cols 922–1008.

[146] See *Agreement between the United Kingdom, the Federation of Malaya, North Borneo, Sarawak and Singapore Concerning the Establishment of the Federation of Malaysia*, UK Cmnd 2094 (Federation Agreement); see also, *Malaysia Agreement Exchange of Letters*, Singapore Legislative Assembly, Misc 5 of 1963 dated 26 July 1963. The Federation Agreement was given statutory force by the enactment of the UK Malaysia Act (11 & 12 Eliz 2, c 35).

[147] Federation Agreement, Art 1.

[148] Turubull, History, at 280.

[149] See The Sabah, Sarawak and Singapore (State Constitutions) Order in Council 1963, SI 1963, No 1493, as published in the *State of Singapore Government Gazette* Sp No S 1 of 1963.

Order in Council, the judicial branch of the government was treated as a federal matter and did not exist as part of the State Constitution. Notably, the protection of minorities clause which had been part of the 1956 All-Party delegation's memorandum had now been inserted into the Constitution as law. Initially, it had been rephrased in the Preamble to the 1958 Constitution as follows:

> And whereas it was further agreed at the said conference, and it is hereby expressly affirmed, that it shall be the responsibility of the Government of Singapore constantly to care for the interests of racial and religious minorities in Singapore, and in particular that it shall be the deliberate and conscious policy of the Government of Singapore at all times to recognise the special position of the Malays, who are the indigenous people of the Island and are in most need of assistance, and accordingly, that it shall be the responsibility of the Government of Singapore to protect, safeguard, support, foster and promote their political, educational, religious, economic, social and cultural interests and the Malay language.

This manifested as Article 89 of the 1963 Constitution of the State of Singapore in the following terms:

> 89.(1)— It shall be the responsibility of the Government to care for the interests of the racial and religious minorities in the State.
>
> (2) The Government shall exercise its functions in such manner as to recognise the special position of the Malays, who are the indigenous people of the State, and accordingly, it shall be the responsibility of the Government to protect, support, foster and promote their political, educational, religious, economic, social and cultural interests and the Malay language.

On 2 August 1963, the Singapore Legislative Assembly approved the Malaysia Agreement, and this was followed on 8, 10 and 21 August by approval in the legislatures of Sabah, the Federation and Sarawak respectively. On 26 August, the Yang di-Pertuan Agong gave his Royal Assent to the Malaysia Bill, and on 29 August, His Majesty signed a Proclamation fixing 16 September as Malaysia Day. Malaysia Day was originally fixed for 1 June 1963. This date was later changed to 31 August, which coincided with the sixth anniversary of the Federation's independence. A further postponement was engendered by President Sukarno's challenge to the Malaysia plan. In order to give time for the United Nations team to determine if Malaysia was being formed against the will of the Borneo peoples, the Tunku agreed to postpone Malaysia Day till 16 September 1963.

These constant delays irritated Lee Kuan Yew who, not only criticised the Tunku's decision to postpone Malaysia Day, but against strong advice from the Tunku, urged Sabah and Sarawak to proclaim their de facto independence on 31 August. Thus, on 31 August 1963 – Malaysia Solidarity Day – he declared Singapore independent. Technically, the Proclamation of Malaysia Day signed by the Yang di-Pertuan Agong did not bind Singapore since Singapore was not yet part of the Federation; and since the British Act had prescribed 31 August 1963 as the day on which the Crown relinquished sovereignty and jurisdiction over

Singapore, there was an anomalous 15 days in which Singapore was technically independent as a unitary state.

VII. CONCLUSION

The internal politics of the Federation and the PAP's disastrous foray into federal politics was to prove fatal to the merger. Soon personal suspicions, fuelled by the increasing communist and communalist threats brought relations between the central government and the Singapore government on a steadily downhill path. The general population in Singapore were also beginning to resent the strains and irritations which the merger involved and this was worsened by incidents created by the Indonesian confrontation.[150] It was clear that worsening relations and tensions created by racial politics would prompt the Tunku to do something drastic. He had only two options: to depose the Singapore government and lock up Lee Kuan Yew (as several of his right-wing colleagues demanded) or to eject Singapore from the Federation. In August 1965, delegations from the Federal government and the Singapore government – led respectively by their deputy Prime Ministers – commenced negotiations for the cession of Singapore. These talks were highly secretive as neither government wanted the British to get a wind of the 'Separation' plan for fear that the British might intervene to prevent it. On 9 August 1965, Singapore's independence was proclaimed.[151]

As we noted at the beginning of this chapter, Singapore's independence was ushered in without any constitutional fanfare. The new government of Singapore simply took its existing State Constitution from 1963 and augmented it with parts from the Federation of Malaysia Constitution. This constitutional repackaging remained unfinished until 1969 when the last piece of the puzzle – provisions relating to Singapore's judiciary – was put in its place. As such, the State Constitution of 1963 did not have any provisions relating to the judiciary, section 8 of the Singapore Independence Agreement of 7 August 1965 made a 'temporary provision' for the 'jurisdiction and procedure of the Singapore' as follows:

> 8. Until other provision is made by the Legislature of Singapore, the jurisdiction, original or appellate, and the practice and procedure of the High Court and the subordinate Courts of Singapore shall be the same as that exercised and followed immediately before Singapore Day, and appeals from the High Court shall continue to lie to the Federal Court of Appeal of Malaysia and then to the Privy Council in like manner.

Two things may be observed from this clause. First, that it was meant to be a temporary measure to ensure the continuity of judicial function in the

[150] Turnbull, n 22 above, at 290.
[151] See Independence of Singapore Agreement, 1965, GN No 1824 of 9 Aug 1965.

newly-independent state; and second, that Malaysia's judicial system remained as part of independent Singapore's judicial structure and hierarchy. This clause was repeated in section 11 of the Republic of Singapore Independence Act 1965. At the Second Reading of the Constitution (Amendment) Bill, Prime Minister Lee Kuan Yew stated laconically that 'it would be in the interest of the administration of justice' for the 'continuance of appeals from the High Court to the Federal Court and thence to the Privy Council.'[152] This anomaly was not fixed till the introduction of the Supreme Court of Judicature Act in 1969. Law Minister EW Barker lamented the delay in the introduction of the Bill, saying that it 'should really have been introduced soon after we left Malaysia'. Unfortunately, 'the many and varied problems' which Singapore had to deal after leaving Malaysia 'forced' the government 'to continue with the existing system of administration of justice until the present day.'[153] Barker elaborated:

> All that the Bill purports to do is to set out logically the consequences that flow from our becoming independent on our own with an independent system of administration of justice separate from the system that was introduced while we were part of Malaysia and which had since continued in use. Such anachronistic references to the Federal Court of Appeal, for example, would be done away with. The Supreme Court now consists of the Court of Appeal, the Court of Criminal Appeal and the High Court. The Bill generally does no more than to revert to the position obtaining before we joined Malaysia. The powers of jurisdiction of the Supreme Court are the same as heretofore, before we joined Malaysia and after we left Malaysia.[154]

In 1979, the Constitution was amended to empower the Attorney-General to issue a consolidated Reprint of the Constitution amalgamating such 'provisions of the Constitution of Malaysia as are applicable to Singapore, into a single composite document.'[155] The first of these Reprints was issued in 1980 and for the first time, Singapore's constitutional foundational documents finally found expression in a single document.

[152] *Singapore Parliamentary Debates, Official Reports*, vol 24, 22 Dec 1965, col 442.

[153] *Singapore Parliamentary Debates, Official Reports*, vol 29, 12 Jun 1969, col 74.

[154] Ibid.

[155] This was the old Art 93(1) (now Art 155(1)) that had been inserted into the Constitution by the Constitution (Amendment) Act 1979, Act 10 of 1979. See Reprint No 1 of 1980, published on 31 Mar 1980.

8

The Making of Brunei's 1959 Constitution

BA HUSSAINMIYA

INTRODUCTION

BRUNEI DARUSSALAM, AN oil and gas-rich State, is the smallest country in the Association of Southeast Asian Nations (ASEAN) group of nations. A Sultanate of old vintage, it is ruled by a monarch who serves both as head of state and head of government, ie, the Prime Minister. Despite its relatively small size and a population of about 400,000, Brunei constitutes an interesting political and a respectable international entity by holding membership in major international forums including the United Nations, Association of the Commonwealth of Nations, Organisation of Islamic Cooperation, and ASEAN etc. Inspired by the much touted philosophy of MIB (Melayu Islam Beraja) rendered in English as 'Malay Islamic Monarchy', the Brunei Sultanate derives its legitimacy to rule on the basis of a written constitutional framework which was first promulgated in September 1959. As the government's official website puts it 'Brunei Darussalam's political system rests on the twin pillars of the country's written Constitution and the tradition of Malay Muslim Monarchy. These two facts dominate both the formal political life and its government ethos.'[1]

'A new nation but an ancient country' is as aptly described kingdom by the ruler, HM Sultan Haji Hassanal Bolkiah, in his address to a Commonwealth Prime Ministers' Conference in the Bahamas in 1999.[2] Arguably one of the oldest sultanates in Southeast Asia, Brunei's history can be conventionally traced back to the fourteenth century CE, coinciding with the spread Islam in the region. The present Sultan and Yang Di-Pertuan Negara, Haji Hassanal

[1] www.information.gov.bn/Media%20Document%20Library/Brunei%20Today/brunei%20in%20brief_FINAL%202.pdf accessed 1 November 2017.

[2] Cited from AVM Horton, *Turun Temurun: A Dissection of Negara Brunei Darussalam*, (Worcestershire: Bordesley, 1998) 15.

Bolkiah Mu'izzaddin Waddaulah, is the 29th of a continuous line of sultans who have ruled the sultanate for over 600 years.

In its heyday, in the sixteenth century, Brunei's hegemony extended to almost all the northern Borneo states and even parts of the Sulu Kingdom in the southern Philippines.[3] Present day Brunei, however, is confined to some 5,675 sq km of territories in two enclaves – Brunei-Muara on one side and the Temburong District hemmed in by the Malaysian Sarawak district of Limbang. The early sprawling territories shrank to its present borders culminating in the annexation of Limbang in 1890 by the Brooke regime in Sarawak. Brunei became a British Protected State following the signing of a Protectorate Treaty in 1888 that was further reinforced by a supplementary Treaty with the British in 1906. The then hapless Brunei Sultan Hashim Jalilul Alam reluctantly gave up his traditional sovereignty – by allowing the British agent, styled as Resident whose advice the Sultan must take in all matters except religion – a precedent already set under a similar Pangkor Treaty in Malaya in 1873.[4] The Resident formed a State Council in 1906–1907 which comprised of selected state dignitaries who rubber-stamped the Resident's decisions.[5] Little was done to lay the foundations for a democratic society. This sanctioned the perpetuation of a model of autocratic centralisation with rule by administrative decree. As a modern writer stated 'the actual constitutional system that was in operation in all of the Malay States in the early twentieth century was the British Resident and Adviser system.'[6]

Though ravaged by abject poverty on the eve of the Residency Rule, Brunei later emerged as a rich country with the discovery of a large oil field at Seria in 1929 by the British Malayan Petroleum Company (later Brunei Shell Petroleum Company). Consequently, next to Burma, Brunei became the second largest oil-producer in the Commonwealth. State debts to Malaya, incurred in the early years of Brunei residency rule, were repaid and the Sultanate accumulated a good surplus of wealth.

I. THE BEGINNINGS OF THE PROPOSALS

In the post-War era, slow changes began to take place in British colonial policy towards Brunei, where the ruling class began to question the status quo

[3] For a concise history of Brunei, See Graham Saunders, *History of Brunei* (Singapore Routledge Curzon, 2002); and DS Ranjit Singh, *Brunei 1839–1983 The Problems of Political Survival* (Singapore: Oxford University Press, 1984).

[4] *Cf* AVM Horton, 'The Signing of the 1905–1906 UK-Brunei Treaty' (1986) 6(2) *Brunei Museum Journal* 125–127.

[5] Details in BA Hussainmiya, 'Manufacturing Consensus: The Role of the State Council in Brunei Darussalam' (2011) 31(2) *Journal of Southeast Asian Studies* 321–350.

[6] Johan S Sabaruddin, 'A Background of Federalism in Malaysia', in Clauspeter Hill & Jorg Menzel (eds) *Constitutionalism in Southeast Asia*, vol 3 (Singapore: Konrad Adenauer Stiftung, 2009), at 135.

of British-Brunei relations of the past. Sultan Ahmad Tajuddin's (1913–1950; r 1924–1950)[7] plea to revise the 1905–1906 Treaty fell on deaf ears.[8] But the British Colonial Office could not ignore the same demand from his successor Sultan Omar Ali Saifuddin (1914–1986; r 1950–1967).

In 1950 when, Sultan Omar Ali Saifuddin, *Sa'adul Khairi Waddien* (SOAS III), ascended to the throne of Brunei as its 28th ruler, the little Sultanate was already a leading oil-producing country and was on its way to becoming a super-rich State. For better or worse, the Western-style government introduced by the British had long ended the political instability caused by a disunited and too frequently self-seeking nobility, particularly among the old territorial chiefs. More importantly, the British administration laid the foundation for a strong and centralised state machinery which helped in the revival and the prestige of the Brunei monarchy itself.[9]

Unlike his two predecessors – Sultans Muhammad Jamalul Alam and Ahmad Tajuddin – who were victims of British overlordship, Sultan Omar possessed a strong personality with a will of his own; traits that enabled him to gradually erode and supplant British influence in his kingdom's internal affairs. Britain now resorted to the Sultan's goodwill to secure imperial economic interests that had been ravaged by World War II. Dollar earnings from Brunei's oil investment income in the UK provided a solid source of finance for British coffers. Following their experience in pre-War Malaya, where the British learnt the importance of a profitable alliance with the Malay ruling class and its aristocratic establishments, the British began to loosen its purse strings to restore an improved monarchic lifestyle in Brunei. With increased privileges, the Brunei aristocracy stood firmly behind the Sultan in resisting any threat to their privileges. At the same time the new assertive ruler began to gain gradual control over the mushrooming benefits of oil income while enjoying political stability under the aegis of the protective British umbrella. Time and tide were in his favour, and he himself was a headstrong personality on whom 'were to fall the demands of a mounting nationalism, as well as the task of mobilising Brunei for a step into the modern world, independent action, and the problems of prosperity'.[10]

Sultan Omar was the first Brunei ruler to receive a Western-style education at the Malay College ('the Malay Eton') in Kuala Kangsar in the Malay state of Perak. He later fulfilled cadet service in government before succeeding his brother as Sultan in 1950. Besides, he was a practicing Muslim and possessed a stronger vision and action plan for royal ascendancy than his immediate predecessors.

[7] Bob Reece, 'The Little Sultan': Ahmad Tajuddin II of Brunei, Gerard MacBryan, and Malcolm Macdonald' (2009) *Borneo Research Bulletin* 2–39.

[8] Sultan Ahmad Tajuddin was invited at last to London to discuss about the revision of the Treaty in mid-June 1950 when he fell ill on his way in Singapore and died.

[9] See BA Hussainmiya, *The Brunei Revival of 1906: A Popular History* (Bandar Seri Begawan, Brunei Press 2006).

[10] DE Brown, 'Brunei: The Structure and History of a Bornean Malay Sultanate' *(Monograph of the Brunei Museum Journal* (1970) 160.

It was during the early years of Sultan Omar's rule that the genesis for the making of the Brunei Constitution was solidified. Whether he proposed the idea or not, Brunein children are taught to recognise him as the '*grantor*' of the Constitution which earned him the epithet of 'the Architect of Modern Brunei'.[11]

The making of the Brunei Constitution is a fascinating case study since it symbolises a unique end game in the history of decolonisation in Southeast Asia. From the imperial point of view, constitution-making was a concomitant process as preparations had to be made for the former colonies towards independence whereas for those who were colonised, it was a symbol of their freedom and sovereignty. In some parts of Asia, including Malaysia, the process of drafting a post-colonial constitution was a somewhat smoother and speedier exercise because the concerned parties coalesced together towards a common goal for decolonisation. However, Brunei's case deviated from this pattern. Not only did the constitution-making discussions prove troublesome and protracted, but the final version turned out to be a watered-down document that failed to do justice to the original ideals its British promoters desired for Brunei's democratisation and liberalisation.

As Nicholas Tarling once remarked about the British: 'In the plenitude of their power, their policy had been one of sufficiency unto the day, of doing no more than seemed necessary to meet their interests'.[12] Indeed, theirs was a deliberate policy of cushioning the local society from the disruptive effects of development and 'over-education' that helped to maintain a status quo of conservatism and general backwardness among the people.

The idea of drafting a Brunei Constitution started in the late 1930s.[13] At that time the Colonial Office treated the plan as 'premature', and it stood little chance of success due to several reasons. First, the Sarawak and North Borneo governments were unlikely to voluntarily liquidate their sovereignty and be reduced to Crown Colonies. While the British thought that Sultan Ahmad Tajuddin was a weak ruler[14] who could have been coaxed into accepting this idea, British officials discouraged it. Second, the takeover of these administrations would be

[11] See, eg, as a well-respected Bruneian Blogger writes 'Almarhum Sultan Haji 'Omar 'Ali Saifuddien Sa'adul Khairi Waddien is the person who played important roles in the realization of the existence of constitution and to clear a way towards Independent Brunei.' The late monarch declared a plan to set up the written Constitution for Brunei in early May 1953.' http://bruneiresources.blogspot.com/2009/10/constitution-of-brunei-darussalam-50th.html. Accessed 1 November 2017.

[12] Nicholas Tarling, *The Fall of Imperial Britain in South-East Asia* (South-East Asian Historical Monographs Oxford University Press Singapore and New York, 1993) at 131.

[13] Cecil Clementi who became the Governor of the Straits Settlements (including Labuan), High Commissioner for the Malay States and for Brunei, and British Agent for Sarawak and North Borneo) made a proposal as early as 1931 to form a federation of Labuan, Sarawak, North Borneo, and Brunei. *Cf* Nicholas Tarling, 'Sir Cecil Clementi and the Federation of British Borneo,' (1971) 44(2) *Journal of the Malaysian Branch of the Royal Asiatic Society* 1–34.

[14] Sultan Ahmad Tajuddin who was deemed to be 'hardly an asset' and one who evoked 'surprisingly little respect or even interest in the Sarawak Malay's mind'. See Clementi to Tuan Muda, 6 Aug 1930, Clementi papers, quoted in Tarling, 'Sir Cecil Clementi and the Federation of British Borneo', ibid, at 33.

costly for the miserly British government. Third, the general backwardness of political development in these territories presented yet another stumbling block. What bothered the British most was that they bore overall responsibility for the Borneo territories in international forums but in fact had little executive authority (except perhaps in Brunei). The Colonial Office also felt it absurd to prolong the four separate administrations and tariff systems in British Borneo that had impeded progress of the territories and made it difficult to attract personnel to run the services.[15]

In the aftermath of the Pacific War, the Federation idea gained steam as British priorities for Southeast Asia changed. After losing India, the proverbial 'Jewel of the British Crown' the British will to sustain its empire by coercive means slackened. Their main concern shifted to holding the empire together by economic, commercial, and financial ties, by constitutional links to the Crown, by common democratic and participatory concepts of government and by defence collaboration.

The little Brunei, dubbed as 'the mother State of Borneo' was touted as the nucleus of a future united administration in Borneo.[16] After the 1930s, Brunei's economy surpassed those of Sarawak and North Borneo – her two neighbours which suffered heavy losses during the War and – which had become a liability to British economic and strategic interests. Consequently, it was Brunei's riches that Britain targeted to cement closer cooperation among the three Northern Borneo territories and pay for the development of the three territories. If Brunei were to agree, it became necessary to return some of her former lost territories. Thus in 1944 Brigadier CFC Macaskie (formerly in Colonial Service in North Borneo, and Head of the Borneo Planning Unit during the War years) suggested restoring to Brunei its former districts, including the 5th Division of Sarawak. Thus placated, the Sultan might agree to a new treaty that would in effect grant direct jurisdiction to the British monarch along the lines of the treaties proposed for Malaya.[17] By distributing the oil riches from Brunei to benefit more people, the new State could become 'a compact territorial unit with a well-balanced economy'.[18]

With a view to re-introduce civil administration in Malaya and the Borneo territories at the end of the War, the British War Cabinet set up a committee whereby the pre-War arrangements in the Borneo territories and Malaya were to be scrapped.[19] The British government was to take over the administration

[15] CO 531/29 (File 17) JM Martin's Memorandum, 14 Feb 1940.

[16] The description of Brunei as 'the mother State of Borneo' was made by Sir John Martin at a Colonial Office meeting with H.H. the Sultan of Brunei in 1957. CO 1030/460, note of a meeting with HH the Sultan of Brunei, 11 Sep 1957.

[17] CO 825/42, (File 55104/3/1943–44, item 37) Macaskie to Wodeman, (Secret) Memorandum, 4 Dec 1944.

[18] Ibid.

[19] CO 825/43 (File 55104/15, item 22) Draft Report of War Cabinet Committee on Malaya and Borneo, 24 Apr 1944.

in North Borneo and seek the cession to the British Crown of full jurisdiction over Brunei and Sarawak. In view of an increased awareness of racial or other communal differences in the territories, the previous concept of a 'United Borneo' did not receive much emphasis. In its place was the idea to subordinate the three administrations to a Singapore-based Governor General for Malaya and Borneo. When Sarawak and North Borneo became Crown Colonies in 1946, Brunei's future hung in the balance. The Colonial Office hoped, though it did not overtly declare, that the two Crown Colonies and Brunei would in due course be brought under some sort of unified administration. 'A public declaration at that time would have had a bad effect on public opinion in Sarawak and would have played into the hands of the anti-secessionists'.[20]

On this occasion Brunei survived and retained its status as a separate entity largely due to fortuitous circumstances. Sir Harold MacMichael, who forced the Malayan Sultans to surrender their jurisdiction to the British Crown and hurriedly introduced the controversial Malayan Union in 1946, was recalled to go to Malta on another mission before he reached Brunei.[21] Thereafter the Brunei question was shelved until a Governor General (of the Malayan Union and the new Colony of Singapore) was appointed to devise 'the possibility of the union of Brunei with the other Borneo territories'.[22] The sudden and unexpected surge of Malay nationalism in Malaya, against the imposition of the Malayan Union plan in 1946, may have cautioned the British against repeating the experiment in Brunei.[23] Malcolm MacDonald, the Governor-General, who had a soft spot for Brunei,[24] warned against amending the 1905–6 Anglo-Brunei Treaty 'since this might tend to arouse an opposition party to our proposals and perhaps defeat our proposals altogether'.[25] Besides, Brunei was 'too small a State' to administer. Therefore, MacDonald devised a plan for Brunei to be 'joined for administrative and any other necessary purposes with a neighbouring colony, without any derogation in theory from the former's present Constitutional position'.[26] Brunei was then placed under the Governor of the British Colony of Sarawak who became the High Commissioner for Brunei, an arrangement

[20] CO 1022/61, A Colonial Office Paper 'Political Objectives in British Territories of South-East Asia,' Secret, 10 Mar 1953, p 157. As early as 1946 it had been intended (though overtly not declared) 'that the two newly created colonies of North Borneo and Sarawak and the State of Brunei should in due course be brought under some form of unified administration.' CO 1022/61(item 24), memorandum (n.d. unsigned). The anti-secessionist movement in Sarawak is well described in RHW Reece, The Name of Brooke, *The Name of Brooke: The End of White Rajah Rule in Sarawak*. (Kuala Lumpur, Oxford University Press, 1982), 246–277.

[21] For MacMichaels' mission in Malaya see Albert Lau, *Malayan Union Controversy:1942–1948* (Singapore OUP 1991) 109–122.

[22] CO 537/2244 (Item 23), Memorandum by Secretary of State for Colonies, 24 Dec 1947.

[23] For details, see Albert Lau (n 21).

[24] See, BA Hussainmiya, 'Malcolm MacDonald and Brunei: Diplomacy with intimacy' (2014) 45(3) *Journal of Southeast Asian Studies* 393–418.

[25] CO 537/2244 (item 14,) Para 2, Telegram, Secret, Governor-General to CO, 23 Oct 1947.

[26] CO 537/2244, (item 5), Secret, Governor-General to CO, 16 May 1947.

that came into effect from 1 May 1948.[27] The High Commissioner seated in Kuching was to direct general policy and administration in both territories. The Resident in Brunei was placed under the authority of the High Commissioner. Also, in place of Malayan civil servants, Sarawak-based officers were seconded for service in Brunei.[28] Advocates of this scheme no doubt had in mind the ultimate fusion of the three Borneo territories either on a unitary or federal basis, but public endorsement of such a plan was wisely eschewed, in view of the animated opposition from the Sarawak anti-secessionists and the Brunei Malays.

The Sarawak-Brunei administrative merger, on the other hand, initiated much against the will of the Bruneians later blighted all subsequent efforts by the British government to bring Brunei into any federal plan with the British-dependent Borneo territories. More importantly, that arrangement hampered smooth progress of the constitutional negotiations that were to follow soon after.

Apart from the 'federal' solution, the British initiative to draft a Brunei Constitution was forced by a turn of domestic events since the beginning of 1950 when the British hold on Brunei began to slacken. The British Resident could scarcely exercise his executive authority under a new Sultan Omar Ali Saifuddin who wanted to gain the lost sovereignty of his predecessors under the British. The 1906 British-Brunei Treaty which stipulated that 'Resident's advice must be taken on all matters except Islamic religion' increasingly turned into a liability rather than an asset. No one was more concerned with the change of events than the new British Governor of Sarawak cum High Commissioner for Brunei, Sir Anthony Abell (1906–1994) who was in office from 1950 to 1959 and felt that there was much at stake for the British power. Until then a single 'Advice Clause' had been sufficient to restrain the royal autocracy.

Anthony Abell grew apprehensive when the State Council which had been from its inception managed under the thumb of the Resident but now dominated by the Brunei aristocracy,[29] was becoming too obstructive an institution for the

[27] Details in BA Hussainmiya, *Sultan Omar Ali Saifuddin and Britain: The Making of Brunei Darulssalam* (Kuala Lumpur: Oxford University Press, 1995), ch 2. Also in BA Hussainmiya, *The Brunei Constitution of 1959: An inside history* (Bandar Seri Begawan: Brunei Press Sdn. Berhad 2000) ch 2.

[28] The following official cadres of the Sarawak Establishment were seconded for service in Brunei: British Resident; Assistant Resident, Controller of Customs & State Treasurer; State Engineer and Officer-in-Charge, Electrical Department; State Medical Officer; Chief Police Officer; State Forest Officer; State Education Officer; Senior Assistant Resident; OCPD Kuala Belait; Assistant State Engineer; 2 Nusing Sisters; Medical Officer; Grade II Matron; Health Sister; State Surveyor; Immigration Officer; Police Officer, OCPD Brunei; Health Sister; Marine Officer; Deputy Legal Adviser. B(runei) A(rchives) /1258/83, (SUK Series 5, Box 97), annexed Sch II to Sarawak Brunei Agreement, 17/22 Apr 1948.

[29] Ie, excluding HH the Sultan, the State Council included six Pengirans, ie, Duli Pengiran Bendahara Pengiran Anak Abdul Rahman (the 1st Minister), Duli Pengiran Pemancha Pengiran Haji Mohammed Alam (the 2nd Minister), Pengiran Haji Mohammed Salleh (the Chief Kathi), Pengiran Kerma Indera, and Pengiran Maharaja Leila. Other members were the British Resident,

colonial administration to carry on minimal functions for the sake of good government. By contrast, the Sultan and his aristocratic followers yearned for self-administration under Britain's protective umbrella and were not interested in self-government. The solution that came to Abell's mind was the dissolution of the State Council and eliminating the role of 'those Malay members' of the State Council who were 'patently unfit for such responsibilities.'[30] As Abell saw it, only under a new Constitution could this be achieved; it was an idea that found favour with the Colonial Office. Such a Constitution would create provisions for new instruments of governance such as a Legislative Council, an Executive Council, and a ceremonial Privy Council. Hopefully, Brunei would move towards a representative form of government which would limit the Sultan's autocratic powers in exchange for some share to the people's participation in self-rule.

II. RATIONALE BEHIND THE MAKING OF THE CONSTITUTION

A Constitution could further facilitate the Sultan to initiate administrative modernisation and power consolidation. The British may have had an altruistic agenda, but the Sultan's motive was otherwise and saw the Constitution as an entrenchment of his sovereignty and an instrument to preserve his dynasty. By agreeing to the proposal for a constitution, he was thinking of the existing constitutional model in the Unfederated Malay States of Johor and Kelantan where the sovereign status of the Sultans was more apparent than his own under the thumb of the British Resident. Moreover, the Sultans in the Federated Malay States (FMS) had a local *Menteri Besar* (Chief Minister) to oversee the administration, albeit guided by the British advisors. Whereas the term Resident whose functions were akin to these of British Advisers in the Unfederated Malay States (UFMS) as in the case of Brunei, became anathema to the Sultan and his aristocratic circles.

Once the Sultan became obsessed with revising the British-Brunei Treaty of 1906, the High Commissioner seized upon the idea to promote the Colonial Office stratagem to prepare a Constitution for Brunei which, in any case, was the Sultan's prerogative, as the sovereign Head of State, to *grant* a Constitution. While agreeing initially to the British proposals for a Constitution the Sultan also bargained for an assurance on dynastic succession of his family by asking the British government to formally and simultaneously regulate succession to the Brunei throne.[31] In fact, the Agreement of 1888 and the Supplementary

The State Treasurer, Pehin Orang Kaya Di-Gadong, Pehin [U]dana Laila, and Pehin Dato Perdana Menteri Haji Ibrahim Jahfar. BA/0260/83 (SUK Series 3, Box 20), The Minutes of the State Council, 30 Sep 1952.

[30] CO 1030/113, Anthony Abell to CO, No 47 (secret), 23 Mar 1954, para 7.

[31] A Brunei scholar highlights the significance of this issue. Quoting an interview with (Pengiran Pekerma Setia Di Raja Sahibul Bandar) Pengiran Dato Haji Ali, a close associate of SOAS III, 'One may argue that the reason why Sultan Omar Ali intended to give Brunei a Constitution was to

Agreement of 1905–6 had specifically recognised that the British government would ensure the due succession to the throne in Brunei. The Sultan was desirous that 'the unwritten law and traditions governing the succession shall be evidenced in a clear and unambiguous manner by an enactment which shall come into force on the same date as the new Constitution'.[32]

As for replacing the Treaty with a Constitution, the Colonial Office showed little inclination. Abell knew of the Sultan's determination to do away with the Treaty and if that could be achieved, he would be amenable to offer his goodwill and cooperation for a speedy resolution to the State's administrative needs by accepting a Constitution and to reform the outmoded feudal basis of his government. Explaining his stand, Abell briefed the Colonial Office as follows:

> His Highness [the Sultan of Brunei] is most anxious to obtain a revision of the treaty whereby he can be given greater responsibilities for the internal affairs of the State. … I have insisted that a revision of the treaty cannot be contemplated until His Highness has established a Constitution on democratic and acceptable lines.[33]

In place of the abhorrent advice clause in the Treaty, it was decided to tie the Sultan down with statutory obligations, through a provision in the Constitution whereby the Sultan would uphold his commitments not as an autocrat, but as a Constitutional Ruler and so on.

The need for a Constitution was also considered a useful step to right the wrongs committed by the previous British administration in Brunei. For example, there were lapses in the manner which previous legislation was passed in Brunei on behalf of Her Majesty's government. By 1949 the British realised that crucial aspects of their authority in the Sultanate stood on flimsy legal foundations – a discovery that they kept pretty much to themselves.[34] CH Dawson, the Acting Governor (Sarawak)/High Commissioner (Brunei), on the advice of Mr Grattan-Bellow, the Attorney-General of Sarawak, was one of the early officials to raise this issue. According to Dawson, there were serious procedural lapses in the way that the Residents had been passing laws for Brunei.

> In so far as can be ascertained the Sultan of Brunei is an autocratic sovereign, and he alone (unless he delegates his powers) can make laws for the Government of the State.[35]

regulate the succession issue'. … This alluded to the succession issue before SOAS was appointed as the Sultan in 1950. Matassim Haji Jibbah, *Political Development in Brunei with Reference to the Reign of Sultan Omar Ali Saifuddien III (1950–67)*, Unpublished MA Thesis (Hull University, 1983) 23, at n 7.

[32] CO 1030/113, Anthony Abell to CO, No 46 (Secret), 23 Mar 1955.

[33] Ibid.

[34] CO 717/76, no 72483. Memorandum by WS Gibson, nd. Possibly Sultan Ahmad Tajuddin's proposed visit to the UK in 1950 to negotiate with the Colonial Office regarding a revision of the Treaty prompted British authorities to review their legal status in Brunei.

[35] CO 943/1,59706, Item 1, CH Dawson to A Creech Jones, the Colonial Secretary for the Colonies, No 7, 14 Oct 1949, para 2. (Parenthesis in original.) CO 943/1, 59706, JC McPetrie, Minute to Sir Kenneth Roberts-Wray, 20 Jun 1950, para 3.

The Protectorate Agreement of 1888 and the Supplementary Agreement of 1905–06 had not provided the Resident with the authority to pass legislation for Brunei. Yet, besides being the de facto executive authority, the Resident had arrogated law-making powers for himself through the Brunei State Council mainly on the strength of the advisory clause in the Agreement. As in the case of the Malayan States, a Colonial Office legal adviser observed:

> The power of legislation has been exercised without being questioned since 1909, but the authority for its exercise, while perhaps a matter of legitimate inference, is indirect and implied … [i]t seems therefore unfortunate that the jurisdiction for the exercise of one of its main functions should be a matter of inference and implications only.[36]

By invoking the Sultan's name, the Residents in Brunei were, from 1907 onward, quite accustomed to pass laws – known as Enactments – through the medium of the Brunei State Council where the Sultan was expected to preside in person. The controversial land legislation in Brunei between 1907 and 1909, passed even against the protests of the Ruler, marked the beginning of this trend. This practice surprised the Colonial Office legal expert, JC McPetrie, who in 1950 highlighted the fact that the State Council had no legal authority to function in this manner:

> It appears that, subject to the Treaties, the Sultan is an absolute sovereign, and that the law making power must be vested in him. The Council has no legal status, or at least is not provided for in any written law. There is no Constitution, or at least no written Constitution, for the State, and the form and method of legislating are not prescribed anywhere.[37]

Apparently, Brunei did not have written laws formulated in the Western pattern before the introduction of the Residency administration.[38] Only from 1907, when the State Council began passing laws, did they take written form. Each printed version carried the enacting words 'It is hereby enacted by His Highness the Sultan in Council as follows …'. The Resident placed his signature at the head of each Enactment, though the words 'I assent' were not used. His signature was presumed to merely testify to the fact that the Enactment had been passed by the Sultan in Council. What was the validity of such an Enactment if

[36] CO 717/76, no 72483, memorandum by WS Gibson, nd.

[37] CO 943/1, 59706, JC McPetrie, Minute to Sir Kenneth Roberts-Wray, 20 Jun 1950, para 3.

[38] Local scholars refer vaguely to the practice of traditional law codes which existed prior to the arrival of the British. See BA Hussainmiya, Some Observations on pre-colonial legal system and practices in Brunei, *Journal of Southeast Asian Studies, Selected papers in Economic and Social History*, FASS, UBD, Brunei, 7., No. 1, 2007 pp. 27–37. There is no detailed information available on the use of traditional legal codes such as the *Hukum Kanun* or of Islamic Shari'a laws in Brunei. Versions of the former have been found in Brunei, but in the opinion of Liaw Yock Fang, of the National University of Singapore, they are no more than copies of the Undang-Undang Malacca, which he edited and published. See Liaw Yock Fang, *Undang-Undang Malacca* (Dodrecht, Hague: Foris Publications, 1978); and RO Winstedt, 'A Brunei Malay Code' (1923) 1 *Journal of the Malayan Branch of the Royal Asiatic Society* 251.

the Sultan was not present in the Council? If the Enactments had been passed under such circumstances by the *Resident* in Council, as had been the case more often than not since the War (with Sultan Ahmad Tajuddin often absent from the State Council) their validity was in question. The Sultan appears at no stage to have expressly delegated his legislative powers to the Resident. Even if he had done so, the printed copies of the laws did not purport to be passed by the Resident in Council.

When the Enactments thus passed in the Brunei State Council from 1907 to 1930 were revised and collated in book form, and the book was alleged to be issued 'by authority', it was not in fact backed by any statutory authority. Nevertheless, as the (law) courts officially accepted all such public statutes, there was no doubt that the book would be accepted as authentic. But Enactments passed after 1930 had not even been collated in book form until 1949, and this created a real legal issue. The individually printed copies of the Enactments did not claim to be printed 'by authority' and did not bear the name of any authorised printer (Brunei did not have a government printer until 1951). In this event, if an Enactment were to be challenged in a court of law, it would at least have been necessary for the Resident to present himself in the court to produce a certified copy. Furthermore, if an Enactment were to be challenged on the ground that it was not passed by the Sultan in Council it would also be necessary to prove that the Sultan had in some way delegated his legislative powers or that he had assented to the Enactment at some stage of the proceedings. Drawing attention to these problems, the Acting High Commissioner CH Dawson concluded his despatch as follows:

> I think that you will agree that these matters which fundamentally affect the legal and Constitutional position in Brunei should be examined ... It may well be that no question would be raised or challenge made for years to come, but, as High Commissioner for Brunei, I am not happy about the position, and would like it to be put on proper footing as soon as possible.[39]

These and other questions were discussed at length among the policy makers in the Colonial Office, and there must have been a great sigh of relief within its walls that no one had so far ever challenged any of the Enactments thus passed.[40] The Colonial Office in late 1949 came up with several suggestions to rectify this legal wrangle. First of all, it was deemed necessary to give retrospective statutory validity to the laws already passed, by means of an Interpretation and General Clauses Ordinance. Second, a government printer was appointed to issue a government Gazette (in 1951). Third, the decision was made to publish a revised edition of the Law Enactments. Fourth and, more importantly, to advise

[39] CO 943/1, 59706, Item 1, CH Dawson to A Creech Jones, the Colonial Secretary for the Colonies, No 7, 14 Oct 1949, para 11.

[40] Ibid, JC McPetrie, Minutes dated 20 Jun & 9 Aug 1949; and GC Whiteley, Minute dated 9 Aug 1950.

the Sultan to grant a Constitution which would determine once and for all the respective statutory functions of various government bodies to be created for the better running of the government. The last item was the most cumbersome and sensitive. It would require time for drafting and implementation. The new High Commissioner to Brunei was expected to lay the groundwork by approaching the Sultan to raise the need for a written Constitution.

Prompted by the Colonial Office and the High Commissioner, Sir Anthony Abell, in May 1953, the Sultan yielded to British pressure to announce his intentions as follows.

> For some time, it has been my intention and desire to grant to my people a written Constitution by means of which provision can be made for the Government and wellbeing of the State of Brunei. It is my wish to set out in this Constitution firstly the laws by which the succession to the Sultanate shall be secured, and such other matters relating to the Sovereign and his family as is right and proper; and secondly the composition, powers and duties of the State Council together with rules for the conduct of the State business and for the making of laws ...[41]

Good intentions apart, the constitution-making for Brunei turned out to be a nightmare of an exercise because of conflicting spheres of interest on the part of the British and the Sultan. At any rate both the traditional elite and the British administration took their task seriously and set to work urgently. Both sides struggled to enshrine their dominance in the Constitution – the Brunei side to uphold the principles of a Malay Islamic Monarchy and the British side to establish a quasi-democratic polity in transition from a semi-colonial set-up. The struggle between these two opposite forces ended in a strange amalgam that in the end satisfied the aspirations of neither.

Had it been implemented in the heyday of their power, ie before the outbreak of World War II, the outcome might perhaps have been different. The machinery necessary for self-government would have evolved over the years as in the case of the Malayan States.[42] On the contrary, the existing Brunei State Council, a relic of the past originally manipulated to the benefits of the British administration, proved hardly a sufficient training ground for local elites in the art of governance.

[41] CO 1030/ 113, The Sultan's Titah. Also the speech is reproduced in BA Hussainmiya & Nicholas Tarling (eds), *Brunei: Traditions of Monarchic Culture and History: RH Hickling's Memorandum upon the Brunei Constitutional History and Practice* (Bandar Seri Begawan: Brunei Press Sdn) Berhad, 2011) 79–81 [hereinafter 'Hickling Memo'].

[42] Until 1948, only Johor and Trengganu among the Malayan States possessed written Constitutions, although they developed certain fixed Constitutional conventions, especially after contacts with British rule. Ibid, at 85. However, one should also take note of the fact that both were promulgated by pre-colonial monarchies as an indirect means of frustrating colonial intervention. JM Gullick, Personal communication, 10 Jan 1995.

Brunei's case was clearly a contrast to the Malayan Sultanates where the rulers willingly or unwillingly were ready to give up their executive powers.[43] The Brunei Sultan never intended to give up his powers despite British machinations to transform his status into that of a constitutional ruler. The end result was when the British ideals of practicing universal suffrage and democratic institutions took a backseat allowing Brunei monarchy to entrench its absolute powers.[44]

III. THE MALAY CONSTITUTIONAL COMMITTEE (*TUJUH SERANGKAI*)

As soon as the Sultan's made his announcement, both the British administration and local elites set about drafting the proposals. In July 1953 the Sultan nominated a seven-member Bruneian Constitution Committee, known as *Tujuh Serangkai* (literally 'branches').[45] Their task was to ascertain public views on a Constitution, prepare a detailed report, and advise the Sultan not only on drafting the Constitution but also establishing District Councils, and reorganising the State Council.[46] Abell reported that:

> … the result was a body which appeared to satisfy public opinion and certainly represented a wide variety of views ranging from the very advanced opinions of the teaching profession to the strictly orthodox and reactionary convictions of the mosque officials.[47]

The Committee toured the four districts of the State, holding meetings with the people. They welcomed the Sultan's proposal which engendered considerable public interest and was inundated with suggestions. Apart from expressing their political aspirations, the people everywhere treated the committee as a forum in which to air their grievances against the government. As usual, the nationalist school teachers came to the forefront to press their demands in vociferous

[43] G Braighlinn's interesting but incomplete study, *Ideological Innovation under Monarchy: Aspects of Legitimation Activity in Contemporary Brunei*, (Amsterdam: VU University Press, 1992), addresses these important issues in a veiled manner. See especially ch IV, 'The Modern Brunei Polity', at 12–17. ('Braighlinn' is the pseudonym of a Western author who lived in Brunei in the 1980s.)

[44] 'The uniqueness of Brunei is highlighted … by the fact that the Sultanate entered the Commonwealth, upon recovering 'full independence' … in January 1984, without the institution of a popular franchise, and within weeks had even abolished the Legislative Assembly', ibid, at 12.

[45] The State Legal Officer was appointed as their adviser. The committee included persons from aristocratic background but also some commoners: Pengiran Maharaja Leila Muda Kahar (Chairman), Pengiran Haji Yusuf bin Pengiran Haji Abdul Rahim, Pengiran Di Gadong Sahibul Mal Pengiran Haji Muhammad Salleh (The Chief Kathi), Pehin Orang Kaya Di Gadong Haji Yusuf, Pehin Orang Kaya Shahbandar Haji Ahmad, Pengiran Haji Ali bin Pengiran Haji Daud, and Haji (Later Pehin Penyurat) Abu Bakar Bin Haji Jambul (from Tutong).

[46] CO 1030/113, Anthony Abell to CO, Savingram No 104, 5 Aug 1954.

[47] Ibid, at para 2.

terms, especially with their favourite nationalist slogan, 'Brunei for Bruneians'. The meetings produced an important dividend to the administration in tapping the actual feelings of the young educated element, and thus serving as a 'safety valve' for an outburst of hidden sentiments.[48]

In January 1954, the Committee also spent two weeks visiting Johore, Negeri Sembilan, Kedah, and Kelantan to study these State's Constitutions. The Committee's final report of 23 March 1954, some 50 pages in length (in Malay), was passed on for the British administration's comments.[49] The authorities, finding the report 'sound and moderate in tone',[50] were surprised that the Committee arrived at unanimous conclusions. 'The minor political differences were subordinated to the strongly nationalist views held by all members of the Committee from the Chairman … down'.[51]

The British, however, were not inclined to accept all the proposals of the Constitution Committee, which tried to adopt as a model the Constitution of Johor. The main recommendations forwarded by the Committee were summarised as follows:

> The State of Brunei is an independent Malay State under a Malay … Sultan and is under the protection of Britain in terms of friendship. … The Sultan, according to-be-made treaty may receive a British Adviser (whose appointment must first be approved by the Sultan in Council) who will be responsible to advise the Sultan in Government and political matters but not … interfere with the religion (Islam) and customs of Brunei Malays and the Sultan may listen to his advice which he considers good and beneficial for the progress of the state of Brunei … The Malay Language must be accepted and used as the official language of the Brunei Government. Islam must be the official religion of the State. There is, however, freedom of worship for other religions.[52]

A main reason why the Johor model appealed to the Malay Constitutional Committee was as mentioned earlier that the Johor Sultanate was an unfederated Malay State where the Sultan's advisor did not carry the much-abhorred nomenclature of the Resident. In addition, a local Menteri Besar was seemingly in charge of the Sultan's administration following Sultan Abu Bakar's Constitution introduced in 1896. Brunei's system, on the other hand, was very much akin to other FMS which were all under the executive power by the British Residents.

[48] Ibid, at para 3.

[49] The report was divided into 8 parts: (A) Government and matters affecting it; (B) The Sultan, His Heir, Minister and 'chetria' (noble officials below the rank of Wazir); (C) Council of State; (D) District Council; (E) Town Council; (F) Brunei Citizenship; (G) Chief Penghulu, Penghulus and Headmen; (H) Other Reports. See CO 1030/114, Full Report of the Brunei Constitution Committee. Annex I in Anthony Abell to CO, Secret, 23 Mar 1955.

[50] Ibid, Ms Fairlie, Minute, 26 Aug 1954.

[51] Ibid, at para 2.

[52] Ibid., 'Government and Matters Affecting it', Part A of the Brunei Malay Constitution Committee report. Parts 'G' and 'H' of the report are omitted from the summary.

A second source of input came from the British side. Reginald Hugh (RH) Hickling, then an Assistant Attorney General in Sarawak came to Brunei in late 1954 to prepare his own report as an *aide memoire* to help colonial officials familiarise themselves with conditions in Brunei.[53] In his report it was pointed out that Brunei had had a sort of unwritten Constitution encompassing monarchic traditions and conventions that guided the affairs of the state from ancient times. The basic principles of such an unwritten Constitution were based on land laws and traditional land ownership of the royal class which were swept off during the tenure of early Residents making way for British sponsored reforms. In his report, Hickling looked at the traditional Brunei institutions with some empathy in making his own recommendations. His final report and some recommendations of the Malay Constitutional Committee then became the basis for the first draft of the Constitutional proposals.

The Malay Constitution Committee's insistence on removing the Resident's advisory role was turned down by the Colonial Office even though the British High Commissioner, Abell, argued strenuously against retaining the advice clause to placate the Sultan's traditional advisers which would smoothen the progress of constitutional discussions. In its place, Abell suggested that it would suffice to commit the Sultan in the new Agreement 'to observe the provisions of the new Constitution Enactment in letter and spirit and to exercise powers and authority in accordance therewith'.[54] But from the point of view of the Colonial Office that if the Brunei Sultan was allowed such a concession, it might precipitate similar demands from Malayan Sultans who too were subject to similar 'Advice' clauses in their agreements with the British. The Malayan Alliance Party manifesto had also requested that the post of British Advisers/Residents in the Unfederated and the Federated Malay States be abolished, although 'there were no indications as yet that the Rulers themselves would wish to dispense with their British Advisers'.[55] At most, the Colonial Office was willing to consider re-wording the advice clause to make it sound less onerous, as in Malayan agreements.[56]

IV. THE EARLY DRAFT PROPOSALS

The first draft of the Constitution Enactment made ready by Abell and his colleagues (JH Ellis, the Secretary to the High Commissioner, George Strickland QC the Legal Adviser, and RH Hickling) seemingly accommodated the nationalistic aspirations of the local Malay Constitutional Committee in so far as they

[53] Details in Hickling Memo (n 40).

[54] Ibid, at para 14.

[55] Ibid.

[56] For a useful discussion on the wordings of the Malayan Agreements see JM Gullick *Rulers and Residents: Influence and Power in the Malay States, 1870–1920* (Singapore Oxford University Press, 1992) at 29–31.

did not compromise the British hold over Brunei. On 16 and 17 December 1954 Abell met the Sultan and his two Ministers, Pengiran Bendahara and Pengiran Pemancha, at the Istana in the presence of the Resident, JO Gilbert, and RH Hickling. The drafts, said to have been unanimously approved, subject to minor amendments, were then forwarded to the Colonial Office for comments and recommendations before preparing the necessary legislation. Abell saw 'nothing very spectacular about these first tentative steps but they [did] represent a considerable readjustment of outlook in the last remaining stronghold of Malay feudalism'.[57] However, the draft fell far short of the expectations of the Malay Constitutional Committee members.

The original proposals on which a common agreement was reached between the Sultan and the British administration were as follows: Three separate bodies were to be formed. A Legislative Council consisting of 28 members, including 10 official members and 14 unofficial members with two ex-officio members (Legal Adviser and State Treasurer) and the Resident to act as Chairman. The Legislative Council would debate and legislate on matters of public interest (subjects exempted and needing the prior consent of the High Commissioner were Succession, Religion, Finance, Constitution, Justice, Ceremony, Defence, and Public Service).

The Sultan would lead the Executive Council, which was to consist of seven members, including the Resident, Legal Adviser, and State Treasurer as ex-officio members, and one official and three unofficial members chosen from the Legislative Council. Its function was mainly to advise and formulate policy, except on those matters lying within the purview of the Privy Council.

The Privy Council would also be headed by the Sultan and would include the Resident and the Legal Adviser as Ex-Officio Members. Others in the Council would be members of the Royal family and selected persons of royal blood. There would be no express qualification for membership but, for reasons of prestige, care would be taken to avoid appointment of members from the Executive and Legislative Councils or from Local Councils. Its main functions would be to advise on royal succession, exercise prerogatives of mercy, appointment of regents, state ceremonial and honours, remission of sentences, etc. As noted earlier, four to six Local Councils would also be established, along with a Public Service Commission with the Resident as its Chairman, along with two official and two unofficial members.

That very first draft ran into a snag as soon as it reached London. The Sultan felt something was amiss in the despatched proposals which led to a severe misunderstanding between him and the High Commissioner Abell. Someone[58] must

[57] CO 1030/113, Anthony Abell to CO, Secret No. 46, 23 Mar 1955, para 2.

[58] Most probably some oil company official who was close to the Sultan and the administration was behind this fiasco which needs to be supported by further research. This chapter also avoids discussions on the role of the oil company which shunned any concessions to the Brunei People's Party's propositions so as to dilute the Sultan's powers which they were propping up to safeguard their economic and strategic interests.

have tipped off the Sultan about the tinkering of mutually agreed proposals in the draft Constitution. What happened was that during the palace discussions, Abell did not elaborate his rationale behind some key proposals. Understandably, his aim was to eliminate the governing role of the two principal Wazirs to the Sultan, something his predecessors tried to do earlier that century.[59] Rather than accommodating the Wazirs in the proposed Executive and Legislative Councils, (to be established according to colonial State models), Abell proposed a Privy Council to give ceremonial representation to people of high noble ranks. This was intended to diminish the political importance of the Pengirans (nobles) who then would not 'interfere with or obstruct the day-to-day business of the State'.[60] Furthermore, he recommended indefinite retention of the posts of both the High Commissioner and the Resident, while maintaining some special veto powers for the British representative in the Constitution. Abell also referred to the need for a Nationality Enactment to enfranchise British protected persons residing in Brunei, who were mainly Chinese. These were some of the detailed matters which Abell chose wisely or unwisely not to disclose to the Sultan nor his advisers. When uncovered, the High Commissioner's attempt to bypass the Sultan on such important issues permanently damaged their relationship, especially their dealings on constitutional matters.

In mid-1955, faced with the ire of Sultan in a defiant mood, Abell had no choice but to give in to the Sultan's demands to amend the proposals to accommodate his two principal Wazirs in both Legislative and Executive Councils, lest their prestige and influence in the traditional Malay polity suffer. For all intent and purposes, this nullified the British principle of reorganising the law-making bodies in Brunei. Once the flood gates were opened, the Sultan, thereafter, began to escalate his demands further to revise the original draft proposals which made the entire constitution-making exercise a farce as seen from the correspondence that went on between Abell and the Colonial Office.

A key recommendation of the Constitutional Committee was to replace the British Resident with a *Mentri Besar*, which was 'one of the strongest aspirations of the politically minded section of the Malay population of Brunei'.[61] At the outset the Sultan accepted the British view that Brunei did not have a qualified Muslim Malay to fill the post of *Mentri Besar*, so that such a change would be impracticable for some time. Moreover, the Sultan trusted Abell's assurance that the controversial 'advice' clause found in the Agreement of 1905–06 would be taken out from the proposed new Agreement. Despite initial agreement, the Sultan began to drag his feet when he knew the British would not to get rid of the advice clause, which made the whole Constitution making process a burdensome effort.

[59] Ibid.
[60] Hickling Memo (n 40), at para 9.
[61] Ibid, at para 12.

If everything had gone along the Sultan's way, a Constitution could have been finalised within two years of his original announcement, by which time many of his constitutional committee's proposals would be implemented,[62] especially the transfer of power from the Resident's hands to those of a Brunei Malay *Mentri Besar.* However, a new political reality dawned in 1956, complicating the constitution-making process further. Among other difficulties the British had to consider the aspirations of an emerging nationalist force articulated by the newly-formed People's Party of Brunei (PRB) seeking a share in the government.[63] Shaikh AM Azahari founded this party on left of centre principles. Since its launch in 1956, it attracted almost 90 per cent of Brunei population into its fold.[64] The PRB's manifesto underscored opposition to 'all forms of colonialism in the political, economic and social spheres' and independence for Brunei through constitutional means. The PRB guaranteed to safeguard the position of the Sultan as a constitutional monarch. It would strive for a Malay nation comprising all states in the Malay Archipelago. In the economic sphere the PRB stood for worker's welfare and equal distribution of the state's wealth.[65] They also demanded general elections based on secret ballots and a ministerial form of government and so on which were considered too radical to be included in the constitutional proposals. In the presence of a defiant and uncompromising party the colonial officials were left helpless despite sympathising with the PRB's stand which led the Sultan to become increasingly less cooperative in accepting the British proposals.

The PRB demands aside, the early constitutional draft now ran into further problems because of the Sultan's insistence on introducing more and more amendments. For example, the British government had other priorities to consider before giving up their prerogatives for restraining the Sultan's power. For instance, as 'closer association between the three Borneo territories' was in sight, they wanted to safeguard the High Commissioner's veto and some executive powers, but even in that instance they were forced to give in to the Sultan's insistence on eliminating several original key proposals, including their

[62] It is important to note that the files relating to this period, 1956, have been closed indefinitely to public scrutiny by the Public Record Office. The files CO 1030/ 238 to 243 are retained by the department under s 3(4). It is likely that these refers to many emerging disputes between the British administration and the Sultan during this critical period. One should also note that the PRB's emergence also occurred in this year, and the files may contain many unpalatable details on personalities and events during the period.

[63] For the rise of PRB See, Zaini Haji Ahmad, *Perumbuhan Nasinalisme di Brunei (1939–1962)* (Bandar Seri Begawan Asia Printers, 2004), Zaini Haji Ahmad (ed), *Partai Rakyat Brunei: The People's Party of Brunei – Selected Documents / Dokumen Terpilih.* (Petaling Jaya, Insan, the Institute for Social Analysis, 1987). CO 1022/396, Anthony Abell to the Secretary of State for the Colonies, Savingram (Confidential), No 54, 13 May 1953.

[64] Zaini Haji Ahmad (ed), *Partai Rakyat Brunei: The People's Party of Brunei – Selected Documents / Dokumen Terpilih.* (Petaling Jaya: Insan, 1987).

[65] Document No. 3/PRB/56 Cited in Ibid., 95–98. See also *Borneo Bulletin,* [Brunei] 28 Jan. 1956 and 25 Feb 1956.

vital veto power. Moreover, the Sultan objected to the inclusion of one significant amendment from accepting the advice of the High Commissioner on immigration and citizenship matters (stipulated under Section 39, clause 2, (a) and (b) of the draft Constitution).[66] By giving in to the Sultan's demands, the British virtually gave up their responsibility to protect the citizenship rights of the recent migrant communities, particularly the Chinese. There were also several other matters in which the Sultan's will prevailed over those of the British proposals.

Bombarded with so many amendments that undermined both the letter and spirit of the original drafts of the Constitution and Agreement, a dispirited Abell warned that the proposed amendments were an attempt to tire them out with the expectation that they (the Colonial Office) might give up the whole exercise or yield to the Sultan the maximum power and privilege.[67] Abell was resentful that the Sultan 'bows more and more to the clamour of Brunei for the Bruneians and out with the foreigners'.[68]

Abell's efforts to bring Brunei out of its feudal past may have been sincerely motivated. However, he failed to appreciate the fact that popular sentiment in Brunei was as much supportive of the Sultan as they were of the PRB's demands. Being a foreigner, he hardly distinguished between popular allegiance to the party and the people's love of their monarch. In the *Mentri Besar* issue, for example, although the PRB opposed it, there was also a considerable body of opinion in the State supporting the appointment, to be rid of the discredited Residency system.

What distressed Abell most was that the revised draft Agreement submitted by the Sultan included a clause under which he would communicate directly with the Secretary of State whenever he did not accept the High Commissioner's advice.[69] Abell feared that this would bring the business of government to a standstill. Highlighting the need to safeguard British interests in the oil industry, he thought this could be achieved only if 'the British element in the Government is strong and has the power to act'.[70]

The Sultan's principal strategy was to extract maximum concessions from the British to establish his own supremacy as the de-facto local sovereign. By the middle of 1957, some four years after Sultan Omar made his first announcement, enthusiasm for constitutional reforms in Brunei had worn off. As the situation came to an impasse, the Colonial Office invited the Sultan for discussions in the summer of 1957. Despite making several agreements and promises in London, such as the holding of elections under a secret ballot system as demanded by the PRB, the Sultan reneged on these assurances once he returned to Brunei, much

[66] CO 1022/396, Anthony Abell to the Secretary of State for the Colonies, Savingram (Confidential), No 54, 13 May 1953.

[67] Ibid.

[68] Ibid.

[69] Ibid., Anthony Abell to E Melville, 5 Jun 1958.

[70] Ibid.

to the disappointment of local British officials. Another round of talks would thus be needed to finalise the Constitution. The talks lingered on for another two long years as the Sultan introduced more and more amendments to the draft. Both the Resident Gilbert and High Commissioner Abell grew despondent in becoming embroiled in the Sultan's single-minded manipulations and who was hell-bent on gaining power vis-a-vis the people. Allaying their officials' despair, the London Officials, felt it was better to leave the Sultan alone[71] if they were to negotiate on issues of power sharing between the Sultan and Her Majesty's government.[72] Caught in the middle, a frustrated Abell wrote:

> It has been hard and so far, unrewarding work. The ignorance and prejudice are of depth and darkness which are never encountered in Sarawak and unless the ballot box can produce an entirely new type of politician unlike any we have so far seen, I have great doubts of Brunei's capacity to make much progress in the political or administrative field.[73]

A heartbroken Abell even questioned the Colonial Office strategy of appeasing the Sultan on constitutional reforms. When the Sultan began wavering to accept the draft proposals, there was a suggestion that the British government could impose a Constitution under the Foreign Jurisdiction Act of 1890 as it was done in the case of the neighbouring Sarawak in 1953. Having raised that option, Hickling's report also highlighted the fact that:

> The Supplementary Agreement of 1905 and 1906 encroaches upon the sovereignty of the sultan in internal affairs to such an extent that he is required to act upon the advice of the representative of Her Majesty: A state of affairs which would indicate that sovereignty in relation to Brunei is, except in relation to 'those affecting the Mohammedan religion', is vested in the Crown.[74]

At any rate Hickling cautioned his government that 'however neat and secure such a method of promulgation might be, it does not offer the correct solution.'[75]

Unable to break the deadlock, the Colonial Office found it increasingly troublesome to resolve differences that had not been ironed out at source. Their lackadaisical approach had been to 'let things develop' and to allow their High Commissioner to steer the course of political advancement,[76] which became a part of the problem as well. No one seemed to have recognised the dilemma of Abell in Brunei, who was also functioning as the colonial Governor in Sarawak.

[71] Ibid.

[72] Ibid.

[73] Ibid.

[74] Hickling Memo (n 40), at para 142.

[75] Ibid, at para 144.

[76] Thus JB Johnston, who failed to stop the visit of Raeburn to Brunei, commented that 'I think we can only let things develop and leave it to the High Commissioner to decide what sort of treatment he gives to Raeburn', ibid. JB Johnston's Minute to E Melville, 31 May 1957. For details about Walter Raeburn's involvement on the side of the PRB demands in Hussainmiya, *Sultan Omar Ali Saifuddin III and Britain,* Ch 7.

Abell tried his best to get this message across to London by emphasising the wounded Brunei sensitivities on the issue.[77] One of his suggestions, put forward as early as 1955, was to consider separating the Sarawak and Brunei administrations and station a High Commissioner in Brunei exclusively. This idea did not find favour at the Colonial Office, which naively expected the Constitution to be implemented first. Had the Colonial Office heeded Abell's advice at the beginning, there was a good chance that the Constitution might have been approved before the end of 1956. However, the busy senior officials in the Colonial Office, drawing on their previous experience in different colonial situations, and playing cool games on paper did not appreciate Abell's hurry to move faster in the case of Brunei.

All the while the negotiations took place only between two main stake holders namely the Sultan and the British government. In Malaya there were three parties namely the British government, the Alliance Party and the State Sultans involved in discussions for constitution making. In Brunei's case only two parties were involved. The biggest loser was the PRB led by the charismatic leader, Shaikh AM Azahari. Despite valiant efforts, Shaikh Azahari, was never invited for tripartite talks as in the case of Malaya. During 1957, he met with some higher officials in the Colonial Office and that was it. His party's proposals for a representative government under a constitutional monarchy had never been seriously considered. As a matter of policy, the British authorities tried to avoid direct talks with the PRB for fear of alienating the Sultan who by all means shunned the PRB points of view for self-government. Both Abell and the Resident JO Gilbert who entertained and empathised with the PRB's demands for representative politics were rendered impotent by the attitude of indifferent Colonial Office mandarins. In the end the PRB leader Azahari could do nothing but blame the British government for betraying the people's aspirations, and when it was known that agreements had been reached between the Sultan and the Colonial Office to launch a Constitution, he was threatening to stage a kind of 'revolution' to win back power.[78]

If Azahari had anticipated repeating Tunku Abdul Rahman's success in London in 1957, he was sadly mistaken. The British approach to the situation in Malaya was different to that of Brunei. In Malaya the Malay politicians and the Rulers had developed an understanding to work hand in hand towards forming a Constitution and to obtain *Merdeka*, the independence. Besides, Malayan political leaders like Tunku Abdul Rahman as the victorious leader of an Alliance party which swept the 1955 national polls had far more charisma and authority to bargain with the British government. His political associates also were people

[77] Discussed in detail in ch 8 of Hussainmiya (n 27).

[78] Zaini Haji Ahmad, a member of Azahari's delegation to London, later wrote that 'He (Azahari) told his two colleagues of his doubts about British sincerity to give the people of Brunei their freedom and independence by constitutional means. Then agitated, AM Azahari talked about 'revolution' as the only way to seek political changes'. See Zaini Haji Ahmad (ed) *Partai Rakyat Brunei* (n 64), at 13.

of a higher calibre. Malaya and Singapore possessed and used a middle class, intelligentsia, and anti-government newspapers to bring pressure on the British for self-government and, ultimately, independence.[79] Azahari in Brunei had none of these advantages, except perhaps his commitment to anti-colonialism. In the end his party was side-lined by both the British and the Sultan during the constitutional talks.

The Malayan Merdeka talks as well as talks with Singapore which began in 1956 had progressed smoothly despite foreseeable difficulties. The British succeeded in blending their own economic and defence interests with the demands for self-government in Malaya and Singapore. By the same token the Colonial Office did not give Brunei's case the same priority and urgency as Malaya and Singapore between 1955 and 1958. Brunei's case had always been on the backburner because it was too small a territory to gain imperial attention. At any rate they needed to get rid of their protectorate responsibilities in Brunei following the successful conclusion of the Malaya/Singapore constitutional talks.

In Brunei, Abell and the Sultan were on a collision course in 1958 over the constitutional imbroglio. And as if to add insult to injury, the Sultan got the Resident Gilbert transferred back to Sarawak in 1958 despite Abell's protestations, especially since he felt that the British government should come forward to chastise the Sultan.[80] A disillusioned and irate Abell even suggested that 'as you [Eugene Melville] say, the Sultan is the key to most of our political problems here and if he does not see sense soon we must seriously consider whether or not we should build the new agreement and the new Constitution round such an unstable element.'[81] That plea was ignored.

Following the conclusion of Merdeka talks, the British officials could now pay full attention to Brunei's outstanding issues regarding the Constitution. Immediate solutions needed to be expedited on several issues which had been lingering for many years in the past straining Brunei-British rapport. In a bid to finalise a Constitution, as a last resort the Sultan was invited to London in early 1959 to iron out following matters with the Colonial Secretary:

(1) the proposed separation of Brunei and Sarawak;
(2) the timing of the appointment of a Menteri Besar;
(3) the powers of Her Majesty in respect of defence and external affairs and the reserve powers of the High Commissioner;
(4) the franchise and the question of citizenship;
(5) the public service and staffing of key posts, and
(6) the powers of Her Majesty and the British Advisor under the Regency and Succession Enactment.

[79] Iain Lang's (A special Correspondent) comments on Azahari is in *The Sunday Times*, [London]11 Dec 1955.

[80] Hussainmiya, *Sultan Omar Ali Saifuddin III and Britain*, ch 7. pp 192–193.

[81] CO 1030/464, Anthony Abell to JB Johnston (CO), 9 August 1957.

Talks concluded in London from 3 March to 6 April 1959 and a final agreement was reached 'despite so many changes through negotiations and counter proposals.'[82] Keeping in mind the successful conclusion of Malayan independence within the Commonwealth, having passed through the constitutional hurdles, the Brunei Sultan in his final communiqué was constrained to note that 'so far his country had not advanced even one step; therefore, 'the time has come when the first step forward should be made'.[83] The final version of the Constitution fulfilled key demands made by the Brunei Constitutional Committee of 1954, particularly to replace the Resident with the appointment of a *Mentri Besar*. The Constitution would be implemented in stages. In the first stage, a *Mentri Besar* would take over from the British Resident and the latter's functions would be transferred to the former and other officers of the State.[84] It was provisionally agreed to complete the pending legal and administrative details in time to introduce the first stage as early as 1 July.[85] In the second stage, a Nationality Enactment would be introduced, and elections to the District Councils held, followed by the appointment of elected members to the Legislative Council. The whole process was to take two years, but a deadline was set to implement the first stage of the Constitution within six months from 1 April.

Other than the Constitution, more importantly a new Brunei-British Agreement of 1959 came into effect by abrogating the previous treaty of 1888 and the 1905–06 Agreement. Hence forward the Sultanate will have a High Commissioner in place of the Resident with an advice clause still intact, albeit diluted. In letter and spirit, however, the High Commissioner would refrain from interfering in domestic affairs since the 'advice clause' was qualified by an exchange of letters between the Secretary of State and the Sultan specifying the areas for British guidance.[86] The British, nonetheless, retained complete control of external affairs and defence, including internal security until Brunei would be ready to shoulder the responsibilities. A Standing Advisory Council, composed of representatives of Britain and Brunei for defence and security purposes, was formed for consultations as necessary.

The nationalist voices of the local people's party were left muted in the end. The Brunei nationalists, understandably, loathed the 1959 Constitution

[82] *The Times* [London] 7 Apr 1959.

[83] Ibid.

[84] CO 1030/527, Dispatch No 83, Secretary of State to Brunei High Commissioner, 23 Apr 1959, para 5(ii).

[85] DO 35/10034, 'Constitutional Change in Brunei', From Foreign Office to certain of Her Majesty's Representatives, No 56 Intel, 1 May 1959.

[86] For the Constitution and treaty see Brunei Constitutional Documents, Kuala Lumpur, nd [1960]. The treaty is also printed in J de V Allen, AJ Stockwell and LR Wright, (eds), *A Collection of Treaties and Other Documents Affecting the States of Malaysia 1761–1963*, vol 2 (London & New York: Oceana Publications, 1981) at 680. The specified areas for the High Commissioner's guidance were public safety and public order including the efficiency of the police, reinforcement of local security forces, measures for the protection of the state, currency, banking and certain aspects of the Sultan's power of either checking or enforcing legislation.

as a British stratagem to perpetuate their political control and secure oil by entrenching the position of the Sultan vis-à-vis the PRB who argued that the new Constitution was nothing but another colonial type administration meant to pave the way for self-administration and not self-government.[87] For the British, Brunei needed more time to move steadily towards a more liberal Constitution despite slowing the pace in the short term. They were optimistic that a written Constitution would act as a check on an absolute monarch, but what really happened was a repeat of what Sultan Abu Bakar of Johor did in 1895; the Brunei Sultan reasserted monarchical authority against British hegemony. While representing a cautious advance through the 1959 Constitution, the monarchy successfully inherited all the power exercised by the British Resident which the PRB contemptuously dubbed as 'self-administration'. Through the Constitution, the Sultan now gained sovereignty in real and practical ways which left the British with nothing but responsibility without power.

For the Sultan, his view was that his people must learn to walk before they began to run. He thus circumscribed the peoples' rights while the British regretted his obstinacy and the incompetence of his courtiers. This compounded the lack of progress in the modernisation of administration, the liberalisation of government and the closer association of Borneo territories. As Anthony Stockwell says:[88]

> … the principal reason why the British eventually yielded to the Sultan's demands was simply because they had no option short of openly opposing him. His sovereignty underpinned Brunei's status as a protected state; to have challenged that would have challenged the legitimacy of Britain's presence in the state.

Despite several hiccups, Sultan Omar finally agreed to promulgate the first written Constitution on 29 September 1959, which earned him, rightly or wrongly, the epithet 'Architect of Modern Brunei.'

V. A REVIEW OF BRUNEI'S 1959 CONSTITUTIONAL ARRANGEMENTS

The Official religion of the state was to be Islam, adhering to the Shafi' school, but other religions and faiths could be practised in peace and harmony. General administrative duties were to be taken over by a *Mentri Besar* who would hold office during the Sultan's pleasure. Under the *Mentri Besar* there were to be a State Secretary, State Financial Officer (replacing the State Treasurer), and Attorney General (replacing the Legal Adviser.).

Provision was made for the hierarchy of government, with His Highness the Sultan and Yang di-Pertuan as the supreme executive authority of the land,

[87] *The Borneo Bulletin*, 12 December 1959.

[88] AJ Stockwell, 'Britain and Brunei, 1945–1963: Imperial Retreat and Royal Ascendancy' (2004) 38(4) *Modern Asian Studies*), 785–819, at 795.

followed by a Privy Council (*Majlis Mesyuarat Di-Raja*), Executive Council (*Majlis Mesyuarat Kerajaan* became the Council of Ministers, *Majlis Mesyuarat Menteri-Menteri*), and a Legislative Council (*Majlis Mesyuarat Negeri*). The function of the Privy Council was mainly to advise the Sultan in the exercise of the prerogative of mercy, in matters relating to the amendment of the Constitution, and in conferring Malay customary honours and titles etc.

The Executive Council was to be presided over by the Sultan. It would function as the most important body in the State, as all matters of policy would be referred to it. Its most important functions would include approving the annual estimates and supplementary estimates for presentation in the Legislative Council. It could be summoned only by the Sultan and might consider only matters tabled by the Sultan and the Mentri Besar. The Sultan, in the exercise of his powers and duties in the State, must consult the Council, unless the law required him to consult any other authority. He could, however, disregard its advice provided he explained in writing his reasons for doing so. The composition of the Council included seven ex-officio members – the Duli Pengiran Bendahara, Duli Pengiran Pemancha, Mentri Besar, State Secretary, Attorney General, State Financial Officer, and the Religious Advisor. The other members were the High Commissioner and seven unofficial members, six of whom must be elected members of the Legislative Council and one a nominated member of that Council. Thus the Council had a fine balance between official members and unofficial members, leaving the Sultan or the High Commissioner to cast the decisive vote in the event of disputed matters that were voted upon.

The Legislative Council, the principal law-making body in the country, was to consist of the following. Eight ex-officio members – the two Wazirs again, the Mentri Besar, State Secretary, Attorney General, State Financial Officer, the Religious Adviser, and another official to be designated by the Sultan. In addition there would be six officials, three unofficial members to be nominated by the Sultan, and 16 elected members chosen from the District Councillors. Elections to District Councils were to be held not later than two years after the date of the promulgation of the new Constitution, as the nationality law had to be enacted first. Pending the elections, in the interim period, the Sultan would appoint all the members for a period of two years.[89] The Sultan might address the Legislative Council at any time upon any matter he saw necessary. He could by proclamation (published in the Gazette) prorogue or dissolve the Legislative Council or any Committee thereof. Each new Legislative Council has a maximum life span of five years from the date of first meeting. It might be dissolved sooner if the need arose.

All revenues and monies raised or received by the State were to be paid into a Consolidated Fund. Numerous government expenses were to be paid out of

[89] For details see, BA Hussainmiya, *The 1959 Brunei Constitution: An inside History'*, (Bandar Seri Begawan: Brunei Press 2000).

these funds. At the commencement of the year the Mentri Besar would table in the Legislative Council a statement of the estimated receipts and expenditure of the State. No money might be withdrawn from the Consolidated Fund except in the manner provided by law. A State Auditor was to be appointed by the Sultan to audit the accounts of the State. Expenditures such as the Civil List of the Sultan and his consort did not need to be authorised by a supply enactment each year and therefore could not be debated with the annual estimates.

There was also a provision in the Constitution for an executive Public Service Commission. Control of the Public Service was vested in the Sultan, who was required to act in accordance with the recommendations of the Public Service Commission. Apart from these the Brunei Overseas Officers Agreement 1959, gave Her Majesty's government control over appointments to 'key posts' in the State. These included the State Financial Officer, Attorney General, State Engineer, State Education Officer, Chief Police Officer, State Medical Officer, and Officer-in-Charge of the Special Branch. This Agreement also safeguarded the terms and conditions of service, including pension rights of overseas officers who served in the Brunei Administration, and provided for payment of appropriate compensation if the services of overseas officers were terminated on other than specified grounds.

The Brunei and Sarawak (Administration Separation) Agreement 1959, brought to an end the Brunei/Sarawak Staffing Agreement of 1948 under which officers from Sarawak had hitherto been seconded for service in Brunei.[90] It provided for payment of appropriate compensation to those officers of the Sarawak government who were serving in Brunei at the time of the separation, who were not offered a transfer to the Brunei Administration, who were surplus to the requirements of Sarawak, and for whom employment could not be found elsewhere.

VI. IN THE AFTERMATH OF THE PROMULGATION

The 1959 Constitution together with the revised Brunei-British Treaty of 1959 ushered Brunei into a new era of tumultuous politics. The envisaged elections to the District Councils and nominations to the newly-formed legislative councils brought new actors to the political scene in a bid to grab power. A prospect of representative government and the attractions of ministerial posts led to a contest between the conservative 'palace party' of *pengirans* and the radical politicians from Party Rakyat Brunei such as Sheikh AM Azahari, HM Saleh and Hapidz Laksamana and others. Knowing the impending outcome in which the PRB led government may be ushered in to the detriment of monarchical

[90] Details of the final Constitutional arrangements are also in DO 35/10035, Commonwealth Relations Office Memorandum on Constitutional Changes in Brunei, July 1959, 2 Mar 1960.

interests, the Sultan as might be expected, tried to postpone elections beyond the two-year time frame stipulated in the Constitution using flimsy excuses such as a need to enact a nationality legislation that would determine the franchise and so on.

The Constitution provided for a two-tier electoral system: In September 1962 direct elections were held for the 55 seats on the four district councils. The PRB won 54 out of the 55 district council seats and thus secured control of the 17 electable seats on the 33-member Legislative Council. In fact, the 16 PRB nominees were immediately returned to the legislature and a week later even the lone independent member had joined the PRB. Although it did not command an overall majority on the Legislative Council, the PRB had won a sweeping popular mandate which the Sultan would ignore at his peril.

When the Malaysia proposals were announced by Tunku Abdul Rahman in late 1961, politics in Brunei had taken a further drastic turn. The 1959 Constitution faced its first litmus test when the election provision was actualised. The newly-elected Legislative Council became embroiled in the Malaysia issue as Azhari's party had rejected the Malaysia plan.[91] The convening of the Legislative Council was postponed three times from September 1962 to prevent the PRB from totally rejecting the Malaysia proposal. The 'undemocratic' Brunei Constitution also became a further hindrance for the formation of Malaysia. In the meantime, there were several other more critical issues to be dealt with other than the constitutional status of the Brunei Sultan who had to be coalesced to agree to the Malaysia proposals. In other words, the Brunei Constitution was not a main issue to derail the Malaya Federation proposals even though the Malayan negotiators were now and then using the paradigm of a democratic system that things work out according to the democratic Constitution even if men and political parties came and went. In contrast to the principle that the Malayan Sultans were bound by the Federal Constitution, Brunei's Constitution gave the Sultan unfettered executive powers. Brunei continued with an ossified system where no change was expected, and change would be resisted as dangerous and threatening to the system.'[92] While the Sultan feared Malaysia would bring democracy to Brunei, the Tunku was worried that the inclusion of Brunei with an autocracy enshrined into the Constitution exposed the whole of Malaysia to international opposition.

The Brunei Constitution was soon to become a casualty in the face of public controversy about accepting or rejecting the Malaysia proposal. The PRB was thoroughly opposed to the idea. When the Legislative Council was formed after almost two years, events moved fast, exacerbating the fissures inside

[91] For details see, DS Ranjit Singh, *Brunei, 1839–1983: The Problems of Political Survival and Harun Abdul Majid. Rebellion In Brunei: The 1962 Revolt, Imperialism, Confrontation and Oil* (London: IB Tauris, 2007).

[92] See relevant discussions in Ghazali Shafie. *Ghazali Shafie's Memoir on the Formation of Malaysia* (Bangi: Universiti Kebangsaan, 1998).

the government. The Tunku's proposed Malaysia Federation issue shook the Brunei Legislative Council to volcanic proportions. Torn between the British government's coercion and his people's opposition voiced by the majority party PRB, the Sultan could do nothing but to sit on the fence. The fissures created finally exploded in a wasteful rebellion in December 1962.[93] The outbreak staged by the PRB led almost instantly to the suspension of the Constitution by the British. Since that event, Brunei has conveniently adopted emergency rule which even after more than 57 years is still in operation. Interestingly essential State legislation still continuing to be passed using the emergency provisions invoking the original clauses of the 1959 Constitution.

The saga of the Brunei Constitution lingers on thereafter. Since 1984 as Brunei Darussalam assumed full independence and sovereignty, constitutional tinkering went unabated as Sultan Hassanal Bolkiah's government introduced amendment after amendment without much public discussion. Ostensibly keen to maintain the security, peace and prosperity of his kingdom, the Sultan, insists that the government must balance the demands of modernisation with the nationalistic aspirations in a bid to reinforce a distinctive post-colonial and national identity by emphasising the essence of Bruneian-Malay tradition, culture and institutions. The remnants of colonial legacies needed to be superimposed with indigenous Bruneian practices and processes. Inevitably, the post-independent era witnessed a further consolidation of monarchic grip in power. By adopting a pragmatic approach and feeling very secure in throne with little interference from outside powers, Brunei has succeeded in maintaining its international standing as respectable State.

In summing up, the 1959 Constitution had both positive and negative aspects, when viewed against the progress of democratic principles intended by the departing colonial power. As Sheridan states, it marked a degree of progress 'from an essentially autocratic system of government under which the Sultan possessed … almost despotic powers not regulated by any written constitution'.[94] In a State which had no proper laws to govern before, the 1959 constitutional provisions were thus relatively progressive especially since they were meant as interim measures before a revised Constitution would take effect. By strengthening various arms of governance, there was hope for peoples' participation in the legislature that would turn Brunei into a proper constitutional State. Although the monarch's powers were left intact, he was still bound by the advisory functions of the Legislative Council. Notwithstanding the fact that the officials held the majority of one in the 1959 Legislative Council membership, the elective representation could later be increased while a cabinet

[93] Harun Abdul Majid, *Rebellion in Brunei: The 1962 Revolt, Imperialism, Confrontation and Oil* (International Library of Twentieth Century History), (London: I.B.Tauris 2007).

[94] LA Sheridan, (ed) *Malaya and Singapore, The Borneo Territories: The Development of its Laws and Constitution* (London: Stevens 1961) at 120.

form of government could be formed as in other Commonwealth countries. The 2004 constitutional amendments effectively ended that evolutionary process since the Sultan's nominees would always be in an unassailable majority in the newly-constituted Legislative Council.

In other areas such as human rights, the 1959 Constitution was still in its infancy as there was no provision for individual liberties. It also lacks some essential features in implementing a system of public law and of any distribution of powers of the kind associated with a federal system. The judiciary which did not become a fundamental institution of the State had its limits as there were no provisions on the set-up, jurisdictional limits, remuneration, independence and retirement age of the judges. The 1959 Constitution also denied the power of the judiciary to interfere with the constitutional structure through interpretation of its provisions. Instead, Section 86 of the 1959 Constitution provided for the establishment of an Interpretation Tribunal with members appointed by the Sultan, which was vested with the power of interpreting the Constitution.

VII. THE 2004 AMENDMENTS

Further to many periodical amendments made to the 1959 Brunei Constitution in the post-independence period, there was a major revision in 2004.[95] It is important to recognise that amendments to Constitutions are substantive changes which modify or develop the Constitution, and then become part of the Constitution as the applicable basic law of a country. Ideally the original Constitution could be amended that would conform with the theory of Constitutionalism, and ensure a balance between the institutions of governance originally prescribed, the objective being to prevent authoritarianism and abuse of State power. When the major constitutional revision took place in 2004, there was hardly any public discussion which took place before or after the amendments were made. Instead the Sultan himself reconstituted the dormant Legislative Council which had been suspended since 1970 which then became a sort of constitutional assembly to approve the amendments by the members who were all the Sultan's nominees.

The revision exercise and its outcome were considerably drastic in that it moved Brunei even further away from the original provisions that were to lead the country along an evolutionary path towards democracy. Section 84 of the 1959 Constitution specifically preserved and maintained the prerogative powers and jurisdiction of the Sultan to proclaim further constitutional provisions as

[95] The amendments are as follows. S 97/59 amended by S 121/61 E 2/63 E 4/64 E 6/67 S 59/70 S 7/83 S 32/83 S 8/84 S 11/84 1984 Edition, Constitutional Matters I amended by S 20/85 S 32/04 S 47/04 S 65/04 S 69/04 2004 Edition, Constitutional Matters I amended by S 14/06 S 15/06 Revised Edition 2011.

may seem to him expedient while section 85(1) also gave the Sultan the power to amend the Constitution.

It all followed from a speech on the tenth anniversary of Brunei's independence in 1994 when the Sultan announced that the 1959 Constitution would be reviewed. One of the purported objects of the review was to increase the citizens' political participation through the establishment of a national Legislative Council.[96] A Committee to review the Constitution was set up soon after the speech and it prepared and submitted the Constitutional Review Committee in 2000, even though this fact was never publicised. It took another 10 years for it to be instituted. It was in the Sultan's 2004 birthday *titah* that he first made the announcements when he reiterated the fact that the changes were designed to 'strengthen the monarchy and to better regulate the relationship between Government and people'.... [they] 'reflect his sincere wish to provide opportunities to his people to contribute constructively to the nation's development through a formal structure of consultation.'

The 2004 amendments were indeed a far cry from the original provisions in the 1959 Constitution. Changes were made to both the letter and spirit of the previous version.[97] For example, whereas the Constitution of 1959 had provided for 16 seats of a 33-seat Legislative Council to be elected by the people, the 2004 amendments made way for 45 members, even though two-thirds of them were to be the Sultan's nominees over whom the Sultan has absolute power of appointment and dismissal. Provisos were made for the remaining 15 members to be elected sometime in the future to represent the various districts of Brunei. Needless to say that elections in Brunei, yet to be held, are a *sine qua non* toward peoples' participation, a norm for any democracy.

Under the 1959 Constitution, the Legislative Council's consent was required before any law could be passed. The 2004 amendments did away with the provisions in such a way that the Legislative Council became an ineffectual and 'meaningless rubber stamp chamber.' More importantly, it must be noted that the 1959 Constitution did not confer any immunity on the Sultan against civil and criminal proceedings but the amended new section 84b now provides that no criminal or civil proceedings may be initiated against him for things done, or omitted to have been done, during or after his reign, whether in his official or personal capacity.[98] When a state of emergency is in place, the Constitution confers on the Sultan an absolute discretion to make any order which he considers desirable in the public interest. While section 83 of the Constitution does not

[96] Mohamed Yusop Damit, 'Brunei Darussalam: Weathering the Storm', *Southeast Asian Affairs*, (2000) 87.

[97] For a detailed exposition of the various amendments see, Tey Tsun Hang, 'Brunei's Revamped Constitution: The Sultan as the Grundnorm?' (2007) 9(2) *Australian Journal of Asian Law* 264–287.

[98] See also the Succession and Regency (Amendment) Proclamation, 2004 (S 49/2004) which introduces s 25(1)(b), that similarly provides that the Sultan can do no wrong in either his personal or official capacity.

provide an exhaustive list of the orders that the Sultan may make, section 83(3)(l) specifically provides that he may make an order modifying or amending any provision of any written law.

VIII. THE FUTURE

The challenges for Brunei to stay as a viable State are many as the Sultan celebrated the Golden Jubilee of his reign on 5 October 2017. Today's Brunei is very different from the one inherited by the young Sultan in 1967 when the Sultanate was still administered as a British protected State. Solely dependent on oil and gas income for its sustenance, Brunei's GDP growth has always been kept under check, spurred by the fluctuations in oil prices as happened in the recent years. Brunei was once described as a 'Shellfare State' which signified the country's reliance on the sustenance provided by the oil income generated by the Shell Company. The situation is not much different today. As the *Financial Times* states 'the 71-year-old's authority appears as strong as ever but his nation has been buffeted by bigger global trends.'[99] The plunge in world energy prices, Chinese expansionism and a younger generation's restlessness have chipped away at the old model of oil-fuelled consumption and welfarism – presenting the world's longest-ruling absolute monarch with a puzzle.[100] The financial squeeze and rising youth unemployment have added urgency to efforts to wean people off State money. The oil price also threatens Brunei's social contract, to which authorities have forestalled opposition with subsidies for housing, healthcare and consumer goods. The government is making every effort to diversify the economy by promoting entrepreneurship and industries such as eco-tourism, but they hardly take off from the ground. 'The Dutch disease' of oil dependency has held back economic development and made people complacent from seeking hard work.

The State sector does still serve as the most prolific sector to provide employment to people while the private sector, not well developed contributes very little to the GDP growth and employment opportunities. There is hardly a middle class to shoulder at least some of the State's responsibilities in economics or in governance. The Sultan relies upon coteries of his technocrats who have benefitted from the country's welfare scheme. They are almost all appointed by the Sultan as cabinet members while others in the public service are also mostly the Sultan's nominees.

Brunei has shown itself capable of accommodating some if not all the modern needs of its population and providing security and stability.[101] Nonetheless, as

[99] 'The Sultan of Brunei grapples with new oil realities.', *Financial Times*, [London] 3 September 2017.

[100] Ibid.

[101] Naimah S Talib. 'A Resilient Monarchy: The Sultanate of Brunei And Regime Legitimacy In An Era Of Democratic Nation-States' (2002) 4(2) *New Zealand Journal of Asian Studies* 134–147.

a nation-State, the stresses and strains of managing a modern State become apparent. The Sultan must be careful to ensure that supporters of his regime, be they the royal elite, or the working class, continue to validate his regime. In the absence of participation, the Sultan needs to work hard to appeal more broadly to his urban and rural constituencies and continue to gain their trust and confidence as a benevolent ruler. Ranjit Singh opines that there subsists in Brunei 'a latent desire for a representative form of government, sometimes dormant, sometimes active'.[102] Horton, however, states that 'the population has shown, and continues to show, little inclination to do anything serious towards realization of the goal.'[103]

The significance of constitutionalism for Brunei now takes more meaning and importance. How much authority can the monarchy continue to wield through the Constitution? Or will the constitutional controls suffice to keep down the political aspirations of the common people? At a popular level, constitutionality of the government has scarce relevance. Its place is somewhat superseded by state's MIB (Malay Islamic Monarchy) philosophy[104] which makes Islam the national religion, upholds the rights and privileges of the Malay ethnic community, and justifies the hereditary monarchy as a relevant governing system. The *Beraja* – a royal component that sanctifies the absolutism of the monarchy in Brunei – with MIB, provides justification for ignoring the suspension of those chapters of the Constitution that provided for some democratic form of government via a partially elected Legislative Council.

Since independence, the State has actively sponsored the ideology of MIB as a means to encourage loyalty to the nation as well as to prop up the Sultan's political legitimacy; this ideology allows the monarchy to situate itself as the protector of Islam and defended of the Malay rights.[105] The Sultan has declared that 'It is therefore clear that Brunei Darussalam upholds the tenets of Malay Muslim Monarchy or Melayu Islam Beraja (MIB) as a realistic formula to ensure amity among its people.' MIB has thus turned out be an effective alternative to constitutionalism as its proponents often quote the Sultan's *titah* during independence that 'Brunei Darussalam shall forever be a sovereign, *democratic* and independent Malay Muslim Monarchy'.[106] These are not matters ever to be questioned; they certainly are not issues that would be raised by the media, or by academia, or be challenged in the courts.

Some view the existing Brunei Legislative Council is nothing but a 'window dressing', considering its largely appointed character and lack of powers.

[102] Ranjit Singh, 'Brunei Darussalam in 1987', *South East Asian Affairs*, 1988, at 67.

[103] AVM Horton, *Turun Temurun,* 117.

[104] For an official version of MIB, See Mohd Zain Serudin *Melayu Islam Beraja: Suatu Pendekatan.* (Bandar Seri Begawan: Dewan Bahasa dan Pustaka 1996).

[105] Müller, Dominik M. (2010) "Melayu Islam Beraja: Islam, Staat und Politische Kommunikation in Brunei Darussalam". In H. Warnk and F. Schulze (eds.). *State and Islam in Southeast Asia.* Wiesbaden: Harrassowitz. 147–170.

[106] Emphasis added.

Others see it as a controlled step towards a new political culture of public participation. No such culture has existed since a short-lived rebellion in 1962, followed by decades of emergency rule. Members of the public can now bring up concerns to LegCo delegates, who assemble annually. The Council also 'approves' government budgets.[107]

It seems that the approach of the Brunei government can be best characterised as a 'top-down' model that induces a popular inertia that lets the government 'in its wisdom' make decisions in the best interest of the people. The ruler does not only make the decisions but provides the funding to implement all government services. Bruneian citizens pay no taxes, so the services provided by the government are promoted as coming from the generosity and affection that the Sultan has for his people. This generosity in turn requires the gratitude, love and support of the people. This is the opposite of an accountable or 'down-up' approach where the government must respond to the desires and needs of the people as transmitted upwards to them, in a way that the government is conceptualised as acting as the servant of the people.

Quite clearly, there is a significant difference between the original 1959 Constitution and the revised one presented in 2004. A detailed analysis of the 2004 amendments goes beyond the scope of this chapter but it is clear that the original 1959 version comes closer to British ideals of a liberal Constitution than the 2004 amended version which has taken away safeguards against monarchist prerogatives. It further dilutes desirable aspects of progressive power sharing while handing unfettered power to the Sultan. As Tey notes, with his super executive powers, the Sultan, 'has become the foundation or *Grundnorm* of the legal system in Brunei.[108] In that sense a fundamental proposition concerning any constitution (as supreme law) is misconceived in the case of Brunei, which enjoys neither constitutional nor legislative supremacy.[109] It may be characterised as an example of constitutions that 'are not expressions of the will of the respective peoples, but simply drafted to cement a status quo, the power of incumbent leaders / elites and to prevent any kind of fresh start.'[110]

Even so, Brunei's recent history reminds us that the idea of 'constitutionalism' had been forced from above by the British, anxious to move the country towards a liberal democracy. Instead, its efforts were thwarted by a ruler who accepted the British drafts in principle, but resisted all attempts to undermine his supreme authority. Whether the Sultan had the will to devolve powers to his people is open for discussion. Had the 1962 rebellion not taken place, there was a chance that a liberal Constitution – embedded to give broader people's representation – would have become a reality under the British aegis. In the aftermath of the

[107] Dominik M. Muller, Islamic Authority and the State in Brunei Darussalam cited in https://kyotoreview.org/issue-23/islamic-authority-and-the-state-in-brunei-darussalam/.

[108] Tey (n 101) at 276.

[109] Ibid.

[110] Kenneth C Wheare, *Modern Constitutions*, (London: Oxford University Press, 1951) 8.

rebellion, and because of the complicated political issues created by the formation of Malaysia (of which Brunei refused to partake), the British government adopted a lackadaisical attitude towards further constitutional reforms in Brunei. When the 1965 White Paper included a provision for a British style cabinet form of government,[111] Sultan Omar dragged his feet until October 1967 when he abdicated in favour of his young son, HRH Hassanal Bolkiah. After gaining independence in 1984, Brunei's new Sultan did not have to face coercion like his father did in constitutional matters. Further he was happy to continue with emergency rule as stipulated in the Constitution with little rumblings from inside or outside powers. Nonetheless as a respectable member of a modern group of nations the Sultan must heed international opinion to justify the legitimacy of his rule based on a Constitution. As an oil and gas exporting country, Brunei needed international partners, and must be seen as a law-abiding nation. This explains partly why the Sultan Haji Hassanal Bolkiah decided to revise the original Constitution by resurrecting a dormant Legislative Council. He did not have to face any dissenting voice within the country or outside to question the validity of such revisions.

In conclusion, the Brunei Constitution (1959–2004) is a unique document in many ways and has no similarity with the constitutions of any of its Southeast Asian neighbours. Neither does an executive monarchic system exist in any other Southeast Asian nation. ASEAN's principle of non-interference in each other's domestic political affairs favours Brunei's political standing. As for now the Sultanate does not seemingly confront any special pressures to bring the country to accommodate conventional democratic expectations. As Horton aptly states, the Brunei's constitutional [2004] amendments is 'a desire to wrap the kingdom in some of the clothes of a liberal democracy without actually being one.'[112]

[111] Hussainmiya (n 27), ch 7.
[112] AVM Horton, 'Window-Dressing an Islamizing Sultanate,' (2005) 45(1) *Asian Survey* 181.

9

Not Meant to Last: Vietnam's First Constitution

STEIN TØNNESSON

INTRODUCTION[1]

VIETNAM'S FIRST CONSTITUTION was not intended to endure. It was conceived in 1945–46 as a temporary political arrangement for a nation fighting for unity and independence. President Hồ Chí Minh (1890–1969), the founder of modern Vietnam, alluded to the temporary character of the Constitution when addressing the Constitutive Assembly in the afternoon of 9 November 1946, after the full text had been approved in the previous evening with 240 against 2 votes:

> The constitution which you have just approved is the Vietnamese people's first constitution. Even though it is not 100% perfect, it is still satisfactory and appropriate for our young nation. It condones the establishment of the republican and democratic regime.[2]

Constitution-makers are often presumed to engage in a quest to bind future generations to a set of timeless principles. They should therefore make it legally difficult to replace the constitution, and they should compose a text that is sufficiently general to make sense under changing conditions. As Marxists, however, Hồ Chí Minh and his political companions viewed history as a sequence of progressive stages: Feudalism > capitalism > socialism > communism. Ho's reason for acknowledging the imperfection of Vietnam's first Constitution was not that it had been written in haste or contained any flaws. As early

[1] This chapter builds on a conference paper presented to a workshop on Nation-State Formation at the International Conference on Southeast Asia in the 20th Century, University of the Philippines, 28–30 Jan 1998, and (after revision) to the International Conference on Vietnamese Studies and the Enhancement of International Cooperation in Hanoi, Jul 1998.

[2] Hien phap nuoc Viet-nam 'Affaires intérieures', dossier 572 (also in the Museum of Revolution, Hanoi). A contemporary French translation can be found in the file Conseiller Politique supplémentaire, Carton 5, Centre des archives de la France d'Outre-Mer, Aix-en-Provence. The latter also includes French-language minutes from the second session of the Vietnamese National Assembly, 28 Oct to 10 Nov 1946.

as 20 September 1945, he had decided that he himself would chair a seven-member drafting committee. A first draft was published on 10 November 1945.[3] A Constitutive and National Assembly was elected on 6 January 1946. When it met for its first session on 2 March, it elected a larger drafting committee with eleven members, none of whom had been part of the first. The new committee presented its proposal to the second session of the Assembly, which began on 28 October.[4]

For Ho and his comrades the Constitution was a means to an end, and that end was to win a place for Vietnam in the world family of nations. At a later stage, another more advanced constitution would be needed to give Vietnam its rightful place in the world's evolution towards socialism. This was still far into the future. At the present stage, his nation needed unity of all social classes in order to liberate itself from French colonialism.

In contrast to most other imagined futures, the future that Hồ Chí Minh and his fellow Marxists imagined in 1945–1946 would materialise. Vietnam would adopt no less than four consecutive Constitutions, each representing a specific historical stage: 1959, 1980, 1992, and 2013. Yet paradoxically, the progress they dreamt of would turn into a malfunctioning, centrally directed economy heavily dependent on foreign aid, and a one-party state with little room for freedom or democracy. After North and South Vietnam were unified in 1976, the state changed its name from Democratic Republic of Vietnam (DRV) to Socialist Republic of Vietnam (SRV), and the Vietnam Workers Party (Lao Dong), which had been founded in 1951, changed its name to Vietnamese Communist Party (VCP).

Well before Vietnam's present Constitution was adopted in 2013, the new generations of Vietnamese intellectuals had abandoned the Marxist ideas of progress. Some looked back at history and sought inspiration from the 1946 Constitution, which was more democratic than the later ones. Others looked for

[3] The first drafting committee was heavily dominated by leading Vietnamese communists. Its members were: Hồ Chí Minh, Trường Chinh, Nguyễn Lương Bằng, Lé Van Hién, Đặng Thai Mai, Vũ Trọng Khánh, and Vĩnh Thụy (former Emperor Bảo Đại). Alec Holcombe. 'The Role of the Communist Party in the Vietnam Revolution, A Review of David Marr's *Vietnam: State, War, and Revolution*' (2016) 11(3–4) *Journal of Vietnamese Studies* 298–364, at 336. David Marr has found no evidence that this committee ever met. David Marr. 'Response to Alec Holcombe's Review Essay on *Vietnam: State, War and Revolution*' (2017) 12(1) *Journal of Vietnamese Studies* 155–162, at 160. The first draft presented in November was therefore probably written under the auspices of the chair of the drafting committee (Hồ Chí Minh) without ever being discussed by the committee.

[4] The broader committee had the following members, none of whom had been members of the first drafting committee: Nguyễn Thị Thục Viên (1903–84, Viet Minh), Tôn Quang Phiệt (1900–73, Democratic Party), Nguyễn Đình Thi (1924–2003, Viet Minh), Nguyễn Đình Thi (1912–88, Democratic Party), Đỗ Đức Dục (1915–93; Democratic Party), Cù Huy Cận (1919–2005, Democratic Party), Huỳnh Bá Những (Viet Minh), Trần Tấn Thọ (Revolutionary League), Nguyễn Văn Hách (Revolutionary League), Đào Hữu Dương (Revolutionary League), Phạm Gia Độ (Nationalist Party). 'La constitution de la République démocratique du Viet Nam,' 27 pp. French study of Vietnamese constitution-making, and an 80 pp. summary of the National Assembly Debates. Carton CP-sup. 4, Centre des Archives de la France d'Outre Mer, Aix-en-Provence, France.

ideological guidance from older Confucian principles, or from the modernising ideas of the first generation of non-communist nationalists and reformers, such as Phan Bội Châu (1867–1940), Phan Châu Trinh (1872–1926), Huỳnh Thúc Kháng (1876–1947) and Bùi Quang Chiêu (1872–1945), while yet others took a new look at constitution-making in the Republic of (South) Vietnam.[5] Even within the Communist Party there were those who wanted to restore what they saw as genuinely democratic elements in Vietnam's first Constitution. These various tendencies are known under the term 'restoration constitutionalism.'[6]

I. THE DEMOCRATIC REPUBLIC OF VIETNAM

In 1945–1946, the Marxist view of evolution through progressive stages, and the need for Vietnam's revolutionary government to reassure the French, Chinese and US governments, were the two most likely reasons why Vietnam's first republic did not become 'Socialist.' At the time of the August 1945 Revolution, all other republics run by communists were either 'Socialist' or 'People's'. When the Union of Socialist Soviet Republics (USSR) was formed in 1922, each of its members was already a 'Socialist Republic.' In 1924, when communists seized power in Mongolia, they acknowledged the relative backwardness of their nation, established a mere 'People's Republic' and did not seek membership in the USSR. In 1946, Albania, Yugoslavia and Bulgaria also became 'People's Republics.' Hungary and China followed suit in 1949, and Poland in 1952.[7] Vietnam's choice of the term 'Democratic Republic' was not, however, entirely innovative. There had been a Democratic Republic of Georgia from 1918–21 but it switched to 'Socialist' before joining the USSR. Vietnam's choice to be a 'Democratic Republic' reflected at once a kind of modesty ('we cannot yet be Socialist') and a need to rally those members of the Vietnamese society who did not want

[5] See, Ralph B Smith, 'Bui Quang Chieu and the Constitutionalist Party in Cochinchina, 1917–1930' (1969) 3(2) *Modern Asian Studies* 131–150; Hue-Tam Ho Tai. 'The Politics of Compromise: The Constitutionalist Party and the Electoral Reforms of 1922 in French Cochinchina' (1984) 18(3) *Modern Asian Studies* 371–391; Bui Ngoc Son. 'The Introduction of Modern Constitutionalism in East Asian Confucian Context: The Case of Vietnam in the Early Twentieth Century' (2015) 7(2) *National Taiwan University Law Review* 423–463.

[6] Bui Ngoc Son. 'Restoration Constitutionalism and Socialist Asia.' (2015) 37(67) *Loyola of Los Angeles International and Comparative Law Review* 67–116.

[7] Art 1 of the 5 December 1936 Soviet constitution reads: 'The Union of Soviet Socialist Republics is a socialist state of workers and peasants.' Russia moved directly to forming a Russian Socialist Federative Republic (RSFR) in 1918, which united with the Ukrainian, Byelorussian and Transcaucasian Republics in a Union of Soviet Socialist Republics (USSR) in 1922. The USSR adopted its first socialist Constitution in 1924 and its second in 1936. As Marxists gained power in more and more countries after WW2, a kind of constitutional hierarchy emerged, based on the idea of progressive stages of human development: (Bourgeois) Republic, Democratic Republic, People's Democratic Republic, People's Republic, and Socialist Republic. No Marxists dared to declare a Communist Republic, since this would imply having already achieved the classless society marking the happy end of history.

socialism but just an independent, democratic state. In 1949, East Germany followed the Vietnamese example and set up their German Democratic Republic (GDR). In 1964, the Democratic Republic of Congo gained independence from Belgium. Sao Tomé and Principe and Timor-Leste became Democratic Republics when Portugal withdrew from its colonies in 1975, Afghanistan in 1978, and Nepal in 2007.[8]

Vietnam's Constitutive Assembly included representatives of several ideational groups, parties or 'leagues': Marxists, Socialists, Democrats, Viet Minh, a Revolutionary League *(Đồng Minh Hội)*, and Nationalists *(Việt Nam Quốc Dân Đảng (VNQDĐ)*. Yet the Assembly was dominated by veterans of the former Indochinese Communist Party (ICP), who rallied behind Hồ Chí Minh as the unquestionable leader of the government as well as of the front organisation *Việt Nam Độc lập Đồng Minh* (Viet Minh). The communists did not at that stage have an official party organisation of their own. On Hồ Chí Minh's initiative, and for the prime purpose of reassuring Nationalist China, the ICP had officially dissolved itself on 22 November 1945. After that, the communists operated through various front organisations, such as a number of National Salvation Organisations *(Cứu Quốc)*, the Viet Minh and the even broader Vietnam National Alliance *(Hội Liên hiệp Quốc dân Việt Nam (Liên Việt))*. The ICP maintained an under-the-radar existence in the form of Marxist Study Groups, which published a monthly theoretical review *(Sự Thật)* but no daily newspaper. The members of the former ICP formed a tight informal fraternity around Hồ Chí Minh, with a remarkable ability to uphold unity in vision and action.

A key to understanding the intended temporality of Vietnam's first Constitution is a vote taken in the National Assembly on 8 November 1946. Dục Đức, who represented the Democratic Party – a small liberal grouping set up in 1944 in affiliation with the Viet Minh front – proposed to include a provision in the Constitution to specify that Vietnam's 'democratic republican system' *must never be altered*. This proposal went against the essence of progressive thinking. In the public debate about the first constitutional draft, leading communists had

[8] The following took the name People's Republic: Mongolia 1924–90, Albania 1946–76, Yugoslavia 1946–63, Bulgaria 1946–90, Hungary 1949–89, China 1949–, Poland 1952–89, Congo (Brazzaville) 1970–92, Bangladesh 1972–, Angola 1975–92, Mozambique 1975–90, Benin 1975–90 and Kampuchea 1979–89. The Kampuchea of the Khmer Rouge (1975–82) called itself just 'Democratic Kampuchea.' North Korea doubled up with 'Democratic People's Republic' in 1948. Algeria 1962–, (South) Yemen 1967–90, Laos 1976–, and Ethiopia 1974/87–94 followed the North Korean example but in the opposite order: 'People's Democratic Republic.' After a certain interval under democratic or people's rule, a state could graduate and become 'socialist'. Czechoslovakia passed the threshold in 1960, Yugoslavia in 1963, Romania in 1965, and Vietnam in 1976. Albania became a People's Socialist Republic in 1976, Sri Lanka a Democratic Socialist Republic in 1978 and Libya a Great Socialist People's Republic in 1977. See list of Republics in William B Simons, *The Constitutions of the Communist World* (Alphen aan den Rijn: Sijthoff & Noordhoff, 1980).

argued that the Constitution would have to include clauses allowing for it to be changed or even completely replaced.[9] Opponents of Dục Đức's proposal said it violated the principle of popular sovereignty, which in their view implied that the people must have a right to amend or replace a constitution at will. A clear majority of the delegates thus rejected the proposal.[10]

The Marxist idea of a stage-based progress towards communism has survived until this day as a basic doctrine of the Vietnamese Communist Party (VCP). Each of Vietnam's Constitutions was adopted in a specific historical situation, shaped by dramatic events in Vietnam and abroad. These *constitutional moments* differed greatly, and their geopolitical circumstances were reflected in the constitutional texts. The 1946 Constitution lasted 13 years, the 1959 Constitution 21, the 1980 Constitution 11, the 1992 Constitution again 21, and the 2013 Constitution is not more likely than its predecessors to satisfy future generations.

Vietnam's fist Constitution was adopted six weeks before the outbreak of the First Indochina War on 19 December 1946. It was never formally promulgated or subjected to a popular referendum but it served as a legal foundation – or facade – for the DRV government, the Viet Minh front and the *Viet Nam National Defence Army* (from 1950 the *People's Army of Viet Nam)* during the Indochina War. When the war ended in 1954, after the Vietnamese – with heavy Chinese support – had won a decisive battle at Dien Bien Phu, and an armistice agreement had been signed at a great power conference in Geneva – Vietnam was divided on a temporary basis along the 17th parallel, pending national elections to be organised in the whole country under international supervision by July 1956. If these elections had been held, the DRV (North Vietnam) would probably have engaged in a new constitution-making process together with representatives of the French-sponsored State of Vietnam (South Vietnam), and would have established a coalition government for the whole of Vietnam. As things went, the elections were never held. Instead two rival republics were built in the North and the South: the DRV returned to its capital Hanoi, and a new Saigon-based Republic of Vietnam replaced the State of Vietnam. Until 1959, the 1946 Constitution continued to underpin the DRV's claim to represent the nation as a whole.

The Democratic Republic of Vietnam's second Constitution was adopted in 1959, in the year when the Vietnam Workers Party decided, after much hesitation and internal disagreement, to give up the hope to reunify North and South peacefully, and instead engage in a protracted armed struggle to topple the

[9] David G Marr, *Vietnam: State, War, and Revolution* (Berkeley: University of California Press, 2013) 69–70 [hereinafter 'Marr']; and Alec Holcombe, 'The Role of the Communist Party in the Vietnam Revolution, A Review of David Marr's *Vietnam: State, War, and Revolution*' (2016) 11(3–4) *Journal of Vietnamese Studies* 298–364, at 332.

[10] Marr, ibid, at 103 & 105.

US-backed South Vietnamese regime, and force the Americans, who had taken over the French position in the South, to withdraw.[11]

The preparation of the third Constitution began in 1976, after the Vietnam War had ended with the collapse of the Republic of (South) Vietnam. In 1976, Vietnam was formally unified. Its communist leaders could now cash in on a celebrated status in the world's socialist camp, and finally become the Socialist Republic of Vietnam (SRV). However, before the text of a new constitution was ready, Vietnam immersed itself in a bitter conflict with Democratic Kampuchea and the People's Republic of China. In 1978, Vietnam invaded Cambodia and installed a puppet regime in its capital Phnom Penh, where after the new Chinese leader Deng Xiaoping (1925–1997) punished Vietnam with a five-week military invasion across Vietnam's northern border. This influenced Vietnam's 1980 Constitution. It singled out China as Vietnam's historical enemy, and served to underpin Hanoi's aspiration to build a Soviet-style centrally managed economy, closely integrated with Laos, Cambodia, the Soviet Union, the East European states, and Cuba in their two-front struggle with the imperialist states of the West and the Chinese hegemon.

Vietnam's 1992 Constitution came shortly after the dissolution of the Soviet Union, at a time when the world socialist movement was in acute crisis, and Vietnam itself had been forced to reintroduce an export-oriented market economy, inspired by Japan, South Korea, Singapore, Taiwan – and China.[12] Vietnam had withdrawn from Cambodia and signed the Paris peace agreement, which settled the last of the three big wars that ravaged Indochina after World War II (1946–1954; 1959–1975; 1978–1991). Finally, Vietnam could enjoy peace and stability. Vietnam's communist leaders had, on the other hand, been frightened in 1989 by the fall of the communist regimes in Eastern Europe and in 1991 of the Soviet Union's collapse, so Vietnam's fourth Constitution did not just recognise the *Doi Moi* market reforms but also introduced an explicit affirmation of the Communist Party's leading role in state and society. The formalisation of the Party's leading role, which had not been there in the first three Constitutions, was not meant as a temporary expedient. It was dictated by a quest for regime survival. In 1990, the small Democratic Party and Socialist Party, which had existed alongside the Communist Party, were dissolved. However, the formalisation of the Party's leading role created a problem: would the Party's statutes,

[11] Pierre Asselin, *Hanoi's Road to the Vietnam War, 1954–1965*. Berkeley CA: University of California Press, 2013; and Lien-Hang T Nguyen, *Hanoi's War: An International History of the War for Peace in Vietnam* (Chapel Hill NC: University of North Carolina Press, 2012). The former Indochinese Communist Party (ICP), which was dissolved in November 1945, was reconstituted in 1951 as the Vietnam Workers Party (Lao Dong), and separate communist parties were subsequently established for Cambodia and Laos. In its time, the ICP had aimed to liberate the whole of French Indochina, including Cambodia and Laos.

[12] Stein Tønnesson, *Explaining the East Asian Peace* (Copenhagen: NIAS Press, 2017), at 37–42; and Stein Tønnesson. 'Peace by Development' in Elin Bjarnegård & Joakim Kreutz (eds) *Debating the East Asian Peace* (Copenhagen: NIAS Press 2017) 55–77.

as decided at the Party Congress, be an inferior or superior source of law as compared with the Constitution?[13]

This was part of the debate leading to the adoption of the fifth Constitution in 2013, which removed some socialist phraseology, strengthened universal human rights, made small concessions to the principle of judicial independence, and decided that the Party, in spite of its leading role, would operate under the Constitution.[14] Yet this disappointed the new generation of reformers inside and outside of the Communist Party who were advocating a return to the democratic spirit of Vietnam's first Constitution. Most of their proposals were rejected by the party leaders, who preferred to maintain the illusion of having reached a mature socialist stage. They were adamant that the Party must retain its constitutionally defined leading role. Paradoxically, this did not weaken Vietnam's foreign policy leverage. Vietnam's illiberal one-party governance in fact allowed it to align with a new world-wide trend away from pluralistic forms of liberal democracy towards more centralised, authoritarian forms of governance, not least in the Russia of Vladimir Putin (1952–) and the China of Xi Jinping (1953–).

II. THE REPUBLIC OF VIETNAM

Among those who wanted to restore elements of Vietnamese pre-Marxist and non-Marxist constitutional thinking, the history of the Republic of Vietnam (1955–1975) has not been completely forgotten. It had its origin in the State of Vietnam, which had been created in 1949 as a French 'Associated State' under Bảo Đại (1912–1997). He had served as a French-protected emperor from 1926, been kept on the throne by Japan in March 1945 when it seized Indochina from the French, but had abdicated voluntarily during the 1945 August Revolution, and become – a mostly honorific – 'Supreme Advisor' to Hồ Chí Minh. In March 1946, however, he left Vietnam and settled down a little later with a French subsidy in Hong Kong. At first, he resisted French overtures but in 1949 he agreed to come to Saigon as head of a new State of Vietnam. Thus, he tried to withdraw the legitimacy he had bestowed on the DRV when abdicating his throne. His new government was recognised by the UK and the US in February 1950, shortly after the young People's Republic of China (PRC) and the USSR had recognised the DRV. In July 1954, during the Geneva Conference, Bảo Đại appointed the staunchly anti-French and anti-communist nationalist Catholic leader Ngô Đình Diệm (1901–63) as new Prime Minister in Saigon. In the following year, Diệm organised a referendum that drove Bảo Đại into exile once again, where after Diệm established the Republic of Vietnam with himself

[13] Mark Sidel, *The Constitution of Vietnam: A Contextual Analysis* (Portland, Oregon: Hart, 2009) at 8–15.

[14] Bui (n 6) at 111–114.

as President. In 1956, Diệm staged separate elections in South Vietnam and set upon the task to write a constitution.

Both the DRV and the Republic of Vietnam claimed to represent all of Vietnam, while their elections – except for the first one in 1946 – happened only in one half of the country. Both the all-Vietnamese 1946 elections and the southern elections in 1956 allowed a certain degree of competition between several parties, within the confines of a demonstrated loyalty to the incumbent government and its leader. Both elections were legally ambiguous in that they aimed to establish a Constitutive Assembly, which would also serve as a National Assembly, with authority to adopt laws and approve of governments. In the period between 1956–1975, Vietnam thus had two national assemblies and a series of competing national elections: in North Vietnam 1960, 1964 and 1971 and in South Vietnam 1956, 1959, 1963, 1966, 1967 and 1971 (and Senate elections in 1967, 1970 and 1973). South Vietnam had a two-chamber and North Vietnam a one-chamber system. None of the elections were free and fair, since there was little freedom of association, and no general right to stand as candidates.

The main theoretical point to be explored in this chapter is the impact of a constitutional moment on the viability of the resulting document. The case to be analysed is Vietnam's first Constitution, which was adopted under precarious circumstances. The four later Constitutions could easily be subjected to the same kind of analysis but there is no room for that here. The questions to be asked about the first Constitution are: What were its main characteristics? What kind of political process led to its adoption, and what were the main internal and external forces in its formation? And, notably, what can we learn from the case of Vietnam's first Constitution about the impact of historical circumstances on a constitution's viability?

III. CHARACTERISTICS

All of Vietnam's five Constitutions begin with a preamble that provides a summary of its historical context. The 1946 preamble says:

> The (1945) August Revolution won back the sovereignty for the country, freedom for the people and founded the republican democratic regime.

The choice of a republican democratic regime had thus been made amidst the August 1945 Revolution, when Hồ Chí Minh assumed the position of President in a provisional revolutionary government in Hanoi, which claimed to represent all of Vietnam.

This constitutional moment differed from those of the other nations that came under communist rule in the aftermath of World War II. While their constitutional moments were created by Soviet power (perhaps except for Yugoslavia), the founders of the DRV, although inspired by the Soviet Union and its victory over Germany and conquest of Manchuria and North Korea from Japan, did not receive any help from Moscow to carry out their revolution. Some of Vietnam's revolutionary leaders, like Hồ himself, had been trained in Russia and had worked as agents of the Soviet-led Communist International (Comintern), and had important ties to the French and Chinese Communist Parties. The choice to be a 'Democratic Republic' reveals a realisation that Vietnam could not openly join the socialist camp in world affairs. By 1946, moreover, there was still some reason to expect that the Soviet Union would continue to cooperate with its wartime allies. Although President Hồ was emotionally and conceptually devoted to Leninism, he thought of his August Revolution in terms of a liberation from colonialism and the abolition of feudal societal traits, not as a break with capitalism or an opportunity to make a rapid transition to socialism. This would happen at a later stage. The Marxist idea of stages is reflected in the preamble to the 1946 Constitution:

> After 80 years of struggle, the Vietnamese nation has freed itself from the colonialist yoke and at the same time abolished the feudal regime.

This is Marxist language, and it follows implicitly that a future task will be to overcome capitalism and establish a socialist mode of production.

The first draft of the 1946 Constitution was published already in November 1945, under the auspices of a committee put together in September and led by Hồ Chí Minh himself. It is unclear, however, if the committee ever met to discuss and approve the draft, and we do not know who penned it. According to Alec Holcombe, the final version of the Constitution adopted by the Constitutive Assembly one year later, showed 'minimal substantive change' from the November 1945 draft.[15] The final version, however, grew out of a broader, more representative and less top-heavy committee, which was elected by the National Assembly on 2 March 1946, amidst an acute military crisis between the DRV and France. It presented its proposal to the National Assembly's second session on 28 October 1946, three days before the entry into force of a ceasefire agreement Hồ Chí Minh had signed with France for southern Vietnam.

At first sight, the 1946 Constitution appears very democratic. Chapter I places sovereignty in the popular community without any distinctions made as to race, gender, prosperity, class or religion, and states that Vietnam is a united territory of the northern, central and southern regions, which cannot be divided, and have Hanoi as their shared capital.[16]

Chapter II enumerates the 'obligations and rights of the people.'[17] The obligations are to defend the motherland, respect the Constitution, obey laws and decrees, and do military service. The rights include expression, property, commerce, association, thought, and movement both within and out of

[15] Holcombe (n 3) at 333.
[16] 'Đất nước Việt Nam là một khối thống nhất Trung Nam Bắc không thể phân chia.'
[17] 'Nghĩa vụ cơ bản của công dân.'

the country. They also include equality before the law, while allowing for positive discrimination of ethnic minorities to elevate them to the general level of development. At the request of an ethnic minority delegate in the National Assembly, ethnic minorities were given a right to be taught in their own language in primary school and to use it if appearing before a court. Women are declared to have the same rights as men in all domains. Some delegates proposed to omit 'in all domains' since there are clear differences in the humanitarian and social mission of the two sexes, but a solid majority voted to uphold the three contested words. One female delegate wanted to specify that military service also applies to women. This was one step too far at the time. Her wish was rejected.

Property rights are defined in Article 12 but a proposal from a delegate to uphold 'entrepreneurial freedom' and protect the property rights not only of individuals but also of companies, was voted down.[18] The Socialist group in the Assembly put special emphasis on the protection of workers, a subject covered in Article 13. The Constitution puts much weight on the right to education. After a long debate initiated by a Catholic priest, it was decided to allow private schools if they conform with official programmes. Everyone has the right to vote from the age of 18, and to accept elected office from the age of 21.

Chapter III deals with the main organ of popular sovereignty: The National Assembly. It consists of just one chamber, which is the highest authority in the state. There shall be national elections every three years, with one delegate for every 50,000 inhabitants. The National Assembly will have two annual sessions in May and November. Between the sessions, its authority shall be delegated to a 15 member Standing Committee, which has the right to control and criticise the government. There had been much discussion in the drafting committee about the respective roles of the Standing Committee and the executive government, and the final text makes clear that no member of the Standing Committee can simultaneously serve in government.[19] This is the only place in the Constitution that provides for division of powers. The Constitution also includes a highly unusual provision: if one-quarter of the voters in a voting district demand it, they have a right to recall their elected Member of Parliament at any time,

[18] One of two who voted against the Constitution on 9 November, the Haiphong-based industrialist Nguyễn Sơn Hà, did so because he was dissatisfied with the lack of emphasis on economic development and company rights. See Marr (n 9) at 103–105.

[19] The following were elected to the Standing Committee on 9 Nov 1946: Bùi Bằng Đoàn (neutral), Tôn Đức Thắng (Viet Minh), Tôn Quang Phiệt (Communist, Viet Minh), Phẩm Bà Thực (Viet Minh), Dương Đức Hiền (DCD, Viet Minh), Hoàng Minh Châu (Viet Minh), Phan Thành (Socialist), Nguyễn Đình Thi (Viet Minh), I Ngo Ong (Viet Minh of Rhadé minority), Cung Đình Quỳ (VNQDĐ), Dương Văn Dư (Revolutionary League), Trần Huy Liệu (Communist, Viet Minh), Trần Văn Cung (Communist), Hoàng Văn Hòa (?), and Nguyễn Văn Luyện (Socialist). Le Directeur de la Police et de la Sûreté Fédérales en Indochine aux Commissaire Fédéral aux Affaires Politiques et le Directeur du Cabinet du Haut Commissaire, No 8940sg, 15 novembre 1946; and Note sur la 'démocratie vietnamienne', Commissariat fédéral aux affaires politiques, No. PRR/cc/3, Nov 1946, Carton CP-Sup. 5, Centre des Archives d'Outre Mer, Aix-en-Provence, France.

although on the condition that two thirds of the National Assembly approves the revocation.

Chapter IV specifies that the government is led by the President of the Republic who shall be elected by the National Assembly for a five-year term. The President chooses the Prime Minister from among the members of the National Assembly and submits the choice to the Assembly for approval. The Prime Minister then chooses the other ministers, also from among the members of the Assembly. Each minister needs to be approved by the Assembly, and there is no ministerial solidarity, meaning that individual ministers can be dismissed through votes of no confidence without any consequence for the rest of the government.

Chapter V says that provinces, cities and urban communes shall have elected People's Committees, while on the level of each of the country's three main regions (the three Kỳ or Bộ), there shall be an indirectly elected Administrative Committee. It shall be responsible both to the local assemblies who elected it and to the central government.

Chapter VI on the judiciary states that all who are accused of crimes shall have the right to be defended either by themselves or with the help of lawyers, and the other powers must not put pressure on the courts. The judges, however, are to be appointed by the government, and there are no provisions for a jury system.

Chapter VII, the final one, prescribes that constitutional amendments require a two-thirds majority in the National Assembly, and consultation of the population through referendum.

A superficial reading gives the impression that the Constitution provides for an all-powerful unicameral National Assembly. For two reasons, however, this is not quite so. First, it shall have only two sessions per year, in May and November. For the rest of the year, a 15 member Standing Committee will represent it. Second, in practice both the Standing Committee and the government would be controlled by a group of dedicated communists around Ho Chi Minh. They could dominate both the National Assembly and the broadly organised Viet Minh League and its National Salvation Organisations *(Cứu Quốc)*, and when they disagreed with each other they did not display their disagreement publicly. Their constant mantra was unity and total confidence in the President. This meant that the real powers were concentrated in the executive. Ho went as far as to declare in the National Assembly that although he held freedom of expression dear, it would have to be curtailed under the present circumstances, so it would not harm the national interest. The same reason was given for exempting his government from any obligation to answer questions from the National Assembly. Moreover, the independent-minded Nguyễn Văn Tố, who had served as chair of the Standing Committee since 2 March, was replaced in November by a more amenable person. Nguyễn Văn Tố had annoyed the government with attempts to keep in touch with members of the parliamentary opposition, asked critical questions about the government's activities, and protected members of the opposition from being arrested by the police.[20] Discipline was enforced in the DRV by an expanding security apparatus, which in 1946 was controlled by deputy minister of the interior Võ Nguyên Giáp.

IV. THE CONSTITUTION MAKING PROCESS

The history of Vietnam's first Constitution can be divided in four main phases.

Phase I: 24 August 1945 to 6 March 1946

The August Revolution created the DRV, with a provisional government based in Hanoi. That government established a seven-member drafting committee, led by Hồ Chí Minh, and a full proposal was published in record time on 9 November 1945, and widely distributed.[21] A public debate followed in the press, and national elections were held on 6 January. The elected National Assembly met for its first session on 2 March and elected a new government of national union, led by President Hồ Chí Minh. At the same time a new committee of 11 members was established to continue the work on the Constitution. On 6 March 1946, under the threat of a French invasion of northern Vietnam, President Hồ Chí Minh signed an agreement with France, in which Vietnam was recognised as a 'free state', and France was allowed to station troops on its territory.

Phase II: 6 March 1946 to 19 December 1946

While the drafting committee was working, the DRV negotiated with France concerning its status. The talks failed, so the result was just a modus vivendi agreement, signed in Paris by Hồ Chí Minh and the Minister of Overseas France on 15 September. It provided for a ceasefire to enter into force on 30 October. The Constitution adopted at the National Assembly's second session on 8 November, made no mention of France at all. An acute crisis emerged in Vietnam's relations with France, and full-scale war broke out in Hanoi on 19 December 1946.

Phase III: 20 December 1946 to 6 July 1954

This was the period of the First Indochina War, with a turning point in 1950, when the People's Republic of China (PRC) and the Soviet Union (USSR) recognised the DRV, and China began to provide large scale military training and support, so the People's Army of Viet Nam could develop a modern fighting

[20] Marr (n 9) at 57, 64–68 & 95.
[21] Ibid, at 20–21.

force and win a major victory at Dien Bien Phu in May 1954 before the Geneva conference divided Vietnam temporarily into a northern and southern zone. During this whole period, the 1946 Constitution served as a basis for the DRV's claim to represent all of Vietnam. The National Assembly held its third session in December 1953 with the main purpose of adopting a law on land reform. There were no elections in this period.

Phase IV: 7 July 1954 to 31 December 1959

In this period the DRV controlled all of Vietnam north of the 17th parallel, and carried out a radical land reform (beginning in conjunction with the Dien Bien Phu campaign in December 1953), which led to much violence, many executions, and a backlash against the communist government at a time when the population had been forced to undergo enormous hardships to sustain the victory at Dien Bien Phu. The land reform was interrupted in 1956, amidst apologies for widespread abuse but it resumed with the formation of cooperatives from 1958 onward. Meanwhile, South Vietnam refused to fulfil the Geneva Conference's decision that national elections be held by July 1956. Instead it held its own rigged elections. After the Geneva agreements and the return of the DRV government to Hanoi in October 1954, the 1946 Constitution was considered out-dated. It failed to reflect the DRV's position as a member of the Soviet led camp in the global Cold War. So, in December 1959, it was replaced with a new Constitution, and a new National Assembly was elected in 1960.

This chapter concentrates on the first two phases. The presence of a Chinese occupation army in northern Indochina had a heavy impact in the first phase, and the arrival of a French expedition force had an even greater impact in the second. In September–October 1945, nationalist Chinese troops poured into northern Vietnam in consonance with a decision made by the World War II Allies at a July 1945 meeting in Potsdam outside Berlin. The Allies decided that Generalissimo Chiang Kai-shek would be responsible for the war against Japan in Indochina north of the 16th parallel, while the British South East Asia Command (under Admiral Lord Louis Mountbatten) would take responsibility south of that line. Together with the Chinese occupation troops came the exiled leaders of two Vietnamese nationalist parties: The Nationalist Party (*Việt Nam Quốc Dân Đảng*, VNQDĐ), led by Nguyễn Tường Tam and Vũ Hồng Khanh, and the rival Revolutionary League (*Đồng Minh Hội*), led by Nguyễn Hải Thần. The DRV government was now forced to reassure both Nationalist China and its local clients in order to dissuade the Chinese occupation authorities from putting in place a new non-communist government. This was the main background for the decision to dissolve the Indochinese Communist Party. China did not oust Hồ but Chiang Kai-shek signed a treaty with France on 28 February 1946, allowing it to return to the northern half of its colony, and Chiang's representatives put pressure on Hồ Chí Minh and the Nationalist leader Vũ Hồng Khanh to sign an agreement with France on 6 March, allowing French troops to land unopposed.

In the second phase, the DRV negotiated with France in continuation of the 6 March agreement, while the Chinese troops marched or sailed out of Vietnam. Negotiations at Dalat in the Central Highlands during April–May and at Fontainebleau south of Paris during June–August 1946 failed to reach agreement on two main points: The DRV's demand for full national independence, and its claim that Vietnam's three main regions (North, Centre, South) were integral parts of one nation. The southern half of Vietnam had come under British occupation in September 1945, and the British had helped France re-establish its power there from September to March. Communist guerrillas, however, organised an increasingly effective rebellion from March onward. Vietnam's first Constitution was drafted at a time when Hồ Chí Minh was in France as a guest of the French government. The second session of the Vietnamese National Assembly opened shortly after Hồ had returned on a French ship. On 30 October, the ceasefire he had signed in Paris entered into force, and was widely respected by the communist rebels in the south, demonstrating their allegiance to the DRV.

Procedures to establish Vietnam's first National Assembly *(Quốc Dân Đại Hội)* had been published by the government as early as 8 September 1945. All Vietnamese men and women above 18 years old would be eligible to vote in national elections. A committee would formulate regulations for the elections, which should take place within three months. A key purpose was to demonstrate to the Chinese occupation authorities that President Hồ and the Viet Minh League he had founded in 1941 enjoyed massive popular support. It had acquired a widespread following in north and central Vietnam during March–August 1945, at a time when the Revolutionary League and Nationalist Party leaders were still in China. Well knowing that they did not stand a chance in open elections, the two parties refused to take part. Hồ then negotiated a deal with them, allowing the Revolutionary League to appoint 20 and the Nationalist Party 50 delegates in addition to the 329 elected ones.

The elections were held on 6 January. On that day, they generated almost festival-like enthusiasm in most parts of northern Vietnam, while some parts of the French-occupied south were also able to hold the poll despite French attempts to stop them. Of the 329 seats up for grabs 30 were reserved for ethnic minority representatives. The Viet Minh approved all candidates. Yet some were categorised as independents, some as representatives of the Democratic Party or Socialist Party, and some as Marxists. In many places, the voters had a choice between alternative candidates. Although there were many reports of irregularities the 6 January elections were freer than any later ones in Vietnam (with a likely exception for South Vietnam's 1967 elections), but they had been hastily prepared and were dominated by a perceived need to show national unity under Viet Minh leadership.

The National Assembly was given three main tasks. One was to approve a new government, including members of the Revolutionary League and Nationalist Party. The second was to legislate, and the third to prepare a constitution based on the text that had already been worked out. The elected assembly was thus not purely constitutive; it had other tasks as well.

Its first session on 2 March 1946 lasted just four hours. This was because of an acute risk of war between Vietnam, France and China in the days leading up to the 6 March agreement, which was signed only after the French expeditionary forces had arrived in the port city Haiphong.[22] A French fleet had been sent up the coast with a plan to land troops in Haiphong and organise a coup against the DRV government in Hanoi with tacit Chinese acquiescence. Chiang Kai-shek had just signed his deal with France, allowing it to re-establish its sovereignty in northern Indochina, but was not prepared to accept open warfare. Hồ Chí Minh sensed the danger and invited the top leaders of the Nationalist Party and Revolutionary League to join him in a national union government, and the key task of the 2 March National Assembly session was to approve of the new government. It also found time, however, to elect the new drafting committee mentioned above, with seven members representing Viet Minh-affiliated organisations, three the Revolutionary League, and one the Nationalist Party.[23] It worked during April–September, but did not receive much public attention at a time when the government was engaged in its futile negotiations with France. After Ho had signed the 15 September Modus Vivendi agreement, the drafting committee went public with its draft. By this time the Chinese occupation forces had left. In the drafting committee the three Revolutionary League representatives went along with the majority in recommending the draft, whereas the lonely Nationalist, Phạm Gia Độ, opposed it. He favoured a two-chamber system, a less class-based and more inclusive national policy, and stronger protection of basic freedoms.

After the publication of the draft, there was a short but heated debate in the press about the same constitutional issues that had been discussed after the first draft was published in November 1945: Mono-cameralism contra bi-cameralism, whether sovereignty resides in the individual or the community, the role of religion, and how strongly individual citizen rights should be protected.[24] Yet the debate suffered from the fact that so many members of the opposition were unable to take part in the proceedings. While Ho was in France, his diplomatic moderation had come under attack in the Nationalist press. He was accused of selling out to France instead of standing firm on the demand for independence

[22] For a full account of the French 'Operation Bentre', leading to a Franco-Chinese incident in Haiphong and to the signing, under Chinese pressure, of a Franco-Vietnamese accord, see Stein Tønnesson, *Vietnam 1946: How the War Began* (Berkeley: University of California Press, 2010), ch 2.

[23] For its membership, see n 4.

[24] Marr (n 9) at 94.

and unity. This prompted the deputy minister of the interior Võ Nguyên Giáp, as the man responsible for security, to launch police raids against the Revolutionary League and Nationalist Party headquarters, arresting many of their members, and revealing plans for terrorist attacks against French targets. In March, most of the appointed Revolutionary League and Nationalist Party members were present; they had been cordially invited by Hồ Chí Minh. In November, most of them stayed away or could not participate because they were in jail, had fled to China or gone into hiding. While the first session had included a great majority of the 399 delegates, only some 270 were present when the second session convened on 28 October, including just 38 of the 70 Nationalist Party and Revolutionary League representatives, and on 8 November, only 242 took part in the vote over the Constitution.[25]

The delegates were again grouped in accordance with their party affiliation (following the French model): Marxists on the extreme left, then Socialists, Democrats, Viet Minh (in the centre), and Revolutionary League and Nationalist Party delegates on the right but there were fewer delegates present on the right-hand side. These divisions were also somewhat artificial. The Marxists, Socialists and Democrats were just as much Viet Minh as those in the Centre, and the Marxist group did not include the top communist leaders, who either held leading positions in the Viet Minh or the government (like Hồ Chí Minh, Võ Nguyên Giáp, Phạm Văn Đồng and Trần Huy Liệu) or operated in the shadows (like Trường Chinh, who had been Secretary General of the ICP and now did his best to keep up an unofficial 'party' network in the guise of Marxist Study Groups). Those Revolutionary League representatives who showed up at the second session had rallied to the Viet Minh. This was not, however, the case for the Nationalist Party delegates. They were a tiny but real opposition. One of them spoke out against the draft Constitution in the opening meeting, and another, drafting committee member Phạm Gia Độ, explained why he would vote against the proposed text. He also argued strongly against the unicameral system, which he said was a recipe for 'majority dictatorship.' While most of those who took the floor disagreed, there was also one who argued that a people's dictatorship is preferable to a minority dictatorship.[26]

Hồ Chí Minh announced the resignation of his government on 29 October and presented a new government for the National Assembly's approval on 3 November. It no longer included anyone from the Nationalist Party or Revolutionary League but was a consolidated Viet Minh government with communists in control of the key ministries.

[25] 'Note sur la 'démocratie vietnamienne.' Commissariat Fédéral aux affaires politiques, Saigon, Novembre 1946, Archives d'Outre Mer, Carton CP-sup 5, at 2; see also Marr (n 9) at 94–95.

[26] 'La constitution de la République démocratique du Viet Nam,' a 27-page French study of Vietnamese constitution-making, and an 80 pp. summary of the National Assembly Debates. Carton CP-sup. 4, Centre des Archives de la France d'Outre Mer, Aix-en-Provence, France.

One article after the other was voted upon with a show of hands. Some were accepted unanimously without anyone asking for the floor (eg, Articles 1 and 2), while others provoked a heated exchange of views and proposals for change. The main debates were about gender, property rights, protection of the working class, whether the freedom of expression could be curtailed to protect the national interest, bi-cameralism versus mono-cameralism, and the role of the Standing Committee vis-a-vis the executive government. Leading Marxists, Socialists, Democrats, Viet Minh, non-party independents, Revolutionary League, and Nationalist Party delegates stated their general priorities, and apart from the Nationalists everyone opted to approve the proposed text. The constitutional debate in the National Assembly reflected an attempt to develop a kind of pluralistic politics within a framework of almost unanimous support for President Ho and the Viet Minh League.

Because of the Franco-Vietnamese crisis and perhaps because of a lack of resources the National Assembly decided in the afternoon of 9 November to refrain from having a referendum, although Article 21 made this mandatory. This decision, which in fact violated the Constitution the day after it had been adopted, was taken with 227 votes against eight.[27] The delegates also decided to exempt the government from its obligation to organise new national elections. Accordingly, the National Assembly decided to prolong its own term indefinitely, and left to the government to decide when to promulgate the Constitution.[28] This never happened. Yet the Constitution was considered to have entered into force.

V. SUBSTANTIAL FORCES

This short section presents the most important internal and external forces behind the Constitution. Their respective roles will be analysed in the following section.

The main political force was the Viet Minh League, which was dominated by a few thousand communists, many of whom had spent time in French prisons

[27] 'Note sur la 'démocratie vietnamienne.' Commissariat Fédéral aux affaires politiques, Saigon, novembre 1946, Archives d'Outre Mer, Carton CP-sup 5, at 77. Art 21 said. 'The people have the right to referendum on the Constitution and on important issues concerning the destiny of the country in accordance with Arts 32 and 70.' Art 32 said: 'Important questions concerning the destiny of the nation shall be submitted to a popular referendum if so agreed by two-thirds of the total number of deputies.' Art 79 said that any amendments to the Constitution would need a 2/3 majority, and 'The articles to be changed after approval by the National Assembly must be submitted to a national referendum.' Art 32 might perhaps be construed to mean that a 2/3 majority could decide that no referendum was needed, but that was probably meant to apply only for other 'important questions.' If amendments to the constitution 'must' be submitted to a referendum, then it would be strange if the Constitution itself must not. So the conclusion stands: The National Assembly violated the constitution immediately after it had been adopted.

[28] Marr (n 9) at 105.

during World War II, while a few had managed to operate clandestinely inside Indochina or – like Hồ Chí Minh – in exile. The Viet Minh was a broad front organisation founded in May 1941 (as a continuation of a small existing front among Vietnamese exiles in China) and was initially led by Hồ Chí Minh from a hiding place near the Vietnamese border to China. During March–August 1945, after Japan had ousted the French colonial regime and allowed many political prisoners to regain their freedom, the Viet Minh gained a widespread following in north and central Vietnam. It played a leading role in the August Revolution and the founding of the Democratic Republic of Vietnam (DRV). Afterwards, it continued to grow as a support organisation for the government and its People's Committees, with local and regional committees and broad National Salvation organisations *(Cứu Quốc)* for various interest groups, such as workers, youth, peasants, women, etc. Its decision-making system was opaque, but it was believed at the time to be directed by an occult central committee *(Tổng Bộ)*. Its decision-making may have been rather informal, yet concentrated in a group of communists around Hồ Chí Minh. During Hồ's long stay in France in 1946, it seems – as was mentioned above – that the one who called the shots in Hanoi was Võ Nguyên Giáp, whose formal position at the time was deputy minister of the interior.

There are few indications that Trường Chinh, the former Secretary General of the ICP who had been opposed to the dissolution of his party on 22 November 1945, took any active part in top level Viet Minh or DRV decision-making during 1946, although he may of course have been consulted behind the scenes. The main French intelligence services do not even seem to have been aware of his existence. The small 'Marxist' faction in the National Assembly did not include any of the top-ranking members of the former ICP, but played a role as advocates of communist viewpoints at a time when loyalty to the Viet Minh required a high level of doctrinal restraint. The Marxists of course fully supported the Viet Minh League. So, did the small Socialist Party, which made a point of fighting for workers' rights, and the Democratic Party, which – as mentioned – hoped to preserve the DRV as a Democratic Republic and avoid any future transition to socialism or dictatorship.[29]

The Viet Minh League should not in my view be seen merely as a classic communist front organisation, manipulated to back up the party line. It built on a high level of popular enthusiasm, particularly among the young, and managed to create a broad national bloc, united in its struggle for unity and independence, under the leadership of President Hồ. Yet it was dominated by a network

[29] While David Marr thinks the Democratic Party could have played a major role in Vietnam if the Franco-Vietnamese war had been avoided, Alec Holcombe sees the Democratic Party as having been fully controlled by the Indochinese Communist Party through Hoàng Minh Chính (1922–2008), who was general secretary of the Democratic Party. Hoàng Minh Chính became a Moscow-trained theoretician who, in the late 1960s, fell out with the Vietnam Workers Party leadership, and was jailed several times. He became a dissident and tried to re-establish the Democratic Party in 2006, after it had been dissolved in 1991.

of highly disciplined communists who would tighten their control of the movement and reorganise their party from 1947 onward.

The only non-Viet Minh forces that influenced the making of the Constitution were the Nationalist Party (VNQDĐ) and the Revolutionary League (Đồng Minh Hội), which had operated in Chinese exile during World War II but been unable to establish a clandestine presence inside Vietnam in the way the ICP and Viet Minh did. The pro-Japanese political parties, which had operated inside Indochina during World War II, disappeared in the August Revolution, and the political sects in southern Vietnam (Cao Đài and Hòa Hảo) concentrated on their local struggle with the British and French forces, as well as local communist guerrillas, and were not present in central and northern Vietnam. Southern Vietnam had its own complex political dynamics, and was weakly represented in DRV politics.

The Revolutionary League and Nationalist Party entered northern Vietnam together with the Chinese occupation forces in September–October 1945, chased the Viet Minh away from a few border provinces, and established themselves with offices and newspapers in Hanoi and other northern cities. The Nationalist Party was the stronger of the two, and the two parties had different Chinese protectors. Hồ Chí Minh knew their leaders well from his time in China, notably Nguyễn Hải Thần of the Revolutionary League and Vũ Hồng Khanh of the Nationalist Party, and had sought to establish a common front with them already in the 1941–1944 period. In December 1945, he negotiated with them under Chinese military auspices, and made the deal that gave them a right to nominate 70 members of the National Assembly – without taking part in the elections. Vũ Hồng Khanh was made Vice President in a government of national union, and signed the 6 March agreement with France along with President Hồ after Nguyễn Hải Thần, whom Ho had first tried to persuade to sign, had made himself unavailable. Once China and the DRV had allowed the French to re-establish a military presence in northern Vietnam, the Revolutionary League and Nationalist Party sought to outflank the Viet Minh by taking up a more staunchly anti-French position. This allowed the DRV government, after the Chinese occupation troops withdrew to China, to suppress the two groups without meeting French opposition, and secure the Viet Minh's monopoly on power.

In September, during Hồ Chí Minh's absence, Võ Nguyên Giáp sought to integrate the Revolutionary League and Nationalist Party in a new Viet Minh-dominated national bloc (Liên Việt) through a combination of sticks and carrots. The most recalcitrant leaders of the two opposition parties were arrested or driven into exile, while others were persuaded to work with the Viet Minh. The integration effort was most successful in relation to the Revolutionary League. During the second session of the National Assembly Phạm Gia Độ was booed by other members for breaking national unity. He was on one occasion deprived of the right to speak, and not long after he had voted against the Constitution, he was arrested and accused of treason.

As for the influence of external forces, it was not just the China-oriented parties that were influenced by developments in China. The views of the Chinese Guomindang and of the Chinese Communist Party, who were engaged in their own constitutional debates and negotiations leading to the adoption of a new Chinese Constitution on 25 December 1946, are likely to have been known and discussed by the drafters of the Vietnamese Constitution. So, we need to look for positive Chinese influence.

The same goes for France, who affected Vietnamese constitution making in three different ways. The first was inspirational. Many references were made to the French Revolution and French constitutional history in the Vietnamese debates, and the drafters followed the French constitutional debates during 1945–46. The second French effect was obstructive. The French government did not want Vietnam to have its own Constitution. On 24 March 1945, General de Gaulle's provisional government had announced its intention to create an Indochinese Federation with five constituent parts: Cochinchina, Annam, Tonkin, Cambodia and Laos, each with a certain level of autonomy but under a strong federal government led by a French High Commissioner. France was opposed to the principle of Vietnamese unity. It suppressed the revolutionary government in the south through a military counter-revolution, and engaged itself in setting up an autonomous Cochinchinese Republic with a local provisional government. France was also opposed to the Vietnamese claim for independence, and after French troops had arrived in northern Vietnam in March 1946, there was a looming threat of war between France and the DRV. The third influence was transactional. Because it ran a risk of war with China, France had been compelled to sign the 6 March 1946 deal, recognising Vietnam vaguely as a 'free state' and promising a referendum to decide on the question of unity between Vietnam's three parts. The French Socialist Party (SFIO) and Communist Party (PCF) were proponents of a 'policy of accords' and wanted to negotiate for real with Hồ Chí Minh. The attitude of the French centrist Christian Democrats (MRP) was more uncertain. The negotiations between the French and DRV governments from April to August 1946 did not lead to any agreement, and Hồ Chí Minh's 'modus vivendi' of 15 September consisted just of a ceasefire in southern Vietnam to be effective from 31 October, a mutual engagement to respect rights of association and expression, and an intention to resume negotiations in 1947, once the new French Constitution had entered into force and a regular French government been established.

So, although France is not mentioned in Vietnam's first Constitution, the French role in shaping its constitutional moment was crucial.

VI. ANALYSIS

Let me begin by asking from which sources the DRV drew its legitimacy. State sovereignty needs to be confirmed both internally and externally. In the text of the 1946 Constitution, and notably in President Hồ Chí Minh's various statements and communications, we see how the DRV sought to utilise several sources of legitimacy in parallel, internal as well as external. The most obvious was the August Revolution, which by being a general uprising was seen as an expression of popular sovereignty. More formally, it was emphasised that a National People's Congress had been held at the Viet Minh headquarters in 'Tan Trao' (Kim Lung village 85 kilometres northwest of Hanoi) just before the revolution happened, calling for a general uprising and electing a Provisional government. This Congress, which in fact could not influence the revolution as such, since it did not have any means of rapid communication, was referred to later as an institutional source of popular sovereignty. These two sources of sovereignty merged after the seizure of power when the uprising committee in Hanoi transferred its powers to the provisional government elected at Tan Trao. Popular sovereignty was further expressed in the national elections of 6 January 1946 and by the two National Assembly sessions held in 1946.

In addition to emphasising popular sovereignty, the constitution makers derived legitimacy from the Nguyen dynasty, although its founder Gia Long (1762–1820) was seen in nationalist historiography as a usurper who seized power with help from France and Siam. It is noticeable that neither Hồ Chí Minh's 'independence declaration' of 2 September 1945 nor the preamble to the 1946 Constitution declared the creation of a new state. They said that the August Revolution restored a sovereignty that had been stolen temporarily by France. After Bảo Đại's abdication, when Hồ Chí Minh appointed him as a Supreme Advisor, he was invited (as Citizen Vĩnh Thụy) to come up from Hue to Hanoi so he could take part in cabinet meetings. This added to Ho's authority and helped the DRV's claim to represent the whole of Vietnam. The French had divided Vietnam into three units (Cochinchina, Annam and Tonkin) and had kept Cochinchina and the cities of Tourane (Da Nang), Haiphong and Hanoi as directly administered French territories, while Annam, Tonkin, Cambodia and Laos were protectorates. After Japan had ousted the French colonial regime in March 1945, Bảo Đại and his new Prime Minister, the historian Trần Trọng Kim, had obtained from Japan the right to annex all the French sovereign territories to the State of Vietnam. This meant that the DRV could inherit a claim to an already unified nation.

Every new State seeks international recognition. Hồ Chí Minh did this by writing to the leaders of the great powers: Chiang Kai-shek, Josef Stalin, Clement Attlee and Harry S Truman, but received no answers. It would take until 1950 before Vietnam obtained international recognition, and then it had two rival governments, which were recognised by either side in the global Cold War.

When we now proceed to analyse the impact of external forces, we should first look at China, which influenced Vietnam through its example as well as its military presence in Indochina down to the 16th parallel. The politics of constitution making in the DRV was like a mirror image of a similar process in the Republic of China. While communists dominated constitution making in

Vietnam with a minority role for non-communist nationalists, the opposite was the case in China. In the Chinese constitution-making process, the communists were the minority. The Republic of China had drawn up its first provisional Constitution in 1912. Until 1928 it provided a parliamentary system with a weak president but it did not have much impact since China succumbed to warlordism. By 1928, however, the Guomindang's Northern Expedition, which had at first been carried out in cooperation with the Chinese Communist Party, provided Generalissimo Chiang Kai-shek with control over much of China. A new provisional Constitution was promulgated in 1931, at a time when Chiang Kai-shek was waging war against the communists, forcing them to venture on their 'Long March,' and shortly before Japan occupied Manchuria. Perhaps surprisingly, the 1931 Constitution provided for a one-party system inspired by Leninist principles, with effective power held by the Central Executive Committee of the Guomindang. It was meant as a provisional arrangement, to be in force until China had been pacified and the people sufficiently educated to participate in a truly democratic government. In 1936 China's Republican government published a new draft Constitution. Then came the Sino-Japanese war in 1937, which forced the Guomindang to collaborate once again with the Chinese Communists, who were operating from headquarters in Yenan in northern China. When Japan surrendered to the Allied powers, the Guomindang, with substantial input from Communist representatives, produced a democratic Constitution that would end one-party rule. The two parties held a convention where both presented their views, and a communist demand for a popular election of a National Assembly (Legislative Yuan) was accepted. The new Constitution was adopted by the National Assembly on 25 December 1946, and promulgated by the National government on 1 January 1947. This Constitution was seen as the third and final stage of the Guomindang's Chinese renaissance. However, by the time the Constitution entered into force, it no longer seemed possible to avoid civil war. Although the Chinese communists had participated in drafting the document and had attended the constitutional convention in May 1946, they declared that they would not recognise the new Constitution. It remains in force though in the Republic of China (Taiwan) today, although it was revised substantially in 1991 and 2005.

The Chinese and Vietnamese constitutional processes thus ran in parallel, and both included difficult negotiations and debates between nationalists and communists. The difference was that the nationalists controlled the government in China, where the communists formed a vocal minority, while the opposite was the case in Vietnam. I have not (yet) found any evidence in French archives or in the literature as to whether or not the parallel process in China influenced the drafting of the Vietnamese Constitution, but I find this likely. All the Chinese provisional and draft Constitutions from 1912 to 1946 were based on Sun Yat-sen's *Three Principles of the People* (Sān Mín Zhǔyì): nationalism, democracy, and social livelihood. A perhaps interesting similarity between the Chinese and Vietnamese Constitutions of 1946 is that they did not define a clear division of power between the various branches of government. In both cases the question was resolved in practice by the authority of the main leader (Hồ Chí Minh and Chiang Kai-shek). For this reason, China and Vietnam would both have strong presidents and avoid the pitfalls of the French Fourth Republic, with its symbolic presidency, strong but divided National Assembly, and all-to-frequent changes of government.

It would be interesting to compare systematically the Chinese and Vietnamese 1946 Constitutions and establish to what extent Chinese constitutional developments influenced Vietnamese constitution making, either through the Nationalist Party and Revolutionary League representatives in the drafting committee, or on the drafters belonging to the Viet Minh communist majority.

We should add that Nationalist China in several ways undermined the power and influence of the Nationalist Party and the Revolutionary League in Vietnam. It did this, first, by allowing Hồ Chí Minh to stay in power. The main reason why Chiang Kai-shek decided to tolerate the DRV, although he knew it was dominated by communists, is probably that he and the commanders of the Chinese occupation forces realised that Hồ's government was vastly more capable than any government the Revolutionary League or Nationalist Party might form. If China had decided to oust Hồ from power, the communists might have launched an armed struggle, and this would mean trouble for the Chinese occupation forces and possibly derail Chiang's plan to obtain American shipping so they could be sent to Manchuria and halt the Chinese Communist expansion there.

Next, China undermined the position of its client parties by signing a treaty with France on 28 February 1946, allowing it to regain its colonial sovereignty. In return, France gave up all its extraterritorial rights in China, a concession Chiang had long sought. From the perspective of the Revolutionary League and the Nationalist Party, the treaty of 28 February meant that they were abandoned by their protective power. It must have felt like treason. Critical voices were also heard inside the Chinese Guomindang. It only made matters worse when China put pressure on the Nationalist leaders to join Hồ Chí Minh in a government of national union and take responsibility together with him for his 6 March accord with France.

Third, in June–September 1946, the Chinese occupation forces withdrew from Vietnam, leaving their Vietnamese clients to be persecuted and repressed by the DRV government. Some would later support the Republic of (South) Vietnam but none of them would again receive a prominent political role.

France had an even greater impact on Vietnamese developments. Those who drafted the Vietnamese Constitution no doubt followed the ongoing constitution-making process in France. While Pham Van Dong, who had chaired the delegation that negotiated with France at Fontainebleau during June–August 1946, presided over the National Assembly session in October–November, he had a copy of the new French Constitution on the desk before him.[30] Yet the

[30] 'La constitution de la République démocratique du Viet Nam' (n 23) at 5.

French government did not have any direct influence on Vietnam's drafting committee. By contrast, in Laos and Cambodia, constitutions were conceived in the French language and translated into the vernacular.

France went through a difficult constitution-making process in 1946, with four successive provisional governments in less than one year. A leftist constitutional proposal supported by the Communists and Socialists was rejected in a referendum on 4 May 1946, while an amended proposal was adopted in a referendum on 13 October, despite heavy opposition from General de Gaulle. De Gaulle's own government, which had been established after the liberation of Paris in August 1944, had resigned on 20 January 1946. All the next three governments were coalition governments between Christian Democrats (MRP), Socialists and Communists, but under different Prime Ministers. The text that was rejected in May did not get the MRP's support, while the successful one was recommended by the MRP. To gain such support, however, the leftist proposal from May underwent radical change, including a reduction in the degree of autonomy offered to members of the French Union.[31]

Constitution-making in France and Vietnam was related in two ways: First, some of the same thinking went into the French and Vietnamese drafts, although there were also major differences.[32] The French Constitution was bicameral and the Vietnamese mono-cameral. The French spoke only of citizens' rights. The Vietnamese spoke of rights and duties. The French provided for a mainly ceremonial president and concentrated powers in a vibrant National Assembly that would elect the leader of the government (Président du Conseil). The Vietnamese National Assembly would have just two short annual sessions and be represented for the rest of the year by a Standing Committee. Alec Holcombe suggests that the idea of having a small and controllable Standing Committee must have been taken from the Soviet Constitution of 1936. Holcombe finds similarity in the structure of the relevant paragraphs in the Soviet Constitution and the November 1945 Vietnamese draft. Yet the content was different. The Soviet 1936 Constitution was actually the most democratic of the two – formally speaking – since it provided the Presidium of the Supreme Soviet with real powers vis-a-vis the executive. By contrast, the November 1945 draft of the Vietnamese Constitution subjects the Standing Committee to the power of the President.[33] This may reflect the situation at the time when the draft was written.

[31] Yet, out of the 18,213 French citizens in Indochina who voted, 14,456 heeded de Gaulle's call and voted no. In the overall French tally, the constitution was adopted by a small majority of 53%. See Tønnesson (n 22) at 85–86.

[32] Marr (n 9), at 106.

[33] The key Art 49c of the 1936 Soviet Constitution says that the Standing Committee has the authority to dissolve the Supreme Soviet (Union Assembly) and order new elections. The corresponding Art 15c of Vietnam's 1946 Constitution says, by contrast, that 'when confronted with a problem that the Representatives cannot solve, the Standing Committee may dissolve the People's National Assembly and request [a solution] from the President of Vietnam.' (italics added by ST). See Holcombe (n 3) at 334–335.

While Stalin could afford a degree of democratic formality in 1936 since he had taken full control of the USSR, Hồ Chí Minh needed to formalise a unity of action around his leadership, since he faced a situation just as threatening as the Bolsheviks had done during the Russian Civil War (1918–1921). A huge Chinese army was occupying northern Indochina while Britain helped France suppress the revolution in the south. Paradoxically, Hồ Chí Minh's preferred Constitution resembles the 'presidential republic' favoured by General Charles de Gaulle, whose failure to persuade the main French political parties to adopt a constitution with a strong, independent executive had driven him to resign as leader of the French government in January 1946. Later in the year, de Gaulle urged the French people to reject the constitutional proposals that were subjected to referendums in May and October. De Gaulle thought they gave too much power to the party-dominated National Assembly and would prevent effective national leadership.

The adopted version of the Vietnamese Constitution retained the principle of a strong president and of a National Assembly that would meet only for short sessions. Yet the text on the Standing Committee was very different from the one that had been proposed in November 1945. A Standing Committee had already been set up on 2 March. Its leader, Nguyễn Văn Tố, had disturbed Ho Chi Minh and his close confident Võ Nguyên Giáp with several independent initiatives. Nguyễn Văn Tố thus lost his job but in Articles 27–28 and 36, the 10 November 1946 Constitution gave the Standing Committee an important role as a watchdog, with a right to 'control and criticise' the government.

Second, the French Constitution included a section on the French Union, of which an Indochinese Federation was supposed to be a key member. Vietnam's place in the French Union was deeply contested both in Vietnam and France and between them, and a bone of contention in their negotiations. As it were, the Vietnamese Constitution would not include any reference to France, the French Union, the Indochinese Federation, Laos or Cambodia but became a purely national framework for a unified and independent Vietnam. Hence the French and Vietnamese Constitutions were in conflict from the start.

One of the most controversial matters in the French Constitution was colonial reform. The French Union was to have its own assembly consisting of representatives from both metropolitan and overseas France. Cochinchina, Annam and Tonkin were supposed to belong to the French Union through their membership in the Indochinese Federation. The French Constitution made an opening for decolonisation within the French Union by creating a new category of 'Associated States' in addition to overseas territories. To understand Vietnam's constitutional moment, we must remember that no one knew there would be full-scale war between the DRV and France from December 1946. They knew there was a risk, and preparations were made for a protracted war of resistance, but the main prospect for the DRV leaders was one of continued negotiations in 1947. The Marxist Nguyễn Văn Thao said it this way in the National Assembly on 31 October: 'We must sincerely endeavour to arrive at a durable understanding with France … but must not submit ourselves in an excessively credulous or absolute confidence.'[34]

From December 1946 to April–May 1947, the French High Commissioner in Saigon feared that a new French government, led by a Socialist Prime Minister, would make new concessions to Hanoi, and perhaps give Vietnam a status as Associated State. This convinced the Gaullist High Commissioner and his team that a more aggressive French strategy was needed, and that he had to take the initiative to a conflict with the DRV without waiting for new government instructions. The crisis leading to the outbreak of war in Hanoi on 19 December 1946 took off immediately after the Vietnamese National Assembly members had gone home. The effective implementation of the ceasefire that took effect in southern Vietnam on 30 October 1946 had demonstrated that the local guerrilla fighters took their orders from Hanoi. This gave the Hanoi government a degree of legitimacy in the south that killed the French-initiated experiment with Cochinchinese autonomy. On 10 November, the president of the Cochinchinese Republic hanged himself. Then France provoked a conflict with the DRV over customs in Haiphong, and proceeded to occupy the strategically important cities of Haiphong and Langson, partly with the help of heavy artillery, leading to huge casualties. In the night between 19 and 20 December the Vietnamese army retaliated by attacking French garrisons in Hanoi and many other places. Hồ Chí Minh had left Hanoi in advance. The First Indochina War was now on. By the autumn of 1947 France abandoned its attempts to re-establish contact with Hồ Chí Minh, and instead began to construct a political alternative around former Emperor Bảo Đại. By 1949–50, the Indochina War became a hot war in the Cold War, with the US providing massive support to France.

To sum up, although the revolutionary history of France provided inspiration for Vietnamese constitution makers, the French impact was mostly destructive. Its colonial war deprived the Vietnamese population of a chance to benefit from the democratic aspects of their first Constitution and pushed them into the Soviet-led Cold War camp. This no doubt satisfied the ideological aspirations of the Vietnamese communist leaders at the time[35] – yet Vietnamese history might have followed a more peaceful course, perhaps also more democratic, if the 1946 Constitution had been given a chance.

What about Soviet inspiration? Vietnam's second Constitution in 1959 was deeply influenced by the Soviet and East European models. One might assume that this was also the case for the first Constitution in 1946. The Vietnamese communists, not least Hồ Chí Minh, staunchly admired the Soviet Union and its two successive leaders Vladimir Lenin and Josef Stalin. Hồ Chí Minh's own

[34] French-language minutes from the second session of the Vietnamese National Assembly, 28 October–10 November 1946. Carton Conseiller Politique Sup-5, Centre des Archives de la France d'Outre-Mer, Aix-en-Provence, at 31.

[35] See Tuong Vu, *Vietnam's Communist Revolution: The Power and Limits of Ideology* (Cambridge: Cambridge University Press, 2017).

clandestine journal during World War II, *Việt Nam Độc Lập,* brought a series of glowing reports about Soviet battlefield victories. Yet there was no direct contact between Moscow and the Viet Minh or ICP leaders during World War II, and in 1943 the Communist International (Comintern) was dissolved. When the August Revolution happened in 1945, it was barely noticed in the Soviet and international communist press. Stalin was keenly interested in the fate of the French Communist Party, but could not care less about Indochina. He failed to respond to letters from the new Vietnamese President – and may not even have seen them.

When looking for external influences on Vietnamese Constitution making in 1946, we find more imprints from China and France than from Russia. To be sure, as pointed out by David Holcombe, there are some similarities between the Soviet Constitution of 1936 and the Vietnamese of 1946. Both provided for People's Committees on the local, and for a Standing Committee on the national level. Neither Stalin nor Ho must have wanted to face questions and opposition from a National Assembly on a regular basis. Yet the Vietnamese Constitution of 1946 bears little resemblance with the Soviet Constitution of 1936, which was federal and explicitly socialist, and did not protect property rights.[36] By contrast to the DRV moreover, the USSR had a two-chamber system. As mentioned, the choice between a uni- and bi-cameral system caused intense debate in Vietnam. A Socialist Party delegate argued that the upper house in a bicameral system always defends the ruling classes. Phạm Gia Độ of the Nationalist Party retorted that uni-cameralism meant 'dictatorship by the majority.' When a Viet Minh delegate countered that in Vietnam's current dangerous circumstances it was vital to possess a strong central power capable of making decisions quickly, an opponent interjected, 'Just like the dictatorship of the [French] Convention of 1792.' After the debate, 200 delegates supported uni-cameralism and just ten bi-cameralism.[37] The language in the Soviet Constitution was full of Marxist expressions, while this was not the case in the Vietnamese. One Việt Minh delegate scolded those who referred to foreign models in the constitutional debates, saying, 'the Constitution is for Vietnam, not Russia or the United States.'[38] By 1959, however, when Vietnam adopted its second Constitution, the Soviet influence was infinitely greater.

VII. ROLE IN MODERN VIETNAM'S FORMATION

The 1946 Constitution did not play a prominent role in Vietnamese nation building because the war with France broke out so shortly after its adoption.

[36] For an English translation of the Soviet constitution of 1936, see: https://constitutii.files.wordpress.com/2013/01/1936-en.pdf.

[37] Marr (n 9) at 101.

[38] Ibid, at 106.

In addition, only few people were engaged in debating the Constitution. It was never promulgated and was rarely referred to in a period when the DRV fought for its survival. When Hồ Chí Minh returned to Hanoi in 1954, after the victory at Dien Bien Phu and the Geneva agreement, the 1946 Constitution was already considered out-dated. The Communist Party had been reconstituted as the Vietnam Workers Party (Lao Động) in 1951, and with Soviet and Chinese backing the DRV could not engage in the construction of an outright socialist state. Eventually this new situation was codified in Vietnam's second Constitution of 1959.

What this study shows is that a constitution does not have much chance of long-term survival if it is written by people seeing it as a temporary arrangement. This may seem obvious. If constitution makers see a constitution as temporary, it is likely to become temporary, and if a constitution is written under an assumption of peace, and war breaks out shortly afterwards, it is likely to quickly lose relevance. A war is an emergency; hence laws are set aside. Constitution makers are peacemakers only if there is a peace to codify, or if they look beyond their contemporary conflicts and create a solid legal framework for managing and resolving future conflicts.

The impact of a Constitution depends on:

(a) The constitutional moment: is it a moment in the nation's history when something new and durable can be formed?
(b) The ability of the drafters to think beyond the moment and formulate general principles and institutional procedures with sufficient flexibility to endure.
(c) The involvement of representatives of all social and interest groups in reaching out for compromises, which are not only acceptable on a temporary basis.
(d) Symbolic value: If the Constitution becomes a symbol of the nation, along with its flag and anthem, if the Constitution Day is actively celebrated and remembered every year, then it may survive even though it has shortcomings.

The moment – or interregnum – between the end of World War II and the onset of the Cold War, which in the Vietnamese context was the period between the August Revolution and the outbreak of war with France on 19 December 1946, included several dramatic changes. The characteristics of the constitutional moment were summarised in the preamble to the Constitution, which reveals how much it depended on a set of circumstances, and therefore was unlikely to survive:

> The August Revolution regained the country's sovereignty, freedom for the people *(nhân dân)*, and the foundations of a Democratic Republic. After eighty years of struggle the Vietnamese people *(dân tộc)* have escaped from colonial oppression and simultaneously cast aside monarchism. The country *(nước nhà)* has stepped onto a

new path. The responsibility of our people in this era is to protect all territory, achieve full independence, and build the nation *(quốc gia)* on democratic foundations.[39]

The drafting committee had not in fact proposed to have a preamble. This came up as a suggestion from one of the representatives in the National Assembly. The idea was put to a vote and accepted by a clear majority. Then the preamble was quickly drafted, discussed and endorsed. This set a precedent for Vietnam's later Constitutions. Their preambles facilitate the task of the historian when seeking to describe each constitutional moment. We may simply compare the 1946 preamble with the later ones.

The preamble to the 1959 Constitution says:

> Vietnam is a single entity from Lang Son to Ca Mau ... From 1930 onwards, under the leadership of the Indochinese Communist Party – now the Vietnam Lao Dong [Workers] Party – the Vietnamese revolution advanced into a new stage ... Our State is a people's democratic State based on the alliance between the workers and peasants and led by the working class ... The new Constitution defines the political, economic and social system of our country ... and provides for the taking of the North towards socialism ... and the building of a stable and strong North Vietnam as a basis for the struggle for the peaceful reunification of the country. ... Our people are resolved to strengthen further solidarity and unity of mind with the brother countries in the socialist camp, headed by the great Soviet Union, and to strengthen solidarity with the peoples of Asia and Africa and peace-loving people all over the world.

The preamble of 1980 contains the following explanation:

> Throughout their four-thousand-year history, the Vietnamese people have worked hard and fought heroically to build and defend their country ... Our country, formerly a colony and a semi-feudal country, has become an independent, reunified, socialist state, a member of the world socialist community ... The victories of the peoples of the three Indochina countries, and the Vietnamese people, in the war against US aggression, heralded the complete bankruptcy of neo-colonialism, contributed to the consolidation and extension of the world socialist system, encouraged the national liberation movements and the workers' and democratic movements, and accelerated the offensive of the three revolutionary currents of the present era ... No sooner had they emerged from thirty years of liberation war than our people, who were longing for peace to build their homeland, were confronted with the Chinese hegemonist aggressors and their henchmen in Cambodia. Promoting our glorious national traditions, our army and people won resounding victories in both wars for national defence against the aggression by Cambodian reactionaries on the south-western border and the Chinese hegemonists on the northern border, safeguarding our independence, sovereignty, unity and territorial integrity. Credit for the great successive victories of the Vietnamese revolution goes to the Communist Party of Vietnam which has creatively applied Marxism-Leninism ... Let our entire people strengthen unity ... and ... establish the system of socialist collective mastery and large-scale socialist

[39] Marr (n 9) at 103–104.

> production … The Socialist Republic of Vietnam needs a Constitution institutionalizing the current line of the Communist Party of Vietnam in the new stage, namely a Constitution for the period of transition to socialism on a national scale. Continuing and developing the Constitutions of 1946 and 1959, the present Constitution … specifies the relationships between the Party's leadership, the people's mastery, and State management in Vietnamese society.

The reference to Vietnam's long history was retained in the 1992 preamble:

> In the course of their millennia-old history, the Vietnamese people, working diligently, creatively, and fighting courageously to build their country and defend it, have forged a tradition of unity, humanity, uprightness, perseverance and indomitableness for their nation and have created Vietnamese civilization and culture … In successive periods of resistance war and national construction, our country adopted the 1946, 1959, and 1980 Constitutions. Starting in 1986, a comprehensive national renewal advocated by the 6th Congress of the Communist Party of Vietnam has achieved very important initial results. The National Assembly has decided to revise the 1980 Constitution in response to the requirements of the new situation and tasks. This Constitution … institutionalizes the relationship between the Party as leader, the people as master, and the State as administrator. … In the light of Marxism-Leninism and Ho Chi Minh thought … the Vietnamese people vow to … carry out a foreign policy of independence, sovereignty, peace, friendship and cooperation with all nations.[40]

Finally, the 2013 preamble sticks to the illusion of progress towards socialism, and claims to be the embodiment of all the previous constitutions:

> With the will and strength of the entire nation and the assistance of friends around the world, our People have gained great victories in the struggles to liberate the nation, reunify the country, defend the Fatherland and fulfil international duties, and have recorded resounding achievements of historical significance in the cause of renewing and building the country toward socialism. Institutionalizing the Platform for National Construction during the Period of Transition toward Socialism, and perpetuating the 1946, 1959, 1980 and 1992 constitutions, the Vietnamese People create, implement and defend this constitution to achieve the goal of a prosperous people and a strong, democratic, equitable and civilized country.

Interestingly, the 1946 Constitution begins its account of Vietnamese history in 1945 (the August Revolution) and the 1959 Constitution in 1930 (the ICP's founding), while the 1980, 1992 and 2013 preambles trace national origins thousands of years back in time. The 1946 Constitution mentions neither the ICP nor the Viet Minh but emphasises unity among all social classes, while the 1959 Constitution affirms that Vietnam is in transition to a centrally managed socialist system. The 1980 Constitution claims that Vietnam is already an

[40] Constitutions of Vietnam 1946–1959–1980–1992, pp 11–12, 35–38, 73–77, 131–132. The Constitution of the Socialist Republic of Vietnam (2013): http://vietnamnews.vn/politics-laws/250222/the-constitution-of-the-socialist-republic-of-viet-nam.html#TDPrWdkA6TwvgOr3.99f.

accomplished socialist country led by a Party, which – by implicit contrast to the Chinese 'hegemonists' – has correctly interpreted Marxism-Leninism.

The 1992 and 2013 Constitutions represent a return to a situation somewhat reminiscent of 1946, with a diversified economy and a non-aligned foreign policy. Yet, on the background of the communist demise in Eastern Europe and the dissolution of the Soviet Union, the 1992 Constitution affirms the leading role of the Communist Party in state and society. The affirmation of its leading role is kept unchanged in Article 4 of the 2013 Constitution while two caveats are added: The Party shall be 'accountable to the People for its decisions' and shall 'operate within the framework of the Constitution and the law.' At any rate, from a liberal point of view there is little doubt that the 1946 Constitution remains the most democratic of the five.

During 1947–54, however, the 1946 Constitution was somewhat irrelevant since the DRV was at war. The state became a war machine, geared towards controlling as much as possible of the countryside and recruiting soldiers for an all-out struggle.[41] Yet the Constitution did play a role as an expression of national legitimacy at a time when France sought to create a new Associated State of Vietnam centred in southern Vietnam. During this period, the Viet Minh leaders got into some trouble with Moscow, who criticised them for having failed to carry out a radical land reform in 1945–46, and above all for having dissolved the Communist Party. During 1949–51, when the DRV received massive aid and military training from the new People's Republic of China, the 1946 Constitution was no longer considered relevant, so when the Communist Party rebuilt itself, while pretending to have existed all along, and then constituted the Vietnam Workers Party (Lao Dong) in 1951, the DRV began to think about writing a new Constitution, directly inspired by the Soviet and East European ones. A French-language copy of the 1946 Constitution that was filed at the time in the Vietnamese National Archives was annotated as follows:

> This constitution was adopted at a time when Vietnam was in a particularly difficult and complex situation … From the point of view of a People's Democracy, this constitution contains a few imperfections and lacunae which have been corrected later through legislative measures implemented by the Resistance Government. Therefore, it clearly no longer corresponds to the social situation of Vietnam.[42]

Yet it remained formally in force until 1959. This was five years after the PRC had promulgated its first Constitution in 1954. A likely reason for the delay in producing Vietnam's second Constitution is Hồ Chí Minh's hope that it would be possible to unite peacefully with South Vietnam, achieve a dominant position

[41] Christopher G Goscha, *Vietnam: A New History* (New York: Basic Books, 2016).

[42] 'Cette constitution a été votée à un moment où le Vietnam se trouvait dans une situation particulièrement difficile et complexe … Du point de vue d'un Etat démocratique populaire, cette Constitution présente de nombreuses imperfections et lacunes qui ont été mises sur pied et les mesures législatives qui ont été prises par le Gouvernement de la Résistance. C'est pourquoi il est hors de doute qu'elle ne répondra plus à l'état social du Viet Nam.'

in a coalition government and then compose a new national Constitution for all of Vietnam. By 1959 this hope was gone.

In the Đổi Mới period from 1986, when the 1992 Constitution was written, some intellectuals regained interest in the democratic aspects of the 1946 Constitution but Vietnam's top leaders were shocked by the fall of the communist regimes in Eastern Europe in 1989 and even more by the dissolution of the USSR in 1991, so they decided to affirm the Party's leading role in state and society. Instead of allowing themselves to be inspired by Russian openness *(glasnost)*, the Vietnamese adopted the Chinese combination of a relatively open and competitive economy with a one-party system of governance, and normalised relations with China. A need was therefore felt to replace the anti-Chinese 1980 Constitution with a new one, again reflecting changing times. In the 2000s, when Vietnam made great strides towards prosperity and no longer belonged to any specific camp in world affairs, calls for a restoration of the 1946 Constitution and non-Marxist constitutional principles of a Confucian or liberal kind were stimulated by public debates in internet forums. Yet another Constitution emerged from these debates in 2013, and some concessions were made to the concept of universal human rights,[43] but for all practical purposes it remained an authoritarian Constitution, with few checks and balances and a weak judiciary. So be it that Vietnam today, along with China, has a Constitution that sustains an authoritarian one-party regime in a capitalist market economy. How long is this meant to last?[44]

[43] Bui Ngoc Son. 'The Global Origins of Vietnam's Constitutions: Text in Context.'

[44] 'It can be anticipated that in a long run, the discourse on restoration constitutionalism in Vietnam may move beyond Ho Chi Minh and his 1946 Constitution to elucidate the meaning of conceptions and social movements by other early Vietnamese constitutionalists.' Bui Ngoc Son (n 6), at 115–116.

10

The Lao Constitution of 1947/1949: Creating a Nation-State

MARTIN STUART-FOX

INTRODUCTION

PRIOR TO THE first Lao Constitution (drafted in 1947, ultimately promulgated in 1949), Laos as constituted within its present boundaries did not exist as a unitary and integrated political entity. As a French possession, Laos comprised two separate components: the protectorate of the Kingdom of Luang Prabang in the north, where French officials advised the royal administration, and provinces in the centre and south directly administered from the French colonial capital of Vientiane. In practice, France controlled the entire territory, but under quite different legal mandates. This anomalous situation was only resolved in the aftermath of the Second World War when French jurisdiction was re-imposed following the Japanese surrender. The solution, contrived by the French, but subsequently endorsed by the Lao people, was embodied in the 1947–1949 Constitution. In a very real sense, therefore, this first Constitution created the modern nation-state of Laos.

I. THE HISTORICAL CONTEXT

The Lao Kingdom of Lan Xang was founded in the mid-fourteenth century with Xiang Dong Xiang Thong (now Luang Prabang) as its royal capital. In 1560, for reasons both strategic and administrative, the capital was moved to Viang Chan, the City of Sandalwood, or as the French later called it: Vientiane. By this time, Lao settlers had spread over most of the basin of the middle Mekong, and Lan Xang was a powerful player in the politics of mainland Southeast Asia, its geographic frontiers defined by the watersheds of the basin to the east with Vietnam and to the west with Siam. Its apogee came in the seventeenth century, when the first European missionaries and merchants arrived, leaving awed accounts of the kingdom's power and wealth.[1]

What shifted the balance of advantage in mainland Southeast Asia was maritime trade, with both China and Europe, from which Lan Xang, as a landlocked kingdom, was excluded. But the nail in the coffin of Lao decline was provided by the bitter succession dispute that followed the death of King Surinyavongsa. The outcome by 1713 was the division of Lan Xang into three separate kingdoms centred on Luang Prabang in the north, Viang Chan in the centre, and Champasak in the south. Within a century each had been forced to acknowledge Siamese suzerainty. Lao kings paid tribute to Bangkok, in return for which they were allowed to administer their respective territories.

The nadir of Lao fortunes came in 1827 when Chao Anuvong, the last king of Viang Chan, attempted to throw off the Siamese yoke and re-establish Lao independence. He was supported by his son, whom Bangkok had recently appointed King of Champasak, but not by the King of Luang Prabang. The Siamese response was immediate and brutal. The Lao armies were defeated and Viang Chan destroyed. Tens of thousands of Lao families were forcibly resettled in what is now northeast Thailand.[2] In Luang Prabang the royal line continued; in Champasak a new king was appointed, loyal to Bangkok; but in both kingdoms real power lay with two Siamese 'commissioners'. Meanwhile Viang Chan ceased to exist as a political entity, its territory disaggregated into small 'fiefdoms' (*meuang*) paying tribute to either Bangkok or Hue, or like Luang Prabang, to both.

This was the situation when the French arrived towards the end of the nineteenth century. France made little secret of its interest in Lao territories east of the Mekong, which it sought to acquire in order to 'round out' its Indochinese empire. In 1887, under an agreement with Bangkok, the first French consul was appointed to Luang Prabang. Six years later, as French gunboats blockaded Bangkok, the Siamese were persuaded to surrender jurisdiction over all territories east of the Mekong to France.[3]

By this time the French were well aware that the Kingdom of Lan Xang had once included all the basin of the middle Mekong, including almost the entire Khorat Plateau (now northeast Thailand), which imperialists in Saigon and Paris argued strenuously France should proceed to annex. In the event, however, treaties between France and Siam in 1904 and 1907 added only two territories west of the Mekong,[4] comprising the province of Xainyaburi in the north and a small

[1] Martin Stuart-Fox, *The Lao Kingdom of Lan Xang: Rise and Decline* (Bangkok: White Lotus Press, 1998).

[2] Mayoury and Pheuiphanh Ngaosyvathn, *Paths to Conflagration: Fifty Years of Diplomacy and Warfare in Laos, Thailand and Vietnam, 1778–1828* (Ithaca: Cornell University Press, 1998).

[3] Martin Stuart-Fox, *A History of Laos* (Cambridge: Cambridge University Press, 1997).

[4] L de Reinach, *Recueil des traités conclus par la France en Extrême-Orient* (E Laroux, 1902–1907, Tome 2).

area in the south taking in the former royal capital of Champasak. Had the imperialist lobby been successful, the boundaries of the Lao state would today have been very different. But with storm clouds of war gathering in Europe, Paris lost interest in expanding its remote protectorate of Laos.

II. FRENCH LAOS

The French Indochinese empire consisted of a federation of five 'countries' (*pays*) – the colony of Cochinchina and the protectorates of Annam and Tonkin together comprising Vietnam, plus the protectorates of Cambodia, and Laos – all presided over by a Governor-General resident in Hanoi. Laos was the last *pays* to be included, when in 1899 the decision was taken to establish Vientiane as the French administrative capital and to appoint a *Résident Supérieur*. Laos was divided into eleven provinces, each governed by a French *Résident*, plus the protectorate of Luang Prabang, where a French Commissioner advised the King.

A single French administration did little to overcome Lao regionalism. While all Lao acknowledged a common heritage in Lan Xang, the two centuries that had elapsed since its demise had fostered strong regional loyalties, especially in the south. The acquisition of the town of Champasak and surrounding territory by France in 1904 left much of the former kingdom in Siamese hands, though the king elected to become a French subject. Rather than create another royal enclave, however, the French allowed Chao Nhouy to retain the title of 'prince' and named him Governor of the province of Champasak – a move that did nothing to diminish his royal status in the eyes of his erstwhile subjects.[5]

The anomalous dual legal status of Laos was never resolved by the French. The 'special protectorate' status of Luang Prabang was confirmed in 1917 but the kingdom remained under threat of direct administration. In 1930 the French Legislative Council moved to rescind the protectorate, reduce Luang Prabang to a province, and directly administer the whole of Laos. So strenuous were the objections of King Sisavangvong, however, that the following year the decision was rescinded.[6] But regaining his kingdom did little to enhance his standing or influence elsewhere in the country: during the period of French colonisation the Luang Prabang monarchy never provided a symbol of Lao unity.

Within a decade the situation in Indochina had radically changed. France was not just at war, it was left defeated and diminished. French authorities in Indochina declared loyalty to the Vichy regime, and signed a modus vivendi with Japan. This did not, however, prevent Thailand from taking advantage of French

[5] P Lintingre, 'Permanence d'une structure monarchique en Asie: le royaume de Champassak' (1972) 216 *Outre-Mers: Revue d'histoire* 411–431.

[6] F Iché, *Le Statut Politique et International du Laos Français: sa condition juridique dans la communauté du droit des gens* (Rousseau, 1935).

weakness to launch an irredentist border war to recover former territories in both Laos and Cambodia previously ceded to France. Under the terms of the Treaty of Tokyo brokered by Japan, Laos lost all territories west of the Mekong.[7]

The loss was felt particularly in Luang Prabang, as the royal teak forests of Xainyaburi reverted to Thai control. In compensation, France extended the kingdom to include all of northern Laos down almost to Vientiane, while formalising its separate status as a French protectorate. But the damage had been done. The aura of France as the invincible protector of Laos from its powerful and avaricious neighbours had been shattered. Nationalist sentiments, rare in Laos before 1940, began to be openly expressed.

III. THE AFTERMATH OF WAR

On 9 March 1945 Japanese forces throughout Indochina, fearing that the French administration was about to switch allegiance from Vichy to General de Gaulle's Free French, carried out a coordinated *coup de force*. French forces were disarmed and French nationals interned. Resistance was limited, and easily suppressed. Only in Laos were some French troops able to withdraw to jungle hideouts, where they were supplied by loyal Lao supporters. This allowed the French to retain residual influence, even though under Japanese duress, in Luang Prabang King Sisavangvong issued a formal declaration of Lao independence.

In the power vacuum created by the Japanese interregnum, various Lao nationalist groups began to form, modelled on anti-Japanese resistance movements in either Vietnam or Thailand. With the sudden Japanese surrender on 15 August 1945, these coalesced to form the Lao Issara, or Free Lao. Its leader was Prince Phetsarath Rattanavongsa, hereditary *uparat* ('deputy king') of Luang Prabang, formerly the highest-ranking Lao official in the French administration, and since 1941, Chief Minister of the Royal government of Luang Prabang.

In the month that followed events moved quickly. In Luang Prabang, the King welcomed back the French in the person of Colonel Hans Imfeld, Commissioner *ad interim*, and abrogated his declaration of independence. In Champasak Prince Boun Oum, son of Chao Nhouy, also reiterated his allegiance to France. In the central Mekong towns, Free Lao forces backed by local Vietnamese seized power; while in Vientiane Prince Phetharath not only reaffirmed Lao independence, but also proclaimed the unification of Luang Prabang and the southern provinces, thus creating for the first time a single Lao political entity.[8]

As the French gathered their forces in the south, Phetsarath sought royal approval for his actions. On French advice, the King responded by relieving

[7] Conventions et Traités entre la France et le Siam relatifs au Laos (1983–1947), (1988) 16–17 *Péninsule* 115–138.

[8] For a more detailed narrative of these events, see Stuart-Fox, *A History of Laos* (n 3).

Phetsarath of his official position and titles. The Lao Issara thereupon appointed a provisional National Assembly, which first named a government of eight ministers, led by the Governor of Vientiane, Khammao Vilai, then deposed the King and proclaimed a provisional Constitution.[9] Though Phetsarath held no official position in the Lao Issara government, his was the guiding hand.

Dialogue over differences between the Lao Issara government in Vientiane, the court in Luang Prabang, and French authorities represented by Colonel Imfeld, dragged on into 1946. By the end of January, however, it was clear that France, intent on re-establishing its Indochinese empire, had no intention of negotiating the independence of Laos with the Lao Issara. In March French forces pushed north from Pakse. Savannakhet was abandoned, but Free Lao forces made a brief stand in Thakhek. Within two days it was all over, and the French resumed their advance. In response, almost the entire Lao Issara government and administration crossed the Mekong to exile in Thailand. On 24 April French troops marched into Vientiane.[10]

IV. UNIFYING THE KINGDOM

The primary goal for the French in regaining control of the Lao capital and central provinces was to reconstruct French Indochina, both territorially and administratively. The former was achieved in November 1946 at the Washington Conference, when Thailand was obliged to hand back those parts of Laos and Cambodia it had acquired in 1941. The latter took the form of a new Indochinese Federation to be included within the French Union, as the French colonial empire reconstituted by General de Galle was henceforth known.

To include Laos in the Indochinese Federation, however, ran counter to the nationalist appeal of the Lao Issara, which rested on the twin foundations of unification and independence. The French had no intention of facilitating Lao independence, though they did realise they would have to go some way towards meeting the expectations of the Francophile elite for a greater say over internal affairs. Unification, by contrast, was something the French could endorse to undercut the revolutionary appeal of the Lao Issara; and the obvious way to achieve it was for the King of Luang Prabang to become King of Laos. But before they could engineer this they had first to solve the 'southern problem'.[11]

[9] This provisional Lao Issara constitution combined French and Thai elements, but had no legal standing as it never received royal assent.

[10] In the intervening month, the provisional National Assembly reinstated King Sisavangvong as constitutional monarch of all Laos, in return for royal recognition of the legitimacy of the Lao Issara government in the absence of France, and of its Constitution as an interim measure, a compromise that freed the Lao Issara from the taint of treason.

[11] Outlined at the time by Charles-Henri Duparc in 'Le problème politique laotien' (1947) 5 *Politique Étrangère* 529–556.

At the heart of the problem was the different treatment of the kings of Luang Prabang and Champasak. Chao Nhouy had not only been King of Champasak: he was also the last direct descendant of the rulers of Viang Chan. His son, Prince Boun Oum, thus had as much right to be proclaimed King of Laos as did the King of Luang Prabang, and perhaps greater support insofar as he represented the more populous centre and south of the country.

What shifted the balance in favour of Luang Prabang was the fact that in southern Laos the Japanese surrendered to British forces, who quickly handed control over to the French; while in the north, French influence was contained by a Nationalist Chinese army of occupation that favoured Lao independence. Moreover, even the Lao Issara government had sought legitimacy by proclaiming allegiance to King Sisavangvong. And finally Prince Phetsarath, the de facto leader of the Lao Issara, was a cousin of the King. So despite the King's fidelity to France, the royal family of Luang Prabang became a symbol for those seeking greater Lao independence.

But while there was widespread support in the north for the King of Luang Prabang to become the King of Laos, the south was more ambivalent. If the matter were treated as a fait accompli, the French feared they might lose support in the south. Some form of plebiscite would be necessary to test 'the will of the people'. In the meantime, the newly appointed French Commissioner, M Jean de Raymond, obtained the cooperation of Prince Boun Oum, who in return for the position of Inspector-General of the Kingdom for life, and third in royal status after the King and Crown Prince, agreed to renounce any claim to the throne. A secret protocol to this effect was duly drawn up and signed.

V. THE MODUS VIVENDI OF 1946

The first step in the constitutional process to establish the Kingdom of Laos was to convene a joint Franco-Lao Commission with the task of setting out interim Lao rights and responsibilities within the new Indochinese Federation. This met on 8 July 1946, jointly chaired by Crown Prince Savang Vatthana representing the King and by Commissioner de Raymond for France.

When the Commission's deliberations were published on 27 August in the form of a *modus vivendi*,[12] it was immediately clear that French interests had prevailed, and that the future Kingdom of Laos would remain firmly under French control. For while the preamble reiterated the status of Laos as a unified kingdom, presided over by a constitutional monarch, and with the right to form a government, elect a parliament, and determine its own constitution and electoral law, the body of the text carried a different message.

[12] See 'Text of the Agreement between France and Laos arranging a provisional Modus Vivendi – Vientiane, 27th August 1947' (1947) 149 *British and Foreign State Papers* 615–622 (in French).

The *Résident Supérieur* was renamed Commissioner of the French Republic in Laos,[13] while the *résident* of each province was replaced by an advisory 'counsellor'. But these were little more than cosmetic name changes; the powers exercised by France remained virtually unchanged. Core provisions laid out the division of services between French and Lao, and the relationship between French advisors and Lao officials. But the French had the final say.

In fact under the modus vivendi, the French Commissioner enjoyed greater power than the King. He was responsible for the maintenance of public order with command not just of French forces stationed in Laos, but also, if necessary, of the newly created Lao National Guard. He was also in charge of all federal services, and appointed all French officials working in Laos. While officially the King's chief advisor, he could demand an audience at any time and could veto any Lao legislation. Likewise at all levels of the administration, in provinces and ministries, Lao officials were required to seek the advice of their French 'counsellors' before making any expenditure or taking any decision.

As for the division of services, only 'Lao justice', prisons and police, primary education, health, small-scale public works, agriculture, sport and the arts were placed under Lao authority (in consultation with French advisors). Finance, customs and immigration, defence and foreign relations, higher education, postal services and communications, and large-scale public works all remained federal matters, and so under French control. No wonder the agreement was denounced by the Lao Issara government-in-exile in Bangkok.

VI. THE PROVISIONAL GOVERNMENT AND CONSTITUENT ASSEMBLY

The next step towards unification and a degree of independence came with the appointment of a Provisional government, whose primary task was to decide on procedures for the election of a Constituent Assembly to draw up a Constitution for the kingdom. To head the provisional government, the King turned to Prince Souvannarath, a younger half-brother of Prince Phetsarath. Souvannarath had been a minister in the former Royal government of Luang Prabang, as had several other members named. Two new portfolios were created, covering national economy and national education, both of which also went to members of aristocratic families from Luang Prabang. Not one appointment went to a southerner.

So as Nhouy Abhay, scion of a prominent aristocratic southern family pointedly asked: 'What therefore of the promises of equality [between regions] and the [principle of] appointment of ministers and high officials on the sole basis of merit, to the exclusion of all considerations of origin or birth?'[14] The real

[13] Commissioner de Raymond was responsible in turn to the French High Commissioner for Indochina in Saigon, which had replaced Hanoi as the capital of the Indochinese Federation.

[14] Quoted in Duparc, 546.

surprise, however, was not that the King had appointed only northerners, but that the French had allowed this imbalance in the first government purporting to represent the whole of Laos.

On 15 December 1946 elections were held for a 44-member Constituent Assembly on the basis of male suffrage (excluding Buddhist monks, members of the royal family, and the military). The level of education required to stand for election ensured that successful candidates were for the most part members of leading families or senior civil servants. Candidates from the south were required to declare their support for the unification of Laos under the auspices of the Luang Prabang monarchy, on the assurance that this was what Prince Boun Oum (then overseas) and their French masters had agreed upon.

The purpose of the Constituent Assembly was first to ratify the unification of Laos, and then to draft a Constitution. Its inaugural session was held in Vientiane on 15 March 1947, and was addressed by members of the government, most of them royal princes. The outcome was never in doubt. The Assembly unanimously agreed that King Sisavangvong should become King of Laos, and appointed a Commission of its members to draw up a Constitution for the new kingdom.

The members of the Commission were guided at all times by French advisors.[15] In fact the text was first written in French, and then translated into Lao. Unsurprisingly, the outcome of its deliberations was a Constitution embodying similar democratic values and institutions to those enshrined in the Constitution establishing the French Fourth Republic the previous year. The text was accepted by the King, and promulgated by royal decree on 11 May 1947.[16]

This was not, however, the end of the process. While it was quite acceptable for a Lao Buddhist King to bestow a form of governance on his subjects, for the French, constituent power derived not from a monarch, but from the people. So as per the terms of the Constitution, elections on the basis of universal suffrage were held on 24 August for 35 deputies to a new National Assembly. All candidates ran as independents, not under the banner of any political group. In its inaugural session, the Assembly's first task was to ratify the King's nomination of Prince Souvannarath as Prime Minister along with his cabinet, which thereupon took office as the first Royal Lao government.[17]

[15] The senior French adviser to the Constituent Assembly who guided the drafting of the Constitution between 15 March and 10 May 1947 was Pierre Marie Louis Lebel de Girard de Chateauvieux. Philippe Preschez, 'Le Laos depuis 1941: État des travaux' (1966) 16 *Revue française de science politique* 588. See also http://anom.archivesnationales.culture.gouv.fr/ark:/61561/hj998wrx-wre.num=20.geogname=Ban+Na+Phao+%28Laos%29.geogname=Cammon+%28Laos%29.geogname=Thakhek+%28Laos%29.geogname=Laos.form=complexe.

[16] An English translation of the text is provided in Amos J Peaslee, *Constitutions of Nations*, 2 ed, vol II (The Hague: Martinus Nijhoff, 1956) 564–569. Not all English translations in this article are taken from Peaslee: some are by the author from the original French (see n 18).

[17] In his speech, the king committed Laos to membership of the French Union, implicitly conceding continued French control over the country's external affairs and defence. Geoffrey C Gunn, *Political Struggles in Laos (1930–1954)* (Bangkok: Editions Duang Kamol, 1988) 177–178.

The second task of the National Assembly was to nominate three members of the nine-member King's Council, to join the six appointed by the King. The task of the King's Council, as set out in the 1947 Constitution, was to act as a house of review to examine laws passed by the National Assembly, and to advise the King on their purpose and implications. The first task of the appointed Council, however, was to combine with the elected National Assembly to form a Constitutional Congress, which met intermittently between 16 August 1948 and 30 April 1949 to deliberate upon and very slightly modify the 1947 text.[18] Formal adoption of the new text by the Constitutional Congress at its final sitting certified the Constitution as the expression of the will of the Lao people, and it was as such that it was definitively promulgated by the King on 14 September 1949.[19]

VII. THE 1947–1949 CONSTITUTION

Because promulgation of the Constitution in 1949 marked the completion of the process of drafting and popularly ratifying the Constitution, and because the two texts are all but identical, the first Lao Constitution is best referred to not as the 1947 Constitution, but as the 1947–1949 Constitution. The text consists of a preamble and 44 articles divided into seven sections dealing with general principles, the role of the King, the Council of Ministers (government), the National Assembly, the King's Council, the administrative and financial organisation of the kingdom, and final matters (on constitutional amendment and interpretation).

Even a cursory reading of the text reveals that its guiding principles and values were those of French democracy: it contains little that derived from traditional Lao forms of governance and legitimation.[20] The debt to France is particularly evident in the preamble and the general principles enshrined in the opening section. Though the powers of the King were considerable, he was a constitutional monarch, for national sovereignty resided in 'the Lao people' (Article 3): the King exercised sovereignty only in accordance with the provisions of the Constitution. Admittedly the King did have the power to dissolve the National Assembly, but new elections had to be held within 90 days (Article 33). And while the King's Council acted as a house of review, its objections could be overridden by a vote of two thirds of the popularly elected National Assembly (Article 30).

[18] The only differences occur in Arts 25 and 31. Art 25 changed the starting date for the annual three-month session of the National Assembly from February to October; while in Art 31 on the powers assigned to the Secretariat of the National Assembly to act on its behalf when the Assembly was not in session, an unnecessary reference to Art 13 was omitted.

[19] The French text is available online at http://mjp.univ-perp.fr/constit/la1949.htm.

[20] See Martin Stuart-Fox, 'Marxism and Theravada Buddhism: The Legitimation of Political Authority in Laos' (1983) 56 *Pacific Affairs* 428–454.

French influence is evident too in the balance achieved between democratic principles and royal prerogatives. In framing the Constitution French advisors were well aware of the need to counter the continuing nationalist appeal of the Lao Issara government-in-exile in Bangkok, whose members included some of the most respected names in Laos. Because of his previous position as Inspector of Political and Administrative Affairs, the most senior Lao civil servant, Prince Phetsarath, de facto leader of the Lao Issara, was better known through most of the country than was King Sisavangvong. Indeed, Phetsarath was widely believed among the peasantry to possess semi-divine powers.

The Constitution had thus to go some way towards meeting moderate nationalist demands, but in a way that transferred only limited powers to the hands of a Francophile political elite educated to believe that Laos was too weak to ward off powerful neighbours without continuing French protection. Other considerations were the debt the French owed the King, and Crown Prince Savangvatthana, for their loyalty during the difficult years of 1945 and 1946; and the need for a respected head of state. Both could be covered by reinforcing the status of the Luang Prabang monarchy and making it the focus of national unity – thereby also ensuring a conduit for continuing French influence.

Constitutional unification not only resolved the legal anomaly of the dual protectorate, it also met one of the two key demands of the Lao Issara, so opening the way for moderate members in exile in Thailand to begin indirect communication with French authorities to sound out possibilities for amnesty in order to return to take part in the political process. In the meantime, a trickle of Lao Issara supporters who had fled the French invasion began returning to Laos.

Such political considerations gained importance after 19 December 1946 when war broke out in Vietnam between the communist Vietminh led by Ho Chi Minh and French forces of occupation. The Vietminh served as a magnet for extreme nationalists and the French were desperate to prevent fighting spilling over into Laos and Cambodia. In both countries, therefore, they set out to reinforce traditional monarchical institutions, while at the same time instituting democratic frameworks which would both allow moderate nationalists to pursue their ultimate goal of independence through political means, and permit them at the same time to manage some of their country's internal affairs.[21]

For France, full independence for Laos was out of the question since this would undermine the Indochinese Federation Paris was intent on creating. So even though the preamble of the constitution declared that Laos was 'an independent state', it also confirmed that it was a member of the French Union.

[21] Though as the French High Commissioner reminded Lao deputies in his address at the end of the first session of the National Assembly on 25 March 1948, legislative and executive powers should not be conflated. Arthur Dommen, *Conflict in Laos: The Politics of Neutralization* (New York: Praeger, 1964) 34.

There was no reference in the Constitution to the Indochinese Federation, but as everyone was aware who had read the terms of the Franco-Lao modus vivendi, inclusion within the Federation constituted a continuing restriction on Lao independence.

Unification, by contrast, could be delivered immediately and in full. It was proclaimed in both the first paragraph of the preamble, and in Article 1 of the Constitution itself, which declared Laos to be a 'unitary, indivisible and democratic Kingdom'. The preamble went on to affirm the loyalty of the Lao people both to the monarchy in the person of King Sisavangvong, and to democratic principles of government. An oblique reference to Lao history made no mention of the Kingdom of Lan Xang or its previous extent. The Constitution established Laos as a nation-state, but within boundaries established by French conquest and diplomacy.

VIII. KEY PROVISIONS OF THE 1947–1949 CONSTITUTION

The core of the Preamble to the Constitution consisted of a set of fundamental rights and duties to be enjoyed and accepted by all Lao citizens. Rights included equality before the law, individual liberty, and the freedoms of conscience, communication, assembly and association – none of which reflected traditional Lao Buddhist concepts. Duties included service to the country, respect for conscience, social solidarity, fulfilment of family obligations, application to work and education, personal probity, and observance of the law. None of these individual rights and duties was further mentioned in specific articles of the Constitution.

The proclamation of Lao unification is enshrined in Article 1 of the Constitution proper, which declares that Laos is 'a unitary, indivisible and democratic Kingdom', in which sovereignty, 'emanates from the Lao people', and is exercised on their behalf by the King in accordance with the constitution (Article 3)

The remainder of the first title (section) sets out 'general principles' pertaining to citizenship, suffrage, religion, language, and the flag as a national emblem. Even though not more than 60 per cent of the Lao population at the time were Buddhist (most minorities being animists of one kind or another), Buddhism was designated 'the state religion' (Article 7), with the King, who was required to be a 'fervent Buddhist' (Article 8), as its 'high protector', both of which conform to Lao tradition. Lao was named the official language, but French was also given official status (Article 6).

Vientiane was designated the national capital. This was the obvious choice, as the city had been the administrative capital of French Laos. The problem was that the King, who had such a central constitutional role to play in the Lao political process, refused to leave Luang Prabang. The consequent separation between Vientiane as the political and administrative capital and Luang Prabang as the royal capital not only complicated Lao politics, but even significantly altered their course at crucial times.[22]

The second title spelled out the role of the King as supreme head of state. Article 8 declared the King's person to be 'sacred and inviolable', a provision reflecting the Lao Buddhist conception of kingship. The succession was a matter for the King and the royal family to decide (Article 9), not involving either the King's Council or the National Assembly. The King's Council was, however, responsible for the appointment of a Regent in the event of royal incapacity, physical or mental (Article 10).

The King was commander-on-chief of the army, conferred all promotions, civil and military, and could commute sentences. He nominated the Prime Minister (referred to in the Constitution as the president of the Council of Ministers), who in turn nominated members of his government and presented them to the National Assembly. Once they had obtained the confidence of the Assembly, ministers were appointed by the King, who was empowered to preside over their deliberations.

The selection of ministers followed the French model, rather than the American (where secretaries [ministers] of government departments cannot at the same time be members of Congress) or the British system (where they must be elected members of Parliament). In Laos, ministers could be deputies elected to the National Assembly, or drawn from outside of it (Article 20). Either way, ministers were responsible to the Assembly, which could force the resignation of the entire government by carrying a vote of no confidence by a two-thirds majority (Article 22).

The popularly-elected National Assembly acted as the constitutional restraint on monarchical power. Deputies were elected by universal suffrage and served four-year terms. During their time in office they were immune to arrest and prosecution, unless indicted by two-thirds of members, or in the case of *flagrante delicto*. All were immune to prosecution or investigation for any opinion expressed or vote cast in the Assembly, an immunity also extended to printing and disseminating whatever was said (Article 35).

The Assembly was normally to meet for three months a year, each session being convoked, opened and closed by the King. At other times its affairs were handled by a 'permanent secretariat' (Article 31) elected at the beginning of each annual session. The Assembly was responsible for legislating the 'organic laws' of the Kingdom, passing the budget, granting amnesty and agreeing to the ratification of treaties (Article 28).

Under the terms of the 1947–1949 Constitution, the National Assembly functioned as a unicameral legislature: there was no provision for an elected upper house or senate. Instead legislation was reviewed by the King's Council, the one institution of government demonstrating continuity with traditional

[22] Eg, in 1960 Captain Kong Le was able to carry out a successful coup d'état in Vientiane largely because almost the entire government was in Luang Prabang consulting with the King.

royal advisory bodies, from the Royal Council (*Senam Luang*) comprising the King's closest counsellors (ministers, generals, and on occasions, senior abbots) going back at least to the early sixteenth century,[23] to the Supreme Administrative Council (*Hosanam Luang*) of the Kingdom of Luang Prabang, consisting of three senior princes and three members of the nobility, each with specific administrative responsibilities.[24]

Under the 1947–1949 Constitution, the Council acted as an upper house of review, tasked with examining all bills and proposals submitted and advising the King on whether they should be passed into law. Proposals for new legislations could originate from the King, or from the Council itself, but had to be referred to the National Assembly to become law. Members of the King's Council enjoyed the same rights, prerogatives and remuneration as deputies to the National Assembly (Article 37).

In exceptional circumstance not further defined in the Constitution, the King's Council could sit as a High Court (Article 38). The judicial system is not detailed in the Constitution. There is no mention in the Constitution of a High or Constitutional Court to which questionable legislation might be submitted for a ruling on its validity.[25] Instead establishing the judicial system was left to the National Assembly, which was also responsible for interpreting the Constitution itself. All that the Constitution required regarding the legal system was that the establishing legislation should 'guarantee the independence of the judicial power in relation to the legislative and executive powers' (Article 42), which provided only relatively weak constitutional support for the separation of powers.

The Constitution enshrined the administrative division of the Kingdom into an unspecified number of provinces,[26] each administered by a *chao khoueng* or governor 'assisted by a provincial council elected on a territorial basis' (Article 40). Each province was responsible for its own 'autonomous' budget covering revenue and expenditure, the operation of which would be fixed by law [enacted by the National Assembly] (Article 41).

The inclusion in the Constitution of provisions for local government exercising a degree of autonomy is significant, especially in comparison to the almost cursory treatment of the judiciary. Clearly this was an attempt to address the concerns of southern provinces that unification of the country could serve as a cover for domination of the south by the north. Two centuries of regional separatism still cast a long shadow.

[23] Stuart-Fox, *The Lao Kingdom of Lan Xang* (n 1), at 64 & 73. On occasions the *Senam Luang* administered the kingdom during an interregnum, while deciding to whom to offer the throne.

[24] Stuart-Fox, *A History of Laos* (n 3), at 30–31.

[25] The final say over interpretation of the Constitution was left to the National Assembly (Art 44). No required majority was specified, which left the Assembly, or a subsequent one, to pronounce on the implications of its own, or previous, legislation.

[26] There were in fact 12 provinces, later increased to 16 through dividing four of them.

The final title of the Constitution set out the procedure for revision, a request for which could come from the King, the King's Council, or an absolute majority of deputies. The Council and the Assembly then combined to form a Congress, which required a two-thirds majority to carry an amendment. No amendment would be permitted, however, that challenged the nature of the state as a unitary kingdom, the 'representative character of the regime', or the principle of the liberty and equality of all citizens (Article 43).

In summary, from the viewpoint of constitutional law, the 1947 Lao Constitution was a minimalist document, drafted in some haste with the political goal of unifying the separate indirectly administered territories of Luang Prabang and the directly administered central and southern provinces to form a single kingdom. At the same time it was designed to reward those Lao who had remained loyal to France, particularly the royal family of Luang Prabang, while neutralising regionalist sentiment in the south (through the secret protocol agreed to by Prince Boun Oum). A second goal was to undercut the nationalist appeal of the Lao Issara government-in-exile in Bangkok.

National unity was achieved through the institutions specified in the Constitution – a monarchy with nationwide jurisdiction, a national legislature, and uniform local government. The political process of popular endorsement that followed royal promulgation of the 1947 text transformed the Constitution into a document whose constituent power derived not from the Luang Prabang monarchy but from the Lao people as a whole, north and south.

The Constitution achieved what it set out to do. By the time the amended version was promulgated in 1949 the widening war in Indochina was driving increasing ideological polarisation. The Lao Issara government-in-exile in Bangkok split between moderate and extremist factions. Most moderates recognised that the Constitution provided a framework within which to work towards independence by political means, and so were prepared to return to Laos.[27] By doing so, they accepted the Constitution as the legal foundation for the Kingdom of Laos as a modern, democratic nation-state.

IX. FROM THE 1947 TO THE 1949 CONSTITUTION

What intervened, between the drafting of the 1947 Constitution and promulgation of the 1949 Constitution on 14 September of that year, was the signing on 19 July 1949 of a General Convention between France and Laos regarding the independence of Laos.[28] It was actually the greater independence promised

[27] The notable exception was Prince Phetsarath, who refused to return until all his privileges and titles (including that of *uparat*) were restored by the King, which he was not prepared to do until 1957.

[28] This was based on an exchange of letters between King Sisavangvong and French president Vincent Auriol pursuant upon the promulgation of the 1947 Constitution. The French text is included in (1949) *155 British and Foreign State Papers* 405–411.

by this document, rather than the Constitution per se, that convinced wavering moderate nationalists that further progress was possible through political means.

Under the terms of this Convention, France recognised the independence of Laos, while Laos re-affirmed its membership of the French Union and committed itself to its defence. Two circumstances were significant in the lead-up to this Convention. The first was the unification in May 1949 of Cochinchina, Annam and Tonkin to create the unified state of Vietnam within the French Union, along with the replacement of the Indochinese Federation by the much looser Associated States of Indochina (associated only through common membership of the French Union); the second was the military success of communist forces in China, their impending arrival on the northern borders of Vietnam and Laos, and the consequences this was likely to have for the war in Indochina.

The Convention set out the commitments entered into by both parties. France would defend the frontiers of the kingdom from invasion, assist Laos in establishing diplomatic relations with other states, support any Lao application for membership of the United Nations, and provide financial and technical aid. In return, as an Associated State, Laos agreed to permit French Union troops to be stationed on Lao territory, step up military recruitment, and allow French nationals and nationals of neighbouring Member States of the French Union (that is, Vietnam and Cambodia) the same rights as Lao citizens with respect to the administration of justice, freedom of movement, and commercial activity – a benefit to be enjoyed reciprocally by Lao nationals in those countries.

At the same time Laos agreed to be part of an internal monetary and customs union with Vietnam and Cambodia, and to join them in further negotiations with France over such matters as communications, immigration and trade.[29] But while these commitments limited Lao freedom of action, they did not detract from the fact that the Convention marked a clear step forward towards the goal of independence.

Or at least so concluded the moderate members of the Lao Issara in Bangkok. Since the November 1947 coup that returned the military to power in Thailand, Thai support for Lao nationalism had waned. Forays into Laos by Issara insurgents were discouraged. In March 1949 division within the Lao Issara came to a head over Prince Souphanouvong's refusal to curtail military activity and unauthorised financial expenditure. As a result. the moderate faction expelled Souphanouvong, so precipitating the revolutionary wing of the organisation into the arms of the Vietminh.

The 1947 Constitution needed no amendments to take account of the General Convention, for the preamble already declared Laos to be an independent state and member of the French Union. Changes in relationships between

[29] Concluded with the signature of the Pau Convention between France, Vietnam Laos and Cambodia in December 1950.

the states of Indochina had no place in an amended Lao Constitution. What the Franco-Lao General Convention signalled was the willingness of France to grant Laos an additional degree of independence. In October the moderates, led by Khammao, Katay Don Sasorith and Souvanna Phouma, accepted a negotiated amnesty and returned to Laos.[30] Their goal of full independence through political means was achieved four years later on 22 October 1953 with the signing in Paris of a 'Treaty of Friendship and Association between France and Laos'.[31]

The 1947–1949 Constitution continued to provide the constitutional and legal basis of the Kingdom of Laos over the following years. It was amended to take account of political agreements to establish the First and Second Coalition governments and promulgated afresh on 11 May 1957 and 30 July 1961. Discussion of provisions required to accommodate the formation of the Third Coalition were cut short by the communist Pathet Lao seizure of power in 1975. The Constitution was finally abrogated on 3 December 1975 by a vote of the National Congress of People's Representatives convened to inaugurate the Lao People's Democratic Republic.[32]

X. CONCLUSION: THE SIGNIFICANCE OF THE 1947–1949 CONSTITUTION

Constitutions are drafted and promulgated within the context of historical and political circumstances, and none were more pressing than those surrounding the drafting and promulgation of the 1947–1949 Lao Constitution. Those circumstances included the defeat of France in the Second World War, the outbreak of the First Indochina War between French forces and the Vietminh, which threatened to spill over into Laos, victories of communist forces in China, and the beginning of the Cold War.

Political circumstances included Lao nationalist demands to unify the Kingdom of Luang Prabang and the directly administered provinces to form a single entity, as first proclaimed by the Lao Issara; the need to counter the nationalist appeal of the Lao Issara government-in-exile in Bangkok; and French determination both to limit real transfer of power, and to make sure that any powers that were transferred would be exercised by the loyal Francophile elite.

Unification was complicated by two things: lack of widespread support elsewhere in the country for the Luang Prabang monarchy; and the equal hereditary claim of Prince Boun Oum na Champasak's to become King of Laos. The former was managed by sending King Sisavangvong on a tour of the south; the latter through a secret protocol.

[30] These events are covered in some detail in Stuart-Fox, *A History of Laos* (n 3), at 70–74.

[31] A 'Military Convention' signed at the same time committed France to the continued defence of Laos. Both texts were published in (1953) *160 British and Foreign State Papers* 658–666.

[32] Stuart-Fox, *A History of Laos* (n 3), at 168–172.

The Constitution was drafted in order to establish Laos as a constitutional monarchy, whose independence was circumscribed through membership, along with Cambodia and a unified Vietnam, of France's Indochinese Federation (and later as an Associated State of the French Union). Equal emphasis was placed therefore on the King and the National Assembly as the two key institutions. Both symbolised the unity of the new state: the King as constitutional head of state of a unified country; the National Assembly as representing all Lao citizens. Both were reinforced through the process of popular endorsement that took place between when the Constitution was promulgated by royal decree in 1947 and when it was legislated by the popularly elected National Assembly in 1949.

The 1947–1949 Constitution was remarkably successful in achieving what it set out to do, which was to create a unified constitutional monarchy. It was a minimalist document in that it did not detail individual rights and freedoms, or institute an independent judiciary, or define legal guarantees for a free-market economy. Yet the values it enshrined informed the institutions it created, including the legal basis for rule of law, the exercise of individual rights and freedoms, and the functioning of an open economy. The 1947–1949 Constitution endured until the Kingdom of Laos was replaced by the Lao People's Democratic Republic, during which time it was amended, but never revoked. Not until the change of regime in 1975 was the 1947–1949 Constitution finally abrogated: and not until 1991 did a new one take its place.[33]

A radical disjuncture occurred in 1975 between the Kingdom of Laos and the Marxist Lao People's Democratic Republic. When after 16 years a new Constitution was eventually promulgated, the regime had already embarked on free-market reform (under the slogan *chintanakan mai* or 'new thinking')[34] and the Soviet Union was on the point of dissolution. It was not surprising, therefore, that the 1991 Lao Constitution differed from the earlier Constitutions of the Socialist Republic of Vietnam and the People's Republic of Kampuchea (Cambodia), which were both modelled on the Soviet Constitution.[35]

Though the 1991 Lao Constitution owed very little to its predecessor – and any influence would certainly have been denied by its authors – there do exist a couple of intriguing similarities. One is the name 'National Assembly', which was only adopted in the third draft of the 1991 Constitution: in drafts one and two it had still been called the Supreme People's Assembly.[36]

[33] The text of the 1991 Constitution of the LPDR is available at http://confinder.richmond.edu/admin/docs/laos.pdf.

[34] Norihiko Yamada, 'Legitimation of the Lao People's Revolutionary Party: Socialism, *Chintanakan Mai* (New Thinking) and Reform' (2018) *Journal of Contemporary Asia*, published online: DOI: 10.1080/00472336.2018.1439081.

[35] See Martin Stuart-Fox, 'The Constitution of the Lao People's Democratic Republic' 1991) 17(1) *Review of Socialist Law* 299–317.

[36] Ibid, at 311.

A second possible influence is that in both Constitutions the National Assembly can determine the fate of a government through a vote of no confidence, an unusual provision for a Marxist State that was retained in both the 2003 and the 2015 amended Constitutions.[37] In the 1947–1948 Constitution such a vote could only be taken when the Prime Minister first presented his cabinet to the Assembly, and required a two-thirds majority to be carried (Article 22). In the current Constitution of the LPDR, the Assembly has the right to pass a vote of no confidence in the Government, or a member of it, if a quarter of its members call for such a vote to be brought on. The President may then request the National Assembly to reconsider, but if an absolute majority supports a second no confidence vote, then the government or member of it must resign (Article 75). Thus in fact the circumstances, timing and majorities required for a no confidence vote all differ between the 1947–1948 Constitution and subsequent LPDR Constitutions, which undermines any likelihood of direct influence.[38]

The provisions of the 1947–1949 Constitution no longer reverberate in modern Laos, though they still do among the Lao diaspora. During its existence from 1949 to 1975, the 1947–1949 Constitution demonstrated its resilience through incorporating the changes necessary to accommodate the first two coalition governments formed as a result of international negotiations and internal agreement between opposing political forces. It created a democratic system of government in the face of the challenging circumstances of war and revolution. The liberal democratic principles at its core have not survived in the single-party state that Laos has become; but as the founding document of the Kingdom of Laos, and thus of the Lao nation-state, it served the country well.

[37] The 1991 Constitution of the LPDR was amended in 2003, and again in 2015. The 2003 Constitution added a new chapter dealing with National Defence and Security, strengthened commitment to a market economy by promoting foreign investment in the economy, education, health and tourism, and protecting foreign capital, assets and intellectual property. The 2015 Constitution added new chapters covering the State Audit Authority and the Electoral Commission, strengthened the powers of the President and made provision for representative administrative assemblies at the province, city and village levels.

[38] The difference between the majorities required is less significant than might appear, since the LPDR always was, and remains, a single-party state, a fact that makes Art 75 of the current Constitution of little more than academic interest, since it is hardly likely to be acted upon by elected representatives of the ruling Lao People's Revolutionary Party to remove a government endorsed by their own Party.

11

The First Constitution-Making in Cambodia: Colonialism, Modernism, Nationalism and the Implications

TEILEE KUONG

INTRODUCTION: THE THREE '-ISMS' IN CONTEXT

CAMBODIA'S 1947 CONSTITUTION was the first Constitution that bore the feature of a Western-style form of government, allegedly modelled after that of the French Fourth Republic.[1] It was a product of many different interacting factors. Nationally, it was a time when colonial rule was on the decline, especially with the impending collapse of the various European colonial powers. At the same time, many Cambodian elites, well exposed to Western philosophy and thought, sense of justice and ideologies, had returned to challenge Cambodia's prevailing values and way of life. Most of these elites were nationalists, advocating revolutionary change, rather than the restoration of the past advocated by the traditional knights. Nationalism was also on the rise throughout Asia and Southeast Asia and some of these nationalist movements had very deep and direct influences upon them. Indeed, many of them fell under the ideological influences of the communist and anti-French movements. Globally, colonialism was also being vilified and with the US leading the charge, efforts were made within the United Nations system to put an end to colonialism.[2]

Cambodia's promulgation of the first western-style Constitution in 1947 can be legally and politically viewed from these perspectives. At the national

[1] Claude-Gilles Gour, *Institutions Constitutionnelles et Politiques du Cambodge* (Paris, Librairie Dalloz, 1965) at 51–53. The observations were, however, superficial and brief. It may be more accurate to refer to the similarity in some institutional designs and nominations.

[2] United Nations Charter 1945, Arts 73–74.

level, the anti-colonial sentiment – home-grown and externally-inspired – formed the backbone of the rising nationalism, while regionalist and internationalist trends were not so much about relinquishing national sovereignty but rather about modernisation and a return to local thoughts and values. In this context, Cambodia differed from its other Southeast Asian neighbours in terms of its relationship with the former colonial suzerain. For reasons discussed below, colonialisation in Cambodia was sometimes considered, perhaps falsely, as a genuine mission of civilisation and of the provision of security and protection against its immediate neighbours who had a long history of interfering in Cambodia's domestic politics and territory. Some conservative interests, particularly those who were proud of their close connection with the French, felt that their connections could help protect and modernise the fading Khmer Empire of the past. I consider this group of individuals as I do the colonialist.

This chapter looks at the making of Cambodia's first Constitution by focusing on the interactions among three streams of political thought and interests. It includes a brief review of the political and legal background leading up to the making of the 1947 Constitution including efforts to bring about constitutional changes to fend off the post-War project to restore some pre-colonial governmental features and values. We will also consider how some constitutional provisions reflect the different streams of thought embodied by three '-isms': Colonialism, Modernism, and Nationalism. In doing so, we examine the changing concept of sovereignty and evaluate the Constitution's continuing legacy in the nation-building and constitution-making.

I. POLITICAL AND LEGAL BACKGROUNDS

There is a serious lack of writing about the 1947 Constitution and about Cambodia's legal system between 1940 and 1970. Information on the political situation of this period is found mainly in historical accounts but none of these works consider the context of constitution-making seriously enough. Instead, it was treated in passing as one of many occurrences in the process of the State's historical and political development.

One exception is Claude-Gilles Gour's *Constitutional and Political Institutions of Cambodia*, which was published in French. Gour, who was Professor of Law at the Faculty of Law and Economical Science of the University of Aix-Marseille had, for a time, taught at the Faculty of Law and Economics in Phnom Penh. The book, entitled *Institutions Constitutionnelles et Politiques du Cambodge*[3] was published in Paris in 1965. Gour's book introduces us to some essential features of constitution-making during this period and highlights

[3] Claude-Gilles Gour, *Institutions Constitutionnelles et Politiques du Cambodge* (Paris, Librairie Dalloz, 1965 [hereinafter 'Gour'].

some controversies arising from that process and offers us a relatively detailed description of the Constitution's main provisions. I will critically examine some of the issues raised in Gour's book in three parts. The first considers the political and legal backgrounds at the time of constitution-drafting; the second briefly introduces Cambodia's pre-1947 constitutional structure; and the third examines some controversies and tensions that arose during the constitution-making process.

A. Political and Legal Backgrounds

The 1947 Constitution was preceded by the formation of a government under the colonial rule. Gour divides the colonial era into two different periods: the pre-1884 and the post-1884 periods. The pre-1884 period was defined by the Cambodian-French treaty of 11 August 1863,[4] which created a typical protectorate relationship between Cambodia and France. The first Article provides that 'His Majesty the French Emperor accords his protection to His Majesty the King of Cambodia.'[5] The Treaty did not allow France to intervene in the internal autonomy of Cambodia, as Article 16 states:

> His Majesty, the Emperor of France, recognizing the sovereignty of the King of Cambodia … is committed to maintaining the order and peace inside the States and guarding against all outside attacks, helping him perceive the rules of commerce, and giving him all facilitation for establishment of a communication between Cambodia and the overseas.[6]

Gour stated that institutionalisation of the protectorate at that time was not aimed at changing, in fact or in law, the internal constitutional equilibrium of the kingdom. But it was the need to modernise the governmental system that led the King to promulgate a number of reforms using his own legislative power.[7]

[4] Concluded as a friendship and commercial treaty signed at the Royal Palace in Udong, then the capital city of Cambodia, by the Cambodian King Norodom and a French rear admiral posted as the Governor and Commander-in-Chief for Indochina, representing the French government, on 11 August 1863.

[5] It is important to note here that the protection was conferred to the King, as the traditional thought had it that the King was the King of the earth, who ruled over all living thereupon. For some introduction to this concept, see Jean-Marie Crouzatier, *Les Institutions Politiques and Institutionelles du Cambodge* (Institut Maurice Haurio, Universite Toulouse 1 Capitole, 2014) 19–24.

[6] This might have been the provision that made Gour argue that the Treaty gave France the right to exercise Cambodia's international competence but the kingdom's internal autonomy was fully preserved. The French senior Resident Representative in Cambodia had no power to intervene directly in the internal affairs of Cambodia. He could only ask for consultation or ask questions. The decision-making power belonged exclusively to the Cambodian King, who alone would have the power to execute the laws of the country without having to follow instructions from the French authority. See Gour (n 3) at 28.

[7] Ibid, at 28–29.

These reforms resulted in a series of Royal Ordinances dated 15 January 1877. It put into operation several important changes in the judicial, administrative, fiscal and constitutional law areas. With regard to constitutional matters, the Ordinances introduced an important reform. It enabled the Council of Ministers – then comprising five of the most senior officials overseeing the implementation of laws – to deliberate in council without the King's presence.[8] Gour saw this as an attempt not only to compromise the absolute power of the King but a means of strengthening the freedom of action by the protecting authority.[9] This actually paved the ground for the later transfer of the presidency of the Council of Ministers meeting to the French senior Resident Representative (*Resident supérieur*) by order of the Governor General for Indochina on 3 October 1889.[10]

This marked a critical departure from the earlier competence of the Governor-General vis-à-vis Cambodia. The open intervention had been encouraged by a France-Cambodia Treaty of 17 June 1884 between King Norodom and the then Governor-General Charles Thomson.[11] The first Article of this 1884 Treaty states:

> His Majesty the King of Cambodia accepts all administrative, judicial, financial and commercial reforms which the Government of the French Republic considers in the future to be useful to proceed for the accomplishment of its protectorate.

This Treaty also made special budgetary arrangement for the King, the princes and the royal family. The civil list for the King and the financial allowances for the princes and the royal family was to be fixed and charged to the national budget of the kingdom.[12] This was obviously an attempt to de-personalise the monarch as an institution and to introduce the western concept of state and government to replace the traditional system of government by the absolute power of the King. Here, it is important to recall the provisions of the 1863 Treaty which started with the statement that 'His Majesty the French Emperor accords his protection to His Majesty the King of Cambodia.' The target of the protection was not Cambodia as a state or nation, but the King of Cambodia.

[8] Ibid, at 29.

[9] Ibid. It seems Gour took a very formalist view on the issue of interventionism. He seemed to argue that, until 1884, all reforms were made by the Cambodian King, and the politics of pressuring for multiple times (as Gour himself stated) Cambodian King to promulgate ordinances for reforms had not changed the juridical structure of the protectorate and the relationship between Cambodia and the protecting power. He wrote that 'France did not always have the permanent legal instrument which allowed it to intervene directly into the administration and the government of the Kingdom'. See Gour, p.30. It is however unclear as to what extent the 1863 Treaty was used to justify the French exercise of political pressure on Cambodian King to act in a way acceptable to the protecting power.

[10] For more details, see Gour (n 3) at 31.

[11] Convention entre la France et le Cambodge, le 17 juin 1884, pour régler les rapports respectifs des deux pays.

[12] Art 7 of the 1884 Treaty.

To secure some level of coherence with the 1863 Treaty, the 1884 Treaty provided in its Article 2 that:

> His Majesty the King of Cambodia will continue, like in the past, to govern His states and to direct their administration, except for those restrictions which result from this Convention.[13]

Those treaty restrictions formed the bases for subsequent reforms and restructuring of the Cambodian government and administration under the French colonial supervision. By October 1889, the transition towards a government supervised by the protecting authority culminated in the successful nomination of the French senior Resident Representative as President of the Council of Ministers. Meetings of the Council started to take two different forms: those presided by the Prime Minister to conduct different studies known as 'permanent commissions'; and those presided by the Senior Resident Representative to issue decisions, known as 'plenary commissions'.[14] This paved the way to establish a government that was technically separate from the royal palace and manned by technocratic elites instead of members of the royal family or their clients. The King remained the supreme leader but exercise of the day-to-day administrative power was now under the direct control of the French Governor-General in Indochina through the office of the Senior Resident Representative.

The resulting ruling mechanism could therefore be considered the foundation of the governmental system stipulated by the 1947 Constitution. In the following section I will examine some basic features of this pre-1947 ruling structure based on Gour's accounts before looking into the detailed provisions of the 1947 Constitution and the extent to which these pre-1947 norms and practices found or failed to find their way into the first Constitution.

B. Some Features of the Pre-1947 Constitutional Arrangements

i. The Executive and the Administration

Soon after the war in Europe erupted, Cambodia was allowed to regain some level of internal legal autonomy. Kram No 1 of 1 June 1940, redefined the roles of the cabinet and sought to 'free the sovereign from regulating administrative issues of little importance and to define more accurately the rights and prerogatives of the ministers'.[15] Governmental work was classified into different subject matters and levels of importance. They were submitted to different procedures

[13] Art 2 of the 1884 Treaty.

[14] Gour (n 3) at 34. Gour considered a Royal Ordinance of 11 Jul 1897, regarding the reorganisation of the governments as the real constitutional charter of Cambodia under the French protectorate. See Gour, at 31.

[15] Cited in French by Gour, ibid, at 36.

for solution. Some could be decided by the King alone (with the consent by the French Senior Resident Representative) while others had to be decided after consultations with the Council of Ministers (also with the consent by the Senior Resident Representative).[16] For less important issues, the Council of Ministers or the ministers concerned had power to decide.[17]

ii. The Legislature

A Royal Ordinance of 18 March 1913 established a consultative assembly which was later changed into the House of People's Representatives in April 1940 but suspended by the Vichy government in June that year.[18] At the local level, attempts to introduce commune level elections started in the early 1900s, partly for the purpose of rationalising revenue generation and French controls at the local level.[19] The councils did not have any legislative mandate. The only legislative power remained with the King who continued to govern through royal ordinances and by delegating some regulatory powers to the Council of Ministers and subordinate governmental institutions. The normative hierarchy of legal instruments was reorganised by Kram No 1 mentioned above.[20]

C. The Political Tensions and New Realities

The Darlan-Kato Agreement signed by the Japanese and the Vichy French government on 29 July 1941 allowed for the setting up of a Japanese military presence in Cambodia. This new change in the colonial reality in Cambodia caught the attention of some leading nationalist figures in Phnom Penh. They called for an anti-French demonstration which then took place on 20 July 1942 and was joined by about 2,000 ordinary Cambodians and around 500 monks.[21] When the Japanese military staged a coup de force against the French military and civilian officials in Cambodia in early March 1945,[22] the Cambodian

[16] Ibid.

[17] Ibid.

[18] Ibid, at 37.

[19] For more details, see Roderic Broadhurst, Thierry Bouhours, Brigitte Bouhours, *Violence and the Civilizing Process in Cambodia* (Cambridge: Cambridge University Press, 2015) at 84–88.

[20] Gour (n 3) at 36. The hierarchy was reportedly as follows: Kram (Royal Code), Kret (Decree), Samrach (decision), Prakas (Proclamation), Deka (Instruction).

[21] The demonstration was originally planned by a nationalist monk called Hem Chieu to demonstrate the anti-colonial sentiment. But the plan was interrupted by the colonial authority ending in the arrest of Chieu on 17 July. The demonstration then took place on July 20 to call for immediate release of Chieu along with other nationalist agendas. For more details, see David Chandler, *A History of Cambodia*, ... and Justin Corfield, *The History of Cambodia* (Santa Barbara: Greenwood Press, 2009) at 39–40.

[22] The incident was marked by the demand made by the Japanese military in Indochina in early March 1942 to the French Governor-General in Saigon that the French troops in Indochina be put under the Japanese command. After the demand was not met, the Japanese took action to disarm and detain a number of French officials of the Vichy government.

government, then under the young King Norodom Sihanouk, was confronted with a difficult situation. It had to decide whether to continue being loyal to its French 'protector' or to side with the Japanese military who at that time was already in desperate straits. Opting for the latter would, of course, presented the nationalists an opportunity to declare Cambodia independent from France. The option of an independence declaration would obviously be resented by the French, but give credit to the Japanese and please the domestic nationalist sentiments which was then running high.

The King decided on the second option. He issued a royal decree on the morning of 12 March 1945 to declare his assumption of the office of the French Senior Resident Representative[23] and later that day, issued another royal decree to denounce the 1963 France-Cambodia Treaty and to declare Cambodia independent.[24] The declaration as cited in French by Gour stated that 'the treaties and conventions on the establishment and organization of French protectorate in Cambodia shall all and entirely be abolished from the date of signature of this declaration'.[25] The next thing the King did was issue Royal Decree No 9 on 17 March 1945, which in fact reproduced the Royal Decree No 1 of 1 June 1940, except that it made no reference to the French Senior Resident Representative.[26] This meant the return to the traditional absolute monarchy in a more modern governmental setting, structured during the years of the French protectorate up to 1945. The King created an advisory post for Prince Sisowath Monireth and offered Son Ngoc Thanh – a nationalist leader who just returned from exile in Japan – the position of foreign minister.[27] Ung Hy was made the first Prime Minister after the 1945 independence. In early August, a large demonstration in Phnom Penh resulted in Thanh seizing power from Hy and becoming Cambodia's second Prime Minister.[28] During the Thanh government, King Sihanouk promulgated Royal Decree No 88, dated 14 August 1945, to eliminate the two forms of Council of Ministers meeting, ie the distinction between the permanent and the plenary commissions, making it a clear mandate for the Prime Minister to be answerable to the King and be responsible for directing the government of the kingdom.[29]

[23] Gour interpreted this act as a way to secure the legal continuity of the constitutional status of the State. See Gour, (n 3) at 40.

[24] See David P Chandler, 'The Kingdom of Kampuchea, March-October 1945: Japanese-sponsored Independence in Cambodia in World War II' (1986) 17(1) *Journal of Southeast Asian Studies* 80.

[25] Gour (n 3) at 40.

[26] Ibid, at 41.

[27] For a brief biography of Thanh, see Sakou Samoth, *Histoire du Cambodge et Elites Khmères*, (publication in Khmer) (Phnom Penh: Editions Angkor, 2013) at 450–457 [hereinafter 'Sakou Samoth'].

[28] On this coup, see Chandler (n 24) at 83–89.

[29] Gour (n 3) at 41.

However, the pronounced independence was short-lived. After Japan was defeated in World War II in August 1945, the French attempted a return to Cambodia to resume its protectoral mandate. To thwart Thanh's further action to make the independence irreversible, the British military, who entered Cambodia as care-taker authority, arrested him on 14 October 1945 on grounds of his earlier collaboration with the Japanese during the War. A new cabinet was established and led by Prince Sisowath Monireth.[30] Given Prince Monireth's pro-French attitude, his government was able to allow renegotiation with the French government to proceed more smoothly with regard to the resumption of French influence and the future of the France-Cambodia relationship. A provisional modus vivendi was concluded between Cambodia and France on 7 January 1946.[31]

This document was aimed at restoring substantive French influences on the Cambodian government with some modifications and specific provisions on the roles and functions of the French officials inside the Cambodian governmental machinery. A Commissioner of the French Republic was nominated to represent France and the Indochinese Federation in Cambodia and to serve as advisor to the Cambodian King; positions of French advisors attached to the Ministers and Heads of Cambodian public services and French advisors at regional levels were specified; positions of the former French Resident Representatives and Heads of the 14 provinces in Cambodia were eliminated; and, provisions related to the organisation of public service in Cambodia were stipulated. It was an obvious attempt to restore the pre-War system of protectorate while dictating some details of the governmental organisation and functioning in Cambodia. These features were later reflected in the preamble and the first articles of the 1947 Constitution.

II. THE CONSTITUTION-MAKING: THE DELIBERATIONS AND THE FINAL PROCESS

The idea of a modern Constitution for Cambodia was originally suggested by the French authority in November 1945. King Sihanouk gave it his support without any reservation. A Franco-Khmer commission was then set up to conduct studies on constitutional drafts. The Commission met for the first time on 23 November 1945. The Commission elaborated and submitted to the King the draft Constitution, which was accepted with some modifications by the King and the Commission itself to become the second draft. But for political reasons

[30] Prince Monireth was educated in France and finished his studies at the military school of Saint CYR in 1934. He later joined the French army as a military officer during the WW II and was awarded the *Chevalier de la Legion D'honneur*. See Sakou Samoth (n 27) at 426–427.

[31] Accord fixant le modus vivendi proviso ire entre la France et le Cambodge, 7 Jan 1946.

that emerged after the establishment of the Consultative Assembly (as will be further explained below) the draft did not become the Constitution adopted in 1947.

According to Gour, this first draft was poorly drafted and modelled after some states in the Middle East. He stated that the Commission took into account the incontestable fact that political maturity was absent among the Cambodian people and that it would be impossible to transplant the western democratic institutions to Cambodia in so sudden a manner.[32] The draft included a limited form of democratic system with a national assembly to be elected indirectly by the provincial councils, which in turn would have to be elected by the commune councils. Only the commune councils would be elected by a universal suffrage.[33] The legislative powers were to be exercised by the King and the right to initiate laws belonged to the King, the Council of Ministers and the National Assembly under conditions specified by law.[34] All constitutional amendments had to be agreed to by the National Assembly but the initiative for constitutional amendment could only come from the King.[35] The National Assembly therefore had only a consultative function in this draft. In addition, Article 24 reportedly introduced a hereditary monarchy instead of the selective system which had already been practiced in Cambodia for several centuries.[36]

When the draft reached the hands of the King, it was accepted with only a few modifications. Gour mentions two relatively significant changes. The first was the removal of the hereditary monarchy and referring the matter of succession to custom. This indicated the return to the elective system in which the King would be elected by a Throne Council, comprising members designated by the Constitution. The second change was to stipulate that members of the National Assembly would be elected by a direct universal suffrage to be specified by an election law.[37]

Instead of exercising his ordinary legislative power to promulgate the Constitution, the King decided to refer the draft to a consultative assembly of representatives for their opinion. Gour thought that this was due to some political reasons considered necessary by the King.[38] However, what really

[32] Gour (n 3) at 44.

[33] Art 51 of the draft read 'En Attendant que l'évolution du pays permette l'élection de l'Assemblée nationale au suffrage universel, ses membres sont élus par les conseillers provinciaux, cuex-ci étant eux-mêmes choisis par les conseillers communaux et ceux-ci élus au suffrage universel'. Gour, p.45.

[34] Art 17 stated, 'Le Pouvoir législative est exercé par le Roi. L'initiative des lois appartient au Roi, au Conseil des ministers et à l'Assemblée dans les conditions fixées par leur statut'.

[35] Art 69(1) stated 'Aucun amendment ne peut être approté à la Constitution du Royaume sans l'accord de l'Assemblée. L'initiative des amendments ne peut venir que du Roi. L'Assemblée n'a pas le pouvoir de modifier les projects dontelle est saisie, mais elle peut présenter au Roi des propositions ou contre-propositions sous forme de voeux'. Gour, p.45.

[36] Gour, p.45. There was no way to verify the accuracy of this statement as the original Art 24 was not made available by Gour.

[37] Gour, p.46.

[38] Gour, p.46.

mattered was the unexpected turns that occurred in Cambodian politics afterwards. The King's decision to submit the draft to the National Assembly changed the course of political transition in Cambodia for the next decade. The decision was announced in a Royal Proclamation dated 13 April 1946. Some interesting paragraphs were reproduced in French by Gour as follows:

> A France-Khmer Commission, presided over on the Cambodian part by the Head of our government, has been organized to prepare this Constitution based on the Khmer tradition as well as the necessity and the trends of modern life. But before granting this Constitution to our country, we consult our people on its provisions which is considered to be of interests to the whole nation.
>
> In this regard, we have ordered our government to arrange, within the shortest period, for the convention of a provisional National Assembly to be made up of representatives elected indirectly by voters of all the Khums (*communes*) of the Kingdom.
>
> This Assembly will review the draft Constitution elaborated with our consent by the Franco-Khmer Commission. It will be able to explain its views freely about the various articles of the draft and to present observations as it may believe proper. Let us then study these views and observations in order to adopt, in the best interest of the nation, the final text of the Constitution which we will endow to our people.[39]

Although the Proclamation mentioned a provisional National Assembly to be elected indirectly by the local communes, an election law promulgated on 31 May 1946 provided for a direct universal vote for the Assembly. Gour thought that this change was intended to evade the possible incidents of corruption that might occur through the two levels of indirect votes, namely at the communal and the provincial levels. But he also pointed out that this was a politically controversial move, as it would be an overkill to have an assembly directly representing the people just to give opinions.

Whatever the controversies, elections were organised on 1 September 1946. Three political parties contested and, with a turnout of 60 per cent, 50 of the 67 seats went to the Democratic Party, 14 went to the Liberal Party and the remaining three seats were won by independents. The Progressive Party gained no seats at all. The Democratic Party was established by leading nationalists and young elites, led by Prince Sisowath Youtevong, who not only held a doctoral degree in physical science from France but also married a French wife, worked for the French government and was for many years an active member of the French Socialist Party. The Party leadership included some radical nationalists who used to operate the first nationalist newspaper, *Nagaravatta* that was generally known as leftist and openly anti-colonial.[40]

[39] Gour, p.47. Note that in Khmer, when the King addressed this subjects, he referred to himself as 'we' instead of 'I'.

[40] In contrast, the Liberal Party was led by another well-known prince, Norodom Norindeth, who had been a French military officer and a modest nationalist favouring gradual achievement of national independence in consultation with the French. The party platform was pro-landowners and accepted the policy-lines taken by the royal government.

The National Assembly dominated by the Democratic Party refused to work solely on the Draft Constitution referred to them by the King. They took on a more legislative role, claiming the parliamentary mandates in the Western countries.[41] The royal government on the other hand did not simply accept that argument. A compromise was reached between the government and the newly-elected Assembly, wherein the constitutional draft adopted by the Assembly would be submitted to a committee comprising the King, his personal advisor, the President of the National Assembly, representatives of the political parties and the Commissioner of the French Republic. As a result, the draft worked and was adopted by the National Assembly and promulgated as the final Constitution, after some minor touches.[42]

III. THE CONSTITUTION IN A NUTSHELL

The Constitution was made up of 10 chapters and 107 articles. It started with provisions on the nature of the State, rights and obligations, definition of law and powers and the monarchy. Chapters 5 and 6 deal with the legislative organs, namely the National Assembly and the Senate. Chapter 7 contained provisions on the government and Chapter 8 defined the judicial power. Chapters 9 and 10 contained general and transitional provisions respectively. This section will make a quick summary of the contents for each chapter and list some important features therein.

The first chapter consisted of two articles to define the nature of the State as a monarchy and its status as an independent State adopting Khmer as the official language and French in its relationship with the French Federation. Article 2 reflects Cambodia's commitment to the French Federation stated in the short Preamble.[43] This chapter demonstrates a fine compromise between the colonial interests and the nationalist view of governance based on the basic characteristics of a monarchy in the Cambodian context. The emphasis on the use of Khmer as the official language of the land was obviously a nationalist denial of the colonial influence of eight decades. Nonetheless, the colonialist was able to place a constitutional limit and set the scope for this nationalist agenda.

Chapter 2 on freedom, rights and obligations of Khmers comprises 13 articles. Article 3 defined in general terms the meaning and scope of freedom and legality. Freedom was defined as the possibility to do everything provided its enjoyment would not infringe upon the rights of others. The condition for

[41] One substantive impact was the replacement of the Prime Minister after the election, giving the position to Prince Yutevong as the leader of the majority in the Assembly. This was not expected in a literal election for consultative assembly, at least not until the Constitution would be promulgated.

[42] Gour (n 3) at 49.

[43] The Preamble declares Cambodia to be an Associated State of the French Union while Art 2 states that while the 'official tongue is Cambodian', French is the official language 'for the proceedings concerning the French Union'.

enjoying freedom shall be stipulated by law. Whatever action not required by law shall not be forced upon any individual. Thus, no one was obliged to do anything not required by law. These provisions obviously put legality in the way of a paternalistic society led by power and arbitrariness. Article 4 further defined legality and due process in the context of criminal matters and exercising public powers. The principle of *sina lege sina pene* in case of arrest and detention was embedded in Article 4(1). Review of legality by judges in the case of detention was explicitly required to ensure propriety in the process. Torture and inconsequential coercion at the time of arrest; physical maltreatment and mental duress imposed on detainees; or, any treatment that exacerbated punishment already proclaimed by the court in conformity with the law against the convicts shall be prohibited by law. Perpetrators, ringleaders and conspirators alike were individually responsible for these acts. Article 5 provided for the principle of presumption of innocence and corrective nature of imprisonment and confinement of offender's freedom.

Subsequent articles dealt with substantive issues, including freedom from expulsion, freedom of movement, religious freedom, freedom of speech, freedom of association and assembly. The right to privacy was partly protected by Article 11 regarding residence and Article 12 regarding communication in the form of letters. Article 13 provided for non-discrimination in joining the public service. The only determining factors were qualifications and competency of the individuals concerned. This was an attempt to modernise the public administration by prioritising efficiency and merits over traditional systems of patronage and clientele. It was obviously a constitutional design to redefine elitism in the transition towards a modern westernised nation. There had been increasing numbers of new intellectuals outside the royal and noble families who had been educated abroad and they resented the traditional mode of public administration that had been in place since the 1930s.[44]

Article 14 gave Khmer individuals a right to file administrative petitions to public authorities to solve problems of either individual or public interest. This was the first reference to a modern form of administrative adjudication in Cambodia. However, it was far from being a clear model of administrative litigation based on a third-party dispute settlement mechanism. Its significance could be perceived from the viewpoint of the transitional elitism implicated by Article 13 mentioned above. Article 15 declared the non-derogability of rights protected by the Constitution, with the exception of Articles 4–9, 10 and 12. Invoking limits in the exercise of freedom and rights had to be based on legality and in special circumstances, including time of crisis, public interests and security.

Gour cited two doctoral dissertations completed in France during the 1940s and 1950s suggesting theories about the significance of these human rights

[44] Some of these intellectuals were later to become leading figures within the Democratic Party. Those included Prince Yuthevong, Son Ngoc Thanh, Sim Var, Eav Keus, etc.

provisions in the 1947 Constitution. One was by Phung Ton arguing that these provisions were introduced by the newly rising elites of the time to forestall any possible loss of their emerging privileges, ie those of the democratic bourgeois. The other thesis by M Larché argued that these provisions actually indicated a progressive trend in the constitution-making of Cambodia from the perspective of a comparison to the country's own history. Any comparison with the more advanced European nations would not be appropriate.[45] Both theories seem to have pointed to one same direction, namely the influence of 'modern western civilisation' upon the political thought in Cambodia at the time of the constitution-making. It was the injection of the modernist agenda, be it the project of the new generation colonialist hoping to obtain and secure their portion of privilege from the conservatives or that of the revolutionary elements hoping to change the power structure of the traditional State.

Chapter 3 was about law and power. It laid down most general principles of law purportedly as part of an attempt to modernise legal thinking and the system of the country following the model of Western constitutional law development. Among them, Article 17 seemed to be most fundamental. It stated:

> Law is the expression of the national will. Law shall be applicable to all individuals, be it the law to protect, to condemn or to coerce.
>
> Law guarantees all Khmer citizens the exercise of all freedom and rights stipulated in the previous chapter. In no way may law infringe upon these freedom and rights.

Article 18 guarantees the right of all individuals to be heard by the court. It further emphasised that 'shortage in resources shall not obstruct the receiving of a hearing by the court'. Article 19 provided for non-retroactivity of legal effects, except for any law that would explicitly provide otherwise. These articles reflected some basic values of modern legality that had no identifiable roots in the traditional concept of public-private relationship in Cambodia. The idea of a national institution that would guarantee everybody's access to justice was a sharp contrast to the perception of a traditional system of kingship in which delivery of justice had been at the discretion of the royal court based on the degree of favouritism held by the King and his entourage.[46]

Articles 20 to 24 dealt with the entry into force of a promulgated law; the source of powers coming from the King and the constitutionality of the exercise of these powers, including by the legislative, executive and judicial institutions

[45] Gour (n 3) at 145.

[46] Citing historian's accounts and his own observation, Stephen Marks wrote 'Patronage and clientship at the village level remained an essential part of the social structure up to the nineteenth century, as the 'rectitude and permanence of these relationships had been drummed into people from birth'... In addition to the King, his high-ranking officials (*Okya*), and the village leaders (*Chaovay sruk*), members of the royal family were an influential connection between the people and their king'. Stephen P Marks, 'The Process of Creating a New Constitution in Cambodia' in Laurel E Miller (ed) with Louis Aucoin, *Framing the State in Times of Transition: Case studies in Constitution-Making* (Washington, DC: United States Institute of Peace, 2010) at 209.

as agents of the King. More analyses of these articles will be made in the next section. Chapters 5–8 dealt with state institutions, including the King, the National Assembly, the Senate, the Ministers and judicial power. It is beyond the scope of this chapter to introduce each article although some of them will be highlighted for analysis later on.

The National Assembly was elected every four years[47] through direct universal votes cast by male citizens not younger than 20 years old, except for active military servicemen and monks.[48] Only male citizens aged 25 and above are eligible to run for election.[49] A position in the public service was incompatible with the membership in the National Assembly.[50] Article 54 provided for immunity of members of the National Assembly, except for the case of *frangrate delicto*.[51] The National Assembly was the only institution that had the right to express views on law-making. This right could not be delegated to any individual.[52] The national budget and national loans with interest had to be approved and the national balance of payment had to be consented to by the National Assembly.[53] However, the National Assembly could not discuss the amount of national budget to be assigned to the coffers of the Royal Palace.[54] A valid National Assembly session required a quorum of two-thirds of the total members.[55] Except for special requests for a closed-door session made by the government, the President of the National Assembly or at least five members of the National Assembly, all sessions had to be open to the public.[56]

The Senate – literally called the Council of the Kingdom – consisted of some nominees and some members elected through indirect votes.[57] A senator had to be at least 40 years old and could not serve concurrently as a member of the National Assembly.[58] The Senate comprises 24 members of which two are nominated by the King from among members of the royal family;[59] two appointed by the National Assembly among non-parliamentarians;[60] eight regional and municipal representatives elected by provincial, municipal and local councils;[61] eight representatives of different professions directly elected

[47] Art 50.
[48] Art 48.
[49] Art 49.
[50] Art 49.
[51] Arts 54 and 55.
[52] Art 64.
[53] Art 66.
[54] Art 66.
[55] Art 67.
[56] Art 68.
[57] Art 70.
[58] Art 70.
[59] Art 71.
[60] Art 72.
[61] Art 73.

by members of the professions;[62] and, four representatives elected by all public servants.[63] The Senate was mandated to review legislation adopted by the National Assembly before its promulgation and any issue submitted by the government.[64] Any opinion on or rejection of legislation by the Senate would require reconsideration by the National Assembly. The second vote on legislation rejected by the Senate must be by open ballot and adopted by an absolute majority at the National Assembly.[65]

The Prime Minister would be selected by the King at the end of each parliamentary election or each time a cabinet was dissolved. The King was required to consult with the President of the National Assembly, the President of the Senate, and the heads of political parties.[66] The Prime Minister would then set up his cabinet which was to consist of not more than 12 members, including the ministers and the secretaries of state.[67] A minister could be a member of the National Assembly, a Senator or someone not belonging to the two houses.[68] The Cabinet could take office after they were given a majority vote of confidence en masse by the National Assembly.[69] The ministers were collectively responsible to the National Assembly with regard to the general policy of the Council of Ministers, and individually responsible to the Prime Minister for his/her own acts.[70] A minister had to answer questions posed verbally or in writing by one or more members of the National Assembly.[71] The National Assembly could remove the whole cabinet to by passing a motion to condemn the government. The motion had to be consented to by an absolute majority of the members of the National Assembly.[72] The National Assembly could bring the case of a minister who committed a felony or misdemeanour or wrongdoing in the exercise of his/her duty to a special court.[73] The special court will comprise five members: two Supreme Court judges; one member appointed by the National Assembly; and two other members appointed by the Senate.[74] The appointment must to be made at the beginning of each legislature and lasts until the end of the legislature's life.[75]

[62] Art 74.
[63] Ibid.
[64] Art 78.
[65] Ibid.
[66] Art 80.
[67] Arts 80 and 79.
[68] Art 79.
[69] Art 80.
[70] Art 81.
[71] Art 83.
[72] Art 85.
[73] Art 92. Note that this high-level court was not the Supreme Court at the top of the judicial branch. This was rather an impeachment mechanism.
[74] Art 93.
[75] Art 93.

There were no specific provisions on the courts, but the judicial power.[76] Article 95 of Chapter 8 on the judicial power only states that 'the organization and duties of the courts shall be stipulated by a special law'. Article 96 provides for the establishment of a Supreme Judicial Council, which would ensure that judges observe discipline and operate in unity. The Supreme Judicial Council was made up of seven members. The Minister of Justice presided over the Council, of which two members were nominated by the King; two members appointed by the National Assembly and two members appointed by the courts.[77] Chapter 9 on General Provisions also contained some interesting articles. Article 97 prohibited revision of three fundamental governmental principles: (1) the monarch as the head of state; (2) a governance system based on the people's representatives, and (3) principles of freedom and equality provided by the Constitution. Article 98 then prohibited any constitutional amendment that would reduce the powers of the King already stipulated by this Constitution. The National Assembly had an absolute right in interpreting the Constitution.[78]

IV. THE CHANGING CONCEPT OF SOVEREIGNTY UNDER THE FIRST CONSTITUTION

Sovereignty was not explicitly mentioned in the 1947 Constitution, except for the short preambular paragraph which stated that Cambodia was an 'associate state' and was part of the French Federation.[79] The Constitution was bestowed by the King to His People within the limits of all existing treaties between Cambodia and France.[80] Another important issue which was closely related to sovereignty was the constitutionally-defined official language. The use of French as an official language in Cambodia was the result of French colonialisation of the country. The Constitution took the important step of constitutionally stipulating Khmer as the official language and stating that French would be the official language for use in relation to the French Federation. However, the Constitution also provided for the possibility of using it for other purposes until the Khmer language was lexicographically developed for use in a modern nation.[81]

The Constitution was therefore an important starting point in restoring a post-colonial independent nation with sovereignty – attributed to the monarch

[76] Ch 8.

[77] Art 96.

[78] Art 101. However, Art 105 of Ch 10 on transitional provisions provided that 'the right to interpret constitutional provisions is the duty of the King at the meeting of the Council of Ministers'. These transitional provisions should be understood to be applicable during the period when the new constitutional institutions were yet to be fully operational and the pre-constitution governmental system remained to run.

[79] The first clause of the Preamble of the 1947 Constitution.

[80] The second clause of the Preamble of the 1947 Constitution.

[81] Art 2.

and the 'French Federation' – and in which the Cambodian nation and people would only be a part. Article 21(1) explicitly pronounces the monarch as the only embodiment of sovereignty: 'All powers come from the King' although Article 21(2) requires that the King's powers 'be exercised in conformity with the Constitution'. The Constitution was therefore a tool to restrain the King's exercise of public power but not a restatement of the principle of a national sovereignty attributed to the people. This was more a matter of policy for (good) governance than a constitutional principle based on the conception of modern political democracy.

However, two important historical and political details of the time suggested that significant changes in the concept of sovereignty actually occurred during the constitution-making process in 1947. First was the relationship with the French Federation. If the election organised in the 1940s to elect a constituent assembly to draft this 1947 Constitution was an important political step towards the democratisation of Cambodian politics, the Constitution's acceptance of the dominant position for the Federation in Cambodia's constitutional order might be seen not as a democratic process of accepting a super-national influence or domination, but as a pre-determined national destiny which was made possible by an important traditional Cambodian political fact – the absolute leadership of the God King in national politics. When the King bestowed the first Constitution to his people through the Constituent Assembly, the Federation was an inherent part of that new constitutional reality to be given to the population. Only the sovereign King could decide this matter. The new Cambodian nation, modelled after the modern western form of government, only accepted this political fact when recommended by the King to do so. The Constitution thus embodied the traditional view of an absolute monarchy that sat uneasily with the country's quest for a modern form of government. The combination ultimately gave the Constitution the form it actually took. It was the product of an interaction between traditional nationalism led by the God King and western modernism introduced by French colonial rules – that were sanctioned by many nationalists to reduce the influence of an absolute monarch.

Second was the de facto transition of the power to rule to the citizens, gradually side-lining the absolute monarch. This was provided under Articles 22–24, which provided that the National Assembly, Council of Ministers and courts of all levels exercised the legislative, executive and judicial powers in the Royal name of the King. However, the monarch retained substantive power in his own right. In his relationship with the government, the King had the right to select the Prime Minister[82] and appoint the cabinet members, based on the list submitted by the Prime Minister.[83] He presided over meetings of the Council of

[82] Art 39.
[83] Art 39(2).

Ministers and all meeting minutes of the Council had to be submitted to him.[84] The King had the right to propose law, just like the government and members of the Parliament and he also had the right to initiate constitutional amendments just like the Prime Minister and the Presidents of the two houses.[85]

The King retained these powers because the logic of the traditional monarch – being the source of all powers – continued to be the guiding principle of the 1947 Constitution. The new constitutional order guided by western concepts of citizenship and democratic government did not replace this traditional concept of sovereignty. Rather, it merely removed some important powers from the King and put them under the substantive control of the National Assembly. The importance of general will did not replace but only redefined the substance of the traditionally-established concept of sovereignty. In hindsight, the Constitution was the first written attempt to relativise the absolutism of the sovereign power of the King. Exercise of the powers became a subject matter to be shared between the King and his former subjects. As long as power can be substantively shared, the question of the source of power was no longer important in practical terms.

Of course, this was a very weak form of constitutional monarchy, especially since there was a lack of constitutional reference to standard rules and procedures to clarify the working relationship between the King and his subjects in the exercise of public powers. Two instances demonstrate the failure of a democratic transition under the 1947 Constitution. The first was the lack of substantive consultations between the King and the democratic institutions – including but not limited to the National Assembly – concerning the selection of a Prime Minister after a national election or at the dissolution of a government. The second was the lack of democratic control over the King's power to initiate draft laws or constitutional amendments. This illustrates the difficulty in democratic reforms and in reality, any democratic transition was at the God King's mercy.

If the King thought it important to obtain the consensus from the presidents of the two houses regarding the appointment of the Prime Minister and attempted to achieve that, the consultation would have had a semi-democratic value. Otherwise, no constitutional restraint would have hindered the King from selecting and appointing as Prime Minister, someone of his sole favour. If the King adopted the latter course, the resulting political tension between the King and the National Assembly would manifest in the running of government. The Assembly which considers itself legitimated by the democratic elections would often resist any cooperation with a Prime Minister and Cabinet appointed by the King and could be thought to solely serve his royal interests. The failure to

[84] Art 40.
[85] Art 99.

have a functioning government between 1947 and the early 1950s was therefore a predictable result of this tension.

In case of legislative power, Articles 22 and 99 posed a very interesting theoretical question.[86] On the one hand, being the sole source of sovereign power, the King had power to legislate for his subjects and kingdom. On the other hand, the cabinet led by the Prime Minister were mandated to exercise the executive power on the King's behalf. When both of them had equal powers to propose legislation or constitutional amendments, what rules are there to limit either party's jurisdictional boundaries or to co-ordinate priorities or secure coherence. Being the principal power holder, the King could, at least theoretically, delegate some powers to his agent, but to stipulate a parallel exercise of the same power between the principal and the agent theoretically leads to some technically confusing and controversial circumstances.

V. THE CONSTITUTION IN OPERATION – A QUICK REVIEW

Six years after the promulgation of the Constitution, Cambodia obtained full independence from France. By then, State institutions had been operating on the foundation of the 1947 Constitution. Writing in 1965, Gour described the development of these institutions as they were functioning at that time. The 1947 Constitution largely redefined the State institutions and their functions as they went through several waves of reforms and restructuring under the colonial government since the beginning of the twentieth century. Most institutions were not literally a product of the Constitution, but pre-dated it, particularly provisions regarding the executive branch and the judicial system. Perhaps the exceptions were the National Assembly and the Supreme Council of the Courts. The following paragraphs will briefly introduce Gour's assessment of the actual operation of these two institutions in Cambodia by the mid-1960s in order to evaluate the effects of the Constitution in the first 18 years of its existence.

[86] Art 22: 'The National Assembly exercises the legislative power on behalf of the King. Those having the right to initiate legislative drafting are the King, the Council of Ministers, members of the National Assembly and members of the Council of the Kingdom'.

Art 99: 'Those having the right to initiate constitutional amendment are the King, the Prime Minister, the President of the National Assembly and the President of the Council of the Kingdom, among whom the Presidents of the two houses shall follow the approval of their respective houses, which shall have expressed their views based on a request by at least one-fourths of the members'.

Although unlike Art 99, Art 22 designated the Council of the Ministers, rather than the Prime Minister, to be one of the potential draft legislative initiators, the collective accountability of all ministers to the Prime Minister, who headed the Council, made this difference in wording not much significant in this context. The only factual difference between these two articles was that the initial legislative draft would normally come from the ministry concerned and be submitted to the Council of Ministers for final approval, whereas a proposed constitutional amendment did not have to go through this bottom up process. See the whole Ch 7 of the Constitution.

A. The National Assembly

A little more than two months after the Constitution was adopted in May 1947, the first Prime Minister from the Democratic Party, Prince Sisowath Yuthevong, died of disease. The first parliamentary election based on the Constitution was organised in December 1947. Struggling for power and control among the political leaders and parties inside the National Assembly afterwards led to a change of government almost every few months. King Sihanouk dissolved the Assembly in 1949 and the second parliamentary election was held in September 1951. The King dissolved the cabinet and the Assembly again in June 1952 just to take full control of the government in the final stage of his royal crusade for national independence from France. In all these parliamentary elections, the democrats won the majority of the seats. Collisions between the Assembly and the Cabinet (comprising figures favoured by the King), resulted in dissolution of cabinets and finally the Assembly for new rounds of elections.[87] However, as King Sihanouk was able to claim the final credit in gaining full national independence in 1953, the Democrats saw their popularity decline due to the weakened rhetorical appeal for nationalism and gradual infiltration of young radical members into the party. In the 1955 election, the first one after full independence, only the political movement headed by Sihanouk won all the 91 seats of the Assembly.[88] At the time of Gour's assessment, the National Assembly had already been diminished in power and stature by the prerogatives of the executive branch. In his words, 'the National Assembly is without doubt the body that experiences most of the difficulties to be integrated harmoniously into the constitutional balance of 1956'.[89]

B. The Supreme Council of the Courts

The Council was an institution established by the Constitution following the French model of the *Conseil Supérieur de la Magistrature*. However, until its amendment in 1959, the founding Constitution did not give the King an official position on the Council. The King only had the right to nominate two members and the Council which was chaired by the Minister of Justice. From the modernist perspective, this might have been an attempt to dilute the King's direct influence on judicial nomination and disciplinary actions. But as Gour would later argue, this formula risked pitching the King against the Council on issues

[87] By Gour's counts, Cambodia witnessed 41 governments in 16 years, between 18 March 1945 and 26 January 1961. See Gour (n 3), at 352. However, this number might have included care-taking and other cabinets running from a few days to a couple of months.

[88] By some accounts, this result was allegedly assisted by some frauds and irregularity. See Ben Kiernan, *How Pol Pot Came to Power* London: Verso, 1985) at 158–162.

[89] Gour (n 3) at 215.

of judicial nomination under Article 43.[90] A Royal Decree issued by the King on 31 December 1947 to define the actual operations of the Council therefore made the Council a purely consultative body.[91] After the successful royal crusade to gain full national independence from the French colonial rule, the Constitution was amended in 1959 to give the King an official position as the President of the Council and rename the Minister of Justice as the Vice-President. Other members remained the same with two being nominated by the King, two elected by the National Assembly and two elected by all the magistrates of the country.[92]

VI. CONCLUDING REMARKS: THE LEGACY OF THE 1947 CONSTITUTION

The constitutional order established in 1947 collapsed dramatically in 1970 after a coup that removed the monarchy and changed the way the government would be formed, and the concept of a God King that bestowed the Constitution upon his subjects. Instead, the people became the official source of power and sovereignty that would choose the head of state and the government through elections. This clear break away from traditional ideas about sovereignty allowed the state-citizen relationship to develop in the following years through the different revolutionary periods.

When the Paris Peace Accords were signed in 1991 to pave the way for political settlement of the Cambodia conflict, there was no clear vision of how the post-UNTAC form of government would be. The only constitutional principles stated in the Accords with regard to a post-UNTAC Cambodia left it open as to whether Cambodia would return to a monarchy. Fundamental principles which would have to be stated in the post-conflict Constitution are, among others, respect for fundamental freedom and human rights, liberal democracy on the basis of pluralism, periodic universal and direct votes through secret ballots, judicial independence and legislative approval of any constitutional amendments.[93]

After the Constituent Assembly was elected under the auspices of the UNTAC to draft a new Constitution in 1993, the political parties agreed to restore the monarchy, with a strongly symbolic King[94] and a clear provision on separation of powers.[95] However, many traits of the 1947 Constitution can be

[90] Gour (n 3) at 367. Art 43 of the Constitution stated that 'the King shall appoint all judges upon recommendations by the Supreme Council of the Courts'.

[91] Gour, ibid, at 369.

[92] Gour, ibid, and Art 114 of the amended Constitution translated in French and reproduced in Gour, at 413.

[93] Agreements on a Comprehensive Political Settlement of the Cambodia Conflict, Art 23 and Annex V, Paris, 23 October 1991.

[94] Art 7 of the 1993 Constitution: 'The King reigns but does not rule'.

[95] Art 51 of the 1993 Constitution, the last clause: 'Powers shall be separated among the legislative power, the executive power and the judicial power'.

found among the provisions of the 1993 Constitution. These include the restoration of an elective mechanism for choosing the King; the establishment of a Supreme Council of Magistracy; and the principles for elections and functioning of the Senate, when it was reintroduced by a constitutional amendment in 1998.[96] However, there are many differences in the details between the provisions of these two Constitutions. The re-introduction of a similar institutional milieu after a hiatus of more than 23 years was no less a matter of nostalgia than an issue of necessity. But one thing has definitely changed throughout the years – the concept of sovereignty and the source of constitutional law in Cambodia. The King no longer bestows a constitution to his subject, but the people make it by themselves.[97] All powers no longer belong to the King but to the people.[98] The grand project of change that was triggered off by the 1947 Constitution has come a full circle and moved to a new stage in 1993 as the direct result of Cambodia's turbulent history.

[96] There were two earlier drafts of the 1993 Constitution which were submitted to then Prince Sihanouk for opinions, one officially prepared by the Drafting Committee set up by the Constituent Assembly and the other one presented by Prince Ranaridh largely modelled after the 1947 Constitution. Sihanouk reportedly was more interested in the Ranaridh draft. See John C. Brown and Ker Munthit, 'Sihanouk Backs the Royalist Charter', *The Phnom Penh Post*, 10 September 1993. In his observations on the drafting process and the political influences on it, Stephen Marks wrote that the Constituent Assembly 'completely sidelining its own drafting assembly', 'examined the FUNCINPEC draft edited by Sihanouk for five days, finally adopting the text on September 21, 1993, with a vote of 113 to 5, with two abstentions'. See Stephen P. Marks, 'The Process of Creating a New Constitution in Cambodia' in Laurel E. Miller (ed.) with Louis Aucoin, *Framing the State in Times of Transition: Case studies in Constitution-Making,* Washington, D.C., United States Institute of Peace, 2010, pp. 214–215 and 226–228.

[97] The Preamble of the 1993 Constitution starts with 'We, the People of Cambodia,...' and ends with 'we inscribe the following as the Constitution of the Kingdom of Cambodia:'.

[98] Art 51 of the 1993 Constitution: 'All powers belong to the citizens. The citizens exercise their powers through the National Assembly, the Senate, the Government and the courts'.

12

The 1932 Compromise Constitution: Matrix of Thailand's Permanent Constitutional Instability

EUGENIE MÉRIEAU

ON 24 JUNE 1932, a group of revolutionaries known as the People's Committee overthrew the Siamese absolute monarchy and imposed a Constitution to King Prajadhipok. In its public announcement, the People's Committee stated:

> When this King succeeded his elder brother, the people first hoped that he would be governing with moderation, but its hopes were disavowed. The King still reigns above the law as he has done in the past.... Dear people, it is time to understand that our country belongs to the people, not to the King, as we have always been told ... As for the Head of State, the People's Committee has no desire to steal the throne. Consequently, we are inviting the King to keep his title. However, he must govern the country under the Constitution, and will not do anything without the consent of the People's Representatives Assembly. The People's Committee already informed the King and is now waiting for an answer. If the King refuses, or if he does not reply within the said timeframe, for the selfish reason that he would see his power diminished, we will consider this act as an act of treason, and it will be necessary for the country to adopt a democratic form of government.[1]

This 'democratic form of government' refers to a republican government. In the words of the People's Committee: 'A democratic form of government means that the Head of State will be a commoner elected by parliament for a limited term.'[2] Under the threat of republicanism, King Rama VII agreed to return to Bangkok as a constitutional monarch.

> I have received the letter in which you invited me to return to Bangkok as a constitutional monarch. For the sake of peace, and to spare the country unnecessary blood spills, to avoid chaos and damages to the country, and, moreover, because I have

[1] First announcement of the People's Committee, 24 June 1932.
[2] Ibid.

> already considered making this change myself, I am ready to cooperate to put in place a Constitution, under the authority of which I am ready to serve.[3]

Three days after the Revolution, on 27 June, Siam adopted its first Constitution, unilaterally drafted by the revolutionaries, and most likely by Pridi Panomyong, a jurist educated in France. Yet six months later, the Parliament installed in accordance with Siam's first Constitution discussed and adopted an entirely new charter, the 10 December 1932 Constitution, that is now considered Siam's very first Constitution.

This chapter examines the genesis of Siam's June and December constitutional texts. I will argue that the December 1932 Constitution constituted an ambiguous compromise between two forces, which, being unresolved until today, still impacts Thai constitutional ideas and practices. It is in fact the cause of Thailand's permanent constitutional instability since then, with a new Constitution being drafted every four and a half years in average since 1932. Even though constitutional ideas were imported to Siam as the result of a consensus between revolutionary and royalist forces in a bid to 'civilize' the country through a written Constitution, the constitution-drafting process was marred by irreconcilable understandings of constituent power that led to an untenable and contradictory compromise between the revolutionaries and royalists.

I. CIVILISING SIAM THROUGH THE ADOPTION OF A WRITTEN CONSTITUTION

From the second half of the nineteenth century to the early twentieth century, constitutional ideas spread in elite circles, embraced by royalist forces for the purpose of conservative modernisation, and by revolutionary forces for the purpose of democratisation. Revolutionary forces imposed a first Constitution to Siam but the constitution-making process was finally re-appropriated by the royalists.

A. The Spread of Competing Constitutional Ideas During the Westernisation of Siamese Law

In 1855, Siam signed the Bowring treaty with Great Britain and lost its judicial sovereignty over British subjects on its soil.[4] Many other similar treaties

[3] Charnvit Kasetsiri, *2475 Kan Patiwat Siam [1932, The Siamese Revolution]* (Bangkok: Foundation for the Promotion of Social Sciences and Humanities, 1999) at 144.

[4] Siam signed extraterritoriality treaties with several countries, starting with Great Britain. In 1855, it signed the Bowring treaty and lost its judicial sovereignty over British subjects on its territory. The treaty stated: 'Any disputes arising between Siamese and British subjects shall be heard and determined by the [British] Consul in conjunction with the proper Siamese officers; and criminal

followed.[5] To regain full judicial sovereignty over its territory, Siam was compelled to modernise its legal system. King Mongkut also known as King Rama IV ascended the throne in 1851 and initiated the Westernisation of Siam.[6] His son, King Chulalongkorn (1853–1910), who succeeded him in 1868, accelerated and deepened it. Chulalongkorn's aim was to westernise law through a two-step process: first, hiring foreign advisors to write legal modern codes; and second, sending a young generation of Siamese royal elites to study law in Europe so that they could progressively replace these foreign advisors upon their graduation and return. Chulalongkorn himself travelled extensively in Europe in the second half of the nineteenth century and developed an interest in its laws, including constitutional law.

Like most modern political concepts, the word 'constitution' came to Siam through the English language. It appeared for the first time in 1865 in the *Bangkok Recorder*[7] as a transliteration from English.[8] In a Thai-language article, the American missionary Dan Beach Bradley explained that the constitution was a 'very short law', comparing the role of the American President to that of the Siamese King.[9] In 1866, he translated into Thai the 1787 American Constitution.[10] Later, the transliterated word spread – modestly – to the educated class; but the spelling was always changing, and there was still no Thai word for 'constitution'. Nonetheless, constitutional ideas started to spread in educated circles. Under the initiative of the King himself, foreign advisors, the younger foreign-educated royal elite, and the royal entourage in Siam started to think about a constitution on the Meiji model as a means to escape from the extraterritorial treaties. Meanwhile, the press voiced and echoed an emerging interest in constitutional ideas.

offenses will be punished, in the case of English offenders, by the Consul, according to English laws, and in the case of Siamese offenders by their own laws, through the Siamese authorities. But the Consul shall not interfere in any matters referring solely to Siamese, neither will the Siamese authorities interfere in questions which only concern the subjects of Her Britannic Majesty'. Francis Bower Sayre, 'The Passing of Extraterritoriality in Siam' (1928) 22 *American Journal of International Law* 71.

[5] Siam later signed 12 other treaties of extraterritoriality: with France and the United States (1856), Denmark (1858), Portugal (1859), Holland (1860) and Prussia (1862), Norway, Sweden, Belgium, and Italy (1868), Austria-Hungary (1869) and Spain (1870). Western powers argued that Siamese penal law was too cruel and uncivilised to apply to their own citizens, and affirmed that they would reconsider the treaties once the Siamese would modernise their penal system.

[6] Rama IV created a Royal Gazette to publish laws – in contrast to the former practice of secrecy. More than 400 'modernization laws' were issued during the reign of King Mongkut.

[7] The *Bangkok Recorder* was created by the American missionary Dr Dan Beach Bradley (1804–1873), who had been sent to Siam in 1835 and who lived there until his death. Bradley participated in the development of medicine in Siam, spreading Western ideas of equality, freedom and education.

[8] Bandit Charoenchanakit, *Rattathammanun sathaphana [The founding Constitution]* (Bangkok: Vipassa, 2006) 66 [hereinafter 'Charoenchanakit'].

[9] The article 'Kasat nai muang United States' [*The King in the United States*], was published in the Bangkok Recorder. See Thanet Aphornsuwan, 'Thammai thong mi rattathammanun-lae newkit rattathammanun chak kriksaharat matheung siam' [*Why we need a Constitution – and the concept of Constitution from Ancient Greece to Siam*] *Prachatai* (Bangkok, 21 May 2016).

[10] *Ibid*.

Twenty years later, in 1885, Prince Prisadang[11], then Ambassador in Paris, proposed to King Chulalongkorn that Siam adopt a European-style Constitution, following Japan's footsteps.[12] He argued that the adoption of a Constitution would protect the institution of the monarchy through codification, while still upholding Thai 'royal custom' (*rachaphrapheni*). According to Prisadang, it was urgent to 'civilize' the kingdom through the adoption of a constitution, to build up its resistance against the colonial threat:

> We have to replace our ancient royal traditions by the constitutional tradition, following, as accurately as possible, the European example, like Japan, the only Eastern country to have followed the European way, did. We need to change our traditions, which give the King the power to decide everything, what the British call "absolute monarchy", and replace them by the tradition called "constitutional monarchy".[13] … We have to embrace change as Japan did following the European way like all civilized countries: it is the only way to preserve our country.[14]

Prisadang's project did not entail a limitation of the King's powers, nor the creation of a Parliament. Even so, the King rejected the proposal, and severely sanctioned its author.[15] Four years later, Chulalongkorn disclosed his own constitutional project, called 'law on royal custom.'[16] He drew his inspiration from the French Napoleonic Constitution, which he had ordered translated and summarised.[17] According to the draft, the King was sovereign, as head of the legislative, executive and judicial powers. Article 2 of Chulalongkorn's draft read: 'The King has absolute and discretionary power, to which there is nothing above'. However, unlike Napoleon's Constitution, Chulalongkorn's draft did

[11] Prince Prisadang (1851–1935) was a grandson of Rama III. He was ambassador to several European capital cities before being appointed to Paris.

[12] Chanrochanakit (n 8) at 68.

[13] Saneh Chamarik, *Kanmuang Thai kap Pattanakan Rattathammanun [Thai Politics and constitutional development]* (Bangkok: Foundation for the Promotion of Social Sciences and Humanities, 2006 [1 ed 1986]) 28.

[14] Chanrochanakit (n 8), at 67.

[15] He was called back to Bangkok, and lost his civil servant status. He became a monk in Sri Lanka before returning to Siam where he died in poverty.

[16] Literally, 'first law on royal custom of Siam', 'phrarachakritsadika 1 waduey kanrachaphrapheni krung siam'.

[17] Chris Baker & Pasuk Pongpaichit, *A History of Thailand* (Cambridge: Cambridge University Press 2005) 70; Attachak Sattayanurak, *Kanphlienphleng lokkathat khong chonchan phunam thai tangtae rachakan thi 4 – 2475 [Change of worldviews among the Elite class from the Fourth reign to 1932]* (Bangkok: Chulalongkorn University Press, 1994) 150; Kullada Kesboonchoo-Mead, *The Rise and Decline of Thai Absolutism* (London: Routledge, 2004), at 48, 52 & 193. Kesboonchoo-Mead summarises the absolutism of the Napoleonic Constitution (at 193) as follows: 'The Emperor is an absolute monarch. He is above all the French people and is the ruler of the Kingdom. He does not need to justify his action to anyone. He is respected and must not be slandered. He appoints ministers to various ministries as he wishes. He has the power to grant pardons to convicts. He is the supreme commander of the army and the navy has authority to declare war and to sign treaties of commerce and friendship with other countries. He appoints members of the nobility to administrative positions throughout the kingdom. He has legislative power, and in the absence of his presidency, no law can be passed. Law courts throughout the empire exercise their power in his name. He is the source of righteousness, and without his consent to every clause of a law, that law is null and void.'

not provide for a Parliament. King Chulalongkorn clearly wished to establish an authoritarian Constitution, without a legislature. This Constitution did no more than codify the pre-existing 'royal custom' – a royal government that he wanted to turn into an absolute monarchy. Chulalongkorn's constitutional project was never realised.

Constitutional ideas however continued to spread in educated royal circles. In 1912, a palace coup sought to end the absolute monarchy of King Vajiravudh and enact a Constitution, but failed.[18] His successor, King Prajadhipok, twice ordered to his American advisors to send him constitutional proposals. The first proposal resulted from the King's letter to his advisor Harvard Professor Francis Bowes Sayre Sr (1885–1972) on 23 July 1926[19] in which he asked a series of nine questions. The two first questions dealt with the modes of royal succession; the third, fourth and fifth with the possible importation of the British parliamentary system into Siam.[20] King Prajadhipok was personally against the importation of a parliamentary system, as he specifically disliked the idea of a Parliament:[21]

> Must this country have a parliamentary system one day, and is really the Anglo-Saxon type of Parliamentary Government suitable to an Eastern people? Is this country ready to have some sort of representative government? I personally have my doubts as to the 3rd question. As to the 4th question [an elected prime minister], my personal opinion is an emphatic NO.[22]

Sayre submitted a constitutional draft in English comprising 12 articles, which enshrined royal absolutism. Article 1 provided that 'sovereignty belong[ed] to the King'. The King concentrated all legislative and executive powers in his hands,[23] and appointed judges (Article 10).[24] Sayre's draft also favoured an extremely rigid Constitution.[25]

[18] In 1912, the government uncovered a royal conspiracy to overthrow King Rama VI. Young army officers planned to assassinate the King, disliked for his taste of caning and bohemian lifestyle. Prince Chakraphong learnt about the coup preparation, and immediately proceeded to a series of arrests. The coup plot was conducted by several groups with different objectives. Although evidence is scarce, it seems that one particularly influential group meant to impose a Republic in Siam under the presidency of Prince Ratburi.

[19] Vishnu Khruangam, *Khotmay Rattathammanun*, [Constitutional Law], 3 ed (Bangkok: Nittibanakarn 1987) at 187.

[20] King Prajadhipok, *Problems of Siam, Memorandum to Dr Sayre*, 23 Jul 1926, quoted in Benjamin A Batson, *Siam's Political Future* (Ithaca: Cornell University Press, 1976) at 14–20 [hereinafter 'Sayre's Memo'].

[21] Ibid, at15.

[22] Ibid.

[23] Art 11 stated: 'legislative power is vested in the King', Art 3: 'the prime minister is responsible for the implementation of the general policies of the government according to the Royal will'. The King appointed the Prime Minister who was responsible before Him (Art 2); ministers were high-ranking officials from each ministry (Arts 4 and 5).

[24] Sayre's Memo (n 20), at 23–24. The constitutional draft provided for the establishment of a consultative organ (*aphiratmontri*) appointed by the King, and composed of five members (Art 7).

[25] The draft provided that constitutional revision had to be approved by three quarters of the King's advisor body (*khonmontrisapha*) (Art 12).

The second constitutional draft, written by Raymond Bartlett Stevens (1872–1942) – who had been appointed the King's Foreign Affairs Advisor in 1926 – and his secretary Phraya Sriwisanvaja in March 1932,[26] was called 'An outline of changes in the form of government'. It was no more liberal than its predecessor. It proposed the creation of a consultative organ, (*aphirattamontrisapha)* appointed by the King (Article 1), and a Prime Minister also appointed by the King (Article 2), a legislative Assembly elected or appointed by the King (Articles 6 & 7). The constitutional draft was very short, and did not specify the rules of monarchical succession nor the modes of constitutional revision.[27] Its authors thought that it was too early to grant a Constitution to the Thai people.[28]

Finally, it seems that the King had planned to grant a Constitution to its subjects on 6 April 1932, the anniversary of the foundation of the Chakri dynasty,[29] but he cancelled his plans due to his advisers' opposition.[30] Details are unknown, but it is likely that Prajadhipok's project aimed to institutionalise rather than limit the King's powers and did not provide for a Parliament.[31] Thus, in the early twentieth century, Siam was an absolute monarchy[32] and, as such, an anomaly, especially since it had joined the League of Nations.

Meanwhile, Siamese elites were conscious of the danger represented by the spread of revolutions in continental Europe and China.[33] This awareness partly explains why Siamese students were sent mostly to England, where revolutionary ideas were less radical than on the continent. However, as the needs of the expanding bureaucracy grew, royal elites progressively sent students to further their education in 'revolutionary' countries, such as France and the US. The young Siamese educated class, returning from abroad, started to demand the enactment of a Constitution.[34]

In his autobiography, King Prajadhipok's advisor Francis B. Sayre wrote:

> Students returning from England or France or America often were unhappy and disturbed, with half-baked ideas about democracy and liberty; they wanted Siam to adopt Western forms almost overnight, as if these were but outward garments. Many

[26] Vishnu Khruangam (n 19), at 187.

[27] Ibid, at 191.

[28] Ibid, at 192.

[29] The Chakri dynasty had been founded in Siam in 1782. This would thus have been the 150th anniversary of the Dynasty.

[30] His advisors in the *aphirattamontrisapha* opposed the move. See Vishnu Khruangam (n 19), at 191.

[31] Nattapol Chaiching, *Kho Fanfai nai Fan an leuacheua* [*I would like to dream the impossible dream*] (Bangkok: Fa Diaw Kan, 2013) at 10. Baker and Phongpaichit (n 17) at 111.

[32] In 1927, the King set up a commission tasked to examine the possibility of creating a representative organ. But he rejected the idea of a Parliament and chose to create a committee of advisors (*khammakan ongkamontri*) composed of four members. Vishnu Khruangnam (n 19), at 254.

[33] During the first two decades of the twentieth century, a worldwide wave of revolutions had overthrown so-called enlightened monarchies: China (1911), Russia (1917), Austria (1917), Germany (1918), Turkey (1921), and Greece (1922).

[34] Vishnu Khruangnam (n 19), at 193.

> felt that Siamese culture was outdated, and their minds seethed with modern, Western ideas, often superficial and misunderstood. One of their outspoken demands was for a Parliament and a modern Constitution.[35]

Among the first generation of students sent to France were Pridi Banomyong (1900–1983), who studied law at the University of Paris and Plaek Phibun Songkhram (1897–1964), student at the military academy of Fontainebleau.[36] In 1927, together with five other friends, they planned, from a Parisian hotel room, the overthrow of the absolute monarchy in Siam.[37] They returned to Siam to become civil servants: Pridi a sa judge and Phibun as a military officer. Pridi became the first Siamese to start teaching administrative law at the law school of the Ministry of Justice. Although the teaching of constitutional law was forbidden, he managed to insert a few notions of constitutional law into his course.[38]

In 1931, he published the first administrative law handbook,[39] in which he established a link between democracy and administrative law. The influence of French constitutional thought on Pridi's thinking was obvious. To him, democracy relied on the existence of human rights whose core pillars were freedom, equality and fraternity[40], while resistance to oppression was an inalienable right, inherent in the very idea of a constitution.[41] Pridi's classes educated young elites in the revolutionary ideas of constitutional law and democracy, much to the King's disapproval. As Pridi recalls:

> The Ministry of Justice appointed me to teach administrative law, a new teaching subject that was recently added to the curriculum of the Law School. I took this opportunity to grow my students' interest in the concept of democracy and economic questions, the very basis of society. As for the Constitution as supreme framework of society and the nature of my teachings, King Prajadhipok heard that I was indoctrinating the law students. King Prajadhipok ordered to the Ministry of Justice Chief to inquire about the nature of my teachings. The head of the Ministry came to interrogate me and warned me to be careful.[42]

Less than a year after the Ministry of Justice Chief warned him, Pridi participated in the overthrow of the absolute monarchy. He was helped by his comrade from France, Phibun, as well as about a hundred civil and military officers. They had all been educated abroad, and felt frustrated by their slow

[35] Francis B. Sayre, quoted in Batson (n 20), at 10.

[36] Nakharin Mektrairat, *Kan Patiwat Siam 2475 [The Siamese Revolution of 1932]* (Bangkok: Fa Diaw Kan, 2010) at 208.

[37] They included two other students at French military academies, a science student, a diplomat at the Siamese Embassy in Paris, and a London barrister.

[38] Nakharin Mekrairat (n 36), at 209.

[39] Noranit Settabutr, *Rattathammanun kap kanmuang thai* [*The Constitution and Thai Politics*] (Bangkok: Thammasat University Press, 2007) at 38.

[40] Ibid, at 37.

[41] Baker & Phongpaichit (n 17), at xiii.

[42] Noranit Settabutr (n 39), at 36.

career advancement compared to members of the royal family. Within a few hours, they seized power, took key members of the royal family and royal guard hostage. Two days later, the King signed an amnesty law for the members of the People's Committee, and stated:

> We recognize that the People's Committee wished to bring, in order to prevent damages, a few changes in the current government and the Thai nation, and to develop the country so that it can be in the future equal to the other countries. The People's Committee seized power in order to establish a Constitution; and asked us to accept to reign on Siam according to the Constitution; ... in reality, to reign according to the Constitution was something we already had in mind; the Action of the People's Committee was fair and is in line with our own preferences[43].

The next day, on 27 June 1932, the King promulgated a new Constitution, as drafted by Pridi. However, he added the word 'temporary' on top of the imposed charter to give himself time to re-negotiate a new text.[44] The People's Committee agreed and decided to ease tensions with the King by choosing a Prime Minister from the royal entourage,[45] while inviting senior officials to form the first government. The fully appointed 70-member Assembly also comprised 25 members from the old bureaucracy.

B. The Royalist Re-appropriation of the Constitution Drafting Process

According to the wishes of the King, a new Constitution would be drafted to reflect the King's own constitutional ideas. At the opening session of the appointed Parliament on 28 June 1932, Pridi discarded his Constitution as being a 'temporary document drafted in emergency',[46] and encouraged the drafting of a new text. The appointed Parliament nominated a seven-member drafting committee, composed mostly of judges and presided by Prime Minister Manopakorn.[47] Pridi, who acted as secretary-general, was the only member of

[43] 'Phrarachakamnot nirathotsakam nai khraw phlienphleng kanpokkrongphaendin 2475', 26 Jun 1932. Charnvit Kasetsiri (n 3), at 150.

[44] He had written, next to the title, the word 'chuakhraw' (temporary). See Bandit Chanrochanakit, *Chiuprawat rattathammanun haeng rachaanyachakthai 2475 [A Constitutional Biography of the 1932 Thai Kingdom]* (Bangkok, Research Development Fund, 2007) 1.

[45] Phraya Manopakorn Nithithada was born in 1884. He was educated in England and was trained as a lawyer. Later, he worked as a judge and was a former member of the King's Privy Council. His wife was lady-in-waiting to the Queen.

[46] On 28 June 1932, Pridi stated: 'This Constitution is temporary because it has been an emergency drafting. It may contain weaknesses; therefore one must appoint people with knowledge and expertise to scrutinize and revise the [interim] Constitution', Noranit Settabutr (ed.), *Ekkasan kanphicharana rang rattathammanun 2475 (doi saphaphuthen rassadorn chut rek)* [*Documents for the Drafting of the 1932 Constitution (First Legislature of the House of Representatives)*] (Nonthaburi: King Prajadhipok's Institute, 2009). 4.

[47] Members included Phraya Thepwithun, Phraya Manwarachasewi, Phraya Nitisatpaisan, Phraya Pridanribet and Luang Sinadyotharak. See Chanrochanakit (n 8) at 1; and House of Representatives, *Documents for the Drafting of the 1932 Constitution*, ibid, at 4.

the People's Committee. He was also its youngest member and the only person to have been educated in France, the other members had studied in England.[48] Two new members of the Committee, close aides of King Prajadhipok, were later added.[49] King Prajadhipok wished to 'advise' the drafting of the new text as shown in the minutes of his audience on 30 June 1932:

> You can ask for my advice. I have extensively studied foreign constitutions recently. I even have the text of the Chinese Constitution.[50]

Finally, the King not only influenced but dominated the drafting process, as Manopakorn noted at the disclosure of the draft in November 1932:

> During the constitutional drafting process, the committee was in permanent contact with the King, to such an extent that one can say that the King has participated in the drafting of the constitution submitted to him, and he has approved all points. When I mention that he has approved, it is not only that he approved the content submitted to him, but even more, it is the expression of His royal will.[51]

The Assembly, the majority of whose members were from the People's Committee, examined the draft article by article within only four days,[52] and made almost no amendments. On 29 November, following its adoption by the Assembly in a unanimous vote, Manopakorn restated how important the King's influence was on the final wording of the text.

> During the drafting and discussion of the constitution, I have had the opportunity to be in contact with the King and to benefit from his observations and teachings regarding several aspects of the constitution… consequently, the success of this constitution was peaceful and [this success] owes to royal grace… this we will certainly not forget.[53]

Parliamentarians stood up and shouted, 'Long live the King, hurrah'.[54] The second Constitution of the kingdom entered into force on 10 December 1932 and thus erased the memory of the first charter.

[48] Chanrochanakit, ibid.

[49] The two members are Phraya Siriwisanvaja and Phraya Rachawangsan. See Nattapol Chaiching (n 31), at 12, and House of Representatives (n 46) at 4.

[50] Chao Phraya Mahitorn, quoted in Vishnu Varunyou, *Les sources nationales et étrangères du constitutionnalisme thaïlandais depuis 1932: recherche sur l'instabilité constitutionnelle en Thaïlande [National and Foreign Sources of Thai Constitutionalism since 1932: a research on constitutional instability in Thailand]*, PhD dissertation, Public Law, Paris II, 1987, at 124.

[51] House of Representatives (n 46), at 17. See Chanrochanakit (n 8) at 2.

[52] It took place between 25–29 November 1932. On 29 November, members of the Assembly unanimously adopted the text. The whole process was very short, because the promulgation of the Constitution was scheduled to take place on 10 December. The date had been chosen by astrologers. On 25 November 1932, the president of the constitution-drafting committee asked parliamentarians to respect time constraints '[There is one that I would like to highlight before this Assembly; this Constitution has to be ready as soon as possible; because the ceremony is planned for 10 December. The royal astrologer considered that this day was auspicious; after the King was informed, he asked that [this constitution] be promulgated on this very day]'. House of Representatives (n 45), at 16.

[53] 29 November 1932, Assembly minutes 42/2475, House of Representatives (n 46) at 191.

[54] Ibid.

The two texts of 1932 were fundamentally different. The June 1932 Constitution had 39 articles drafted by Pridi. Devoid of a preamble, it proclaimed the people's sovereignty in Article 1. It created a 'régime of assembly', in which the executive, a sort of parliamentary committee, could not dissolve the unique chamber. It provided for a transitory period: during the first phase, Parliament was to be fully appointed by the People's Committee, then, during the second phase, half the assembly would be replaced by elections, and finally, whenever the Thai population would have reached sufficient levels of primary schooling, the entire assembly would be elected (Article 10).[55] The text proclaimed constitutional supremacy (Article 31) without specifying any specific mode of constitutional revision or organ dedicated to the interpretation of the Constitution. The King's powers were severely curtailed, and there would be an organ dedicated to the interpretation of the Constitution. The King was neither sacred nor inviolable and could be 'tried' by the Assembly (Article 6).

The December 1932 Constitution was much longer, and resembled in large parts the text of June: it proclaimed the people's sovereignty, provided for a unicameral assembly composed of both elected and appointed members according to similar transitory provisions. However, it changed the system from a regime of assembly to that of a parliamentary system. The King acquired the ability to dissolve Parliament (subject to countersignature by the Prime Minister) and the Assembly could dismiss the Prime Minister following a no-confidence vote. It clearly established constitutional supremacy (Article 61), and the Assembly was granted exclusive powers of interpretation over constitutional dispositions (Article 62). Finally, it laid down specific modes of constitutional revision (Article 63). Some of the King's powers were restored, although the countersignature requirement persisted. Significantly, it made the King both sacred and inviolable; the Assembly no longer had power to put him on trial (Article 3).

In the interim June Constitution, the power of the People's Committee was reinforced at the expense of the King in fields traditionally reserved to the monarch such as the right to pardon (Article 30) or the conduct of international relations (Article 36). The King regained both symbolic powers in the permanent December Constitution: right to pardon (Article 55), to declare war and sign treaties (Article 54) as well as others, such as being the Upholder of Buddhism (Article 4) and the Commander of the Army (Article 5).

In both Constitutions, royal veto was suspensive, but only for seven days in June (Article 8) while it became 45 days in December (Article 39). Also, the

[55] The Constitution put in place a gradual process leading to the implementation of general elections within 10 years. During a first period, the 70 parliamentarians had to be appointed by the People's Committee. After six months, each province would vote for a representative, and the elected representative would become a member of Parliament, so that there are as many parliamentarians appointed as elected. When half the population would have reached a sufficient level of education, namely the completion of primary schooling, or within ten years, if the afore-mentioned condition was not achieved, then all parliamentarians would be elected (Art 10).

December text granted the King the right to declare martial law (Article 53), as well as special powers in times of emergency:

> Article 52
>
> When a situation of emergency does not allow the convening of parliament, the King can promulgate decrees having legislative value (*phrarachakamnot*). These decrees will be submitted for approval to the next session of parliament; if decrees are approved they will become laws; if they are not, they will be void, but without retroactive effect.

Finally, there were notable differences between both texts concerning the regency. The interim Constitution gave the People's Committee the prerogative to act directly as regent in case of the King's incapacity (Article 5), while the permanent Constitution returned this power to the King (Article 10).

Thus, the permanent Constitution dramatically increased the King's power at the expense of the People's Committee. Even so, members of the permanent constitution-drafting committee denied that their draft was much different from the June version:

> A first glance at the Constitution could give the impression that it is considerably different from the interim constitution. I would like, however, to affirm that there is no difference regarding fundamental principles. Like the interim text, the new project adopts the system of constitutional monarchy. We chose, nevertheless, a different form, and we have made a couple of modifications. In order to make these changes, the committee has studied with the greatest care the constitutions of other countries and adapted some of their dispositions to the needs of our country.[56]

The royalist drafters of the December 1932 text emphasised continuity over change, as they needed the support of the mostly revolutionary Assembly to pass the draft. But a closer examination of constitution-drafting minutes indicates that both texts drew on very different sources and inspirations and were informed by competing constitutional ideas.

II. COMPETING UNDERSTANDINGS OF THE CONSTITUTION

Pridi's June text belongs to the tradition of revolutionary constitutions, marked by the revolutionary models of France, China and Russia, while the December 1932 text, drafted under the supervision of the King and his entourage, subscribed to the tradition of a granted constitution inspired by Imperial Japan but under the disguise of a borrowing of Westminster-style parliamentary democracy. The textual compromise of 1932 proclaimed both popular and royal sovereignty, a contradiction that led to constitutional crises and eventually to the abdication of the King.

[56] 16 November 1932; House of Representatives (n 46) at 17.

A. Antagonistic Foreign Models: Socialist Revolutionary versus Conservative Modernisation Constitutions

The drafters of the 1932 Constitutions drew their inspiration from constitutions in force at the time of drafting, in particular those which had acquired a certain level of international prestige. The revolutionaries of June 1932 had taken their inspiration from the Soviet, French and Chinese models.[57] Unicameralism was a particularly salient feature of socialist revolutionary constitutions, such as the 1793 French Constitution, the 1912 Chinese Constitution and the 1918 Russian Constitution. The Soviet inspiration was obvious in the choice of terms used: in Pridi's text, the government was called the 'people's committee' (*khanakamakan rassadorn*), the ministers 'people's commissars' (*kamakan rassadorn*), the lower house the 'assembly of people's representatives' (*sapha phuthen rassadorn*). The word for 'people', *rassadorn*, was also indicative of an intention to break with the past. Its use was associated with early twentieth century radical intellectuals,[58] and referred to commoners, *phrai*, while excluding noblemen and members of the royalty. It had been specifically chosen by the 24 June revolutionaries for their group, the People's Committee (*khana rassadorn*).

The interim Constitution proclaims that sovereignty is exercised through four organs: (a) the King; (b) the People's Assembly; (c) the People's Committee; and (d) the courts (Article 2). This peculiar wording reproduces the terms of the revolutionary 1912 Chinese Constitution, especially its Articles 2 and 4.[59] The existence of a transitory period, during which members of the Assembly were to be appointed before being progressively replaced by elected members owes to the constitutional practice of Imperial China from 1908 onwards[60] and that of the Republic of China from 1912 onwards.[61]

The December 1932 Constitution had other sources of inspiration, namely the 1889 Meiji Constitution and a misunderstood 'British Constitution'. The first

[57] The French, Soviet and Chinese revolutions were radical revolutions, held in high esteem by socialist-leaning Pridi Panomyong in the early 20th century, as can be drawn from his biography *Ma vie mouvementée et mes 21 ans d'exil en Chine populaire* [*My turbulent life and my 21 years of exile in China*] (Paris: UNESCO & Bangkok Post, 1972). See also Theda Skocpol, *States and Social Revolutions: A Comparative Analysis of France, Russia, and China* (New York: Cambridge University Press 1979).

[58] Nakharin Mekrairat (n 36), at 222.

[59] Art 2 'The sovereignty of the Chinese Republic is vested in the people' and Art 4 'The sovereignty of the Chinese Republic is exercised by the Advisory Council, the Provisional President, the Cabinet and the Judiciary'.

[60] During the summer of 1908, the Chinese Empire initiated the creation of a constitutional monarchy and adopted a nine-year plan to prepare the adoption of a Constitution. The plan entailed the progressive set up of representative institutions at several levels: local, provincial and national. The national Parliament, the 'Guohui', would also be in charge of drafting a constitution. On 27 August 1908, an imperial edict, 'Xianfa Dagan', 'General Principles of Constitutional Government' was issued. It enshrined imperial sovereignty, on the Meiji's model. In 1911, the 'nineteen articles' came to detail the 'Xianfa Dagan'.

[61] The 1912 Constitution is called 'interim Constitution'. It plans the election of an assembly in charge of drafting the new 'Constitution of the Chinese Republic' (Arts 53 and 54).

handbook of comparative constitutional law ever written in Siam was published straight after the June Revolution, and before the drafting of the December text.[62] Authored by a member of the extended royal family,[63] it analysed and compared the following Constitutions: Russian (1918), Chinese (1928), Turkish (1924), Italian (1848), French (1875), American (1787), Japanese (1889), and British. The author decided to focus more specifically on two case studies: the Meiji Constitution, entirely translated,[64] and the British 'constitution', analysed at greater length.[65]

At first glance, the 10 December Constitution created a Westminster-style parliamentary regime, with a flexible separation of powers, a Prime Minister responsible to the lower house, and appointed members of Parliament. However, the December text was a copy-and-paste version of the Japanese imperial Constitution. Indeed, with the exception of the last title, the structure of the Siamese Constitution reproduces exactly the Meiji text.[66] Also, the same legitimising discourse was used in the Japanese and Siamese texts: the granting of the Constitution was a royal decision taken in consideration of the necessity to modernise ('to civilise') the country.[67] Third, the word chosen for 'the King's sacredness'[68] was a direct Thai translation of the Meiji text.[69] The exact same wording was also used to refer to the 'exercise' of sovereignty, distinguished from the 'ownership' of sovereignty: 'sovereignty is exerted by the King according to the provisions of the Constitution.'[70] Laws, acts and rulings are rendered in the name of the King, and laws and acts are countersigned by ministers.[71] More peculiarly, the Siamese King, like the Japanese Emperor, retained special powers in times of crisis (Articles 52 and 8 respectively). The complicated wording of the

[62] Chakpanisrisilvisuth, known as Visuth Krairik, *Khamathibai thammanun pokkrong phaendin siam priepthiep kap prathet thangthang* [Handbook of the Constitution of the Land Compared with various countries] (Bangkok: Siam Bangkit, 1932).

[63] Chakpanisrisilvisuth (1903–1958) was a son of Prince Mahithon, known as Lo Krairik, one of Rama VII's Privy Councillors. An Oxford graduate, he was a judge at the Ministry of Justice.

[64] Ibid, at 112–126.

[65] The references section is filled with books about British constitutional law, most notably Walter Bagehot's *The English Constitution*; and AV Dicey's *Law of the Constitution*.

[66] In the Meiji Constitution, comprising 76 articles, sections are as follows: the Emperor (s 1), rights and duties (s 2), imperial diet (s 3), ministers and Privy Council (s 4), judicial institutions (s 5), finances (s 6), additional rules concerning constitutional revision (s 7). In the 10 December Constitution, composed of 68 articles, sections are ordered as follows: the monarchy (s 1), rights and duties (s 2), the House of Representatives (s 3), the government (s 4), the courts (s 5), constitutional revision (s 6) and the promulgation of the Constitution (s 7).

[67] The Meiji's Constitution reads: 'In consideration of the progressive tendency of the course of human affairs and in parallel with the advance of civilization, We deem it expedient, in order to give clearness and distinctness to the instructions bequeathed by the Imperial Founder of Our House and by Our other Imperial Ancestors, to establish fundamental laws formulated into express provisions of law'.

[68] Art 3, Meiji's Constitution.

[69] Assembly minutes 35/2475, 25 November 1932, quoted in House of Representatives, *Documents*...31.

[70] Art 4, Meiji's Constitution.

[71] Art 55, Meiji's Constitution, Art 57, 10 December 1932 Constitution.

Siamese article matches perfectly the Meiji text.[72] Fifth, the catalogue of rights, liberties and duties of the Siamese people drew heavily on the Meiji version. For instance, the same terms are used for freedom of religion, which was to be exerted 'within the limits of respect of peace and order and in a manner non incompatible with the duties of citizens /subjects'.[73]

There were nevertheless a couple of formal differences between the Meiji text and the December 1932 Constitution. First, unlike the Meiji model, Siam did choose unicameralism. However, this was more formal than substantial since the unicameral structure of the Siamese Parliament hid a hybrid bicameralism: the Parliament was made up of both elected and appointed parliamentarians, according to the transitory provisions.[74] Second, if the Siamese text read 'the King exerts legislative power with the advice and consent of the Assembly', the Japanese corresponding article only stated 'the Emperor exerts legislative power with the consent of the Assembly'. However, an examination of parliamentary debates show that this article was drafted with the erroneous belief that it reproduced the wording of the Japanese Constitution.[75]

The royalists also made semantic changes to the interim Constitution. They replaced the radical word *rassadorn* with the more conservative *prachachon*. All positions were then renamed: Cabinet, from *kamakan rassadorn* to *rattamontri*, and Prime Minister from *prathan khan kamakan rassadorn* to *nayok rattamontri*. The changes were an express order from the King.[76] As Pridi stated, the Socialist influence had to be expunged entirely:

> The president of the subcommittee says that the King is against the use of this word [rassadorn], as it would make people believe that I am trying to import and spread principles from foreign countries.[77]

Another important significant change was the use of royal vocabulary to refer to the King and King's actions, even though the interim Constitution was written

[72] Art 8, Meiji's Constitution: 'The emperor, in consequence of an urgent necessity to maintain public safety or to avert public calamities, issues, when the Imperial Diet is not Sitting, imperial ordinances in the place of law. Such imperial ordinances are to be laid before the Imperial Diet at its next session, and when the Diet does not approve the said ordinances, the government shall declare them invalid for the future'.

[73] Art 13, 10 December 1932 Constitution, reads: 'Everyone has the right to freedom of religion or belief and to practice their cult in accordance with their beliefs when such practices are not incompatible with their duty as citizen and do not hamper order, peace or public morals'. Art 28, Meiji's Constitution, reads: 'Japanese subjects shall, within limits not prejudicial to peace and order, and not antagonistic to their duties as subjects, enjoy freedom of religious belief'.

[74] The mode of election was indirect suffrage, as provided for in Revolutionary France, according to the 1791 Constitution.

[75] Phraya Manwarachasewi, member of the Constitution-drafting assembly, declared 'In Japan's Constitution, Article 5 related to legislative power states that the King exerts his legislative power by the advice and with the consent of parliament'. The word 'parliament' was a transliteration of the English word 'parliament', what seems to show some confusion between the British and Japanese constitutional models. Assembly minutes 35/2475, 25 November 1932, House of Representatives (n 46), at 41.

[76] Session 34/2475 and 41/2475. 28 members voted in favour of a name change, seven opposed it and 24 abstained. Noranit Settabutr (n 39), at 97.

[77] Noranit Settabutr, ibid, at 96.

in plain language. The King was no longer referred to as *kasat* (King) but as *phramahakasat* (His Excellency the King). The permanent Constitution also opened with the King's full name, over 13 lines of text. The most effective change was, however, not in the constitutional framework laid out by the Constitution, or in the language used, but in its underlying principle of legitimacy, its 'myth of origin' as told in the Preamble.

B. Royal Sovereignty versus Popular Sovereignty

The December 1932 preamble, written by Palace officials,[78] adopted the form of a granted Constitution, a mode of constitutional founding commonly used by resilient absolute monarchies. The 1889 Meiji Constitution, the 1906 Russian Constitution, the 1908 Chinese Constitution, and Meiji's model, the 1848 Prussian Constitution, were all 'granted' Constitutions. These authoritarian texts aimed to anticipate revolutionary movements by setting up assemblies while maintaining the power of the monarch, with the monarch becoming the source of the Constitution – as such, the original constituent.[79] The Siamese preamble subscribed to this tradition and read:

> The King, having considered the moment to graciously give to His civil servants and to the people of His Majesty the possibility to [participate] in the development of the country, has granted (*phrarachathan*) a constitution to Siam according to His will on 27 June 1932.[80]

It is notable that civil servants are distinguished from the rest of the people, a practice inherited from the absolute monarchy and in clear breach with the spirit of the June Constitution. This restoration of the constitutionally enshrined classification of class was also reflected in the disposition that princes were banned from politics to preserve the dignity of members of the royal family – princes being 'above' politics (Article 11).[81] The 27 June 1932 introductory lines told a rather different story:

> By order of King Prajadhipok, following the People's Committee request that the King be placed under the authority of the Constitution for the good of the country,

[78] Statement by Constitution-drafting Committee Manopakorn, 29 Nov 1932. Suphot Dantranakul, *Prawat Ratthathammanun [Constitutional history]* (Nonthaburi: Foundation for the Promotion of Social Sciences and Humanities, 2007) at 23.

[79] Legal theory pertaining to 'granted constitutions' has been developed in 19th and early 20th century France (*charte octroyée*) and Germany, but does not, to the author's knowledge, have been the subject of extensive English-language studies. See works by Paul Bastid for France and Carl Schmitt for Germany.

[80] *Ibid.*

[81] The rationale was that princes had to be 'above politics'. Pridi had proposed the abolition of nobility ranks to the Constitution-drafting Committee, which rejected it. However, Art 12 states that ranks of nobility do not yield any privileges. See Chanrochanakit (n 8) at 7; and Constitution-drafting Committee President, Assembly minutes, 36/2475, 25 November 1932, House of Representatives (n 45), at 53.

> and following the acceptation by the King of demands formulated by the People's Committee, the Constitution is promulgated.[82]

The permanent Constitution preamble highlighted at length the role of the King in granting the Constitution, in line with the '150 years of absolute monarchy under the principles of the ten virtues of a righteous King'.[83] It erased the 1932 revolution by emphasising continuity between the absolute and constitutional monarchy, a continuity embodied in the person of King Prajadhipok. In a granted constitution, constituent power and sovereignty lay with the King as the source of the Constitution. However, the permanent constitution does not enshrine royal sovereignty as clearly as the Meiji Constitution which reads:

> The Emperor is the head of the Empire, combining in Himself the rights of sovereignty, and exercises them, according to the provisions of the present Constitution.[84]

Instead, the permanent Constitution stated that 'sovereignty *emanates* from the people and the King exerts it according the provision of the constitution' *through* the Parliament, government and courts. This is in marked contrast to the wording of the interim charter which stipulates that 'sovereignty belongs to the people and is exercised *by* the King, the People's Assembly, the People's Committee and the Courts'.[85] Both texts distinguished between the *ownership* of sovereignty and the *exercise* of sovereignty. While the interim Constitution gave both, entirely or partly, to the people, the permanent Constitution gave only part of the ownership of sovereignty to the people, as an 'emanation'. Manopakorn, president of the drafting committee, explained before the Assembly:

> In reality, the first part of this article [on sovereignty] is a reaffirmation of our ancient traditions. Indeed, if we open old books, we will notice that the name of the King says he is an elected King; the King ascends the throne upon being invited by the people.[86]

The doctrinal construction is as follows: the King is 'elected' by the people; therefore, people's sovereignty is embodied in the King's sovereignty.[87] The invocation of royal tradition once again justified the theory of the granted constitution. Likewise, royal traditions were invoked to dismiss calls for a constitutional requirement to have the King swear a royal oath to uphold the Constitution. Such requirement would have contradicted the theory of the granted constitution, as it would imply that the King was not the source of the constitution. This question was one of the most controversial during discussions on the

[82] Preamble of the 27 June 1932 Constitution.

[83] Preamble of the 10 December 1932 Constitution.

[84] Art 4, Meiji Constitution.

[85] Words for 'sovereignty' have fluctuated. The interim constitution referred to 'supreme power' (*amnat sung sut*) while the permanent one to 'sovereignty' (*amnatipatai)*.

[86] Ibid, at 362, quoted in Nattapol Chaiching (n 31), at 15.

[87] Nattapol Chaiching, ibid, at 11–17.

constitutional draft. When a member of the People's Committee raised the issue, Manopakorn responded by invoking traditional custom according to which the King swears a royal oath when ascending the throne – and that this suffices to ensure that the King reigns with virtue, which in turn, ensures that the King upholds constitutional principles.[88] Another member of the Committee explained:

> The King swears an oath to representations of Buddhist divinities. Therefore, the [constitutional] text remains silent [on the issue of the oath to the Constitution].[89]

Parliamentarians voted 48–7 against enshrining a royal oath in the Constitution in the constitutional draft, arguing that such an oath was part of customary law.[90] Pridi himself thought that it was unnecessary to write the royal oath into the Constitution, as it was a constitutional convention.[91]

The issue of granted constitution/sovereignty is important because it lays the foundational principles within which the ambiguities of the constitutional text are to be interpreted. The interim Constitution had clearly established the pre-eminence of the People's Committee at the expense of the King in line with the proclamation of popular sovereignty. The power structure created by the 10 December 1932 text was more difficult to decipher, especially since the King had, according to Article 2, exclusive exercise of sovereignty. Royal powers could then be subject to either a royalist or a revolutionary interpretation: a suspensive veto could be read as either absolute (royalist) or non-existent (People's Committee), and emergency powers as empowering either the King (royalist) or the government (People's Committee) at the expense of the Assembly.

Textual ambiguity clouded all discussions of the permanent constitutional draft. On emergency powers, members of the drafting committee referred to the need to have emergency laws promulgated by 'the King' *and* 'the People's Committee'.

> [We have] drafted [this article] to facilitate the work of the administration; so that it becomes possible to pass laws. The word *phrarachakamnot* in this article refers to the law promulgated by the People's Committee and the King without prior vote of the assembly (…) and these dispositions exist in constitutions of foreign countries.[92]

Yet, the *phrarachakamnot* of Article 52 can be understood in different ways, depending on which foreign model is taken as reference. If it was interpreted

[88] Committee President, Assembly minutes, 36/2475, 25 November 1932, House of Representatives (n 46), at 48.
[89] Phraya Rachawangsan, Assembly minutes, ibid.
[90] Ibid at 50.
[91] Chanrochanakit (n 8) at 5.
[92] Committee President, Assembly minutes, 39/2475, 27 November 1932, House of Representatives (n 45), at 145.

along the lines of the Meiji Constitution, then Article 52 gives the King the means to exert legislative and executive power,[93] as in early twentieth-century Siam and Japan, the parliamentary session lasted only a few months. The *phrarachakamnot* can also be understood as a French-type of decree known as *ordonnance*.[94] In this case, the government, not the King, is empowered to pass laws instead of the Parliament.

This ambiguity translated into a very chaotic implementation of the text[95] – the King adopted a monarchical interpretation of the Constitution, determined to exercise his royal veto and emergency powers. The King also considered that he had the right to 'appoint members of parliament on the advice of the government', and had a personal discretion in the appointment of parliamentarians. Prime Minister Manopakorn had apparently accepted such an interpretation.[96] The King also interpreted his suspensive veto as being absolute. He used it several times, requesting vetoed drafts to be entirely withdrawn.[97] He also meant to use Article 52 on emergency powers, or rather, its spirit, with discretion.

In April 1933, he pronounced the adjournment *sine die* of Parliament, the appointment of a new government and the suspension of parts of the Constitution. The act of parliamentary dissolution[98] stated that the decision was the King's own, in light of the emergency caused by the 'calamity' of the economic plan of Pridi.[99] As the country had no Parliament, the King continued to promulgate laws countersigned by the Prime Minister, such as the anti-communist law in 1933. On 20 June 1933, Manopakorn then faced a counter-coup led by Pahonyothin, a member of the People's Committee.

[93] Art 8. 'The Emperor, in consequence of an urgent necessity to maintain public safety or to avert public calamities, issues, when the Imperial Diet is not sitting, Imperial ordinances in the place of law. (2) Such Imperial Ordinances are to be laid before the Imperial Diet at its next session, and when the Diet does not approve the said Ordinances, the Government shall declare them to be invalid for the future.'

[94] The ordonnance of the French Fifth Republic or the décret-loi of the French Third Republic is an authorisation, given by Parliament to the government for a limited period, to take measures by Ordinance that are normally the preserve of statute law.

[95] Nattapol Chaiching (n 30), at 18–19; Suttachai Yimprasert, *Prawatisat phrachatipatai thai [A History of Thai Democracy]* (Bangkok: P. Press, 2008) 33–34; and Chanrochanakit (n 8), at 13.

[96] Nattapol Chaiching (n 31), at 35 & 143.

[97] He used his veto against a law giving the courts the power to hand down the death penalty, as he was the only person in the Kingdom to possess this power of death over his subjects. He was to remain the 'Lord of Life and Death [of his subjects]' (*chao chiwit*). Walter Vella, *The Impact of the West on Government in Thailand* (Los Angeles: University of California Press 1955) at 370. He also opposed a law on succession tax. See also, Nattapol Chaiching, ibid, at 34–35.

[98] It is not the Article 52 *phrarachakamnot* but rather the *phrarachakrisdika* (decree).

[99] In 1933, Pridi proposed a socialist economic plan. The members of the Assembly, including members of the People's Committee, split on Pridi's economic plan. King Prajadhipok and the Prime Minister, Phraya Manopakon, were fiercely hostile to the plan, and adjourned the Assembly sine die; government members in favour of Pridi were dismissed and Pridi went into exile. A new government was appointed. See Nattapol Chaiching (n 31) at 19. The act on the dissolution of Parliament and appointment of a new government passed on 1 April 1933 starts with the following words: 'doy thi song phrarachadamri hen wa', 'According to Royal Will'. This unusual formula hints at a royal decision.

After he was discredited for supporting a failed counter-revolution,[100] King Prajadhipok travelled to Great Britain for eye surgery. In 1935, he requested, in a telegram sent to the government, that several changes be made to the Constitution, especially concerning the royal veto. The text of 10 December had restored many royal prerogatives, yet it had not fully satisfied King Prajadhipok. He demanded that a majority of three-quarters replace the simple majority needed by Parliament to overrule a royal veto (Article 39),[101] and that the Parliament be automatically self-dissolved following the use of a royal veto.[102] The People's Committee rejected these demands, and King Prajadhipok abdicated His abdication telegram read:

> I am disposed to give the powers I have formally exerted to the people in its entirety, but I am not ready to give them back to an individual or group of individuals so that they can be used in an autocratic manner without preoccupation for the voice of the people.[103]

The Royalists and their royalist interpretation of the 1932 text were thus marginalised by the following decade of regency.[104] Prajadhipok's successor, Ananda Mahidol, was a young and unknown man living in Switzerland, who did not show any interest in the Crown let alone power intrigues.

III. EPILOGUE: A CULT OF THE 1932 CONSTITUTION AS SACRED ROYAL OCTROY

The 10 December 1932 Constitution remains to date the most durable Constitution of Siamese-Thai constitutional history. It provided for a parliamentary

[100] In October 1933, a pro-royalist rebellion broke out. Prince Bowaradet led a fraction of the army to the capital city and several government members were captured. However, after a few days of skirmishes, the pro-government forces, under the leadership of Phibun Songkhram, managed to defeat the rebels. The role of King Prajadhipok during this rebellion was controversial. He learnt about the rebellion while he was in his Hua Hin Palace. He then fled with the Queen to the Malay frontier after sending a telegram expressing sorrow for the outburst of violence. He would also have planned to execute members of the People's Committee on 24 June 1933. See Nattapol Chaiching (n 31), at 21–22.

[101] In the same document, the King requested the government to pardon political prisoners, pay compensation to civil servants dismissed because of their political allegiances, cancel trials against civil servants, and to commit not to decrease the army's budget. He also asked to choose appointed parliamentarians himself. Vishnu Khruangam (n 19), at 198.

[102] The Prime Minister Pahonyothin, rejected this disposition: 'The automatic dissolution of parliament following a royal veto is not compatible with a democratic constitutional system' quoted in Suphot Dantranakul, *Prawat Rattathammanun*. 36.

[103] Noranit Settabutr (n 39), at 130; and David Wyatt, *A Short History of Thailand* (New Haven: Yale University Press, 2003) at 238.

[104] Prajadhipok had abdicated without a successor. His nephew, Prince Ananda Mahidol, grandson of Chulalongkorn, who was ten years old at the time and lived in Switzerland, was unanimously chosen by the House of Representatives. This choice offered many advantages: the People's Committee could have a free hand over government, given both the young age and the absence of the new King. Noranit Settabutr (n 38), at 130. The government also chose the members of the regency

monarchy that offered many channels for the King to exercise legislative power, either negatively through the royal veto, or positively with emergency powers. Legislative power is, according to Jean Bodin's seminal definition, 'sovereignty'. The myth of a 'granted constitution', as presented in the preamble, gave royal sovereignty a legitimising force. Yet, there was, from late 1933 onwards, no King to exercise it.

The void left by the disappearance of the figure of the King was filled by the cult of the Constitution, popularly framed as sacred, being a 'king's octroy' (*khong phrarachathan*). Revolutionaries including Pridi Panomyong, who had fought for the recognition of parliamentary sovereignty at the expense of royal sovereignty, nevertheless used the idea of the 'royally granted constitution' to mobilise people throughout the country in its defence. A 'Constitution Association' (*samakhom khana rattathammanun*) presided over by Pridi, and with branches all over the country, organised celebrations and rallies akin to royal ceremonies.[105] Symbolically, constitutional supremacy was replacing royal supremacy, even while drawing its legitimacy from it. A law of 'protection of the constitution' was promulgated in 1933,[106] and another against 'defamation of the constitution' came close to being adopted as well,[107] while the lèse-majesté law protecting the King fell temporarily into oblivion.[108] In 1934, the 10 December became a national holiday and soon supplanted the King's birthday in popularity. Young people could go on romantic dates at Constitution festivals, and admire 'statues' of the Constitution in their provincial halls – a golden 'samutthai', folded book used for Buddhist scriptures, on a two-tier golden tray, used for royal items.[109]

According to some accounts, the regency years were 'undoubtedly the most hopeful years in the Thai constitutional experiment'.[110] Indeed, what is now widely acknowledged as a failed experiment with constitutional democracy contrasts with an assessment of Thailand's constitutional developments in the late 1930s and 1940s, during times of regency. The 1946 Constitution, which

council (Art 10, 10 December 1932 Constitution). Yet two of the three members appointed by the government in 1932 were of princely rank. The regency period lasted more than 10 years. Ananda Mahidol returned to Siam in 1946.

[105] Puli Fuwongcharoen, 'Long live the Rattathammanun', (2018) 52(2) *Modern Asian Studies* 609–644, at 619.

[106] 'Phrarachabanyat chatkan pongkan raksa rattathammanun 2476' The law created a special committee to try people having committed 'acts directed against the constitution or aiming to erode the trust of the people in the constitutional system, including agreements, conspiracies and preparations [aiming toward their realisation]' (Art 3). The offences carried a jail term of 3 to 20 years. It was abrogated by Phibun Songkhram in 1938.

[107] Puli Fuwongcharoen (n 106), at 630.

[108] A trade union leader even sued the King for defamation in 1933. See Somsak Jeemteerasakul on Thawat Ridet's case, available at http://somsakwork.blogspot.com/2006/10/blog-post_26.html [in Thai].

[109] The use of the samutthai aimed to 'make the Constitution look mystical' (*khlang*). It was an idea of King Prajadhipok. Meanwhile, Pridi supervised the overall design of the replicas. Another influential figure in the process of making the Constitution an object of worship was Luang Wichit Wattakan. See Puli Fuwongcharoen (n 106), at 625 and following.

[110] Walter Vella (n 97), at 366.

succeeded the December 1932 text, was not the result of a coup, but of a constitutional revision process undertaken in accordance with the provisions of the 1932 Constitution. As such, it is unique in Thai constitutional history. Drafted under the supervision of Pridi Banomyong, it finally gave Siam its fully elected Parliament. But in 1947, following a royalist-backed military coup, the 1946 Constitution was abrogated and was followed by the drafting of two new charters in 1947 and 1949 respectively. Since then, constitutional texts have followed one after another relentlessly, and political and constitutional instability became the norm.

Eighteen Constitutions have been promulgated since December 1932, but the 10 December remains the only national 'Constitution Day', while the Democracy Monument, in the heart of Bangkok, still represents a 'statue of the 1932 Constitution', an accordion-type golden book on a golden tray, to symbolise both the sacredness of the text and the royal octroy from which it emanated. Today, the genesis of Thai constitutionalism lies at the heart of the historiographical conflict opposing royalist and revolutionaries. To royalists, the events of 24 June 1932 were not a revolution but a 'coup'. In their eyes, the attempt to transplant Western institutions of parliamentary democracy was premature and ill-conceived, and created a path dependency of coups, interim constitutions with amnesties for the coup-makers, and permanent constitutions. To royalists, Thailand's chronic constitutional instability results from the actions of Pridi who would have forcibly railroaded Siam on the path to constitutional democracy even when the Siamese people were not yet ready. Pridi acknowledges, *a posteriori*, his unpreparedness for the consequences:

> In 1925, when we began to organize the nucleus of a revolutionary party in Paris I was only 25 years old. Very young. Too young. Inexperienced. Without experience, I applied theory sometimes dogmatically. I did not take into account the realities in our country. I did not have enough contact with the people. All my knowledge was book knowledge. I did not take into account human elements as much as I should have. In 1932, I was 32 years old. We had a revolution but I was inexperienced. When I had power, I had no experience, but when I had more experience, I had no power.[111]

Pridi's 'original sin' in the aftermath of the 1932 Revolution led to the vicious cycles of coups and constitutions that has plagued Thai constitutional history till today. Yet to revolutionaries, the first coup and the origin of the vicious cycle of Thai politics was the April 1933 dissolution of Parliament by the King and Manopakorn. Royalists argue that there is a fundamental 'impossibility of legal transplants'[112] from the West to Siam. However, the first constitutional text was less inspired by Siam than by China or Russia; while the second owed less to the West than to imperial Japan. During the parliamentary discussion of the 10 December 1932 Constitution, members of the People's Committee were

[111] 'Pridi through a looking glass', interview by Anthony Paul, *Asiaweek*, 4 Jan 1980.

[112] Pierre Legrand, 'The Impossibility of Legal Transplants' (1997) *Maastricht Journal of European and Comparative Law* 111–127.

presented with the British model, while drafters had in reality copied the Meiji model. This confusion allowed royalist and revolutionary forces to reach an agreement.

However, in practice, both forces had different interpretations of each disposition, especially with regards to royal power. Likewise, the political principle on which the Constitution was built – that is, the question of the constituent power – was ambiguous: revolutionary forces considered the people, represented by themselves, to be sovereign and exert constituent power, while royalist forces believed in the theory of the granted constitution, making the King the constituent power and the ultimate sovereign. Consequently, two opposing conceptions of sovereignty coexisted simultaneously – royal sovereignty and parliamentary or popular sovereignty – leading to opposing interpretations of key provisions of the constitution, such as the use and meaning of royal veto.

The founding compromise of Thai constitutionalism can thus be analysed as a dilatory compromise in the Schmittian sense – establishing an unworkable constitution based on contradictory principles of monarchic and popular sovereignty.[113] Until today, Thailand's constitutional politics remains entangled in the questions arising from this unsolved conflict of legitimating principles. The issue of 'granted constitution' versus 'people's revolution' still continues to haunt historiographic and political debates in Thailand.

The promulgation ceremony of the 2017 Constitution of Siam re-enacted the myth of a granted constitution, still referred to in the preamble on the 1932 Constitution's model. The new King, Vajiralongkorn, chose the date of the anniversary of the Chakri dynasty's foundation – the 6 April – to 'octroy' to civil servants and Thai people their twentieth Constitution. He formally 'granted' the *samutthai* Constitution on its golden tray to the civil servants and people. The same month, the bronze plaque commemorating the 24 June 1932 revolution disappeared, to be replaced by a plaque glorifying the Chakri dynasty. Discussion of the plaque incident was criminalised and people were arrested and charged.[114] Indeed, the 24 June 1932 events and its 'interim' constitution remain a very controversial issue in Thai politics, whose academic discussion is subject to harsh prison sentences under the Thai *lese-majeste* law.[115]

[113] Carl Schmitt argues in his *Constitutional Theory* that if a constitution is unilaterally granted by a prince, it rests on the constituent power of the prince. If, for political reasons, it does not adopt the form of octroy and makes it an agreement between the King and the people, then it is a 'dilatory compromise' as long as the prince does not renounce his constituent power. See Carl Schmitt, *Constitutional Theory,* Jeffrey Seitzer (trans) (North Carolina: Duke University Press 2008) at 85–86 & 105.

[114] In April 2017, academic Somsak Jeemterasakul wrote a post on his Facebook page about the 1932 plaque commemorating the Revolution and the 27 June Constitution. Six people who had shared his post were arrested and charged with lese-majeste.

[115] The Thai Lese-Majeste Law is the harshest in the world. It punishes by a prison term of 3 to 15 years any person who insults, defames or threatens the King, the Queen, the Heir or the Regent. In practice, cases of lese-majeste involve prison sentences of up to 60 years. The courts systematically deny bail pending trial, citing security reasons and the gravity of the offence.

Index

Introductory Note

References such as '178–79' indicate (not necessarily continuous) discussion of a topic across a range of pages. Wherever possible in the case of topics with many references, these have either been divided into sub-topics or only the most significant discussions of the topic are listed. Because the entire work is about 'South-East Asia' and 'Constitutions', the use of these terms (and certain others which occur constantly throughout the book) as an entry point has been minimised. Information will be found under the corresponding detailed topics.

abdication, 245, 307, 315
Abell, Anthony, 197–99, 203, 205–7, 209–12
absolute majorities, 270, 274, 289
absolute monarchy
  Brunei, 1, 214, 221
  Cambodia, 281, 291
  Philippines, 28
  Thailand, 297, 300–303, 311–12
absolute power, 203, 220, 278
abstentions, 90–91
accountability, 65–66, 92, 98, 106
activists, 12, 53, 114, 120, 131–33
  former, 126
administration
  British, 114, 123, 127, 174, 193, 199, 202–4, 206
  Brunei, 194–98, 204, 214
  Cambodia, 279
  civil, 27, 195
  colonial, 26, 114, 117–18, 126, 198
  daily, 65
  direct, 133, 259
  French, 259–60
  Indonesia, 65
  Japanese military, 50–51, 53, 56
  of justice, 88, 183, 190, 271
  Laos, 261, 263
  Myanmar, 117–18
  Philippines, 36–37, 40
  Singapore, 186–87, 190
  Thailand, 313
  Timor-Leste, 77, 79, 86, 91–93, 95, 99, 101–2
administrative centralisation, 26
Administrative Committees, 235
administrative powers, 88, 279
advice clause, 197, 199, 205, 207, 213
advisors, 80, 282, 299
  constitutional, 8, 85, 133, 168–69, 266
  French, 263–64, 282
  international, 79, 109
Advisory Council, 58, 165
  Supreme, 57–58
AFPFL (Anti-Fascist People's Freedom League), 123–37
Ahmad Tajuddin, Sultan, 193–94, 201
Albania, 227
alliances, 79, 84, 131
allies, 124–25, 129, 134, 142, 237
American colonial governments, 18, 25, 28
American colonialism, 12, 14, 18, 38
American Governor-General, 27–28, 32–33, 36
Americans, 11–14, 16, 19, 24, 26, 30–31, 34, 38
Amery, Leopold, 123
Ananda Mahidol, 315–16
Angola, 81, 83
Annam, 244–45, 249, 259, 271
annual estimates, 215–16
anti-colonialism, 8, 70, 86, 126, 135, 212, 276
Anti-Fascist People's Freedom League, *see* **AFPFL**
appeals courts
  Singapore, 190
  Timor-Leste, 100–105, 107
armed forces/armies, *see also* **military**
  Indonesia, 65, 68–70
  Laos, 258, 268
  Myanmar, 122–24
  Philippines, 29
  Singapore, 172

Thailand, 306
Timor-Leste, 83, 92, 95–96
Vietnam, 229, 236, 253
arrests, 104, 122, 128–29, 268, 286
ASEAN (Association of Southeast Asian Nations), 1, 191
aspirations
Brunei, 202–3, 205, 207–8, 211, 218, 222
Malaysia, 158
Myanmar, 123–24, 127
Philippines, 13
Associated States, 231, 249–50, 271, 273
Association of Southeast Asian Nations (ASEAN), *see* **ASEAN**
audit, 57–58, 66, 105, 107, 216
August Revolution, 231–33, 236, 242–43, 245, 251–52, 254
Aung San, 112, 114, 122–24, 127–37
Australia, 87, 108, 132, 146–47, 157, 162
authoritarianism, 66, 70, 75, 219
authoritarian regimes, 49–50, 64–71
authority, 10
Brunei, 197, 199–200, 204–5, 211, 215, 221–22
constitutional, 44, 156
executive, 37, 161, 195, 197, 200, 214
Indonesia, 65–66, 68, 70, 72
Malaysia, 140, 148
Myanmar, 114, 117, 127, 129, 131
Philippines, 15, 23, 25–27, 29, 38
Singapore, 163
Thailand, 298, 311
Timor-Leste, 88, 95, 101–2, 105
Vietnam, 232, 234, 247
autonomous state, 134–35
Azahari, Shaikh AM, 208, 211–12, 216

balances, 99, 107–8, 215, 218–19, 256, 258, 262, 266
racial, 184
Bangkok, 258, 263, 266, 270–72, 297, 317
Bảo Đại, 231, 245, 250
bargaining, political, 87, 141
Barker, EW, 162, 190
basic human rights, 63, 73–74
basic law, 49–50, 75, 98, 219
benevolent imperialism, 12–14
Bere, Maternus, 103–5
bicameralism, 33–34, 72, 239, 241, 251
hybrid, 310
bicameral legislatures, *see* **legislatures, bicameral**
bills of rights, 63
Malaysia, 155–56
Philippines, 12, 14, 20–21, 36–38, 44, 47
Timor-Leste, 82, 90–91
Board of Audit, 57–58, 66
Borneo, 53, 195–97, 208, 214
North, 52, 139, 159, 182, 187, 194–96
Boun Oum, Prince, 262, 264, 270, 272
branches
executive, 31, 64, 183, 293–94
judicial, 12, 21, 24, 29, 31, 50, 188
legislative, 31, 71, 135, 164
political, 36–39
British Burma, 113–19, 121, 133
pre-war political factionalism, 116–22
British businesses, 123–24, 127, 129
British Colonial Office, *see* **Colonial Office**
British Commonwealth, 145, 147–48, 152, 156, 158–59, 168, 175, 191–92
British government, 126–27, 129, 169–70, 174, 177, 195, 197–99, 210–12
British India, 113, 116, 132
British Residents, 141, 197–98, 204, 207, 213–14
Brune, Malay Constitutional Committee, 203–6
Brunei, 1, 4, 6, 182, 191–224
1959 constitutional arrangements, 214–16
2004 amendments, 219–21
absolute monarchy, 1, 214, 221
administration, 194–98, 204, 214
advice clause, 197, 199, 205, 207, 213
aftermath of promulgation, 216–19
amendments, 208–10, 215, 218–20, 223–24
appointments, 204, 206, 209, 212–13, 216, 220
aristocracy, 193, 197
aspirations, 202–3, 205, 207–8, 211, 218, 222
beginnings of proposals, 192–98
British government, 195, 197–99, 208, 210–12, 218, 224
citizens, 220
Constitution, 194, 197, 217–19, 224
democracy, 217, 219–20
early draft proposals, 205–14
elections, 209, 213, 215, 220
future, 221–24
governance, 198, 202, 218–19, 221
government, 191, 193, 195, 198–99, 202–4, 208–10, 214, 218–24
legislature, 217–18
legitimacy, 191, 214, 222, 224

parties, 194, 208–9, 211–12, 217
rationale behind making of Constitution, 198–203
religion, 192, 204, 206, 214
self-government, 198, 202, 211–12, 214
sovereignty, 194, 198, 210, 214, 218
treaties, 193, 195, 199–200, 213
Buddhism, 6, 115, 119, 267, 306
budgets, 29, 95, 107–8, 268, 278, 288
Burma, 114, 116–17, 119, 122–23, 125–27, 130, 132–33, 135–37; *see also* **Myanmar**
British, 113–19, 121, 133
Independence Army, 114, 123–24
Lower, 112–13
National Army, 123–24
Northeast, 113
Upper, 112–13, 115
Burmans, 114, 119–20
Burmese, 119, 122–26, 128, 130, 132–33; *see also* **Burmans**
lowland, 114–15, 130
nationalists, 111, 114, 116–17, 119–20, 122–25, 128–29, 132, 135
business interests, 116, 123
businessmen, 16, 120, 132, 144

cabinet members, 33, 54, 221, 291
cabinets, 63, 65, 123, 126, 170, 173, 289, 292–94
cabinet secretaries, 32–33
Cambodia, 8–9, 230, 244–45, 248–49, 259–61, 271, 273, 275–96
absolute monarchy, 281, 291
amendments, 283, 290, 292–96
appointments, 289, 292
autonomy, 277, 279
communists, 275
constitutional provisions, 285–90
Constitution in operation, 293–95
constitution-making, 282–85
courts, 286–87, 290–91, 293–94
elections, 284, 288, 291, 294–96
governance, 285, 291
government, 275, 277–79, 281–82, 284–85, 288–89, 291–95
human rights, 286, 295
kings, 277–83, 285, 287–96
legacy of 1947 Constitution, 295–96
legislature, 280, 289
ministers, 278–80, 282–83, 289, 291–92
National Assembly, 283–85, 288–95
nationalists, 275, 281, 285, 291
parties, 284–85, 289, 294–95
political and legal background, 276–82
political tensions and new realities, 280–82
politics, 284, 291
pre-1947 constitutional arrangements, 279–80
preamble, 282, 285
sovereignty, 277, 290–93, 295–96
Supreme Council of Magistracy, 10, 296
Supreme Council of the Courts, 293–94
treaties, 277–79, 281, 290
candidates, 73, 154, 166–67, 179, 182, 232, 238, 264
capitalism, 41, 75, 225, 233
CAS (civilian affairs service), 122, 124–25, 129
casting vote, 170, 178
Catholic Church, 85–86, 92–93
ceasefires, 233, 236, 238, 244, 250
central government, 25–28, 136, 147–48, 157, 167, 178–79, 187, 189
central Vietnam, 238, 242
Ceylon, 146–47, 154, 156–57
Champasak, 258–60, 262, 272
Chan Htoon, U, 133
Chao Nhouy, 259–60, 262
Chiang Kai-shek, 237, 239, 245–47
Chief Justices, 99, 105, 162–63, 166, 175, 177
Chief Ministers, 143, 167, 170, 198, 260
Chin, 113, 125–26, 130
China, 227, 230–31, 236–40, 242–47, 255–56, 258, 271–72, 307–8
Nationalist, 228, 237, 247
Chinese, 145, 147, 151–53, 164–65, 207, 209, 246–47, 252
Chinese Communists, 233, 244, 246–47
Chinese Constitution, 244, 305, 308, 311
Chinese Nationalist Party, 7, 58, 61
Chinese occupation forces/authorities, 237–39, 243, 247
Chin Hills, 133
Chulalongkorn, King, 299–301
Churchill, Winston, 124
citizens, 6
Brunei, 220
Cambodia, 291
Indonesia, 73
Laos, 267, 270–71, 273
Myanmar, 131
Philippine, 20, 45–46
Singapore, 162, 166, 184, 186

Thailand, 310
Timor-Leste, 82, 91–93, 95, 105
Vietnam, 248
citizenship, 45, 63, 135, 183–84, 212, 267, 292
City Council, 166, 179–81
civil administration, 27, 195
civil servants
Brunei, 197
Laos, 264, 266
Myanmar, 122, 124, 132
Thailand, 303, 311, 318
civil service, 115, 120, 122, 157
civil society, 89, 97, 102, 104–6
organisations, 85, 98, 105, 107
class, 117, 119, 127–28, 144, 149, 222, 226, 253–54
coalition governments, 229, 248, 256, 274
Cochinchina, 244–45, 249, 259, 271
Cold War, 136, 237, 245, 250, 252, 272
colonial administration, 26, 114, 117–18, 126, 198
colonial authorities, 116, 118, 126, 166, 171, 180
colonial governance, 14, 18, 21, 32
colonial governments, 13, 114, 118, 120–21, 179, 293
American, 18, 25, 28
colonialism, 8, 13, 83, 86, 115, 119, 141, 275–76
American, 12, 14, 18, 38
colonial law, 114, 131–32, 136
Colonial Office, 146–47, 150–52, 164–65, 170, 193–96, 198–202, 205–7, 209–12
colonial rule, 32, 112, 117, 119, 128, 141–42, 275, 277
direct, 112, 127
commerce, 47, 115, 165, 168, 170, 172, 233, 277
commitments, 21, 86, 91, 93, 99, 131, 199, 271
constitutional, 40, 43
Committee for the Preparation of Independence, 50, 52–55, 59, 62
Commons Committee on Burma Policy, 124
Commonwealth
British, 145, 147–48, 152, 156, 158–59, 168, 175, 191–92
Philippine, 12, 15, 23–25, 28, 34, 48
communism, 42, 44, 46, 75, 225, 229
communist leaders, 171, 230
Communist Party, 118, 128–29, 227, 230–31, 244, 252, 255
Indochinese, 237, 253
of Vietnam, 253–54
Communist Party of Burma (CPB), 125, 136
communists, 8
Cambodia, 275
Chinese, 233, 244, 246–47
Malaysia, 144
Myanmar, 112, 114, 119, 127–29, 136
Singapore, 171–73
Vietnam, 227–28, 240–42, 245–48
conscience, 74, 99, 102–3, 267
consensus, 87, 91, 96, 99, 103, 122–23, 292, 298
consent, 12, 14, 18, 20, 69, 71, 280, 310
prior, 183, 206
conservatism, 23, 42, 47, 58, 194
Philippines, 20–23
constituent assemblies, 84, 89–92, 94, 128–31, 133–36, 263–64, 291, 295
constituent assembly elections, 129–31, 135
constituent power, 264, 270, 298, 312, 318
constitutional advisors, 8, 85, 133, 168–69, 266
constitutional amendments, *see* **amendments**
constitutional assemblies, 22, 87–88, 219
constitutional authorities, 44, 156
constitutional commissions, 89–90, 139, 163, 166
Malaysia, *see* Malaysia, constitutional commission
constitutional commitments, 40, 43
constitutional conventions, 11, 17, 33, 45, 133, 246, 313
constitutional courts, 5, 71–73, 269
constitutional democracy, 14, 21, 38, 74, 316–17
constitutional design, 9, 286
Philippines, 24–37
constitutional development, 2–3, 7, 157, 164, 166, 178, 182, 247
constitutional drafts, 53–54, 208, 228, 282, 285, 301–2, 313
constitutional history, 1–10, 139–40, 157, 315, 317
constitutional foundings, 5–10
study of, 3–5
constitutional ideas, 2, 298–99, 301, 304, 307
constitutionalism, 2–3, 10, 12, 80, 82, 84, 86, 222–23
Timor-Leste, 78–79, 86, 109
constitutionality, 37, 98, 102, 108, 222, 287
constitutional monarchs, 151, 208, 262, 265, 297
constitutional order, 6, 78, 86, 97, 160, 291–92, 295

constitutional principles, 80, 85, 101, 108, 110, 256, 291, 295
constitutional reforms, 116, 142, 146, 209–10, 224
constitutional structure, 98, 143, 166, 219, 277
constitutional values, 2, 5, 7–8
constitution-making, 1, 6–8, 10, 79, 84, 194, 276, 287
  processes, 8–9, 85–87, 89, 208, 229, 246–48, 291, 298
constitutions, granted, 307, 311–12, 316, 318
Constitutive Assembly, 225, 228, 232–33
consuls, 55, 258, 299
consultation, 82, 89–90, 129, 131, 170, 175, 213, 220
control, 21–22, 32, 34, 46–48, 95–96, 169–70, 172–73, 294
  French, 261–63
cooperation, 18, 22, 128, 131, 144–45, 195, 199, 246
Council of Ministers, 82, 92, 167, 265, 268, 278–80, 283, 289
coups, 84, 239, 271, 280, 295, 317
courts, 2, 5
  appeals, 100–105, 107, 190
  Brunei, 201, 222
  Cambodia, 286–87, 290–91, 293–94
  constitutional, 5, 71–73, 269
  Indonesia, 58
  Laos, 261
  lower, 100, 102–3
  military, 92, 98, 100
  Philippines, 35–36, 39–40, 44
  Singapore, 165, 177
  Supreme Courts, 35–39, 57–58, 99–100, 102, 105, 107, 175, 177
  Thailand, 308, 312, 318
  Timor-Leste, 91, 94, 98–100, 102–3, 105–8
  Vietnam, 234–35
CPB (Communist Party of Burma), 125, 136
crimes against humanity, 93, 100–101, 104
Crown Colonies, 194, 196
Cuba, 11, 13, 230
culture, 60, 74, 86, 114, 152, 155, 218, 223

Darlan-Kato Agreement, 280
Dato Onn, *see* **Onn, Dato**
decolonisation, 6, 8, 81, 132, 135–37, 194, 249
defence
  external, 95–96, 168, 170, 172, 174
  national, 63, 90, 95–97, 253
de Gaulle, General, 244, 248–49
delegates, 15–18, 20–23, 29–37, 40–41, 43–48, 234, 238, 240–41
democracy, 1
  Brunei, 217, 219–20
  constitutional, 14, 21, 38, 74, 316–17
  Indonesia, 60, 62, 75
  liberal, 59, 64, 223–24, 231, 295
  Malaysia, 153, 156–57, 160
  parliamentary, 62, 147, 155, 307, 317
  Philippines, 27
  Singapore, 162, 179
  Thailand, 302–3
  Timor-Leste, 78
  Vietnam, 226, 246
democratic government, 35, 166, 222, 246, 292, 297
democratic institutions, 203, 283, 292
Democratic Party, 15, 167, 228, 238, 242, 284–85, 294
democratic transition, 74, 292
democratisation, 49–50, 194, 291, 298
  Indonesia after, 71–75
de Raymond, Jean, 262
development
  economic, 11–12, 149, 158, 221
  political, 164, 195, 276
Dewan Rakyat, 187
Dewantoro, Ki Hadjar, 60
Diệm, Ngô Đình, 231–32
Dien Bien Phu, 229, 237, 252
dignity, 91, 93, 147, 311
District Councils, 179, 203, 213, 215–17
districts, 34, 36, 89, 133, 135, 203, 220
Dorman-Smith, Governor Reginald, 122–24, 127–29
dos Santos, Armando, 101–3
drafting, 50, 81–82, 84–85, 88–90, 133–34, 202–3, 304–5, 308–9
  committees, 226, 234, 236, 239, 247–48, 253, 304, 312–13
DRV (Democratic Republic of Vietnam), 9, 226–33, 236–38, 242–45, 247, 249–52, 255
Dục Đức, 228–29
due process, 39–40, 43, 286
duties
  Brunei, 202, 215
  Cambodia, 289–90
  Indonesia, 64, 74
  Laos, 267
  Philippines, 14, 43
  Singapore, 169, 185–86

Thailand, 310
Timor-Leste, 85, 90, 92
Vietnam, 248
Dyarchy government, 120, 132

East Timor, 1, 6–7, 79–81, 88, 96–97, 100–102, 104–6, 108; *see also* Timor Leste
East Timorese, 77, 81, 84–89, 93–96, 98, 101–8
economic development, 11–12, 149, 158, 221
economic resources, 47, 109
economic rights, 86, 108
Economic Stabilisation Fund case, 107–8
education
Indonesia, 63, 74
Laos, 263–64, 267
missionary, 118–19
Myanmar, 112, 114, 116–17, 121
Philippines, 18, 20, 40
Singapore, 183, 187
Thailand, 302
Timor-Leste, 82
Vietnam, 234
elections, 10
Brunei, 209, 213, 215, 220
Cambodia, 284, 288, 291, 294–96
constituent assembly, 129–31, 135
general, 17, 69, 72–73, 145, 166, 181, 208
Indonesia, 66
Laos, 263–64
Malaysia, 143–45, 149, 151
Myanmar, 121, 129, 131, 133
parliamentary, 289, 294
Philippines, 15, 20, 42
popular, 88–89, 246
Singapore, 165, 167, 171, 173, 175, 179, 181–82
Thailand, 306
Timor-Leste, 84, 89, 100
Vietnam, 229, 232, 237–38, 243
elites, 20, 81, 84, 112–14, 118, 120, 223, 275
local, 115, 202–3
municipal, 18–19
political, 70, 109, 113, 129, 155, 266
provincial, 18–19
royal, 222, 299, 302
traditional, 114, 117–18, 202
urban, 18–19, 115
western-educated, 115, 131
young, 115, 284, 303
emergency, 37, 43, 65, 93, 170, 304, 307, 314
powers, 155, 169, 181, 313–14, 316
states of, 65, 77, 93, 97, 220
English language, 113, 115, 117–18, 299
environment, intellectual, 2, 8, 149
equality, 44, 63, 73, 168, 186, 263, 267, 270
equal rights, 153, 184
estimates, annual, 215–16
ethnic groups, 51, 113, 119, 126, 131
ethnicity, 82, 111–12, 119, 127, 131, 136
ethnic minorities, 113, 118, 127, 234
Eurasians, 118, 169
executive authority, 37, 161, 195, 197, 200, 214
executive branch, 31, 64, 183, 293–94
executive councils, 129, 131, 198, 206–7, 215
executive government, 187, 234, 241
executive powers, 30, 32–33, 35, 203–4, 208, 217, 293, 301
exile, 122, 231, 242–43, 261, 266, 281
ex-officio members, 165, 167, 170, 206, 215
experience, 17, 20–21, 95–96, 140, 146, 148, 154, 317
expropriation, 43–44
expulsion, 128–29, 171, 286
of international judicial actors, 105
external affairs, 172, 183, 212–13
external defence, 95–96, 168, 170, 172, 174
external forces, 232, 241, 244–45
external influences, 8–9, 79, 251

factionalism, political, 116–22
FALINTIL (Forças Armadas para a Liberação Nacional do Timor Leste), 83, 96–98
family, 60–61, 64, 82, 104, 198, 202
Family Principle, 7, 59–64, 70
farmers, 16, 42, 62–63, 121
federal government, 12, 21, 25, 161, 183–84, 186–87, 189, 244
Federated Malay States, 164, 198, 205
Federated Malay States (FMS), 164, 198, 204–5
Federation of Malaya, 142, 147, 155, 167, 172, 174, 182, 187
Federation of Malaysia, 1, 163, 185, 187, 189
Filipinos, 11–14, 18–21, 26, 30, 32–34, 41, 45–46
financial provisions, 145, 184, 186
First Indochina War, 229, 236, 250, 272
Five State Principle, 51
flags, 14, 25, 94, 160, 252, 267
FMS (Federated Malay States), 198, 204–5
Fong, Swee Suan, 171, 180
Forças Armadas para a Liberação Nacional do Timor Leste (FALINTIL), *see* **FALINTIL**

forces, external, 232, 241, 244–45
foreign affairs, 20, 169–70, 174, 177, 187
France, 236–39, 242–45, 247–52, 257–63, 270–72, 277, 281–82, 302–3
France-Cambodia Treaty, 278, 281
Franco-Khmer Commission, 282, 284
freedom, 73–74, 226, 232, 267, 273, 278, 285–87, 290
  of assembly and association, 64, 74
  of association, 63, 286
  of expression, 63, 74, 82, 235, 241
  of movement, 271, 286
  of religion, 52, 63, 74, 92, 286, 310
  of speech, 64, 286
  of thought, 73, 82
French administration, 259–60
French advisors, 263–64, 282
French authorities, 259, 261, 266, 282
French colonialism, 6, 226
French colonial regime, 242, 245
French Constitution, 244, 247–49, 300, 308
French control, 261–63
French forces, 243, 260, 263, 266, 272
French government, 238, 244, 248–50, 282, 284
French language, 248, 255
French Laos, 259–60, 267
French Union, 248–49, 261, 266, 271, 273
FRETILIN, 81–85, 89–91, 95, 104
Frontier Areas, 130–31, 133, 136
functions, 5, 7, 28, 35, 99–101, 177, 179, 215
  main, 32, 178–79, 200, 206
fundamental rights, 90, 93, 134, 156, 161, 267

GCBA (General Council of Buddhist Associations), 115–16, 118–19, 121
gender, 233, 241
General Council of Buddhist Associations, *see* **GCBA**
general elections, 17, 69, 72–73, 145, 166, 181, 208
general principles, 82, 252, 265, 267, 287
genocide, 93, 100–101, 103
German Democratic Republic (GDR), 228
God King, 291–92, 295
Gour, Claude-Gilles, 276–79, 281, 283–84, 286, 293–94
governance
  Brunei, 198, 202, 218–19, 221
  Cambodia, 285, 291
  colonial, 14, 18, 21, 32
  Indonesia, 61
  Laos, 264–65
  Malaysia, 140, 142
  Myanmar, 112–13, 117–18, 124, 128, 131–32
  structure, 82–83
  system, 118, 290
  Timor-Leste, 78, 83, 86–88, 90, 92–95, 100, 106, 109
  Vietnam, 231, 256
government
  British, 126–27, 129, 169–70, 174, 177, 195, 197–99, 210–12
  central, 25–28, 136, 147–48, 157, 167, 178–79, 187, 189
  coalition, 229, 248, 256, 274
  colonial, 13, 114, 118, 120–21, 179, 293
  democratic, 35, 166, 222, 246, 292, 297
  executive, 187, 234, 241
  federal, 12, 21, 25, 161, 183–84, 186–87, 189, 244
  French, 238, 244, 248–50, 282, 284
  Japanese, 50–53, 123
  local, 27–29, 72, 166, 169, 178–79, 181, 269–70
  of national union, 239, 243, 247
  Philippine, 12, 24–26, 28, 31–32, 37, 40
  provisional, 232, 236, 244–45, 248, 263
  representative, 198, 211, 216, 222, 301
  revolutionary, 33, 227, 232, 244
  royal, 260, 263–64, 285, 301
  stable, 15, 145
Governor-General, American, 27–28, 32–33, 36
Governors, 125, 127, 129, 167–68, 174, 179, 259, 269
granted constitutions, 307, 311–12, 316, 318
Guided Democracy, 49, 68

Haiphong, 239, 245, 250
Hamid, Abdul, 147, 149–51, 156, 172, 181, 186
Hanoi, 229, 232–33, 236–37, 239, 242–43, 245, 250, 252
Hatta, Mohammad, 49, 52–54, 63–64
Hayden, Governor-General Joseph Ralston, 16–18, 21–22
health, 74, 82, 263
  public, 39–40, 179
Hickling, RH, 155, 202, 205–6, 210
High Courts, 189–90, 269
highlands, 113–15, 130, 134
Hồ Chí Minh, 225–26, 228, 231–33, 236, 238–40, 242–45, 247, 249–50
House of Local Representatives, 72

House of People's Representatives, 56–57, 72, 280
House of Representatives, 15, 17, 21, 183
humanity, crimes against, 93, 100–101, 104
human rights
basic, 63, 73–74
Brunei, 219
Cambodia, 286, 295
fundamental, 73–74
Indonesia, 50, 54–55, 63–64, 70, 73–74
movements, 87, 109
Thailand, 303
Timor-Leste, 86, 104

ICP (Indochinese Communist Party), 228, 237, 240, 242–43, 253–54
identity, 3, 13, 45, 86, 112, 114, 118–19, 141
national, 86, 218
political, 3, 119
ideology, 2, 60, 62, 119, 131, 136, 222, 275
communist, 119
national, 7
impeachment, 33–35, 37, 71, 73
imperialism, benevolent, 12–14
independence, 13–15, 50–55, 99, 125–28, 145–46, 157–62, 269–73, 293–95
declarations, 54, 245, 281
Indonesia, 50–51, 53, 62, 75
judicial, 9, 36, 104–5, 231, 295
Lao, 258, 260–62, 267, 270–71
Singapore, 161, 164, 189
Independence Missions, 15–16
India, 113, 116–17, 125, 133, 144, 147–48, 156–57
British, 113, 116, 132
Indian community, 141, 145, 154, 157
individualism, 7, 59–60, 63–64
individual liberty, 7, 219, 267
Indochina, 6, 237, 242–43, 245, 251, 259–60, 270–72, 278–79
Indochinese Communist Party, *see* **ICP**
Indochinese Federation, 244, 249, 261–62, 266–67, 271, 273, 282
Indonesia, 6–7, 9–10, 49–50, 55–59, 61–62, 71–72, 75, 104
1945 Constitution, 49–75
after democratisation, 71–75
amendments, 49–50, 52–53, 57, 70–75
appointments, 65, 67
armed forces/armies, 65, 68–70
articles supporting authoritarianism, 65–66
authoritarian regimes, 49–50, 64–71
authority, 65–66, 68, 70, 72
Board of Audit, 57–58, 66
Committee for the Preparation of Independence, 50–55, 59, 62
constitutional provisions and origins, 55–64
courts, 58
democracy, 60, 62, 75
drafting of 1945 Constitution, 50–55
education, 63, 74
Family Principle, 7, 59–64, 70
founding fathers, 58–59
governing structure, 56–59
government, 49, 56, 58–59, 61, 63, 66, 68, 70
human rights, 50, 54–55, 63–64, 70, 73–74
Investigating Committee for the Preparation of Independence, 50–52
legislature, 57, 62, 68, 70–72
meaning of Constitution, 54–55
ministers, 57–58, 72
MPR (Peoples's Consultative Assembly), 55–59, 62, 65–73
MPRS (Provisional People's Consultative Assembly), 67–68
nationalist leaders, 51, 54, 61
nationalists, 59, 61
occupation of Timor-Leste, 77, 83–85, 90, 109
organisational representatives, 62–63, 67–70
parties, 49, 58, 68–70
preamble, 54–56
Presidents, 53, 56–58, 62, 64–73, 75
religion, 51–52
separation of powers, 50, 58–59, 71
State principle, 51, 55–56
structures, 51, 55–56, 72
Supreme Court, 57–58, 66, 72
treaties, 65
instability, 30, 129
constitutional, 297–98, 317
political, 71, 193
institutions, 6, 8–9
Brunei, 197, 218–19
Cambodia, 278, 288, 293–94
democratic, 203, 283, 292
Indonesia, 58–59, 62
Laos, 264, 268, 270, 273
legislative, 71, 73
Malaysia, 148
Myanmar, 118
Philippines, 12, 14, 16
political, 30, 49–50, 55, 57, 59, 64–65, 72, 74
state, 2, 72, 131, 288, 293

Thailand, 300
Timor-Leste, 109
Insular Government, 14, 17, 20–21, 24–26, 31–33, 38, 40, 45
Insular Legislature, 26, 32, 34–35, 45
integralism, 61
intellectual environment, 2, 8, 149
intellectuals, 8–9, 62–63, 115, 119, 132–33, 256
intentions, 2, 23, 96, 147, 176, 202, 244, 261
interests, legitimate, 148, 153–54
interference, 36, 39, 105–6, 218
internal security, 46, 95–99, 167, 169–70, 172, 174–75, 178, 187
Internal Security Council (ISC), 174, 178
internal self-government, 168, 170
international advisors, 79, 109
international judges, 100, 102, 105–6
interventions, 12, 38–39, 102–3
international, 109
Investigating Committee for the Preparation of Independence, 50–52
ISC, *see* **Internal Security Council**
Islam, 52–53, 56, 191, 204, 214, 222
Islamic laws, 52–53, 56

Jakarta Charter, 51, 54, 56
Japan, 50–51, 123, 125, 230–32, 245–46, 259–60, 281–82, 300
Japanese, 111, 122–23, 125–26, 132, 280–82, 309–10
Japanese government, 50–53, 123
Japanese invasion, 16, 31, 122
Japanese military administration, 50–51, 53, 56
Japanese surrender, 50, 257, 260
Java, 51, 53, 55–56
Jennings, Sir Ivor, 147–50, 156, 158, 160, 169
Johore, 143, 153, 164, 204
Jones Law, 15–16, 21, 26, 30, 32–34, 39
judges, international, 100, 102, 105–6
judicial branch, 12, 21, 24, 29, 31, 50, 188
Judicial Committee of the Privy Council, 145, 175, 183
judicial independence, 9, 36, 104–5, 231, 295
judicial nomination, 294–95
judicial review, 36, 66, 72
judicial sovereignty, 298–99
judicial structure, 100, 106, 165, 190
judicial systems, 99–100, 103, 107, 190, 269, 293
judiciary, 35–37, 57, 65–66, 71–72, 98–101, 103–6, 134–35, 160–61
independent, 66, 157, 175, 273
Timor-Leste, 99–106
Jumat, Hamid, 169
jurisdiction, 4–5, 40, 72, 104, 177, 187–90, 196, 200
justice, 88, 91, 93, 100, 190, 287, 294–95, 303
military, 98–99
social, 40, 42–44, 58, 86, 91, 144
transitional, 93, 101, 109

Kachin, 125–26, 130
Karens, 113, 118–19, 125, 131, 133, 135
Kayin, 125–26
kingship, 140, 268, 287
Klibur Oan Timor Asuwain (KOTA), 85, 104
KOTA, *see* **Klibur Oan Timor Asuwain**

labour, 47, 121, 151, 170, 183–84, 187
labourers, 63, 121, 141
Labour Front, 167, 179
Labour Party, 151, 157–58
land reform, 121, 124, 237, 255
language, 81, 86, 91, 93, 101, 103, 118–20, 153–54
choice, 81, 93
English, 113, 115, 117–18, 299
French, 248, 255
Malay, 141, 169, 188, 204
official, 87, 93, 154, 156, 167, 204, 285, 290
Lan Xang, 257–59, 267
Lao citizens, 267, 271, 273
Lao independence, 258, 260–62, 267, 270–71
Lao Issara, 8, 260–63, 266, 270–72
Lao People's Democratic Republic, 272–73
Laos, 1, 4, 6, 8–9, 84, 244–45, 248–49, 257–74
1946 *modus vivendi*, 262–63
1947–1949 Constitution, 265–67
key provisions, 267–70
significance, 272–74
from 1947 to 1949 Constitution, 270–72
administration, 261, 263
aftermath of war, 260–61
amendments, 265, 270–71
appointments, 263, 268
armed forces/armies, 258, 268
autonomy, 269
citizens, 267, 270–71, 273
civil servants, 264, 266
education, 263–64, 267
French, 259–60, 267
governance, 264–65
government, 261–62, 264–65, 267–68, 274

historical context, 257–59
Kingdom, 262, 270, 272–74
Kings, 258–70, 272–73
legitimacy, 262
military, 264, 268, 271
ministers, 261, 263, 265, 268–69
National Assembly, 265, 268–69, 273–74
parties, 271
preamble, 262, 265–67, 271
provisional government and Constituent Assembly, 263–65
treaties, 258, 268
unification, 264, 267
unification of Kingdom, 261–62
Laurel, Jose, 24, 30–31, 34–35, 40, 44, 48
leaders, 60–61, 109–10, 167, 169, 173, 243, 245, 248–49
communist, 171, 230
nationalist, 49–52, 54, 56, 167, 238, 247, 281
political, 9, 16, 20, 45, 97–99, 131, 211, 294
revolutionary, 97, 109, 233
leadership, 117, 119, 123, 125–27, 129, 242, 249, 253
Lee Kuan Yew, 162, 172, 185, 187–90
legal basis, 102, 272–73
legislative branch, 31, 71, 135, 164
legislative institutions, 71, 73
legislatures, 2
bicameral, 34, 125, 147, 157
Brunei, 217–18
Cambodia, 280, 289
Indonesia, 57, 62, 68, 70–72
Malaysia, 145, 149–50, 154–55
Myanmar, 126
Philippines, 17, 21, 26, 28–33, 35, 38–39, 42
Singapore, 182, 188
Thailand, 301
Timor-Leste, 92
legitimacy, 10
Brunei, 191, 214, 222, 224
Indonesia, 68, 71
Laos, 262
Myanmar, 127
Philippines, 18
Thailand, 311, 316
Timor-Leste, 80, 83, 88, 110
Vietnam, 231, 244–45, 250, 255
legitimate interests, 148, 153–54
Lennox-Boyd, Sir Alan, 144, 146, 159, 170, 172–73, 175
lese-majeste, 318
liberal democracy, 59, 64, 223–24, 231, 295
liberty, 14, 23, 39, 63, 85, 90, 302, 310
individual, 7, 219, 267
Limbang, 192
Lim Chin Siong, 170–73, 180, 182
Lim Yew Hock, 170–74, 176, 178–79, 181–82
local autonomy, 28, 131, 183
Philippines, 26–28
local elites, 115, 202–3
local governments, 27–29, 72, 166, 169, 179, 181, 269–70
Singapore, 178–81
local officials, 27–28, 179, 210
local representatives, 27, 57, 72, 148, 165
Locsin, Jose, 42–43
Lower Burma, 112–13
lowland Burmese, 114–15, 130
loyalty, 116, 122, 144, 153–54, 222, 242, 259, 266–67
Luang Prabang, 257–64, 266–67, 269–70, 272

Magna Carta, Timor-Leste, 85–88, 90–93, 99–100, 103, 106, 109
majorities, absolute, 270, 274, 289
Malacca, 145, 151–53, 164, 184
Malay, privileges, 141, 150, 158
Malaya, 139–44, 147–49, 151–60, 172–74, 182, 185–87, 195–96, 211–12; *see also* **Malaysia**
Malayan Chinese Association, *see* **MCA**
Malayan Democratic Union, *see* **MDU**
Malayan Indian Congress (**MIC**), 140, 144, 159
Malayan Union, 142, 164, 196
Malay Constitutional Committee, 203–6
Malay Islamic Monarchy, 191, 202, 222
Malay language, 141, 169, 188, 204
Malay States, 141, 183, 192–93
Federated, 164, 198, 205
Unfederated, 164, 198, 204
Malays, 141–43, 145, 148–55, 157–59, 169, 184–86, 188, 204
Singapore, 183, 186
Malaysia, 1, 3, 6, 8, 139–62, 164, 185–90, 217
appointments, 146
aspirations, 158
authority, 140, 148
autonomy, 147
British government, 153, 158
central government, 147–48, 157
colonial and constitutional precursors, 142–46

communists, 144
Constitutional Commission, 139–40, 146–48, 151–52, 156–58
deliberations, 149–51
creation, 185–89
democracy, 153, 156–57, 160
elections, 143–45, 149, 151
governance, 140, 142
government, 140, 146, 150, 153, 157, 159–60
individual or community rights, 152–55
legislature, 145, 149–50, 154–55
Malayan context, 140–41
parties, 143, 155
ruling and reigning, 151–52
self-government, 142–46
sovereignty, 142, 144, 151–52
Supreme Court, 141
treaties, 141, 153
Westminster-style parliamentary democracy, 155–59
Manila, 19, 25–27, 32, 40
Manila Bay, 11, 13
Manopakorn, 304–5, 312–14, 317
Marshall, David, 163, 167–74, 176, 178
Marxists, 81, 225–28, 238, 240–42
Mayors, 179–81
MCA (Malayan Chinese Association), 140, 144, 150, 157, 159
McGillivray, Sir Donald, 139
McKell, Sir William, 147, 149
McKinley, President William, 12–15, 21, 28, 48
MDU (Malayan Democratic Union), 165
Meiji text, 309–10
Mekong, 257–58, 260–61
Melaka, 140
Melayu Islam Beraja, *see* **MIB**
Mentri Besar, 207–8, 213–16
***merdeka*,** 145, 160, 170, 211–12
merger, 166, 178, 182–83, 185, 189
MIB (Melayu Islam Beraja), 191, 222
MIC (Malayan Indian Congress), 140, 144, 159
migration, 130, 140–41
military, *see also* **armed forces/armies**
Laos, 264, 268, 271
Myanmar, 122, 124–25
Timor-Leste, 82, 92, 94–99, 109
Vietnam, 243, 245
military courts, 92, 98, 100
military justice, 98–99
military role, Timor-Leste, 95–99
military service, 233–34
ministers
Brunei, 206, 215
Cambodia, 278–80, 282–83, 289, 291–92
deputy, 236, 240, 242
Indonesia, 57–58, 72
Laos, 261, 263, 265, 268–69
Myanmar, 117, 126
Singapore, 163, 167–68, 170, 174, 177, 181
Thailand, 301, 308–9
Timor-Leste, 82, 92
Vietnam, 235
minorities, 17, 111–14, 126, 134, 150, 155, 162–63, 169
ethnic, 113, 118, 127, 234
religious, 188
minority parties, 21, 35
missionary education, 118–19
mobilisation, 9–10
moderates, 180, 266, 270–72
modifications, 23, 69, 164, 178, 282–83, 307
***modus vivendi*,** 244, 259, 262–63, 282
monarchs, 31, 191, 209, 264, 278, 290–91, 306, 311
constitutional, 151, 208, 262, 265, 297
monarchy, 56, 113, 115, 117, 149, 222, 285, 295
absolute, 1, 214, 221, 281, 291, 297, 300–303, 311–12
hereditary, 222, 283
Mongkut, King, 299
Monireth, Prince Sisowath, 281–82
monks, political, 120–21
MPR (Peoples's Consultative Assembly), 55–59, 62, 65–73
and constitutional foundations of authoritarianism, 66–71
MPRS (Provisional People's Consultative Assembly), 67–68
MRP, 244, 248
municipal elites, 18–19
municipalities, 27–28, 43
murder, 100–101, 104
Muslims, 52–54, 56, 147, 193
mutual help, 61, 68
Myanmar, 1, 4, 111–37; *see also* **Burma**
1885–1942, 112–16
1945–1947, 126–32
administration, 117–18
appointments, 118
armed forces/armies, 122–24
aspirations, 123–24, 127
authority, 114, 117, 127, 129, 131
autonomy, 114, 128, 130–31, 134

British government, 126–27, 129
CAS (civilian affairs service), 122, 124–25, 129
central government, 136
civil servants, 122, 124, 132
communists, 112, 114, 119, 127–29, 136
drafting the Constitution 1944–1947, 132–35
Dyarchy government, 120, 132
education, 112, 114, 116–17, 121
elections, 121, 129, 131, 133
ethnicity, 111–12, 119, 127, 131, 136
Frontier Areas, 130–31, 133, 136
governance, 112–13, 117–18, 124, 128, 131–32
government, 116–20, 123, 129–31, 135, 137
highlands, 113–15, 130, 134
legacies of 1947 Constitution, 135–37
legislature, 126
military, 122, 124–25
ministers, 117, 126
nationalists, 111, 114, 116–17, 119–20, 122–25, 128–29, 132, 135
parties, 111, 116–17, 125, 130–31
political factionalism in pre-war British Burma, 116–22
preamble, 135
religion, 119–20, 130, 135
rural communities, 119–20
Saya San Rebellion, 121
self-government, 124–25, 128
Simla government in exile, 122–23, 125, 127
socialists, 112, 114, 127, 136
Supreme Court, 123
war-time planning, 122–26

Nacionalista Party, 34–35
National Assembly, 9
Cambodia, 283–85, 288–95
Laos, 265, 268–69, 273–74
Philippines, 34–35
provisional, 261, 284
Vietnam, 226, 228, 232–39, 241–43, 245–51, 253–54
national defence, 63, 90, 95–97, 253
national identity, 86, 218
nationalisation, 44, 47
nationalism, 9, 44, 133, 153, 246, 275–76, 294
nationalist appeal, 261, 266, 270, 272
Nationalist China, 228, 237, 247
nationalistic aspirations, 205, 218
nationalist leaders, 49–52, 54, 56, 167, 238, 247, 281
Indonesia, 51, 54, 61
nationalist movements, 60, 115, 119–20, 275
nationalists, 7
Brunei, 204
Cambodia, 275, 281, 285, 291
Indonesia, 59, 61
Malaysia, 144
Myanmar, 111, 114, 116–17, 119–20, 122–25, 128–29, 132, 135
non-communist, 227, 246
Vietnam, 228, 239, 241, 246
nationality, 13, 145, 183–84
national sovereignty, 99, 106, 265, 276, 291
national unity, 106, 154, 238, 243, 266, 270
natural resources, 41, 45–46, 108–9, 113
Navarro, Vicente Ruiz, 11, 16–17
negotiations, 164, 169, 185–86, 211, 213, 244, 246, 249
New Deal, 40, 43, 48
New Order, 49
New Zealand, 157, 162
Nguyễn Hải Thần, 237, 243
Nguyễn Văn Tố, 235, 249
nominations, judicial, 294–95
non-communist nationalists, 227, 246
non-Malays, 141, 143, 149, 153–54, 157
North Borneo, 52, 139, 159, 182, 187, 194–96
Northeast Burma, 113
northern Vietnam, 236–38, 243–44
North Vietnam, 229, 232

obligations, 20, 41, 52–54, 61, 233, 235, 241, 285
observers, 17–18, 81, 97, 99
official language, 87, 93, 154, 156, 167, 204, 285, 290
officials, 27, 124–25, 143, 164–65, 169, 210–11, 215, 218
local, 27–28, 179, 210
senior, 9, 152, 211, 278, 304
Omar Ali Saifuddin, Sultan, 193–94, 197, 199, 209, 214, 224
Ong, Eng Guan, 180–81
Ong, Pang Boon, 180
Onn, Dato, 142–43, 145
opposition parties, 182, 196, 243
organic acts, 14, 20–21, 26, 32, 34, 36, 39, 44
organisational representatives, 62–63, 67–70
organs of sovereignty, 99, 105–6, 109
Osmeña, Sergio, 15–17, 20–22, 24, 32, 45

Pakistan, 146–48, 156–57
Pancasila, 52, 55–56, 70–71
PAP, 162, 171–73, 179–82, 184
Paris Peace Accords, 230, 295
parliamentarism, 32–33, 58
parliamentary democracy, 62, 147, 155, 307, 317
parliamentary elections, 289, 294
parliamentary politics, 63, 68
parliamentary sovereignty, 316
parliamentary supremacy, 157
parliamentary system, 32, 56, 58, 246, 301, 306
parties
alliance, 144, 211
Brunei, 194, 208–9, 211–12, 217
Cambodia, 284–85, 289, 294–95
Indonesia, 49, 58, 68–70
Malaysia, 143, 155
minority, 21, 35
Myanmar, 111, 116–17, 125, 130–31
opposition, 182, 196, 243
Philippines, 22, 37
Singapore, 167, 169–70, 181–84
Timor-Leste, 81, 83, 85–87, 89–92, 95, 99, 104, 109
Vietnam, 228, 230–32, 238, 242–43, 246, 253–56
Party Rakyat Brunei, 216
peace, 11, 60, 65, 144, 176, 214, 218, 252–54
Penang, 145, 151, 164, 184
People's Committees, 235, 242, 251, 297, 304–8, 311–15, 317
People's Consultative Assembly, *see* **MPR**
people's representatives, 33, 56–57, 72, 272, 280, 290, 308
People's Republic of China (PRC), 230–31, 236, 255
Phetsarath, Prince, 260–63, 266
Phibun Songkhram, 303
Philippine-American War, 13, 18–19
Philippine Assembly, 21, 31, 34
Philippine citizens, 20, 45–46
Philippine citizenship, 45
Philippine Commission, 13, 21, 27, 32–34, 36, 45
Philippine Commonwealth, 12, 23–25, 28, 34, 48
Philippine government, 12, 24–26, 28, 31–32, 37, 40
Philippine Legislature, 15, 31
Philippines
1935 Constitution, 11–48
absolute monarchy, 28
administration, 36–37, 40
administrative centralisation, 26
amendments, 24, 36–37
appointments, 29, 34–36
armed forces/armies, 29
aspirations, 13
authority, 15, 23, 25–27, 29, 38
autonomy, 15, 25–28
benevolent imperialism, 12–14
Bill of Rights, 37–47
calling of Convention, 15–24
central government, 25–28
conservatism, 20–23
constitutional design, 24–37
Convention safeguards, 20–24
courts, 35–36, 39–40, 44
delegates to Convention, 16–20
democracy, 27
education, 18, 20, 40
elections, 15, 20, 42
government, 11–14, 18–19, 21–23, 25, 27–29, 32–33, 41–45, 47–48
Insular Government, 14, 17, 20–21, 24–26, 31–33, 38, 40, 45
Insular Legislature, 26, 32, 34–35, 45
Jones Law, 15–16, 21, 26, 30, 32–34, 39
legislature, 17, 21, 26, 28–33, 35, 38–39, 42
local autonomy, 26–28
mandatory provisions, 16, 20, 23
National Assembly, 34–35
nationalism and nationalisation, 44–47
organic acts, 14, 20–21, 26, 32, 34, 36, 39, 44
parties, 22, 37
police power and due process, 39–40
presidential approval, 23–24
Presidents, 12, 22, 24, 29, 31–33, 35, 37–38
progressivism, 38–44
separation of powers, 28–37
social justice, 40–44
sovereignty, 11–14, 19, 25, 28
substance of 1935 Constitution, 37–47
Supreme Court, 35–39, 43
treaties, 11, 13, 18, 20
unitary state, 24–25
philosophy, 47, 59, 61–62, 75, 222
Phnom Penh, 230, 276, 280–81
phrarachakamnot, 304, 307, 313–14
police, 95–99, 104, 121, 171, 236, 263
power, 38–39
political aspirations, 124, 203, 222
political autonomy, 114, 128
political bargaining, 87, 141

political branches, 36–39
political developments, 164, 195, 276
political elites, 70, 109, 113, 129, 155, 266
political factionalism, 116–22
in pre-war British Burma, 116–22
political identity, 3, 119
political instability, 71, 193
political institutions, 30, 49–50, 55, 57, 59, 64–65, 72, 74
political leaders, 9, 16, 20, 45, 97–99, 131, 211, 294
political monks, 120–21
political parties, *see* **parties**
political power, 37, 71, 90
political process, 88, 179, 232, 266–67, 270
political progress, 124–25, 128, 158
political rights, 14, 83, 85, 91
political stakeholders, 126, 133
political systems, 54, 57, 72, 191
politics, 20, 64, 99, 117, 119–20, 217, 245, 257
parliamentary, 63, 68
popular elections, 88–89, 246
popular sovereignty, 229, 234, 245, 311, 313, 318
Portugal, 81–85, 100, 228
Portuguese, 77, 81, 85, 87, 93, 109, 140
powers
absolute, 203, 220, 278
administrative, 88, 279
constituent, 264, 270, 298, 312, 318
emergency, 155, 169, 181, 313–14, 316
executive, 30, 32–33, 35, 203–4, 208, 217, 293, 301
King's, 291–92, 300, 302, 306–7
police, 38–39
political, 37, 71, 90
public, 286, 291–92
real, 168, 235, 248, 258
separation of, 33, 35, 58–59, 92, 94–95, 99, 104–5, 107
sovereign, 38, 56, 292–93
power structures, 78, 110, 287, 313
Prajadhipok, King, 297, 301–3, 305, 311–12, 315
presidentialism, 32–33, 72
presidential system, 33, 48, 56, 58
Presidents
Indonesia, 53, 56–58, 62, 64–73, 75
Philippines, 12, 22, 24, 29, 31–33, 35, 37–38
Timor-Leste, 82, 92, 95, 99, 104–7
Vietnam, 232, 235, 248, 250
prestige, 111, 118, 148, 193, 206–7, 308
Pridi Panomyong, 298, 303–4, 306–7, 310, 313–14, 316–17
Prime Ministers, 82, 104–6, 174–77, 235, 289, 291–93, 306, 309–10
Prisadang, Prince, 300
privileges, 14, 113, 118, 130, 139, 153–54, 172, 175
Malay, 141, 150, 158
Privy Council, 145, 159, 175, 183, 189–90, 198, 206–7, 215
progress, political, 124–25, 128, 158
Progressive Party, 165–66, 284
progressivism, 38–44
property, 39–40, 42, 44, 46, 171, 233
rights, 39–40, 74, 234, 241, 251
taxation, 27
prosecution, 93, 100, 268
prosecutors, 101, 105
protectorates, 192, 200, 245, 257, 259–60, 277–78, 281–82
protests, 17, 104–5, 120, 200
provinces, 27–28, 72, 130, 235, 257–59, 263, 269, 282
southern, 260, 269–70
provincial councils, 27, 269, 283
provincial elites, 18–19
provisional government, 232, 236, 244–45, 248, 263
Provisional People's Consultative Assembly, *see* **MPRS**
public health, 39–40, 179
public opinion, 37, 196, 203
public powers, 286, 291–92
public service, 153, 206, 212, 216, 221, 282, 286, 288
Public Service Commission, 145, 206, 216
Pusat Tenaga Rakyat, *see* **PUTERA**
PUTERA, 144
PVO (People's Volunteer Organization), 132

Quezon, Manuel Luis, 12, 15–17, 20–22, 24, 33–34, 37, 42, 48

race, 82, 153, 163, 165, 233
Rakhine, 126
Rangoon, 115–16, 121, 123–25, 128, 133
Rao, Sir Benegal Narasinga (BN), 133
recall, 234
reconstruction, 109, 124–26, 135
Recto, Claro M, 22–23
referenda, 88–89, 184–85, 229, 231, 235, 241, 244, 248–49

reformers, 75, 114–15, 120–21, 123, 132, 227, 231
reforms, 71, 98, 114, 120–21, 131–32, 165, 199, 277–79
constitutional, 116, 142, 146, 209–10, 224
land, 121, 124, 237, 255
regency, 212, 307, 315–16
Reid, Lady, 149
Reid, Lord, 146, 149–51, 154, 157–59
Reid Commission, *see* **Malaysia, Constitutional Commission**
religion, 8
Brunei, 192, 204, 206, 214
freedom of, 52, 63, 74, 92, 286, 310
Indonesia, 51–52
Laos, 267
Malaysia, 157
Myanmar, 119–20, 130, 135
official, 204, 214, 267
Singapore, 163
Timor-Leste, 82–83, 93
Vietnam, 233, 239
Rendel Commission, 166–67, 178, 182
representation, 82, 91, 103, 112, 116–17, 131, 145, 151
representative government, 198, 211, 216, 222, 301
representatives, 53–54, 62–63, 72, 85, 131, 134–35, 182–83, 283–85
local, 27, 57, 72, 148, 165
people's, 33, 56–57, 72, 272, 280, 290, 308
republicanism, 56, 297
Republic of Vietnam, 231–32
Residents, 192, 197, 199–201, 204–8, 213
resistance, 9
Laos, 260
Philippines, 12
Thailand, 300, 303
Timor-Leste, 77, 83, 85–87, 89, 92, 94, 96, 98
Vietnam, 249
resources, 40, 47, 106, 108, 116–18, 241, 287
economic, 47, 109
natural, 41, 45–46, 108–9, 113
revenues, 27–29, 107–8, 186, 215, 269, 280
review, judicial, 36, 66, 72
revolutionaries, 8, 11, 13, 84, 87, 297–98, 308, 316–17
Revolutionary Congress, 17
revolutionary government, 33, 227, 232, 244
revolutionary leaders, 97, 109, 233
revolutions, 2, 6, 78, 80, 232–33, 245, 249, 317–18
rights
bills of, 12, 14, 20–21, 36–38, 44, 82, 90–91, 155–56
economic, 86, 108
equal, 153, 184
fundamental, 90, 93, 134, 156, 161, 267
human, *see* human rights
individual, 37, 267, 273
political, 14, 83, 85, 91
property, 39–40, 74, 234, 241, 251
of secession, 126, 134
special, 154, 186
rigidities, 157–58
riots, 121, 150, 156, 171
Roxas, Manuel, 15–16, 22–23, 25, 28, 33–34, 37, 47–48
royal elites, 222, 299, 302
royal families, 206, 264, 268, 278–79, 288, 304, 309, 311
of Luang Prabang, 262, 270
royal governments, 260, 263–64, 285, 301
royalists, 8, 298, 310, 313, 315, 317–18
royal oath, 312–13
royal sovereignty, 307, 311–12, 316, 318
royal veto, 306, 314–16, 318
rule of law, 91
Russia, 42, 231, 233, 249, 251, 307–8, 311, 317

Sabah, 185–86, 188
Saigon, 53, 229, 231, 250, 258
Sarawak, 182, 185–88, 195–97, 199, 205, 210, 212, 216
Saya San Rebellion, 121
Sayre, Francis Bower, 299, 301–2
secession, 130, 135
right of, 126, 134
security, 90, 99, 177, 183, 218, 221, 276, 286
internal, 46, 95–99, 167, 169–70, 172, 174–75, 178, 187
Security Council, 88, 172–73
self-administration, 198, 214
self-government
Brunei, 198, 202, 211–12, 214
internal, 168, 170
Malaysia, 142–46
Myanmar, 124–25, 128
Singapore, 165–68, 170, 172, 176
self-rule, 15, 115–16, 125–28, 198
semi-presidential system, 9, 92
senates, 10, 26, 34, 183, 232, 285, 288–89, 296
senators, 24, 33, 288–89
senior officials, 9, 152, 211, 278, 304

separation, 14, 28, 57–59, 116, 160, 164, 212, 216
separation of powers, 35
  Cambodia, 295
  Indonesia, 50, 58–59, 71
  Laos, 269
  Philippines, 28–37
  Timor-Leste, 92, 94–95, 99, 104–5, 107
Shan States, 125–26, 128, 130–31, 133–34
Siam, 245, 257–58, 298–304, 309–11, 316–18; *see also* **Thailand**
Sihanouk, King Norodom, 281–82, 294
Simla, 122–23, 125, 127
Simla Reconstruction Department, 123–24
Singapore, 1–3, 6, 8, 10, 159, 161–90, 196, 212
  1946–1955, 164–68
  1956 constitutional talks, 168–70
  1957 constitutional talks and self-government, 170–76
  1958–1961, 178–82
  1958 Order in Council, 176–78
  1959 general elections, 181–82
  administration, 186–87, 190
  amendments, 162–64, 166, 169, 187, 190
  appeals courts, 190
  appointments, 168, 174, 181
  armed forces/armies, 172
  autonomy, 169, 183–84, 186
  British government, 166, 169–70, 172, 174, 177, 185, 187
  central government, 167, 178–79, 187, 189
  citizens, 162, 166, 175, 181, 183–84, 186
  City Council, 166, 179–81
  communists, 171–73
  courts, 165, 177
  and creation of Malaysia, 185–89
  delegation, 169, 173, 175
  democracy, 162, 179
  education, 183, 187
  elections, 165, 167, 171, 173, 175, 179, 181–82
  'founding' constitution, 161–64
  government, 161–67, 169–70, 172, 174, 176, 178, 182–83, 186–90
  independence, 161, 164, 189–90
  Independence Act, 163, 190
  Independence Agreement, 189
  legislature, 182, 188
  Legislature, 162–63, 175, 189
  local government, 178–81
  Malays, 183, 186
  merger terms, 182–85
  ministers, 163, 167–68, 170, 174, 177, 181
  parties, 167, 169–70, 181–84
  preamble, 188
  Rendel Commission, 166–67, 178, 182
  road to merger, 178–82
  State Constitution, making of, 164–76
Supreme Court, 175, 177, 190
Singapore Day, 162, 189
Sisavangvong, King, 259–60, 262, 264, 266–67, 272
Smith, Robert Aura, 17–18, 20
social classes, *see* **class**
socialism, 42, 46, 75, 225–26, 228, 233, 242, 253–54
Socialist Party, 230, 238, 242, 251
Socialist Republic of Vietnam (SRV), 9, 226, 230, 254, 273
socialists
  Indonesia, 58
  Myanmar, 112, 114, 127, 136
  Singapore, 180
  Vietnam, 227–28, 240–41, 248, 251–53
social justice, 40–44, 58, 86, 91, 144
social welfare, 40, 63
Soeharto, 49, 65, 68–71, 75
Soekarno, 49, 52–53, 55–56, 58, 62–65, 67–68, 70–71, 75
Soepomo, 52, 54–55, 58–59, 61–65
Soetatmo Soeriokoesoemo, 60
Southeast Asia Command, 124
South Vietnam, 226, 229, 232, 237–38, 255
sovereign powers, 38, 56, 292–93
sovereignty, 7, 9
  Brunei, 194, 198, 210, 214, 218
  Cambodia, 277, 290–93, 295–96
  changing concept, 276, 290
  defence of, 95–98
  Indonesia, 59
  judicial, 298–99
  Laos, 267
  Malaysia, 142, 144, 151–52
  Myanmar, 111
  national, 99, 106, 265, 276, 291
  parliamentary, 316
  Philippines, 11–14, 19, 25, 28
  popular, 229, 234, 245, 311, 313, 318
  royal, 307, 311–12, 316, 318
  Singapore, 162–63, 187
  Thailand, 301, 308–9, 312–13, 316, 318
  Timor-Leste, 77, 99, 105–6, 108–9
  Vietnam, 232–33, 239, 245, 253–54
Soviet Union, *see* **USSR**

Spain, 11, 13, 19, 25, 28, 41–42
Spanish-American War, 11, 13, 19
Spanish colonial rule, 12, 19, 25–28
Special Panels for Serious Crimes in East Timor, 101–2, 104
speech, freedom of, 64, 286
Sri Lanka, 154–55
Sriwisanvaja, Phraya, 302
SRV, *see* **Socialist Republic of Vietnam**
stability, 94, 193, 221, 230
stakeholders, 112, 116, 118–19, 121–23, 126–27, 130, 132
  political, 126, 133
Stalin, Josef, 47, 245, 249–51
Standing Committee, 234–35, 241, 248–49, 251
state-building, 1–2, 4, 95, 103, 106, 108–9
state institutions, 2, 72, 131, 288, 293
State principle, 51, 55–56
states of emergency, 65, 77, 93, 97, 220
Stevens, Raymond Bartlett, 302
Straits Settlements, 135, 141, 151–52, 164, 184
structures
  Indonesia, 51, 55–56, 72
  judicial, 100, 106, 165, 190
  Malaysia, 139, 157
  Myanmar, 131
  Philippines, 24, 47
  Singapore, 168
  Thailand, 309
  Timor-Leste, 77, 83, 92–94, 100–101, 106, 108
  Vietnam, 248
students, 120, 147, 171, 302–3
Suai, 104
succession, 198–99, 202, 206, 212, 258, 268, 283, 301–2
Sultanate, 140–41, 191–92, 199, 202, 213, 221, 224
supremacy, parliamentary, 157
Supreme Council of Magistracy, 10, 296
Supreme Council of the Courts, 293–94
Supreme Courts
  Cambodia, 289
  Indonesia, 57–58, 66, 72
  Malaysia, 141
  Myanmar, 123
  Philippines, 35–39, 43
  Singapore, 175, 177, 190
  Timor-Leste, 99–100, 102, 105, 107
  United States, 3, 25–26, 37, 43
suspensive veto, 313–14
symbolism, 91, 94, 103, 180
symbols, 7, 91, 94, 109, 121, 252, 259, 262

Taman Siswa, 60
Tan Cheng Lock, 152–53
Tan Trao, 245
taxes, 28, 116–17, 179, 183–84, 186–87, 223
tenure, 92, 99, 177, 205
Thailand, 1, 3, 6, 8, 259–61, 266, 271, 297–318; *see also* **Siam**
  1932 compromise constitution, 297–318
  absolute monarchy, 297, 300–303, 311–12
  administration, 313
  adoption of written constitution as civilising process, 298–307
  amendments, 305
  appointments, 314
  armed forces/armies, 306
  authority, 298, 311
  civil servants, 303, 311, 318
  competing understandings of Constitution, 307–15
  constitutional instability, 297–98, 317
  courts, 308, 312, 318
  cult of 1932 Constitution, 315–18
  democracy, 302–3
  education, 302
  elections, 306
  government, 302, 304, 308, 312–16
  Kings, 297, 299–302, 304–18
  legislature, 301
  legitimacy, 311, 316
  ministers, 301, 308–9
  politics, 317–18
  preamble, 306, 311, 316, 318
  Royalist re-appropriation of constitution-drafting process, 304–7
  royal sovereignty v popular sovereignty, 311–15
  socialist revolutionary v conservative modernisation constitutions, 308–11
  sovereignty, 301, 308–9, 312–13, 316, 318
  spread of competing constitutional ideas, 298–304
  treaties, 298
Thakin Soe, 118, 128
Timorese People, 86, 90–91, 103
Timor-Leste, 77–110, 228
  1975 Constitution, 80–84
  1998 Magna Carta, 85–88, 90–93, 99–100, 103, 106, 109
  2002 Constitution, 88–94

administration, 77, 79, 86, 91–93, 95, 99, 101–2
amendments, 82, 85, 93–94
appeals courts, 100–105, 107
appointments, 88, 106
armed forces/armies, 83, 92, 95–96
authority, 88, 95, 101–2, 105
citizens, 82, 91–93, 95, 105
constitutionalism, 78–79, 86, 109
constitutional practice, 94–108
courts, 91, 94, 98–100, 102–3, 105–8
democracy, 78
drafting of Constitution, 88–90
economic and financial organisation, 106–8
Economic Stabilisation Fund case, 107–8
elections, 84, 89, 100
FRETILIN, 81–85, 89–91, 95, 104
governance, 78, 83, 86–88, 90, 92–95, 100, 106, 109
government, 80–82, 84, 88, 92–93, 95, 98–99, 105–7
human rights, 86, 104
Indonesian occupation, 77, 83–85, 90, 109
judiciary, 99–106
legislature, 92
legitimacy, 80, 83, 88, 110
military, 82, 92, 94–99, 109
military role, 95–99
ministers, 82, 92
parties, 81, 83, 85–87, 89–92, 95, 99, 104, 109
preamble, 86, 90–92, 94
Presidents, 82, 92, 95, 99, 104–7
relevance, 79–80
resistance, 77, 83, 85–87, 89, 92, 94, 96, 98
separation of powers, 92, 94–95, 99, 104–5, 107
sovereignty, 77, 99, 105–6, 108–9
structures, 77, 83, 92–94, 100–101, 106, 108
Supreme Court, 99–100, 102, 105, 107
Tonkin, 244–45, 249, 259, 271
trade, 16, 113, 115, 129–30, 153, 170, 172, 186
traditional elites, 114, 117–18, 202
traditional systems, 278, 286–87
transition, 1
Brunei, 202
Cambodia, 279, 286
democratic, 74, 292
Myanmar, 111
periods, 20, 25, 94, 111, 124, 254
Philippines, 24
Timor-Leste, 88, 94, 102–3, 106
Vietnam, 242, 254
transitional justice, 93, 101, 109
treaties
British-Brunei, 197–98
France-Cambodia, 278, 281
Tujuh Serangkai, 203
Tun, Sir Paw, 123, 127–28
Tunku Abdul Rahman, 143–47, 149–50, 154–55, 159–60, 173, 188–89, 211, 217–18
Tydings-McDuffie Act, 15–17, 20, 23

UMNO (United Malays National Organisation), 140, 142–44, 153–54, 180
Unfederated Malay States, 164, 198, 204
unicameralism, 33–34, 251, 308, 310
Union of Socialist Soviet Republics, *see* **USSR**
unitary state, 1, 52, 161, 189
Philippines, 24–25
United Kingdom, Colonial Office, 146–47, 150–52, 165, 170, 194–96, 198–202, 205–7, 209–12
United Malays National Organisation, *see* **UMNO**
United Nations, 8, 77, 79, 85, 109, 188, 191, 271
Convention on the Law of the Sea (UNCLOS), 108
Security Council, 88, 172–73
United States, 11–13, 16, 20, 28, 37–39, 100, 132, 250–51
Congress, 14–15
rule, 13, 20, 26–27, 32, 35–36, 47
Supreme Court, 3, 25–26, 37, 43
unity, 60–61, 225–26, 228, 240, 242, 244, 249, 253–54
national, 106, 154, 238, 243, 266, 270
UNTAET (UN Transitional Administration in East Timor), 84, 88–90, 100–103
UN Transitional Administration in East Timor, *see* **UNTAET**
Upper Burma, 112–13, 115
urban elites, 18–19, 115
USSR (Union of Socialist Soviet Republics), 132, 134, 136, 227, 230–33, 236, 249–51, 255–56

Vajiralongkorn, King, 318
Vajiravudh, King, 301

values, 6, 8–10, 74, 106, 119, 265, 273, 275–76
constitutional, 2, 5, 7–8
traditional communitarian, 6–9
VCP (Vietnamese Communist Party), 226, 229, 250
veterans, 82, 92–93, 95, 97–99, 228
veto, 170, 263
royal, 306, 314–16, 318
suspensive, 313–14
Viang Chan, 257–58, 262
vice-presidents, 24, 45, 54, 57, 295
Vientiane, 257, 259–61, 264, 267
Viet Minh, 228, 238, 240–43, 245, 247, 251, 254–55, 271–72
League, 238, 241–42
Vietnam, 1, 3, 6, 8–9, 225–56
amendments, 235
analysis, 244–51
armed forces/armies, 229, 236, 253
Associated States, 231, 249–50
August Revolution, 231–33, 236, 242–43, 245, 251–52, 254
authority, 232, 234, 247
autonomy, 244, 248
ceasefires, 233, 236, 238, 244, 250
central, 238, 242
central government, 235
characteristics of constitutions, 232–36
communists, 227–28, 240–42, 245–48
constitution-making process, 236–41
Constitutive Assembly, 225, 228, 232–33
courts, 234–35
democracy, 226, 246
divided, 237, 245
elections, 229, 232, 237–38, 243
forces behind Constitution, 241–44
governance, 231, 256
government, 228, 232, 234–36, 238–42, 246–49
legitimacy, 231, 244–45, 250, 255
military, 243, 245
nationalists, 228, 239, 241, 246
North, 229, 232
northern, 236–38, 243–44
parties, 228, 230–32, 238, 242–43, 246, 253–56
People's Committees, 235, 242, 251
preamble, 232–33, 245, 252–54
Presidents, 232, 235, 248, 250
religion, 233, 239
role of 1946 Constitution in formation of modern Vietnam, 251–56
socialists, 227–28, 240–41, 248, 251–53
South, 226, 229, 232, 237–38, 255
sovereignty, 232–33, 239, 245, 253–54
Standing Committee, 234–35, 241, 248–49, 251
treaties, 237, 247
War, 230
Vietnamese Communist Party (VCP), 226, 229, 250
Vietnam Workers Party, 226, 229, 252, 255
violence, 29, 42, 88, 97, 121, 141, 237
Võ Nguyên Giáp, 236, 240, 242–43, 249
votes, 89–90, 94, 116, 234–35, 238, 240–41, 272, 274

wars, 112, 122–27, 132, 195, 229–30, 244, 251–53, 259–60
Philippine-American, 13, 18–19
Spanish-American, 11, 13, 19
welfare, 39, 46, 136, 170, 221
social, 40, 63
western-educated elites, 115, 131
West Irian, 68
women, 43, 45, 51, 113, 234, 238, 242
workers, 46, 127, 136, 171, 234, 242, 253
World War II, 111, 114, 117–18, 130, 230, 232, 242–43, 251–52

Yang di-Pertuan Agong, 162, 176, 183–84, 188
Yang di-Pertuan Besar, 148, 150, 152–53
Yang di-Pertuan Negara, 162, 174–78, 183, 191
YMBA (Young Men's Buddhist Association), 115, 117–18
young elites, 115, 284, 303
Young Men's Buddhist Association, *see* **YMBA**